I0291595

HYWEL DDA
THE LAW

A Welsh Law Court in Session
from British Library Manuscript Add. 22356,
written in the Teifi Valley in the 15th Century.

HYWEL DDA
THE LAW

LAW TEXTS FROM MEDIEVAL WALES
TRANSLATED AND EDITED

Dafydd Jenkins

First published in harback by Gomer, 1986
This paperback edition, 2025

© Copyright Y Lolfa Cyf., 2025

The contents of this book are subject to copyright, and may
not be reproduced by any means, mechanical or electronic,
without the prior, written consent of the publishers.

ISBN: 978 1 80099 688 5

Published and printed in Wales
on paper from well-maintained forests by
Y Lolfa Cyf., Talybont, Ceredigion SY24 5HE
website www.ylolfa.com
e-mail ylolfa@ylolfa.com
tel 01970 832 304

To my fellow-members
of the Colloquia and Seminars
on Welsh Medieval Law
in gratitude

CONTENTS

Preface	ix
Introduction	xi
Note on the Text and Translation	xxxix
Bibliography and Abbreviations	xliii
THE LAW OF HYWEL DDA	1
Book I: The Laws of Court	3
Book II: The Laws of the Country	43
Book III: The Justices' Test Book	139
Source References	211
Notes	219
Glossary and Index to Notes	309
Index to Sources	395
Index to Text and Introduction	399
The Colophon	427

Illustrations

A Welsh Law Court in Session	*frontispiece*
Map of Wales (8th—16th centuries)	viii

Môn
(Anglesey)

Aberffraw •

• Bangor

St. Asaph •

Clwyd

G W Y N E D D

Dinlle •

Conwy

Yr ▲
Wyddfa

Dee

Llŷn

Meirionnydd

Mathrafal •

Severn

Dyfi

P O W Y S

Offa's Dyke

Genau'r
Glyn

Pumlumon
▲

C E R E D I G I O N

Llanddewi
Brefi •

Wye

Teifi

Llanwenog •

Cantref
Mawr

Towy

St. Davids •

Taf

D E H E U B A R T H

Llandeilo •

Llandovery •

Usk

D Y F E D

Whitland •

Kidwelly
Lordship

Dinefwr •

G W E N T

M O R G A N N W G

Llandaf •

Miles
0   10   20   30

N
↑

0 10 20 30 40
Kilometres

PREFACE

WHEN the Welsh chronicler came to record the death (in 949 or 950) of King Hywel the Good, son of Cadell, he called him *pen a moliant yr holl Frytaniaid*—'the head and glory of all the Britons'; and the body of law which has come to be known by his name is one of the great glories of medieval Wales. As the Introduction will show, we cannot say exactly what Hywel did for the legal system of Wales. He certainly left his mark on it, but he must share the glory with a body of skilled lawyers who worked to develop and adapt the law before and after his time.

The law texts are of interest to Welsh readers as part of their national heritage, but they are valuable material also for students of social history and anthropology, of legal history, jurisprudence, and comparative law. The present selection aims at providing, for those who cannot read the medieval Welsh of the original text, an English translation of the most important and interesting material. Its main source is the 'Iorwerth Redaction' (earlier known as the 'Venedotian Code'), which presents the classical law of the thirteenth century in its fullest form. This Redaction was last published in translation in 1841; it is here newly translated in its entirety, with material from other classical-law texts and a selection of earlier and later statements of principle and practice. In the Notes and Glossary the requirements of readers with various levels of interest have been borne in mind, with the result that some observations will seem to some readers to state the obvious, while others are so technical that they will hardly interest the general reader. Much of the technical material is included here because it is not elsewhere available readily, if at all. The detailed references are given primarily for those who need them for specialist purposes, but they will also give the general reader clues to further reading.

3 March 1986   D.J.

ACKNOWLEDGEMENTS

The publishers and the editors gratefully acknowledge the courtesy and assistance of the following:

the National Library of Wales for permission to use for the cover illustration the drawing of the King on his throne from Peniarth MS. 28;

the British Library for the illustration of a Welsh law court in session from BL Add. MS. 22356;

Mr Gareth Bevan and his colleagues of Geiriadur Prifysgol Cymru for access to the Dictionary slips;

Dr Rachel Bromwich, Dr T. M. Charles-Edwards, Mr Robert Davies, Dr David Dumville, Professor Dafydd Evans, Professor Geraint Gruffydd, Mr Daniel Huws, Dr Christine James, Dr E. D. Jones, Dr William Linnard, Miss Morfydd Owen, Dr Huw Pryce, Dr Patrick Sims-Williams, Mr J. Beverley Smith, Dr Aled Wiliam, and Professor J. E. Caerwyn Williams, for discussion, help, and information given over many years.

In addition thanks are accorded to the staff of the Computer Unit at the University College of Wales, Aberystwyth, for help in the preparation of the indexes; to Peter Lord for his designs and illustrations; to Anne Mainman for drawing the map; to J. G. T. Sheringham for reading the final proof; and to Elgan Davies for design and typographical assistance.

Thanks are also due to the Welsh Arts Council for financial assistance in the form of a production grant to the publishers towards the production of the volume.

INTRODUCTION

THE message of this Introduction can be summarised in a few sentences.

The Welsh lawbooks on which this translation is based were produced by or for lawyers between the early thirteenth and early sixteenth century. The ultimate foundation of nearly all the books is a small core of material put together about the middle of the tenth century, in some way under the auspices of Hywel Dda. There are more immediate foundations in lawbooks put together in the twelfth and early thirteenth centuries, but in all the surviving manuscripts material has been added to the core, in order to make the book more useful to the professional lawyer.

Any Welsh law manuscript therefore contains a good deal of material which is later than Hywel's time, and great care is needed before a Welsh lawbook is cited as evidence for tenth-century conditions. But the lawyers were very slow to discard obsolete material: great care is therefore also needed before a Welsh lawbook is cited as evidence for conditions in the century in which it was written.

The sections which follow will develop this theme.

I. HYWEL DDA AND THE WELSH LAW

For perhaps a thousand years the native law of Wales has been known as the law of Hywel—*Cyfraith Hywel* in Welsh, *Lex (or Leges) Hoeli* in medieval Latin. Who was Hywel and what did he have to do with the law? The lawbooks call him 'king of all Wales': he was never quite that, and he was not nearly that until 942, seven years or so before he died. But his career shows up one great feature of medieval Welsh history, a feature which is of some importance for understanding the lawbooks.

Wales was not a political unit in the Middle Ages. It was not a single 'country' under one ruler, but a collection of countries whose pattern was always changing. The ruler of each country was in theory an independent sovereign, no matter how small his country might be; but the chances of inheritance and marriage, of battle and murder, and of sudden death, meant that from time to time a ruler would build up a bigger kingdom—which would break up again when he died. So it happened with Hywel.

xii   The Law of Hywel Dda

Hywel's grandfather, Rhodri Mawr, had ruled over all Wales except Dyfed[1] and the south-east, and his kingdom had been shared by his sons when he died in 878. Hywel himself came to a throne early, for after his father-in-law, Llywarch ap Hyfaidd, died in 904, Hywel became king of Dyfed; by 942, after his father, Cadell, his uncle, brother, and cousin had died, he was king of all Wales except the south-east. But when he died in 949 or 950, this united kingdom split up. In fact, it is wrong to speak of it as a united kingdom: perhaps we should think of it as a personal union of kingships, like that of England and Scotland under the Stewarts, or that of Great Britain and Hanover from 1714 to 1837.

What is most striking about the reign of Hywel is its great peacefulness, by the standards of the age, for it was Hywel's policy to avoid any action which would provoke English interference in his dominions. For some historians, Hywel was an admiring worshipper of the kings of Wessex, for others he was reluctantly accepting unpleasant necessity —but no one doubts his political skill and the fact that he did homage to those English kings and attended their court. [2] His name appears (with the title 'under-king') as a witness to some of their charters, and he seems to have had coins struck for him by an English moneyer.

So Hywel may have been emulating Alfred of Wessex when he went on pilgrimage to Rome in 928, and English example may have encouraged him to pay attention to the law of Wales. When the attacks of the Danes had reduced culture to a low level in England, Alfred had turned to Wales (among other places) for renewal; now perhaps Alfred's code was to inspire a Welsh king to renew his country's law.

But did Hywel copy Alfred? It seems quite certain that Alfred published an authoritative code of law, and the prologues to the Welsh lawbooks of course say that Hywel did the same. The Welsh prologues go into a good deal of detail

---

[1] This medieval Dyfed was much smaller than the administrative county of the same name created in 1974: see the map and the Glossary for this and other areas. For detailed maps of Wales at different dates, see W. Rees, *An Historical Atlas of Wales* (Cardiff, 1951).

[2] For Hywel's relationships with England see A. D. Carr, *A Look at Hywel's Law* (Whitland, 1985), 3-16.

Introduction   xiii

(and some of them go into very improbable, and even impossible, detail) about the process, but the kernel of their
story is that Hywel convened a representative assembly
from all his dominions to Whitland; after long consultation the law was revised and published in its revised form
with Hywel's authority.[1]

There is nothing improbable in the statement that Hywel
convened representatives from his dominions to examine
the law, but historians are cautious about accepting the
statement because the Welsh chronicles say nothing about
Hywel's connection with the law. The earliest evidence
for the assembly is that of the lawbook prologues, and it
cannot be proved that these were composed in any form
much before the oldest surviving law manuscripts were
written, early in the thirteenth century. And lawbooks are
notorious for setting out unreliable history for propaganda
purposes: the Irish law collection, *Senchas Már*, for
instance, has a 'pseudo-historical prologue' which quite
incredibly shows St Patrick giving his approval to the
work.[2] For that matter, it would be unwise to accept at face
value every statement found in the preamble to a modern
British statute.

It has even been suggested that the whole story of
Hywel's 'promulgation of laws for all Wales . . . is not an
historical description of legal unity but a myth of political
unification', apparently created in the twelfth century.[3]
This certainly goes too far, though equally certainly there
was an upsurge of legal activity in the twelfth century, and
though there is in the prologues another element which
suggests the twelfth, rather than the tenth century. This is
the placing of the assembly at Whitland, for Whitland
seems to have been a much less important place in the
tenth century than it was in the twelfth: by then it was the
home of the abbey which became the mother of all the Cis-

---

[1] See p. 1 and Notes; for criticism of the prologues, Sir Goronwy
Edwards's lecture, *Hywel Dda and the Welsh Lawbooks* (Bangor,
1929; reprinted at CLP 137-60). This lecture was given as part of
the celebration in 1928 of the millenary of Hywel's pilgrimage to
Rome.

[2] D. A. Binchy, 'The Pseudo-historical Prologue to the *Senchas
Már*', (1975/76) 10/11 SC 15-28.

[3] A. Harding, [1984] *Juridical Review*, 110; ct. A. D. Carr, *A
Look at Hywel's Law*, 10-12.

The Law of Hywel Dda

tercian houses of western and northern Wales. Whitland was founded by a Norman, but soon became thoroughly Welsh and received the patronage of Rhys ap Gruffudd, 'the Lord Rhys', chief ruler of southern Wales in the second half of the twelfth century. Moreover there was in the thirteenth century a lawbook called *Llyfr y Tŷ Gwyn*, the Book of the White House or Whitland Book. This was almost certainly written in the twelfth century, and for the lawyers of the time it must have been a book which they associated with the Abbey: if it was not still there, it was known to have come from there.[1] And if there was a myth-maker at the time, he may have fastened on the name of the manuscript to supply a location for the meeting-place of his mythical assembly.

Yet though there is no evidence for the importance of Whitland in the tenth century, there must surely have been a royal site somewhere in the neighbourhood. The commote of Peuliniog must have had an administrative centre somewhere in the valley of the Taf, and the Cistercians would be likely to choose a home within reach of that centre, though the abbey's actual site would be in a sparsely-inhabited country place.[2] If Hywel had a court anywhere in this district, he is likely enough to have chosen it as the meeting-place for his assembly, for it was in a 'forward position' in Dyfed, where he would be most at home because it was the first of his dominions. It may seem that representatives from Gwynedd would have been unwilling to travel so far in order to attend the assembly, but it has been ingeniously suggested that they could have fitted attendance at the assembly in to a pilgrimage to St. Davids.[3]

If there was an assembly, it may well have been at Whitland. It is admitted that if Hywel did anything for Welsh law, he probably did it with the help of an assembly—and it seems clear that Hywel must have done something very significant for Welsh law. The evidence for this is indirect: it comes from the nature of the law and the lawbooks, and

---

[1] See 94.1-25n, 141.30n.

[2] See L. A. S. Butler in *Studies in Celtic Survival* (ed. Lloyd Laing), (1977) 37 *British Archaeological Reports* 62.

[3] D. Cyril Jones and Malcolm M. Jones, *Y Cronicl pan oedd Oed Grist yn 947* (Whitland, n.d.), 1.

Introduction

especially from the contrast between the lawbooks of Wales and those of Ireland.[1]

Both Irish and Welsh law are primarily lawyer-made law, recorded in books compiled by professionals, whether practitioners or teachers. These men were working out the application of the customary principles of their people: they were not recording the authoritative legislation of a sovereign, nor were they (like British judges of the present day) making or finding new rules of law by deciding actual cases. But signs of the growing power of the state, which are absent from the Irish material, are clearly to be seen in the Welsh.

Thus all the main Welsh manuscripts seem to share a fairly small core which is concerned with what we now call public law: that is, they provide for punishment by the state of offences and lay down the obligations of the people towards the state, which in the Middle Ages means the king. This suggests that the law was revised at some date with the encouragement of a king who took this opportunity to strengthen his own authority. It is hardly an accident that the first place in all the main texts is given to a form of the same very substantial tractate,[2] which deals with the royal court, and it is hardly an accident that the court reflected in the tractate would need a substantial kingdom to finance it. Anyone who was concerned with the law during Hywel's reign must have realised that his kingdom was likely to break up (as it indeed did) after his death, but fragmentation would be discouraged if the cost of maintaining the king and his officers was a heavy burden. Most of the rules relating to the court and the royal officers are stated in general terms, so that they would apply to any Welsh kingdom, but all the lawbooks make a definite distinction between smaller and greater kingdoms. There is no hint in the books that the king of a small kingdom is not every inch a king, but his lack of inches put him in the second division of the royal class.

'Constitutional law' is thus now weighted in favour of the survival of the larger units. It would naturally be easier

[1] For the contrast between Irish and Welsh law see R. Thurneysen, 'Celtic Law', CLP 50-70, especially 66-70; D. A. Binchy, *Celtic and Anglo-Saxon Kingship* (Oxford, 1970), especially 21-30.

[2] For the name 'tractate' applied to the distinct parts of the lawbooks, see p.xxiv. The name was suggested by Sir Goronwy Edwards: WHR Sp. No., 9.

The Law of Hywel Dda

to establish these larger units if there were no important differences in law between the different parts of a unit, and it may have been under Hywel that the principle was established that the law of Wales was one law. The lawbooks do indeed mention some practices which are confined to particular parts of Wales, but we shall see that their compilers felt quite free to draw their material from any part of Wales with the assurance that it was good law for any other part.

If any Welsh king brought the law together in the way indicated, it must have been Hywel ap Cadell. Only one Welsh king ever ruled more of Wales at the same time than Hywel: this was Gruffudd ap Llywelyn between 1055 and 1063, but his reign was far too stormy for any plan of law reform, whereas Hywel's policy gave him peace enough to allow the carrying out of such a plan. The names of Hywel Dda and Cyfraith Hywel carry some weight, and if a myth of political unification was created in the twelfth century, we may well ask why Hywel was made the hero of the myth unless there was some grain of truth around which this impressive pearl could be made to grow.

So we believe that Hywel turned the course of Welsh law, and if he made the kind of changes which the lawbooks suggest, he must have had them put into writing. But whatever was done under Hywel, we have no record of it as it then was: all our lawbooks show the Hywelian pearl mounted in a rather overwhelming setting of later date. For the growth of Welsh law did not end in Hywel's reign:

it is clear that Hywel's work was carried on by a succession of Welsh lawyers through the three turbulent centuries from Hywel to Llywelyn ap Gruffydd, and . . . through three more centuries to the days of Henry Tudor . . . Law is a living thing which changes to meet the varying needs of a living community, and the Welsh lawyers who succeeded Hywel worked in such a way that we find it hard now to say where his work ended and where theirs successively begins. We see only the final edifice. Hywel's share in the building of it is now largely hidden in the work of those who followed him, but they conceived that they built on foundations which he had laid, and when they rebuilt, that they did so with stones which he had hewn.[2]

[2] J. G. Edwards, CLP 160.

Introduction   xvii

We can flog the metaphor a little further: even Hywel's
stones were not all freshly quarried. Some of them came
from older and cruder buildings about whose architecture
we know nothing.

To sum up, we can say that the history of Welsh law
seems to fall into three periods. The first period ends with
the work of Hywel Dda in the mid-tenth century; the
second with the death of Llywelyn ap Gruffudd in 1282;
and the third with the Act of Union of 1536, by which
English law was made to apply throughout Wales. Interest
in the Law of Hywel then became antiquarian; a hundred
years later it was already becoming scholarly.

The first period should perhaps be regarded as pre-
history rather than history, because there is so little
written material which can safely be ascribed to the period.
There is indeed the oldest surviving piece of syntactical
written Welsh: this is the account of a dispute relating to
some land in Ystrad Tywi, written on the margins of a page
of a manuscript of part of the Gospels (now in Lichfield
Cathedral, but once at Llandeilo Fawr) in the ninth
century; there are other records relating to land on other
pages of the same manuscript; and there is some very
mixed material in the 'Book of Llan Daf'.[1] But for our ideas
of this period we rely mostly on what can be deduced from
the lawbooks of the later periods. There must surely have
been lawbooks of some kind before Hywel's time, for
occasional passages which are found only in comparatively
late manuscripts are so archaic in substance or language
that they must go back to a very early date. Some of these
archaisms are proverbs or triads which could have been
transmitted orally, but others are too complicated for that,
especially when we remember that medieval Welsh legal
practice laid great stress on written statements of law.[2]
Again, there are in the later lawbooks statements of contemporary law which can hardly be understood until it is

[1] For the 'Surexit' memorandum and other records in the Llan-
deilo/Lichfield Gospels, see D. Jenkins and M. E. Owen, 'The
Welsh Marginalia in the Lichfield Gospels', (1983) 5 CMCS 37-
66, (1984) 7 CMCS 91-120. For the Book of Llan Daf, see Wendy
Davies, *An Early Welsh Microcosm* (Royal Historical Society
Studies in History Series no. 9, 1978), and *The Llandaff Charters*
(Aberystwyth, 1979).
[2] See Binchy, 10/11 SC 15 n. 4.

xviii   *The Law of Hywel Dda*

realised that they present a modern adaptation of some
more primitive institution. In the lawbooks, the *mach* is a
surety who may be compelled to pay the debt if the principal debtor defaults; but there are clear signs that in an earlier age, when there was no public machinery for law enforcement, the *mach* was brought in so that the rights of
the parties to a formal agreement could be enforced by him
—by physical means if necessary.[1] For much of this first
period, the principles of law must have been fairly clear,
though central authority was so weak that men relied on
social pressure to conform to those principles. The Irish
parallels show that there was effective encouragement to
submit disputes for arbitration, and the principles which
would be applied in such arbitration are the basis of the
future law.

   In the second period, jurists all over Wales develop the
law with increasing sophistication. Social and political
changes make it necessary to adapt and extend the law, and
political strength seems to stimulate study of the law. So it
is very probable that the rise of Rhys ap Gruffudd to authority over a large part of southern Wales in the second half of
the twelfth century encouraged the production of a revised
lawbook, and it is virtually certain that it was the growth of
the power of the princes of Gwynedd at the beginning of the
thirteenth century which led to the development of what
we can call the classical law.

   For the third period, the most obvious influence is the
Statute of Wales, which imposed some parts of English law
on some parts of Wales. The defeat of Llywelyn ap Gruffudd
led to the creation of the English principality in Wales, but
left untouched the marcher lordships and the realms of the
Welsh princes who had not joined Llywelyn; and nowhere
in Wales was Welsh law totally extirpated at this time. A
fair amount of Welsh law was still in force in Principality
and March, and in some parts of the Principality it was still
important enough for the authorities to appoint specialists
to advise on Welsh law.[2]

   In recent years we have learnt enough about a few of the
Welsh jurists to be able to add some detail to the bare
names which crop up in the lawbooks. Morgenau and Cyf-

----

   [1] See the general note to II.4 (p.247), and 68.22-30.
   [2] See Christine James, 'Golygiad o BL Add. 22356 o Gyfraith
Hywel' (Unpublished thesis, University of Wales, Ph.D., 1984).

Introduction

nerth his son, living near the end of the twelfth century, were members of the tribe of Cilmin Droetu, which held land at Dinlle in Arfon: this tribe produced more lawyers than any other in Wales, and were the ancestors of the Glyns and Wynns of Glynllifon and the Glynnes of Hawarden (now represented by the descendants of Catherine Glynne and W. E. Gladstone). Iorwerth ap Madog was the great-grandson of Morgenau's brother Ednywain; another brother, Ystrwyth, the ancestor of the Glyns and Wynns, served Llywelyn the Great as an administrator.[1] Goronwy ap Moriddig came from somewhere in what is now the county of Clwyd: at an inquiry at St. Asaph in 1274 he gave evidence about procedure which he had seen applied in the 1230s.[2]

Several jurists are named in the record of an inquiry into the applicability of Welsh law, held in 1281 under a commission from Edward I. One of those named was certainly a jurist, not so certainly a judge; for the question put to the witnesses was whether Iorwerth Fychan was not judge in Cyfeiliog and another area in Powys. Prince Llywelyn ap Gruffudd said it was clearer than light that he was; the witnesses said he was not: he was indeed called *ynad*, 'justice', but only by way of compliment because he had been in Gwynedd studying the law of Hywel. According to Llywelyn ap Gruffudd again, the sons of Cynyr ap Cadwgan were judges in Arwystli in Powys—and Cynyr is named as the compiler of a lawbook (found incorporated into a larger text) which he left to his sons. The third man named in this record was presumably the most distinguished of all: he was Einion ap Gwalchmai, who was associated with the King's justices at Westminster and gave judgment with them.[3]

We know nothing of Einon ap Gwalchmai's legal activity at home in Wales, but he seems to have combined in himself two of the medieval Welsh learned professions, law and bardism. Some half-dozen poems of his survive: more than survives from his brother Meilyr, but much less

[1] For this family see CLP 123-33.

[2] O. E. Jones, 'Llyfr Coch Asaph' (Unpublished thesis, University of Wales, M.A., 1968), 72-3, 173.

[3] The record of the commission is printed (in Latin) at LW 518-31, and calendared in English at *Calendar of Chancery Rolls, various, 1277-1326* (London, 1912), 190-210; see also J. E. Lloyd (1915) 25 YC 1-20, (1916) 26 YC 252.

The Law of Hywel Dda

than from his father Gwalchmai; his grandfather Meilyr was less productive but equally famous. And though Einion ap Gwalchmai is the only medieval lawyer whose verse has survived, the two professions are also found in the tribe of Cilmin Droetu. Iorwerth ap Madog had a brother, Einion, who sang the praises of Llywelyn the Great's unfortunate son, Gruffudd; and Gruffudd ab yr Ynad Coch, who composed the great elegy on Gruffudd's son, Llywelyn, was probably the son of Madog Goch Ynad, a second cousin of the other Madog, Iorwerth's father.

A literary connection can also be traced at a later period. One of the great manuscript collections of medieval Welsh literature is *Llyfr Gwyn Rhydderch*, 'the White Book of Rhydderch', and Rhydderch ab Ieuan Llwyd, for whom it was written in the fourteenth century, was deputy-justiciar in Cardiganshire and one of the experts in Welsh law to whom the authorities of the Principality turned for advice. This medieval Welsh lawyer was a man who had a wide cultural background. Another lawyer from this district gave his name, not to a literary manuscript but to a roll of legal material, *Rhol Dafydd Llwyd*, which is named as a source in the fifteenth-century manuscript from the Teifi Valley, Llanstephan MS. 116. The roll seems to have been that of Dafydd Llwyd ap Gwilym, who acted as *dosbarthwr* in 1387-8.[1]

There is one traditional juristic name, however, for which we no longer believe that we can find an owner: Blegywryd. According to some manuscripts, Blegywryd was a cleric who was secretary to the committee of twelve laymen which drafted the law promulgated at Whitland; according to a few of these manuscripts, he was archdeacon of Llandaf and a doctor of both canon and civil law. Archdeacon and Doctor he certainly was not, and few people can now believe that he was secretary of the drafting committee. It was once thought that he was the Blegywryd ab Einion of Gwent, a holy man who is the hero of an incident recorded in the Book of Llan Daf, but it is now generally accepted that his name did not reach the lawbooks until the eleventh or twelfth century, and that we must look for anyone of that name among those who bore it at that kind of date.[2]

[1] Christine James, 'Golygiad . . .' xxxiv; Griffiths, *Principality*, 514.

[2] J. G. Edwards, WHR Sp. No., 1-19. especially 13-16.

II. The Medieval Lawbooks

Any one who sets out to study the law of medieval England in depth can turn to an embarrassing plethora of court records for a picture of the law in action from the twelfth century on. From Wales there are very few records of court proceedings, and we must rely on the lawbooks; they are fortunately a rich source. There are naturally fewer medieval law manuscripts from Wales than from England, but those we have are teaching us a great deal about the way the law grew, as we come to know them more intimately.

There still exist about forty manuscripts of Welsh law written between the early thirteenth and the early sixteenth century, when the Law of Hywel was still a living force in parts of Wales.[1] Six of these manuscripts are in Latin; the rest are in Welsh, and every one is at least slightly different in content from all the others. But every one is a private collection of material which was expected to be useful to someone who needed to have the law in ink on parchment. That 'someone' might be a practising lawyer, who would take his lawbook to court in the sleeve of his gown: several of the most important manuscripts are handy little books which would slip comfortably into a pocket, and most of these show the signs of wear from constant use. They are often quite clumsily written by non-professional hands.

Others are more impressive volumes written by expert scribes. Some are thick books with large pages, which were perhaps kept in an abbey for information on the law relating to its rights; one such book, the British Library manuscript Add. 22356 from which the frontispiece of this book is taken, was probably prepared for a Welshman from the Teifi Valley who acted as official advisor on Welsh law to the royal authorities in Cardiganshire in the fifteenth century.[2] The manuscript from which our main text is taken (BL Cotton Titus D.II) is smaller, but finely written: it is thought to have belonged to Anian, bishop of St. Asaph from 1268 to 1293. He perhaps had it with him when he served on commissions for the king of England, but he

---

[1] There are also some forty later manuscripts, the work of antiquarians and scholars.

[2] Christine James, 'Golygiad . . .', cii-cv.

The Law of Hywel Dda

evidently did not use it very much, for it is still in fine condition.

Another finely-written manuscript is the Latin Peniarth 28 (at Aberystwyth), with its engaging illustrations. This was once at Canterbury, and is probably the text which gave John Peckham, Edward I's archbishop, the idea that the Law of Hywel was contrary to the Ten Commandments and that King Hywel had published it by the authority of the devil. [1]

We know the names of a few of the scribes of these manuscripts. There was Dafydd Ysgrifennydd, 'David the Scribe': about 1325 he wrote for Iorwerth ap Llywelyn ap Tudur of Merioneth a manuscript which is now lost, though we have copies of parts of it. At the end of this manuscript he wrote something which is to be found nowhere else, a criticism of a statement which he had copied into the body of his text.

Then there was Hywel Fychan of Builth, whose hand has been recognised in the Jesus College Oxford MS. 57, a very comprehensive law text. Hywel was also the principal scribe of the Red Book of Hergest, in which were brought together so many treasures of medieval Welsh prose and verse from many sources. Another of the Red Book scribes, whose name we do not know, also wrote a law manuscript, Peniarth 32, which was so finely written that in the seventeenth century it was given the name *Llyfr Teg*, 'the fair book'. [2]

Both Dafydd Ysgrifennydd and Hywel Fychan seem to have been more than mere mechanical copyists acting on instructions, and Gwilym Wasta, who wrote three manuscripts of the 'Blegywryd Redaction', was certainly more than that. Gwilym, whose epithet seems to be *gwas da*, 'good servant', or perhaps 'good lad', had the status of an 'English burgess' of the New Town of Dinefwr at the beginning of the fourteenth century. Writing his manuscripts in a district which had recently come very fully under English administration, he saw that the old laws of court were obsolete and that it would be a waste of ink and parchment

---

[1] Daniel Huws, 'Leges Howelda at Canterbury', (1976) 19 NLWJ 340-44.

[2] Gifford Charles-Edwards, 'The Scribes of the Red Book of Hergest', (1980) 21 NLWJ 246-56.

Introduction   xxiii

to copy them; he boldly cut them out, and so set a pattern
for one branch of the manuscript tradition.

★   ★   ★   ★

When we turn to the content of the manuscripts, we can
start by quoting the words in which one of those manuscripts introduces itself:

> Here is a lawbook which Hywel Dda made at the White
> House on Taf, though there be also other things in it, by
> way of good laws which were made both before that and
> after that. [1]

The scribe of that manuscript knew that it contained material which did not belong to 'Hywel's Book', and so of
course did other scribes. In our own text, the Prologue to
Book III tells us that the compiler drew its contents from
certain named books and 'from the best books that he
found also in Gwynedd and Powys and Deheubarth' (p.
141). Then there are occasional references to the absence of
any provision on a particular matter in Hywel's book,
occasional references to changes in the law introduced by
later rulers, and (perhaps most important of all) occasional
references to a conflict of opinion between different jurists.
   This means that the Welsh lawbooks are compilations of
a kind rare in medieval Europe: they bring together from
different sources all the material which their compilers
thought might be useful to them; and because lawyers are
by nature reluctant to discard anything as obsolete, these
compilers must often have included out-of-date material
in their collections. As a result, it is not safe to assume that
a statement found in a law manuscript of a particular date
gives a fair picture of life at that date: the social or economic conditions implied may be those of an age long past,
and even rules of law must not be taken at their face value.
They may on the one hand be obsolete; on the other hand
they may sometimes set out, not the actual practice of the
time, but what the compiler thought ought to be the practice.

---

[1] *Ban wedy i dynny* (reprinted in *Yny Lhyvyr hwnn*, Bangor and
London, 1902), Aii; similar wording in MS. *Z* (Peniarth 259B),
57v.

The Law of Hywel Dda

Though the material of the manuscripts quite clearly comes from various sources, the arrangement is not haphazard. The texts are built up round 'tractates' dealing with particular subjects, such as the Law of Women (II.1), Theft (III.2), and Corn Damage (III.10). The tractates vary greatly in size, from that on Injury to Animals (II.3) to the Laws of Court (Book I), which divides into sub-tractates and sub-sub-tractates. They vary also in orderliness, with that on Injury to Animals again at one extreme: it seems to have the same form in all the manuscripts, whereas the longer tractates may vary a good deal, because different material has been added to the 'basic' tractate in different manuscripts, or the same material has been inserted at different points in the tractate. Indeed, the same rule may appear in different tractates in different manuscripts, or even more than once at different points in the same manuscript. The rules about medical treatment in our main text are in equally good company in the section on the Physician (at p. 24 in the Laws of Court) and in that on the Human Body (at p. 197).

There are also in most manuscripts many pages of material which has not been put into any logical order: a rule or two about land may be followed by a rule or two about harm done by animals. One of our most important sources is a disorderly collection of this kind, *Llyfr y Damweiniau*; its only unifying principle is the form of many of its rules, which begin with the clause 'If it happens that . . . .

In spite of disorder, a great deal of our manuscript material (probably much more than half of it) has a measure of order. There are enough manuscripts which have the same tractates, in much the same order, to lead us to think of these manuscripts as representing a particular Redaction of the law, and it has long been clear that there are three such Redactions. These we now label the Cyfnerth, Blegywryd, and Iorwerth Redactions (with the abbreviations *Cyfn*, *Bleg*, and *Ior*); the names are taken from persons named in the manuscripts, but are not intended to imply any particular relation between those persons and the Redactions.

Within the Redactions the appearance of order is enhanced by the statements about their content found in some manuscripts. *Bleg* manuscripts tell us that the law was to be written down in three parts, 'first the law of [Hywel's] daily court; second, the law of the country; third, the practice of each of them', and the first two divis-

Introduction

ions appear clearly enough: they are marked, in this edition as in others, by the headings 'Book I' and Book II'. No
manuscript of any Redaction identifies a third part dealing
with practice: our Book III is the 'Justices' Test Book' of
the Iorwerth Redaction, whose foundation is material
taken out of the Laws of Country.

In some manuscripts sections dealing with particular
subjects are marked out by cross-headings (usually in red),
which excuse the practice of modern editors who divide
the Books into chapters. But the cross-headings can be
misleading, for they are sometimes appropriate only to a
sentence or two, while they appear to cover many sentences which are only distantly related to the heading. Like
other features of the manuscripts, this irregularity reflects
the way the texts were handled by the practical men who
used them.

So while most of the manuscripts have a version of one of
the Redactions as their primary text, most of them also
have extra material. This may be inserted into tractates or
between tractates of the Redaction, or added after the Redaction; it may be a tractate taken from another Redaction,
or a rather formless 'tail' of miscellaneous rules of law.
Llyfr y Damweiniau is one such tail: it took shape (apparently in Gwynedd) in the thirteenth century and gained the
dignity of a name of its own in the fourteenth. It is found, in
some form, in association with each of the three Redactions.

There is still much work to be done on the relation between the Redactions and on the relation between the
manuscripts of each Redaction, but our ideas on some
points are already fairly clear. It can be said that the least
developed Welsh law is found in the core of the Cyfnerth
Redaction; that the Blegywryd Redaction shows clear signs
of the influence of the Church, and more doubtful signs of
the influence of English legal procedure; and that the Iorwerth Redaction was surely put together in Gwynedd in
the early thirteenth century, when the political successes
of Llywelyn the Great created a favourable environment
for the development of more sophisticated law, such as we
find in that Redaction.[1] The Blegywryd Redaction is for the
most part a re-translation from a Latin text which was
perhaps first put together in southern Wales about the

[1] See T. Jones Pierce, 'The Laws of Wales—the Kindred and the
Bloodfeud', *Medieval Welsh Society* (ed. J. Beverley Smith;
Cardiff, 1972), 295-6.

xxvi   *The Law of Hywel Dda*

third quarter of the twelfth century when Rhys ap
Gruffudd was 'suzerain' (164.24, and see 203.31n). Our
oldest copies come from about 1300; by then southern
Wales was all under Anglo-Norman rule, and the Iorwerth
Redaction never came into general use there, though some
material, such as the tractate on Joint Ploughing (III.9) was
taken into later manuscripts based on the Blegywryd
Redaction. These later manuscripts, of which BL Add.
22356[1] is probably the most important survivor, were in
practical use until Welsh law was finally suppressed in
1536.

There seems to be nothing in medieval legal literature
which is quite like these Welsh lawbooks, in which a sort
of textbook is combined with a sort of legal commonplace
book. They perhaps find their closest parallel in the manuscripts put together by members of the Inns of Court in six-
teenth- and seventeenth-century London. Of course the
kind of law they present is very different from post-Renais-
sance English law, but they show the same enthusiasm for
snapping up unconsidered trifles, and the reference to what
Goronwy ap Moriddig used to say about the right of a
cuckold to compensation (p.48) is just the sort of note
which might be found in a seventeenth-century manuscript
from Gray's Inn. The likeness to a barrister's collection is
closest in material like *Llyfr y Damweiniau*, which has no
basic framework of tractates as the Redaction material has;
but even in the Redactions a quite casual examination of
our text will show that the Welsh lawyers were more
concerned to snap up everything than to put it into the best
order when snapped up. That is plainly why our main text
twice states the rule that when a man takes a second wife
the first is freed from him (47.31-2; 57.11-14).

III. THE CLASSICAL AND LATER LAW

The law recorded in the oldest surviving manuscripts in
Welsh has features which justify our calling it classical.
Those manuscripts all contain the Iorwerth Redaction (or,
in one case, its revised edition, 'Llyfr Colan'), with associated material of which the most important is *Llyfr y Damweiniau*. All these manuscripts were written before the fall

---

[1] See p. xxi above.

Introduction

of the princes of Gwynedd, and they were written in Gwynedd; but those who compiled them would certainly have said that any of their rules was law throughout Wales. Some of their material would in time be copied in other parts of Wales, and much of it was derived from books written in other parts: we have seen that the Justices' Test Book drew on books from Powys and Deheubarth, and Llyfr Colan used a Latin manuscript (probably written in southern Wales) and the 'Book of the White House', which may have been that same Latin manuscript and which we have already mentioned as connected with Whitland Abbey.

Gwynedd was nevertheless the great centre of Welsh juristic learning in the thirteenth century. When that witness told the commissioners in 1281 that Iorwerth Fychan was called *ynad* because he had studied in Gwynedd, his answer was probably politically motivated, but it is evidence of the reputation of Gwynedd in popular opinion at the time.

This pre-eminence of Gwynedd in legal studies in the late twelfth and early thirteenth centuries is natural enough under the political conditions of Wales at the time. The relative stability of the heartland of Llywelyn the Great's dominions would have given the jurists a rare freedom to think out solutions to legal problems; economic changes and developing commerce would have raised new problems for solution; and the growing power and ambitions of the ruler would have made it necessary to define his rights and to extend them as much as possible. Our classical texts show 'public law' becoming even more important than it had been, and its character is changing. The 'laws of court' still look like a description of the festive gathering of the Heroic Age, but there are additions which show that the old court had fallen into disuse and that the men who had been the ruler's companions in the chase and at the banquet were becoming parts of the administrative machine of the developing state. There are signs also of the influence of the prince's Anglo-Norman consort and her entourage; this aspect of the Iorwerth Redaction has not yet been studied in detail but it can at least be said that words of French origin are noticeable in the Redaction.

What makes the law classical, however, is not the power of the prince, nor the sophistication of his court, but the professionalism of the lawyers. Though we know very

The Law of Hywel Dda

little about the training of these lawyers and about any professional organisation there may have been, we can venture to say that there were enough lawyers to form a profession capable of setting standards and of working out principles and applying them to problems of the day. If some of those lawyers fell into pedantry as they applied their logic, that is a sign of their professionalism: the chief occupational hazard of any profession is a hardening of the mental arteries which leads to unthinking application of rules.

The concept of classical law of course implies that the system was not finally completed but was still developing, and that this was true can be seen most plainly in the 'Colan' manuscript (NLW Peniarth MS. 30).[1] In that manuscript we have both a revised edition of the Iorwerth Redaction (in which *Iorwerth* tractates have been reworded more concisely, sometimes amended, and often supplemented from another source) and the earliest full copy of that disorderly *Llyfr y Damweiniau.*

This classical law is the source of most of the material translated in this volume, but material has also been drawn from other sources. On the one hand there are passages from the Cyfnerth and Blegywryd Redactions, in which the law is less developed, or differently developed. On the other hand there are passages from later texts in which extraneous influences have affected the native law.

The later material is found mainly in manuscripts written in the fifteenth century, when the authority of Hywel's law was declining, both in the Principality created by Edward I and in the autonomous marcher lordships. In the Principality the Statute of Wales (1284) had introduced English criminal law and had set up an English system of courts and administration, though the Welsh substantive law of property and obligations remained in force; but as time went on there was a growing tendency (especially among the gentry of Gwynedd) to seek assimilation to the English mould. In a marcher lordship the lord claimed to be a king, just as the Welsh ruler whom he replaced had done. He might not be a big king or a powerful one, and he acknowledged the king of England as his feudal superior. In theory, Welsh law should have applied to a marcher lord-

---

[1] The manuscript was given this name by the seventeenth century antiquary William Maurice because it was in two columns: *Col* p.xv.

Introduction

ship, and that would give the lord no authority to change the law, but this would matter little in practice, for the lord would usually be strong enough to get his own way. Thus he could make changes quite freely after such consultations as he saw fit, provided that he did not call the attention of the English king by any flagrant wrongdoing. The records of the lordships show the lords innovating where they saw some advantage in so doing, and upholding long-standing rules of Welsh law (with adjustments on occasion) when that was to their advantage. They were, for instance, very careful to see that when women married or lost their virtue, the fee laid down by Welsh law, the amobr, should be paid.[1]

IV. FEATURES OF WELSH MEDIEVAL LAW

An observer coming to the Welsh lawbooks for the first time is likely to be most sharply struck by the juxtaposition of crudity and sophistication in the texts: this is most obvious in the tractate on the law of women. Here we have the very stark procedure in a charge of rape (p.51), and the satirical agweddi paid to a 'false maiden' (p.49) as survivals from a more primitively robust society. This provision for the false maiden's agweddi is evidence for a mechanical application of legal principle: agweddi of some kind is always due when a marital union ends, even if the woman has no moral merit; in like manner, the seated serjeant is given a mocking compensation for insult because he has no right to sit while on duty (p.35).

At a later stage the wife who deserts her husband without legal excuse is refused agweddi, and the lowly dung maer is refused compensation for insult. And the developing law shows a subtler logic at work, for instance in the detail of the compensation for rape: since rape creates a marital union which is immediately terminated, all the payments which fall due on creation or termination are payable, in addition to the payments appropriate to the insults involved. To social historians, indeed, the law texts seem too much 'concerned to display the subtlety of legal argument': the right of a husband to reclaim his separated wife if he overtook her with one foot out of her intended second

[1] See R. R. Davies, WLW 93-114 and the sources cited.

husband's bed has an 'air of unreality which hardly fosters confidence in the validity of the law-texts as a guide to the central issues of social custom'. The warning is timely, for lawbooks of all kinds tend to give special prominence to exceptional cases, and as the historian here quoted emphasises, the lawbooks were not written for social historians.[1] To the lawyer, the rule in question sounds like the opinion of an advocate who has been arguing that his client is entitled to reclaim his wife, and has been asked by the judge where he would draw the line.

If the general reader is first struck by the contrast of crudity and sophistication, he is likely to be struck also by the fact that homicide appears in the lawbooks as primarily a matter for compensation whereas theft is a matter for punishment. Moreover theft—taking by stealth—is a more serious crime than robbery—taking by force: only theft is a capital offence. Both these are common phenomena in early societies; though the explanation for them is not quite the same, both depend on the primacy of strength in early society. The strong man armed keeps his goods in peace, but trust in society is undermined by the thief who acts in secret. On the other hand, when compensation is paid for homicide, the killer's kindred are buying off the vengeance which the victim's kindred would otherwise take on them, and there are in our books passages enough which show how near the surface the blood-feud still lay.

The society of the lawbooks has indeed begun to treat some kinds of homicide as offences against society and to inflict punishment. But here as elsewhere in Hywel's Law compensation and punishment go together, and the medieval Welsh lawyers seem to have a clearer vision than their English contemporaries (and indeed, a clearer vision that most twentieth-century English lawyers). The English common law was born in the twelfth century, when disorder had become intolerable and the power of the state was put forth to suppress it. The state was more concerned to punish the offender than to compensate the victim, and in English law punishment has ever since tended to take precedence over compensation, and has often excluded it. In the classical Welsh law, punishment was becoming more important as the state grew stronger, but compensation still had priority. It is made quite clear that the ruler has

[1] R. R. Davies, WLW 93-4.

Introduction

the right to mitigate a penalty, but that if he does so, his mercy does not affect the victim's right for compensation for loss.[1]

Compensation and punishment were dealt with in the same proceedings: the ruler took advantage of the proceedings begun by the victim or his kin, and he would not ordinarily bring an independent prosecution. This is nicely brought out in the rules relating to bloodshed (197.11-16n): though the ruler was entitled to a penalty for all bloodshed, he could not prosecute for that penalty unless the shed blood reached the ground; in any other case he would get the penalty only if the victim sued for compensation. Here there may be a survival in secularised form of the magical or sacral aspect of bloodshed: as in Biblical law, the idea perhaps is that the earth is polluted by blood. In general, the basis of penalties for crime was the loss caused to the ruler, as we are told in one passage—though we are not told in what that loss consisted: it was perhaps a loss of reputation, caused by the ruler's failure to protect the victim from wrong.

For the non-historian who knows the working of modern law courts, the most peculiar passages in the Welsh lawbooks will be those dealing with court procedure. He will find especially unacceptable the drastic consequences for a judge of giving a judgment which is reversed on appeal (to put it in modern terms): he pays a heavy financial penalty, and is disqualified from judging ever after. Such punishment would be quite unreasonable (as well as impracticable) under modern conditions; in medieval Wales it was perhaps over-severe, but it was not unreasonable, because the function of the judge was significantly different from that of the modern judge. To put it in aphoristic form: in modern courts, trial precedes judgment; in medieval courts, judgment precedes proof.[2]

In a modern trial, evidence is taken and subjected to testing, especially by the cross-examination of witnesses; the judge or jury makes a subjective assessment of the truth of the evidence, and so determines the facts to which the judge then applies the law. In most cases, the rule of law to

[1] DwCol 435.

[2] The aphorism is Maitland's: *The Forms of Action at Common Law* (Cambridge, 1936), 15. He said it was to be found in 'modern German books dealing with ancient procedure.'

be applied is clear, but if necessary the judge will find a rule, by interpreting some statutory provision, or by comparing the decisions in earlier cases in which the facts were more or less similar to those of the case before him. The judgment thus given after trial of the facts may be reversed because the judge is held either to have determined the facts wrongly (or misdirected the jury about the facts) or to have applied the wrong rule of law; he may have made a mistake without being incompetent or perverse.

In such medieval courts as those of Wales, the judge does not decide who is telling the truth: he decides which of the assertions made by the parties before him are to be proved, and in what way. When he has decided that, the parties will try to fulfil these requirements of proof, and the only question is the purely objective question whether they have indeed fulfilled them. The judgement that a particular form of proof is appropriate of course precedes that proof, and the judgment can be reversed if it is shown that the wrong form of proof was chosen. The judge is in no danger if he takes care to find in a lawbook a written statement of the rule which he applies; there are special provisions for allowing him to consult books if a judgment given by him without reference to a book is challenged.

This contrast between medieval proof and modern trial is well known from many countries. Everyone has heard of the ordeals of hot iron and hot water, and Norman England had trial by battle, in which the parties fought, in person or by champions, with special weapons and according to very formal rules, to decide who was in the right. These methods of proof we moderns call irrational, but there is nothing very rational in our assumption that a judge or jury can always recognise a lie, while ordeal and battle are rational enough for those who have a certain view of the world. It is more accurate to speak of the medieval methods as objective and the modern ones as subjective.

In Wales the classical and earlier lawbooks do not mention ordeal or battle: in a land which was never pagan, perhaps it was never thought proper to tempt God by asking for a miraculous vindication of the accused innocent. But the Welsh methods were objective: they depended on oaths sworn by the parties or by witnesses of various kinds, and the lawbooks tell the judge what oaths are required in the different kinds of case.

Introduction

The general principle was that the party which was most likely to know the truth was required to prove it. Thus criminal charges were most often rebutted by the defendant's oath of denial, though his unsupported oath was seldom enough. It must usually be supported by a prescribed number of compurgators, but these did not swear to the truth of the facts; they swore to the 'cleanness' of their principal's oath.

In other circumstances the oaths were sworn by witnesses of various kinds, who testified to particular facts. In a simple society where everyone knew everyone else, oaths were not very likely to be false, but the classical law shows a determined effort to refine these methods of proof. There is no sign of anything like cross-examination of witnesses (there was none in English law till long after this period), but there are strict rules for the qualifications and disqualifications of witnesses and compurgators.[1] The danger of misuse of compurgation is further reduced by the requirement in many cases that some of the compurgators should be designated in advance.

V. The Significance of Hywel's Law

'All the time you were speaking, I was saying to myself "Africa, Africa".' It was a retired missionary who told the present writer that, after listening to a public lecture on medieval Welsh law. Any social anthropologist would be likely to react in much the same way to the obvious parallels between some features of Welsh law and the practices of a twentieth-century society (and not necessarily of a 'backward' society). Of course this does not mean that Africa has borrowed from Wales or Wales from Africa, nor even that Africa and Wales have borrowed from the same source; it was long ago pointed out that the enumeration of coincidences between Celtic and early English law did not prove that the English had borrowed from the Celts: 'by that method our English medieval law could with little ado be proved to be Greek, Slavonic, Semitic, or, for aught one knows, Chinese.'[2]

[1] See Glossary, s.v. *tyst*, and the references there given.
[2] PM i.xcix

The Law of Hywel Dda

Social anthropologists may be able to learn something from Welsh medieval law. Students of Welsh law can certainly learn one thing from social anthropology: that in different places and different ages human beings react to similar circumstances in similar ways. So some features of Hywel's law are similar to features of other systems simply because the medieval Welsh were human: but others are similar because they were Celts or because they were Indo-Europeans.

Similarities with Irish law have their origin in the common Celtic social pattern, and it is particularly instructive to compare the Welsh lawbooks with those of Ireland. We have seen that these show little sign of the growth of state power; they also deal with the development of the law very differently from the Welsh books. It was evidently the theory of Irish law that the law was unchanging and its expression in words unchangeable; hence the Irish scribes copied the old material in its archaic language—and adapted it to the facts of their own time by gloss and commentary which explained away the difficulties.[1] The Welsh continually revised and added to their original material so that the archaic was transformed: it has often been pointed out that the Irish and Welsh materials complement each other because what appears as a fossil in a Welsh text can be recognised in its living form in an Irish one.[2]

For the legal historian the greatest interest of the law of Hywel lies in an overriding importance which it attached to written lawbooks. On the Continent the medieval lawyers drew a distinction between customary law jurisdictions (pays de droit coutumier) and written law jurisdictions (pays de droit écrit): the latter applied Roman law in some form or other. Wales was a territory of written law jurisdictions: though its law was no form of Roman law, but a well-developed and still developing customary law, the authority of any alleged rule of law depended on its being found in writing in a lawbook. If a Welsh litigant challenged a judge's decision on a point of law, both parties were expected to produce lawbooks in support of their conten-

---

[1] See D. A. Binchy, 'The Historical and Linguistic Value of the Irish Law Tracts', reprinted in CLP 73-107.
[2] See the section of the text on Dadannudd (101.18-104.8) and especially the introductory note.

Introduction

tions, and it is clear that there was a possibility of conflict between lawbooks.

This of course means that the lawbooks did not consist of legislation issued authoritatively by rulers, like the so-called 'barbarian laws' of Germanic kings, such as the Lombard Laws. Nor are they officially-encouraged codifications of customary law, like the *Sachsenspiegel* in Germany, or the Scandinavian books in which a written text recorded the law which had previously been recited from year to year by an officially appointed lawman. They very occassionally refer to changes in the law made by a ruler, and there are many signs of the increasing importance of the state (that is, the ruler); but at no point do the books attribute the authority of the legal rule to the ruler. The rule is law because of the lawbook, not because of the law-maker.

The peculiar virtue of the Welsh law manuscripts is their variability. Because there are three different Redactions, and because there are several manuscripts of each Redaction, it is possible to discern signs which point to its development from a pre-curial law and a society in which state authority hardly existed. When all the manuscripts have been edited and scientifically studied, it should be possible to trace in considerable detail the growth of a system which, by the beginning of the thirteenth century, was coming to a surprisingly sophisticated fruition.

Here we cross the uncertain frontier between legal history and juristic doctrine, and the claim can be made for the law of thirteenth-century Wales that it deserves attention because of its success in applying its principles to meet new situations. Its solutions to the problems are rational, and if some of the jurists are inclined to push logic to the point of legalism, others have the vision which gives priority to justice. If they sometimes seem to be drawing distinctions which are too fine to be practical, they are on the whole primarily concerned with real problems which might arise in their society.

Practical concern for justice is most clearly seen in the application of *cyfraith gyhydedd*, 'the law of equality', according to which the subject-matter of a dispute could be equally shared between the parties: if this principle were formally accepted in modern English law, the judges would be spared a great deal of mental gymnastics. For an example of the application of a general principle to particular cases, we can turn to the rule that for damage unwittingly caused compensation must be wittingly made. This meant that a plaintiff who suffered harm did not have to prove that the defendant caused the harm intentionally or negligently, as the modern plaintiff under English law must do. For the medieval Welsh plaintiff, it was enough that the defendant caused the harm. In modern legal language, liability in tort was based on causation, not on fault. The practical question then is, what amounts to causation?—and such rulings as that on non-liability for the act of a person suffering from rabies (151.34-152.3), or the condition for liability for harm caused by a felled tree (153.29-33) show the Welsh lawyers' skill.

So we Welsh can show good reason for our pride in the native law of our country; and for us (and through us, for other small nations) our old law is of special significance as one of the elements which made it possible for a politically fragmented people to attain a consciousness of nationhood. In a recent study Professor Rees Davies has shown how important a part distinctive forms of law played in the development of national consciousness in thirteenth-century Europe, and nowhere will this part have heen more important than in Wales, where legal unity did much to counterbalance lack of political unity.[1] More than half a century earlier, Sir Goronwy Edwards had said that two things in special had made the Welsh a nation: the language and the law, which in the Middle Ages was 'a potent force, recognized by others as well as by ourselves as marking us off from other people and strengthening our national consciousness'.[2]

The law made its contribution to this strengthening both directly and indirectly. Since Welsh was the language of the law, the Welsh language had a publicly-expressed dignity which English did not have in England at that period, and the technical terms of law which passed into the ordinary vocabulary were natural to the vocabulary, not foreign borrowings as they are in English. If the political fate of medieval Wales had been different, the law's service might have been even greater. It has been argued that if the princes of Gwynedd had succeeded in their aim of establishing

[1] R. R. Davies, 'Law and National Identity in Thirteenth Century Wales', *Welsh Society and Nationhood . . . presented to Glanmor Williams* (Cardiff, 1984). 51-69.
[2] CLP 160

Introduction   *xxxvii*

a unified Welsh state, the Welsh language would have died out, since it was not the first language of the princes' milieu. The lawbooks indeed show traces of the French influence of that milieu, but it is likely that if the rule of the Welsh princes had continued, the prestige of the law would have counterbalanced any tendency in the court of Aberffraw to abandon the language.

If in those hypothetical circumstances the law had not protected the language, it would not have been for any insufficiency in the law. We have already seen that the law of Hywel was proving its capacity to adapt to changing circumstances, which is the great condition for the survival of any legal system; and it was able to adapt because it was a learned law, preserved in writing by a learned profession. Our great regret must be that so many good principles of Welsh law were lost when English law replaced it: there is irony in the fact that some of those principles have found their way into English law in the last hundred years or so, and especially in the present generation. As the right to compensation for the death of a human being is established, and it is accepted that in some cases losses should be shared between the parties to a transaction (as under *cyfraith gyhydedd*), we may even wonder whether English law has not unconsciously adopted the slogan 'Back to Hywel Dda.[1]

---

[1] The point is developed in 'The Significance of the Law of Hywel', [1978] *Tr. Cym.* at 67-72.

xxxviii — The Law of Hywel Dda

Recommended for Further Reading:

Aberystwyth Studies, vol. x (The Hywel Dda Millenary Volume); Cardiff, 1928.

H. D. Emanuel, 'Studies in the Welsh Laws', in *Celtic Studies in Wales* (ed. Elwyn Davies; Cardiff, 1963), pp.71-100.

Welsh History Review, vol. i, Special Number (The Welsh Laws); Cardiff, 1963. Papers given at the first Colloquium on Welsh Medieval Law, Aberystwyth, 1962.

Celtic Law Papers (ed. D. Jenkins), Brussels, 1973.

M. E. Owen, 'Functional Prose', in *A Guide to Welsh Literature*, vol. i (ed. A. O. H. Jarman and G. R. Hughes; Swansea, 1976), especially pp. 267-75.

The Welsh Law of Women (ed. D. Jenkins and M. E. Owen); Cardiff, 1980.

Lawyers and Laymen (ed. T. M. Charles-Edwards, M. E. Owen, and D. B. Walters); Cardiff, 1986.

T. M. Charles-Edwards, *The Welsh Laws* (Writers of Wales, Cardiff, 1989).

T. P. Ellis, *Welsh Tribal Law and Custom in the Middle Ages* (Oxford, 1926; reprinted, Aalen, 1982), is still useful as a lead to the texts, but as a guide to their interpretation it must be used with great caution. It is at its most reliable in dealing with the land law.

Anyone who has difficulty in buying copies of books in Welsh or relating to Wales should send to the Welsh Books Centre, Glanrafon Industrial Estate, Llanbadarn Fawr, Aberystwyth, SY23 3AQ.

NOTE ON THE TEXT AND TRANSLATION

THE text here translated is composite, and in this it follows a long tradition in the handling of medieval Welsh legal material. The practitioners of the later Middle Ages (as we have seen) added material from any source to their basic texts. The lawyer-antiquary William Phillips of Brecon brought together at least two texts in the manuscript which he wrote in 1663. The first printed edition of the material, *Leges Wallicae* (1730) added material from many other manuscripts to a basic text taken from a single manuscript, and the editors have been severely criticised for thus introducing 'a confusion on which learning spent itself in vain'. Perhaps British learning was rather too lazy to fight the confusion, for continental scholars were able to use the text effectively for comparison—but the present editor has taken warning from the criticism, and has tried to avoid confusing the reader.

The starting-point for the present text was Books I to III of *Leges Wallicae*. What the critics regarded as that edition's weakness was its strength for the present editor's purpose: for, since *Leges Wallicae* had added to its basic Iorwerth text extracts from manuscripts of the Cyfnerth and Blegywryd Redactions, his attention was immediately drawn to the relevant passages in those Redactions, and it was usually easy to trace those passages in the modern printed editions. Tracing the classical material from manuscripts not used for *Leges Wallicae* was significantly more laborious.

Since *Leges Wallicae*'s primary source was the same manuscript (*B*, i.e. BL Cotton Titus D.ii) as that used for Aled Wiliam's *Llyfr Iorwerth*, our main text serves as a translation for *Llyfr Iorwerth*. MS. *B* is the only medieval manuscript of its branch of the Iorwerth tradition, which we can call Ior B; the other branch, 'Ior A', is represented by the thirteenth-century manuscripts, *A*, *C*, and *E*, and by the revised edition of Ior, *Col*. The only substantial difference between Ior A and Ior B is in the tractate on Homicide (Galanas: III.1 in this edition); so some material from the A form of the tractate has been added to our text, usually in the form in which it appears in *Col*. A few other additions of Iorwerth material have been made; most of these are taken from *Col*, but some are passages from other Iorwerth manuscripts, not taken into *Llyfr Iorwerth*.

The Law of Hywel Dda

Substantial additions have been made from *Llyfr y Damweiniau* and from *Llyfr Cynghawsedd*, the 'Book of Pleadings' published as Book VII in *Ancient Laws*. Since *Llyfr y Damweiniau* is found in association with *Col* (and part of it in association with MS. *A*), and *Llyfr Cynghawsedd* is found in association with MS. *B*, this material is treated as classical. Other additional material is non-classical: some of it seems to be pre-classical and to reflect an earlier society, while some of it is certainly post-classical and reflects the social changes of the later Middle Ages. Most of the post-classical material comes from the 'tail' which bulks so large in the later manuscripts. Priority has usually been given to the Cyfnerth version, as being more likely to represent an original Welsh text than the Blegywryd version: in *Bleg* some passages are known to be mistranslations of a Latin original, and other passages may be undetected mistranslations.

The insertion of additional material has inevitably broken the continuity of the main text here and there. The arrangement of the text has been designed to minimise the harm so caused; anyone who wants to follow the main Iorwerth text without interruption can do so by ignoring all text which is indented (not set to full measure).

The text has been laid out with the aim of showing, as unobtrusively as possible, from what kind of source each particular passage is derived. Hence:

(a) All material whose Welsh text is printed in *Llyfr Iorwerth* is in this edition set to full measure in 11 point type, like this sentence.

> (b) All other classical material is set to narrower measure in 11 point type, like this sentence.
> (c) All non-classical material is set to narrower measure in 10 point type, like this sentence.

This means that the source of all material set to full measure is *Ior*, so that no indication of source is needed. For all material not set to full measure, the source is indicated at the end of each extract by an abbreviation: because the extract is the unit, the same abbreviation sometimes appears at the end of successive extracts. Full references to the sources are given in the Table of Source References and indexed in the Index to Sources.

Introductory Note

The Translation

As a schoolboy in London the editor was taught the first rule of translation, 'the translation must be English'. If he has broken that rule in this work, he has done so with his eyes at least half-open, because it seemed necessary in order to convey effectively the meaning of the Welsh. The original does not always observe the niceties of grammatical convention, and the translation has been allowed a corresponding liberty. Welsh idiom has occasionally been carried over into English; this is likely to affront native speakers of English less than Welsh speakers, who are (excusably enough) slow to admit that languages grow by sponging on each other. Above all, accuracy has never been knowingly sacrificed to elegance, for all too often the scholar who must depend on an elegant translation draws a false conclusion from which a cruder translation would have saved him.

In the interest of accuracy, a large number of technical terms have been kept untranslated; these are spelt according to modern Welsh conventions, and are explained (as concisely as may be) in the Glossary. They are not italicised. The Glossary also includes some English words and expressions which uniformly translate particular Welsh ones; but one Welsh verb has defied uniform translation and must be explained here. This is *dylyu*, which was a complete verb in medieval Welsh, whereas in modern Welsh only the imperfect and pluperfect tenses survive, with the meaning 'ought'. The basic meaning in the law texts is wider; it has often been possible to convey this by 'to be right', and it is to be noticed that at some points one manuscript has *dylyu* where another has *bod yn iawn*, which has been translated 'to be proper'. The translation 'to be right' for *dylyu* leaves open the question whether the function concerned is a right or an obligation: for the officers of the court, of course, it is clear that they were both bound and entitled to perform the functions specified for them. In other contexts, however, the decision has sometimes to be taken in favour of either 'bound' or 'entitled': fortunately there is seldom or never any doubt which is right, but the reader may perhaps find that a perplexing passage becomes more satisfactory if one of these words is replaced by the other.

One noun also needs special mention: this is *dyn*, which in medieval Welsh always means 'man' in the sense of

xlii *The Law of Hywel Dda*

'human being', but is in modern Welsh also used for 'man' as male. For the avoidance of confusion, *dyn* is always (though reluctantly) translated 'person': in a German translation, *dyn* would naturally be *Mensch*, and *gŵr* would be *Mann*, with the bonus of covering in one word the two senses 'human male' and 'husband'.

Though the translator of course hopes that he has improved on previous translations, he emphatically disclaims anything like final authority for his renderings. He has been disconcerted to find, when editing the Index, some inconsistencies which he cannot defend, though he would readily argue that such variants as 'tilth' and 'tillage' are appropriate to their respective contexts. The notes reveal the gradual clarification of his understanding of some words; some further notes could no doubt be profitably added—on, for instance, the word *mefl*, translated by 'blemish'. The blemishes mentioned in the lawbooks are certainly shameful, and the primary meaning of *mefl* may have been 'shame'.

In the 1990 reprint the opportunity has been taken to make some necessary corrections and amendments; the most significant change is in the interpretation of W. *hebog* and *gwalch*: see the Glossary, s.v. *falcon*.

BIBLIOGRAPHY AND ABBREVIATIONS

A (MS)	MS. N.L.W. Peniarth 29
a	adjective
AL	*Ancient Laws and Institutes of Wales* [ed. Aneurin Owen], London, 1841
AS	Anglo-Saxon
AV	Authorised Version (of Bible)
Arch. Brit.	Edward Lhuyd, *Archaeologia Britannica*; Oxford, 1707, reprinted, Shannon, 1971
Arch. Camb.	*Archaeologia Cambrensis*
B (MS)	MS. B.L. Cotton Titus D.II
BBCS	*Bulletin of the Board of Celtic Studies*
BBleg	*The Laws of Hywel Dda (the Book of Blegywryd)*, tr. M. Richards, Liverpool, 1954
BL, B.L.	British Library
Bd	*Y Beirniad*

Binchy, D. A., *Anglo-Saxon and Celtic Kingship*, Oxford, 1970

Bleg	The Blegywryd Redaction; with specific reference to page and line (for text) or (with p.) to page (for notes), *Cyfreithiau Hywel Dda yn ôl Llyfr Blegywryd*, ed. S. J. Williams and J. E. Powell, Cardiff, 1942, second edition 1961.

Bowen, Ivor, *The Statutes of Wales*, London, 1908

C (MS)	MS. B.L. Cotton Caligula A.XIV
CG	*Crith Gablach*, ed. D. A. Binchy, Dublin, 1941
CLP	*Celtic Law Papers*, ed. D. Jenkins, Brussels, 1973
CMCS	*Cambridge Medieval Celtic Studies*
Col	The 'Colan' revision of the Iorwerth Redaction; with specific reference to numbered sentences (for text) or (with p.) to page (for notes), *Llyfr Colan*, ed. D. Jenkins, Cardiff, 1963
Cyfn	The Cyfnerth Redaction; for specific references see WML

The Law of Hywel Dda

D (MS)	MS. N.L.W. Peniarth 32
Dict.Dupl.	John Davies, *Antiquae Linguae Brit-annicae . . . et Linguae Latinae Dictionarium Duplex*, London, 1632; Scolar reprint, 1968
Dw, Dw Col	'Llyfr y Damweiniau'; with specific reference to numbered sentences, *Damweiniau Colan*, ed. D. Jenkins, Aberystwyth, 1973

E.	English
E (MS)	MS. B.L. Add. 14931
Econ HR	Economic History Review
Ellis, T.P.,	*Welsh Tribal Law and Custom in the Middle Ages*, Oxford, 1926; reprinted Aalen, 1982

F (MS)	MS. N.L.W. Peniarth 34
f	feminine
Fr.	French

G (MS)	MS. N.L.W. Peniarth 35
GC	'Gwentian Code' in AL; specific references to Book, chapter, and verse of that edition
GML	Timothy Lewis, *A Glossary of Welsh Medieval Law*, Manchester, 1913
GPC	*Geiriadur Prifysgol Cymru: a Dictionary of the Welsh Language*, Cardiff, 1950-
Germ.	German

Governance, see Stephenson

Graf and Dietherr, *Deutsche Rechtssprichwörter*, second edition, Nördlingen, 1869; reprint, Aalen, 1975

Griffiths, *Principality* R. A. Griffiths (ed.), *The Principality of Wales in the later Middle Ages*, vol. i, Cardiff, 1972

Grimm, Jacob, *Deutsche Rechtsalterthümer*, fourth edition by A. Heusler and R. Hübner, Leipzig, 1899; reprint, Darmstadt, 1974

H (MS)	MS. N.L.W. Peniarth 164

Bibliography and Abbreviations   *xlv*

HW	J. E. Lloyd, *A History of Wales . . . to the Edwardian Conquest*, second edition, London, 1912; third edition, 1939
Ior	The Iorwerth Redaction; with specific reference to numbered section and un-numbered sentence (for text) or (with p.) to page (for notes), *Llyfr Iorwerth*, ed. A. R. Wiliam, Cardiff, 1960
J	*Cyfreithiau Hywel Dda o Lawysgrif Coleg yr Iesu, Rhydychen LVII* (ed. M. Richards, Cardiff, 1957; revised edition, 1990)

James, Christine, 'Golygiad o BL Add. 22356 o Gyfraith Hywel . . .' (unpublished University of Wales thesis, Ph.D., 1984)

Kingship, see Binchy

LHDd	*The Laws of Howel Dda*, ed. T. Lewis, Aberystwyth and London, 1912
LTWL	*Latin Texts of the Welsh Laws*, ed. H. D. Emanuel, Cardiff, 1967
LW	*Cyfreithjeu Hywel Dda ac eraill, seu Leges Wallicae*, ed. W. Wotton and M. Williams, London, 1730
Lat A, B, C, D, E,	The Latin Redactions of LTWL; references are to page and line of LTWL

Linnard, W., *Trees in the Law of Hywel*, Aberystwyth.

Litt. Wall.	*Littere Wallie*, ed. J. G. Edwards, Cardiff, 1940
Ll (MS)	The lost Llanforda manuscript, see 14 BBCS 89-104

Llyfr Iorwerth, ed. A. R. Wiliam, Cardiff, 1960

m	masculine
ME	Middle English
Mk (MS)	The Bodorgan manuscript of the Cyfnerth Redaction
MS	manuscript (referring to actual reading)
n	noun
NEB	New English Bible

N.L.W.	National Library of Wales, Aberystwyth
NLWJ	National Library of Wales Journal
O.E.	Old English
O.Fr.	Old French
O.W.	Old Welsh
PKM	*Pedeir Keinc y Mabinogi*, ed. Ifor Williams, Cardiff, 1930
PM	F. Pollock and F. W. Maitland, *A History of English Law*, second edition (1898), reprinted with Introduction by S. F. C. Milsom, Cambridge, 1968
PRO	Public Record Office, London
RSV	Revised Standard Version of the Bible
Rec. Caern.	*The Record of Caernarvon*, London, 1838
Rees, W., *A Calendar of Ancient Petitions relating to Wales*, Cardiff, 1975	
S (MS)	MS. B.L. Add. 22356
SC	*Studia Celtica*
SOED	*The Shorter Oxford English Dictionary* (definitions in this are taken direct from the larger OED)
Stephenson, D. *The Governance of Gwynedd*, Cardiff, 1984	
tr.	translated (passages quoted in English translation from Welsh originals)
Tr. Cym.	*Transactions of the Honourable Society of Cymmrodorion*
TYP	*Trioedd Ynys Prydein*, ed. R. Bromwich, Cardiff, 1961, second edition, 1978
U (MS.)	MS. N.L.W. Peniarth 37
v	verb
V	Book V in vol. ii of AL
VC, V.C.	'Venedotian Code' in AL
W.	Welsh

Bibliography and Abbreviations   xlvii

WHR	*Welsh History Review*; Sp. No., Special Number, 'The Welsh Laws', 1963
WLW	*The Welsh Law of Women*, ed. D. Jenkins and M. E. Owen, Cardiff, 1980
WM	*The White Book Mabinogion*, ed. J. Gwenogvryn Evans, Pwllheli, 1907; reprint with introduction by R. M. Jones, Cardiff, 1973
WML	*Welsh Medieval Law*, ed. A. W. Wade-Evans, Oxford, 1909, reprinted Aalen, 1979

Wiliam, see *Llyfr Iorwerth*

YC	*Y Cymmrodor*
Z (MS)	MS. N.L.W. Peniarth 259b

ARRANGEMENT OF TEXT

ALL material which is set to full measure in 11-point type (like this sentence) is translated from the Iorwerth Redaction and corresponds to the Welsh text printed in *Llyfr Iorwerth* (ed. A. R. Wiliam; Cardiff, 1960).

All material set to narrower measure in 11-point type (like this sentence) is translated from other classical material (see pp. xxxix-xl above).

All material set to narrower measure in 10-point type (like this sentence) is translated from non-classical material (see p. xl above).

For material not corresponding to *Llyfr Iorwerth*, the source is indicated at the end of each extract by one of the following abbreviations:

B	MS. B.L. Cotton Titus D.II (passages not in *Llyfr Iorwerth*)
Bleg	The Blegywryd Redaction (as printed in *Llyfr Blegywryd*)
C	MS. B.L. Cotton Caligula A.XIV (Iorwerth Redaction)
Col	*Llyfr Colan* (i.e. the first part of MS. Peniarth 30)
Cyfn	The Cyfnerth Redaction (as printed in WML)
Dw	*Llyfr y Damweiniau* (as printed in *Damweiniau Colan*)
E	MS. B.L. Add. 14931 (Iorwerth Redaction)
G	MS. N.L.W. Peniarth 35
J	MS. Jesus College, Oxford, 57 (Blegywryd Redaction)
S	MS. B.L. Add. 22356 (Blegywryd Redaction)

Full references to the sources are given in the Table of Sources.

THE LAW OF HYWEL DDA

HYWEL son of Cadell prince of all Wales saw the Welsh misusing the laws and called to him six men from every cantred in Wales, to the White House on Taf. These were to be the wisest men in the realm, four of them laymen and the other two clerks. This was the reason for bringing the clerks: lest the laymen should set down anything which might be against Holy Scripture.

The time they came was Lent, and the reason they came in Lent was that it is right for everyone to be holy in that time of holiness, so that he would do no wrong. And by the common counsel and agreement of the wise men who came there they examined the old laws, and some of them they allowed to continue, others they amended, others they wholly deleted, and others they laid down anew. And after they had declared the laws which they adjudged, Hywel gave them his authority and ordered that they should be kept exactly and firmly; and Hywel and the wise men who were with him laid their curse and that of all Wales on anyone in Wales who should corrupt the laws by not keeping them, and laid their curse on the justice who should take the judicial oath, and on the Lord who should give it to him, if he did not know the Three Columns of Law and the Value of Wild and Tame, and what is needed for human practice.

Book I
THE LAWS OF COURT

1. The Court's Members

HE took the court to begin with. It is right that there should be twenty-four officers in it: Captain of the Household; Priest; Steward; Chief Falconer; Court Judge; Chief Groom; Chamberlain; Bard of the Household; Usher; Chief Huntsman; Mead-brewer; Physician; Butler; Doorkeeper; Cook; Candleman; Queen's Steward; Queen's Priest; Queen's Chief Groom; Queen's Chamberlain; Queen's Handmaid; Queen's Doorkeeper; Queen's Cook; Queen's Candleman—and the first officers enumerated above are those of the court, and the last eight are those of the Queen. Three times every year the above twenty-four officers are entitled by law to their woollen clothing from the King and their linen clothing from the Queen—at Christmas, Easter, and Whitsun.

2. The Royal Family

The King and Queen
It is right for the King to give the Queen a third of the goods he gets from land and earth, and in the same way the King's officers to the Queen's officers.

The King's worth is his sarhaed three times. In three ways sarhaed is done to the King. One is when his protection is broken, when he gives his protection to a person and the latter is killed. A second is when two kings meet on their common boundary to negotiate, and in the presence of the two kings a subject of one kills a subject of the other. A third is misuse of his wife, and that sarhaed is increased by a half.

The sarhaed of the King of Aberffraw is paid thus: a hundred cows for every cantred he has, with a red-eared bull for every hundred cows, and a rod of gold as tall as himself and as thick as his little finger, and a plate of gold as broad as his face and as thick as the

6 *The Law of Hywel Dda*

nail of a ploughman who has been a ploughman seven years. Gold is not paid save to the King of Aberffraw.

> The status of the Lord of Dinefwr is also adorned with white cows, each with its head to the tail of the next, with a bull between every twenty of them, so as to fill the space from Argoel to the court of Dinefwr.
>
> *Cyfn, Bleg*

In three ways sarhaed is done to the Queen. One is to break her protection. A second is to strike her a blow. A third is to snatch something from her hand. And a third of the King's sarhaed is paid to her for her sarhaed, but without gold or silver.

The King is entitled to have in his company thirty-six persons on horseback, to wit, the twenty-four officers and the twelve guests, besides his bodyguard and his goodmen and his servants and his musicians and his needy ones; and that is called the King's retinue.

The Edling

The heir-apparent, to wit the edling, who is entitled to reign after the King, is entitled to be the most honoured in the court, except the King and Queen. It is right for him to be a son or a nephew of the King.

His place in the court is between the host and the chief falconer, as one of the six men of the King's mess. His lodging is in the hall, and the pages with him, and the fueller to light a fire and to shut the doors. His provision is unstinted in food and drink, and all his expenses come from the King's coffers, even including his offering; and his horses and dogs and rings and trinkets from the King—and his weapons too. He is not entitled to give away any of that without the King's leave; and when the edling dies he is bound to leave his horses and dogs to the King, since he is not bound to pay any ebediw save that. The reason he is not bound is that he is one of the King's members.

The Royal Family

These are the King's members: his sons and his nephews and his male first-cousins. Some say that each of these is an edling; others say that no-one is an edling save him to whom the King gives hope and prospect. He is one of the three persons who are entitled to hold a banquet in the court, with servants standing before him in his service as before the King. He is not entitled to leave the King for a single night unless the latter himself wills it.

The edling's worth is one third of the worth of the King; his sarhaed is a third of the King's sarhaed, without gold. The edling's protection is to take the person who does the wrong to safety. His horse's fodder is unstinted. His dogs are of the same value as the King's.

The edling and those whom we named above will be of that status until they take land, and after that their status will follow that of the land they take, except for this, that if it happens that they take villein-land the status of their land will rise to make it free land.

No-one has any claim against him for his clothes at the three special feasts, but let them go the way the King wills. No servant has any right against him, and he is entitled to have his service freely.

The Order of the Court

There are fourteen who have chairs in court, four of them below the bar and ten above the bar. First is the King: it is right for him to sit next to the screen; and next to him the cynghellor; after that the host; after that the edling; after that the chief falconer, with the footholder across the dish from him, and the physician at the foot of the column, across the fire from him.

Next to the other screen the priest of the household, in order to bless the food and sing the paternoster; and it is the column above him which it is right

8   The Law of Hywel Dda

for the usher to strike; next to him the court justice; next to him the chaired bard; the court smith at the end of the bench, before the priest's knees.

It is right for the captain of the household to sit at the lower end of the hall, with his left hand to the end door, with those whom he wishes from the bodyguard beside him, and the others on the other side of the door. The bard of the household on one side of him; the chief groom across the screen from the King; the chief huntsman across the screen from the priest.

> From when the steward stands in the hall, and sets the protection of God and that of the King and Queen and the goodmen, and their peace, over the court and the gathering, there is for him who breaks that peace no protection anywhere; for that protection is the general protection of them all, and above the protection of all the protection of the King as highest. And accordingly there is no protection for him from any one of them, nor from relics nor from a church.
>
> None of the court officers can give protection, unless one of them stands for them all and says that it is he who gives protection for them all to everyone who seeks it from him in the name in which it is sought.
>
> The Queen's protection is to take the person to whom she gives protection over the boundary of the country, without prosecution and without pursuit.
>
> *Bleg.*

3. The King's Officers

The Captain of the Household

It is right for the captain of the household to be the King's son or nephew, or a man so high that he can be made captain of the household. It is not right that an uchelwr should be captain of the household; the reason it is not right is, that the captain's status depends on the King, and that no uchelwr's does so. Accordingly the **men of** Gwynedd removed the cap-

The King's Officers

tain of the household from the number of the twenty-four officers under the steward.

His worth is a third of the King's worth. His sarhaed is a third of the King's sarhaed, except for gold. His protection is to take the man who does the wrong to safety. His place is with his left hand to the door of the hall.

It is right for him to put the harp into the hand of the bard of the household at the three special feasts.

His lodging is the largest house in the townland, and the most central, and with him those he wishes of the bodyguard, with the others surrounding him so that it shall be convenient for him to find them at need. He is entitled to have the second most honourable dish in the court, next after the King. His provision is three dishes and three hornfuls of the best drink in the court.

He is entitled to a third of the dirwy for what is done in the lower precinct. If a person commits an offence in the upper precinct, and when fleeing is caught by him or by one of the bodyguard, the captain of the household is entitled to a third of the dirwy.

He is entitled to the King's clothing at the three special feasts, to his horses at all times and his dogs and his hawks and his arms (and his dogs are of the same value as the King's, and so are his hawks), to two shares of fodder for his horse, to his linen clothing from the Queen, and to four horseshoes from the court smith once a year, with their set of nails. He is entitled to three pounds every year from the King as his bounty, and twenty pence from every pound that comes to the King for cases related to land and earth, and twenty-four pence from every man of the bodyguard the first year he rides.

If any man of the bodyguard goes away from the King by reason of anger, it is right for him to invite him to his meal, and to reconcile him with the King. When the bodyguard must go on a raid, or on some

10 · The Law of Hywel Dda

other errand, it is right for him to choose those whom he wants to send, and he is entitled not to be refused.

It is right for him to occupy the hall in the King's absence, and for the servants to wait on him as on the King.

The bodyguard are not entitled to give away their clothing without the captain's leave. It is right for him to go before them everywhere, and that they should do nothing save with his counsel. He is entitled to two men's share of the booty taken from a strange country; and of the King's third, a third is for the captain of the household. He is one of the three persons who are entitled to share with the King: the two others are the Queen and the chief huntsman.

Three persons with whom the King shares by thirds: the Queen, and the captain of the household, and the chief huntsman. This is where he shares with the Queen, to wit everywhere in his realm, but not in a strange country. From the booty of a strange country the captain of the household is entitled to two men's share, and he is entitled to a third of the third which goes to the King. Of the skins of the small wild animals the chief huntsman is entitled to a third of the third which goes to the King; and there are the three places where there is sharing in thirds with the King.

Dw.

He is entitled to three hornfuls of drink, one from the King and the second from the Queen and the third from the steward: it is right that these should be provided for him. He is entitled to a song from the bard of the household when he wants it. He is entitled to free medical care from the physician of the household, except for his blood-clothes, unless one of the three dangerous wounds is involved: these are, a blow to the head reaching the brain, a blow to the body reaching the bowels, and breaking one of the four columns.

The King's Officers

He is entitled to a circuit from the King, after he parts from him at Christmas, together with the bodyguard. And it is right that there should be three parts of the bodyguard, the old part and the middle part and the young part, and it is right for him to be with each of them in turn; and the part with which he is, that is the one entitled to choose the lodging. And as long as he is on that circuit, he is entitled to have officials, a doorkeeper and a cook and a food official; those are entitled to the skins of the animals slaughtered for them, and the cooks are entitled to the tallow and the broken meat and the entrails. And after that circuit is ended, let him come to the King and let him stay with him until the end of a year; and he is not entitled to leave him except on his errands. And here is the reason that he is not entitled to leave him, that the bodyguard is one of three indispensables of a king: the two others are the priest of his household and his court justice.

When the captain of the household dies, the King is entitled to his horse and his arms and his dogs and his falcons, in lieu of his ebediw, since there is no right to any ebediw from a king's member, except his harness.

The Priest of the Household
Second is the priest of the household. He is entitled to his land free, and to his horse in attendance, and his woollen clothing from the King and his linen clothing from the Queen. His place in the hall is across the fire from the King, next to the screen, in order to bless the food and sing the paternoster. His lodging is the sexton's house, with the clerks with him. His sarhaed is according to the judgement of the synod. His provision is a dish and a hornful of drink.

He is entitled to the offering of the King and of all those to whom the King gives an offering at the three special feasts. He is entitled to a third of the King's tithe. He is entitled to the tithe of the bodyguard and to their daered. He is entitled to fourpence for every patent seal which the King gives for land and earth, or for other great matters.

The court priest has three kinds of service to give in sessions: to delete from the roll every case which has been determined; second is to keep in writing up to judgment every case until it is determined; third is to be ready and unintoxicated at the King's need, to write letters and to read them. *Bleg.*

He is entitled to the King's offering at mass every day, and the offering of all the officials, and a third of their service, and two thirds for the place they come from; and similarly for all persons who belong to the court, a third of their service belongs to him.

He is entitled to the clothes in which the King does penance in Lent. He is bound to be always with the King, for he is one of his three indispensables. He is entitled to have his horse from the King as he exhausts it.

The bishop is not entitled to make anyone parson of the King's chapels, save the priest of the household, unless by the counsel of the King.

The Steward

Third is the steward. He is entitled to his land free and to his horse in attendance, and his woollen clothing from the King and his linen clothing from the Queen. His worth is nine kine and nine score kine, with augmentation; his sarhaed is nine kine and nine score pence. He is entitled to the clothing of the captain of the household at the three special feasts.

It is right for him to allot the lodgings, putting himself nearest to the court and having all the officials with him. He is chief over all the officials. He is entitled to twenty-four pence from every one of the officials when they receive their office from the King. He and the officials are entitled to the skins of the cows slaughtered in the kitchen, and two thirds of

The King's Officers 13

them belong to the steward, except for the cows of the maer. The skins of the small livestock belong to the steward and the cook: those are the sheep and lambs, and the kids and bucks and fawns, and every small beast whose skin comes to the kitchen on it, even to the smallest eel.

He is entitled to ten pence from every pound that comes to the King for land and earth. He is entitled to a third of the dirwy and camlwrw of the officials. He is entitled to a third of the dirwy for what is done in the upper precinct. If it happens that a person commits an offence below the bar and flees above the bar and is caught there before getting protection, the steward is entitled to a third of his dirwy. His protection is to take the person who commits the offence to the captain of the household, and he takes him to safety; others say that this is his protection: from when he begins to stand in his function until the last person goes to sleep, to keep the person safe.

It is right for the steward always to control the food in the kitchen and the drink in the mead-store. It is right for the steward to wait on six persons with food, and a seventh with drink: those are the King and his elder and his host and his edling and his chief falconer and his footholder, with the chief groom as seventh for drink; for though he is not entitled to eat with the King, he is entitled to drink with him.

It is right for him to set protection and to attest liquors, and whosoever breaks the common protection which he sets, for him there is no protection.

He is entitled to two shares of fodder for his horse, and four horseshoes and their set of nails once a year from the court smith. He is entitled to a tiercel falcon from the chief falconer every Michaelmas. He is entitled to have from the huntsmen between the middle of February and the first week in March a doeskin, and when they choose, between that day and the middle of October, a hart's skin, for it is at those seasons that hunting goes on.

He has from the chief huntsman a hart's skin in October (to make vessels to keep the King's horns and his cups) before the skins are shared between the King and the huntsmen.   *Cyfn.*

It is right for him to keep the King's share of the booty which comes from a strange country until the King wants to use it, and when the King uses his share, the steward is entitled to the steer he chooses from the King's third.

It is right for the steward to swear for the King, and it is right for him to share out the supper money. The supper money is shared out like this (and the supper money is twenty-four pence for every feast at which there is mead; of this, sixteen pence for the King's officials and eight for the Queen's officials): of the sixteen pence which come to the King's officials, eight for the steward and the cooks, and two shares of that for the steward; and fourpence for the chamberlains, twopence for the hall doorkeeper, a penny for the chamber doorkeeper, a penny for the candleman. Of the eight which belong to the chamber, fourpence for the steward and the cook, and two shares to the steward; a penny for the chamberlain, a penny for the handmaid, a penny for the doorkeeper, a penny for the candleman.

The Chief Falconer

Fourth is the chief falconer. He is entitled to his land free and his horse in attendance, his woollen clothing from the King, and his linen clothing from the Queen. His place in the court is as the fourth man from the King, in his mess. His lodging is the King's barn, lest smoke affect his birds. He is entitled to take a vessel to the court to put his liquor in, for he is entitled only to quench his thirst: the reason for this is, lest he should neglect his birds.

He is entitled to a handsbreadth of wax candle from the steward so as to feed his birds and make his bed.

The King's Officers   15

He is not bound to pay grooms' money, for the King serves him in three places: when he looses his falcon, by holding his horse; this is what is right, to hold his horse while he dismounts, to hold his stirrup while he mounts; and to hold his horse when he goes to relieve himself.

He is entitled to the hearts and lungs of the wild animals killed in the kitchen, for feeding his birds. He is entitled to a dry sheep or fourpence from the King's villeins. He is entitled to a circuit round the King's villeins once a year. He is entitled to a third of the falconers' dirwy, and to the amobr of their daughters. He is entitled to a hart's skin in autumn, and in spring to a doe's skin, to make gloves for carrying his birds and jesses.

He is entitled to be honoured with three gifts on the day his falcon kills one of three birds, a bittern, or a heron, or a crane.

> Whatsoever day the falconer kills a heron or a bittern or a mountain curlew by the power of his falcons, the King does three services for him: to hold his horse while he recovers the birds, and to hold his stirrup while he dismounts, and to hold it while he mounts. Three times the King serves him with his own hand at meat that evening; for he serves him daily by the hand of his messenger, except at the three special feasts and on the day that he kills a notable bird.
> *Cyfn.*

> On the day that he takes a notable bird when the King is not at the place, when the falconer brings the bird to the court it is right for the King to rise before him; and if he does not rise it is right for him to give the raiment he is wearing to the falconer.   *Cyfn.*

He is entitled to the mantle in which the King rides at the three special feasts. His protection is as far as the Queen; others say that it is as far as the last place where his falcon killed a bird. He is entitled to the tiercels, and to the nests of the falcons and sparrow-hawks on the King's land.

From when he puts the falcon into mew until he takes it out, he is not bound to answer any one for a claim, save one of his fellow-officers.

His sarhaed is six kine and six score pence with augmentation; his worth is six kine and six score kine, with augmentation.

> If the falconer kills his horse in hunting, or if it dies by accident, he shall have another from the King.
> *Cyfn.*

> If the falconer is despoiled by law, neither maer nor cynghellor despoils him, but the bodyguard and the serjeant.
> *Cyfn.*

The Court Justice

Fifth is the court justice. He is entitled to his land free, and his horse in attendance, and his woollen clothing from the King and his linen clothing from the Queen. His place is across the fire from the King, next to the priest of the household.

His lodging is the King's chamber, that in which he sleeps, with a pillow from the Queen, and a sheet; and with the cushion on which the King sits by day under his head at night. Others say that he is not entitled to his lodging outside the hall. His horse is entitled to be between the King's horse and the wall, with two shares of the fodder for it.

He is entitled to a throwboard of whalebone from the King, and a gold ring from the Queen and another from the bard of the household, and those idle trinkets he is not entitled to give away or to sell while he lives. He is entitled to a man's share with the officials.

He is entitled to have the chief groom equip his horse from the first nail to the last, and caparison it and bring it caparisoned to him when he is to ride. He is entitled to have the porter open the great gate for him when he comes to the court and when he goes from it, and that he should not send him to the wicket in coming or going.

The King's Officers   17

The court justice does not give money to the chief groom when he gets a horse from the King.   *Cyfn.*

He is entitled to a man's share of the grooms' money. He is entitled to the steer of his choice from the booty which the bodyguard takes in a strange country, after the King has had his third.

> He gets two men's share of the booty which the bodyguard takes even though he does not leave his house.   *Cyfn.*

He is entitled to twenty-four pence, between himself and the justices, for every case on land and earth, with two men's share for himself. He is bound to judge the court and the bodyguard and those who belong to them, free.

He is entitled to a trained sparrowhawk or a tiercel falcon from the chief falconer. He is one of the three indispensables of a king.

He is entitled to twenty-four pence from every justice whom he tests; and where he judges jointly with other justices he is entitled to two men's share.

His protection is as far as the Queen. Whosoever seeks protection from him, he will have protection from when he begins to deal with the first case until the last case finishes on that day.

If it happens that a person pledges himself to the court justice or another, if the person can prove that the judgment which the justice judged was wrong, let him lose his tongue, or buy it from the King for its legal value. If it is he who wins, let his sarhaed be paid to him. This is his sarhaed: six kine and six score pence; his worth is six kine and six score kine with augmentation.

> The court justice is one of the three persons who maintain the status of the court in the absence of the King. He is free of ebediw, since justiceship is better than any temporal thing.   *Cyfn.*

The Chief Groom

Sixth is the chief groom. He is entitled to his land free, and his horse in attendance, and his woollen clothing from the King and his linen clothing from the Queen. His place is across the screen from the King.

His lodging is the house nearest to the barn, because it is right for him to share out the horse-fodder. He is entitled to two shares of the fodder for his own horse.

He is entitled to fourpence for every horse which the King gives, except from three persons, and those are the bishop and the chief falconer and the jester. The reason he is not entitled to the payment from the bishop is that he is the King's parish priest, before whom he rises, sitting down after him, and holding his sleeves while he washes. The reason he is not entitled to it from the chief falconer is that it is right for the King to serve him on three privileged occasions. The reason he is not entitled to it from the jester is that it is right for him to tie the end of the halter (which is on the head of the horse given to him) around his testicles while he goes from the court. And for these reasons they are not bound to pay grooms' money.

He and the grooms are entitled to the foals up to two years old from the King's third of the booty. He is entitled to the King's rain-capes, and his old saddles with coloured wood, and his old black-stained bridles and his old black-stained spurs. It is right for him to carry the King's arms.

He is entitled to an ox's skin in winter and a cow's skin in summer, to make halters. He is entitled to the legs of the cows slaughtered in the kitchen.

No-one is entitled to any of the lees, but the chief groom is entitled to a handsbreadth between drink and lees.

His protection is while the king's fastest horse continues to run.

He is entitled to a third of the dirwy and camlwrw of the grooms, and to the amobr of their daughters. He is entitled to a hornful of drink from the King, and another from the Queen, and the third from the steward; and it is right for these to be his provision, with a dish of food.

His sarhaed is six kine and six score pence; his worth is six kine and six score kine with augmentation.

The Chamberlain

Seventh is the chamberlain. He is entitled to his land free, and his horse in attendance, and his woollen clothing from the King and his linen clothing from the Queen.

He is entitled to have his lodging in the chamber in which the King sleeps. It is right for him to care for the chamber and make the King's bed, and to run errands between the hall and the chamber. It is right for him to pour drink for the King at all times, except the three special feasts. He is entitled to a man's share of the supper money. He is entitled to the King's old bedclothes. It is right for him to eat in the chamber.

His protection is from when he goes to fetch a burden of straw for the King's bed, and after it has been brought he makes the bed and spreads the coverings on it, until he takes them off the next day, to take the person without prosecution and without pursuit.

It is for him to keep the King's treasure, in the form of his cups and his horns and his rings, and to be charged for what he loses.

> From every booty which the bodyguard takes he gets the cattle whose horns are as long as their ears. *Cyfn.*

His sarhaed is six kine and six score pence; his worth is six kine and six score kine with augmentation.

The Bard of the Household

Eighth is the bard of the household. He is entitled to his land free and his horse in attendance, and his woollen clothing from the King and his linen clothing from the Queen.

He is entitled to sit next to the captain of the household at the three special feasts, so as to have the harp put into his hand. He is entitled to the steward's clothes at the three special feasts.

When a song is required to be sung, the chaired bard starts, first of God, with the second of the King to whom the court belongs, and if he has nothing to sing of him, let him sing of another king. After the chaired bard, the bard of the household is to sing three songs of some other kind.

If it happens that the Queen wants a song, let the bard of the household go and sing to her without stint, and that quietly, so that the hall is not disturbed by him.

He is entitled to a cow or ox from the booty which the bodyguard takes in a strange country, after the King has had his third; and it is right for him, when they share out the booty, to sing *The Sovereignty of Britain* to them.

He is entitled to a whalebone throwboard from the King and a gold ring from the Queen. His lodging is with the captain of the household. His protection is as far as the captain of the household.

When he travels with other bards, he is entitled to two men's share. His sarhaed is six kine and six score pence; his worth is six kine and six score kine with augmentation.

The Usher

Ninth is the usher. He is entitled to his land free and his horse in attendance, and his woollen clothing from the King and his linen clothing from the Queen. He is entitled to a man's share with the officials.

The King's Officers

He is entitled to fourpence from every cow which comes by way of dirwy from those who belong to the court.

It is right for him to control the meat and drink under the steward. It is right for him to give service and to call for silence and to strike the post above the priest of the household. It is right for him to stand in the King's service at every place in his absence.

He is entitled to six score pence from every dung maer when he is appointed maer. It is right for him to take charge of the court from the time when the maer is removed until another is put in his place. It is right for him to look to the equipment and to the King's goods in the court, from when he who is maer there goes until another comes thither. It is right for him to collect the King's twnc.

His lodging is with the steward. His protection is from the first silence that he proclaims until the last. His sarhaed is six kine and six score pence; his worth is six kine and six score kine with augmentation.

The Chief Huntsman

Tenth is the chief huntsman. He is entitled to his land free and his horse in attendance, and his woollen clothing from the King and his linen clothing from the Queen.

His place in the court is across the screen from the priest of the household, with the huntsmen with him. His lodging is in the kiln. His provision is three hornfuls of mead and a dish: one hornful from the King, another from the Queen, and the third from the chief of the household.

He is entitled to a third of the dirwy from the huntsmen, and to the amobr of their daughters. He is entitled to twenty-four pence from everyone to whom the Lord grants office.

> He shall have four legal pence from every greyhound huntsman and eight legal pence from every staghound huntsman, when they take office. *Cyfn.*

From Christmas to February it is right for him to be with the King when he wishes it. And from the first week of February it is right for him to take his hounds and his horns and his leashes, and to go to hunt hinds (and it is right for his horn to be of buffalo-horn, and its value is a pound) and to hunt hinds from then until St John's Day at Midsummer. And during that period he is not bound to answer to anyone for a claim he may have on him, save to one of his fellow-officers. And some say that it is not right for him to swear save by his horn and his leash.

He is entitled to an ox's skin in winter to make leashes, and to a cow's skin in summer to make brogues.

The day after St John's Day at Midsummer it is right for him to go to hunt stags. And unless he is found before rising from his bed and putting on his brogues, he is not bound to answer to anyone for the claim that is brought against him. And during that period until the Winter Kalends it is right that there be twelve legal joints in a hart and accordingly they are hunted until the Winter Kalends. And on the ninth day of the Winter Kalends it is proper for him to go to hunt wild boars, and from then until the Kalends of December it is right for him to be hunting them; and for so long a time as that he is not bound to answer to anyone for a claim unless to one of his fellow-officers—unless it is on that day before he gets up that the claim is made to him.

And on the Kalends of December it is right for him to share out the skins and to render to everybody among his fellow-officers his entitlement, doing this before sharing the skins with anyone. After that let the skins be divided into two-thirds and one-third; the two-thirds for the huntsmen and the one-third for the King. Of the huntsmen's two-thirds, two shares for a staghound huntsman and one for a greyhound huntsman; and the chief huntsman is entitled to two shares from the huntsmen, and of the King's third of the skins he is entitled to a third: he is one of the three who share in thirds with the King. And after that it is right for the chief huntsman to show his hounds and his horns and his leashes to the King, and after showing them to go on circuit around the King's villeins, and to be on that circuit until Christmas. And by Christmas let them come to the King to take their status and their place in the court.

The chief huntsman's hounds are of the same value as the King's hounds.

Whosoever has something in common with the King, whether it be the chief huntsman or another, it is right for him to divide and for the King to choose.

The chief huntsman's protection is to take the person who commits the offence so far that the sound of his horn can hardly be heard. His sarhaed is six kine and six score pence; his worth is six kine and six score kine with augmentation.

The Mead-brewer

Eleventh is the mead-brewer. He is entitled to his land free and his horse in attendance, and his woollen clothing from the King and his linen clothing from the Queen.

He is not entitled to a statutory place in the hall. His lodging is with the steward. His protection is from when he begins to make a vat of mead until he ties the cover over it, to take the person who commits the offence.

He is entitled to the cover which is over the vat of mead, or fourpence, at the choice of him who owns the feast. He is entitled to a third of the wax or fourpence instead of it from the steward, or footwear worth fourpence. The wax of the feast is shared thus: a third to the mead-brewer first of all; and the two-thirds are divided into three thirds, two parts to the hall and the third to the chamber.

His sarhaed is six kine and six score pence; his

worth is six kine and six score kine with augmentation.

The Physician
Twelfth is the physician. He is entitled to his land
free and his horse in attendance, and his woollen
clothing from the King and his linen clothing from
the Queen.

His place in the court in the hall is at the base of the
post which is by the screen beside which the King
sits. His lodging is with the captain of the household.
His protection is from when the King asks him to go
to a wounded person, whether he be in the court or
outside the court, until he comes from him, to take
the person who commits the offence.

It is right for him to give medical attention free to
whomsoever is in the court, and to the bodyguard;
and he shall have from them only their blood-clothes,
except for one of the three dangerous wounds. Those
are: a blow to the head reaching the brain, and a blow
to the body reaching the bowels, and breaking one of
the four posts.

These are the two thighs and the two arms.   *Cyfn.*

For each of these three dangerous wounds the
physician is entitled to nine score pence and his food,
or a pound without his food, and also to the blood-
clothes.

He is entitled to twenty-four pence when he applies
a tent. For medication with red ointment, twelve
pence. For medication with herbs for a swelling, fourpence. For letting blood, fourpence. His food every
night is worth three halfpence; his lighting is worth a
penny. The value of a pan for medication, a penny.

It is right for him to take assurance from the
kindred for a wounded man, lest he should die under
the treatment which he gives him; and if he does not
take it, let him answer for his act.

It is right for him to go to the hostings. He is bound

never to go away from the court except with the King's leave.

His sarhaed is six kine and six score pence; his worth is six kine and six score kine with augmentation.

The Butler

Thirteenth is the butler. He is entitled to his land free and his horse in attendance, and his woollen clothing from the King and his linen clothing from the Queen. He is entitled to a share of the supper money.

It is right for him to take charge of the mead-cellar and to keep the locks. He is entitled to what cover there is on the mead vat, or fourpence, at the choice of the owner of the feast. He is entitled to liquor from every feast at which there is mead.

It is right for him to dispense the drink and to give to everyone according to his entitlement. It is right for him to supply the mead-cellar and what is in it. The measure of legal liquor is the vessels in which it is served, full of beer, or half-full of bragget, or one-third full of mead.

He is entitled to eat with the officials. His lodging is with the steward. His protection is from when he begins to dip a vessel into the drink until the banquet ends that night, to take the person who commits the offence. He is entitled to his light unstinted from the steward. His sarhaed is six kine and six score pence; his worth is six kine and six score kine, with augmentation.

The Doorkeeper

Fourteenth is the doorkeeper. He is entitled to his land free and his horse in attendance, and his woollen clothing from the King and his linen clothing from the Queen. He is entitled to a share of the supper money. He is entitled to legal liquor.

It is right for him to convey the messages which are said to him from the gate to the hall, or to another place where the King is. He is entitled to the clothes of the bard of the household at the three special feasts. His lodging is the porter's house. He is entitled to eat with the officials.

He is bound to know all the officers of the court, and not to stop any of them in the gate; and if he stops one, let him pay a camlwrw to the King. If it is one of the chief officers, let him pay him his wynebwerth; if one of the others, fourpence.

His protection is to take the person who commits the offence as far as the porter, who will take him to safety. He is entitled to a hornful of drink from the steward, and a dish, and that is his provision.

It is right for him to clear the way for the King with his mace, and what person soever he strikes from the road with his mace at arm's length, though he claim compensation from him, he is not entitled to have it. It is right for him, after the eating, to send out what it is proper to send from the hall. He is entitled with the officials to a share of the money from the skins.

It is not right for him to sit in the hall, but on his knees to do his errand to the King. His sarhaed is six kine and six score pence; his worth is six kine and six score kine with augmentation.

The Cook

Fifteenth is the cook. He is entitled to his land free and his horse in attendance, and his woollen clothing from the King and his linen clothing from the Queen.

It is right that he should occupy the kitchen. He is entitled to have what he needs from the steward and the dung maer. He is entitled to the skins of all the small animals which come to the kitchen with their skins on; and thus is he entitled: one third for him, and two-thirds for the steward.

It is right for him to take first taste of every dish which he himself seasons. He is entitled to the broken fragments of meat, and the tallow, and the entrails. It is right that he should himself bring in the

The King's Officers 27

last dish and set it before the King, and that the King should then present him with food and drink.

His protection is from when he begins to prepare the first dish until he sets the last before the King, to take the person who commits the offence. It is right for the steward to supply him with herbs for seasoning his dishes, that is, with pepper and other herbs. He is entitled to eat with the officials.

His lodging is with the steward. He is entitled to a share of the supper money. His sarhaed is six kine and six score pence; his worth is six kine and six score kine with augmentation.

The Candleman

Sixteenth is the candleman. He is entitled to his land free and his horse in attendance, and his woollen clothing from the King and his linen clothing from the Queen. He is entitled to a share of the supper money.

It is right for him to hold a candle for the King, across the dish from him, while he is eating. He is entitled to the broken bread and the fragments of meat which spill over the dish. He is entitled to a handsbreadth of the candle which is in his hand. It is right for him to light the candles in the court; and what he takes with his teeth from the wax of the top of the candles, that belongs to him. He is entitled to what is left of the candles when the King goes to his chamber. He is entitled to have the candles he uses from the steward, unstinted.

His protection is from when the first candle is lit until the last is extinguished, to take the person who commits the offence, without prosecution, without pursuit.

When the King goes to his chamber, it is right for him to take a candle with him before him. He is entitled to eat with the officials.

His sarhaed is six kine and six score pence; his worth is six kine and six score kine with augmentation.

28   *The Law of Hywel Dda*

4. The Queen's Officers

Above we have treated of the status and entitlement of the sixteen officers who pertain to the King; here we begin to treat of the eight who pertain to the Queen.

The Queen's Steward

First of those is her steward. He is entitled to his land free and his horse in attendance, and his woollen clothing from the King and his linen clothing from the Queen.

It is right for him to control the food and drink in the chamber. It is right for him to wait on the Queen with food and drink. He is entitled to a third of the dirwy of the Queen's officials. His lodging is with the King's steward.

It is not right for him to sit in the chamber, but to do service between the chamber and the kitchen.

His protection is to take the person who commits the offence as far as the King's steward, who will take him to safety.

He is entitled to have one third from the King's officials to share with his colleagues, with two shares for himself. He is entitled to fourpence from the supper money to share with the cooks, with two shares for himself. He is entitled to all that he uses from the King's steward, unstinted.

His sarhaed is six kine and six score pence; his worth is six kine and six score kine with augmentation.

The Queen's Priest

Second is the Queen's priest. He is entitled to his land free and his horse in attendance, and his woollen clothing from the King and his linen clothing from the Queen. He is entitled to a third of the tithe of the Queen and those who belong to the chamber.

His lodging is with the King's priest in the sexton's house.

The Queen's Officers

He is entitled to fourpence for every patent seal which the Queen issues. He is entitled to the offering of the Queen and of all who pertain to her. He is entitled to the Queen's clothes, those in which she does penance during Lent. It is right for him to bless the food and drink which come to the chamber.

His protection is as far as the nearest church.

His sarhaed is according to the judgement of the synod; his worth is according to the status of his kindred, and so likewise every man in orders.

The Queen's Chief Groom

Third is the Queen's chief groom. He is entitled to his land free and his horse in attendance, and his woollen clothing from the King and his linen clothing from the Queen.

He is entitled to fourpence for every horse which the Queen gives, and it is right for him to give a halter with each one.

His lodging is the house nearest to the barn, with the King's chief groom. His protection, according to some, is as far as the King's chief groom; others say that it is to take the person who commits the offence for as long as the Queen's fastest horse continues to run.

He is entitled to a third of the foals under two years from the booty, two-thirds going to the King's chief groom.

His sarhaed is six kine and six score pence; his worth is six kine and six score kine with augmentation.

The Queen's Chamberlain

Fourth is the Queen's chamberlain. He is entitled to his land free and his horse in attendance, and to the Queen's old cape and his linen, and to his woollen clothing from the King.

He is entitled to a share of the supper money. It is right for him to do errands between the chamber and the hall. It is right for him to serve the Queen with food and drink, except at the three special feasts. It is right for him to keep the keys of the Queen's coffers, and keep the chamber supplied, and to make her bed.

His lodging is the Queen's chamber, with his bed in the garderobe, so as to be ready to serve the needs of the King and Queen. He has the same protection as the King's chamberlain.

His sarhaed is six kine and six score pence; his worth is six kine and six score kine with augmentation.

The Queen's Handmaid
Fifth is her handmaid. She is entitled to her horse in attendance and the Queen's old clothing: her old shifts and her old sheets and her old kerchiefs and her old shoes and her old bridles and her old saddles. She is entitled to a share of the supper money.

Her protection is from when she spreads the coverings on the bed until she takes them off on the morrow.

She is entitled to her bed in the chamber so that she may hear the slightest word which the Queen says.

Her worth and her sarhaed are according to her status.

The Queen's Doorkeeper
Sixth is the Queen's doorkeeper. He is entitled to his land free and his horse in attendance, and his woollen clothing from the King and his linen clothing from the Queen.

It is right for him to bear liquor where there is mead. It is not right for him to sit down in the chamber, but to do his service standing. He is entitled to a share of the supper money.

His lodging is with the King's doorkeeper in the porter's house. His protection is the same as that of the King's doorkeeper.

His sarhaed is six kine and six score pence; his

worth is six kine and six score kine with augmentation.

The Queen's Cook

Seventh is her cook. He is entitled to his land free and
his horse in attendance, and his woollen clothing
from the King and his linen clothing from the Queen.

He is entitled to be supplied by the steward with
what he needs in the kitchen. It is right for him to take
first taste of every dish which he prepares.

His protection is the same as that of the King's
cook. His lodging is with the King's steward.

His sarhaed is six kine and six score pence; his
worth is six kine and six score kine with augmentation.

The Queen's Candleman

Eighth is her candleman. He is entitled to his land free
and his horse in attendance, and his woollen clothing
from the King and his linen clothing from the Queen.

He is entitled to a share of the supper money. He is
entitled to a handsbreadth of every candle which he
holds in his fist. He is entitled to the top of the candles
which he takes off with his teeth. He is entitled to
what is left of all the candles. He is entitled to the
broken bread and the broken fragments of meat which
spill over the Queen's dish.

He has the same protection, and the same sarhaed,
and the same worth, and the same lodging, as the
King's candleman.

5. Additional officers

Above we have treated of the twenty-four officers
who belong to the court; here we treat of the officers
by use and those by custom who are in a court.
First of these is the Groom of the Rein, second is the
Footholder, third is the Dung Maer, fourth is the
Serjeant, fifth is the Porter, sixth is the Watchman,

The Law of Hywel Dda

seventh is the Fueller, eighth is the Bakeress, ninth is the Court Smith, tenth is the Pencerdd, eleventh is the Laundress.

The Groom of the Rein

First of these is the groom of the rein. He is entitled to his land free and his horse in attendance, and his woollen clothing from the King and his linen clothing from the Queen.

He is entitled to the King's rain-capes, in which he rides, and his old bridles, and his old gold-enamelled saddles, and his old spurs, and his old hose, and all his harness. It is right for him to be in every place on behalf of the chief groom in his absence.

It is right for him to hold the King's stirrup when he mounts and when he dismounts, and to take his horse to its lodging and to bring it to him on the morrow. It is right for him to walk near the King in order to serve him when necessary. It is right for him to shoe the King's horses.

His lodging is with the chief groom. It is right for him to accoutre the court justice's horse and to bring it to him to mount; and it is right for the latter to judge his status and his right for him, without charge.

His protection is from when the court smith begins to make four horseshoes and their set of nails until he finishes setting them under the hooves of the King's horse, to take the person who commits the offence. His sarhaed is six kine and six score pence; his worth is six kine and six score kine.

The Footholder

The second is the footholder. He is entitled to his land free and his horse in attendance, and his woollen clothing from the King and his linen clothing from the Queen. And that office comes to him in right of land.

It is right for him to hold the King's feet in his lap from when he begins sitting at the banquet until he

Additional Officers

goes to sleep, and to scratch the King; and for as long a period as that let him guard the King from harm. His protection is from when the King puts his feet into his lap until he goes to his chamber, to take the person who commits the offence. It is right for him to eat from the same dish as the King, with his back to the fire.

He lights the first candle before the King, at meat.
Cyfn.

His sarhaed is six kine and six score pence; his worth is six kine and six score kine.

The Dung Maer

Third is the dung maer. He is entitled to his land free. It is right for him to supervise the court next after the court steward. It is right for him to receive what goods the maer and cynghellor give him in order to hold the court; it is for him to prepare all the court's needs.

To him belong all the dirwy and camlwrw of the maerdref. He is entitled to the ebediw of the men of the maerdref and the amobr of their daughters. When there is a case between two men of the maerdref for land and earth, or for theft, or for fighting, he is entitled to twenty-four pence.

It is right for him to swear for the court land. He is entitled to sixty pence for every prisoner who goes into gaol. He is entitled to entertainments from the men of the maerdref. To him belong the skins of the cows which are in his care for three nights before being slaughtered. No one is entitled to the cattle skins of the dung maer save himself, whether the King be in the court or not.

The dung maer has the suet and lard from the court.
Cyfn.

Even if the servants insult the dung maer while carrying food and drink from the kitchen and the mead-cellar to the hall, they will not compensate him for that.
Cyfn.

The Law of Hywel Dda

His protection is to take the person who commits the offence over the boundary of the court land. His lodging is the food-house. His sarhaed is six kine and six score pence; his worth is six kine and six score kine.

The Serjeant

Fourth is the serjeant. He is entitled to his land free; and when the King is in the court he is entitled to a dish of food.

It is right for him to stand between the two posts and to watch lest the house should burn while the King is eating, and it is right for him to drink with the officials. He is not entitled to sit down while the King is eating or drinking in the hall, and he is not entitled to strike the post on the King's side.

He is entitled to the fill of the vessels which are used for serving in beer, and half the fill in bragget, and one third in mead. He is entitled to the legs of the oxen and cows which are got by his accusation, to make brogues reaching to his ankles; and on the ninth day of the Winter Kalends he is entitled to have a smock and a shirt and breeches without mixed fabric; and it is right for his clothes to be as long as to the knot of his breeches. At the Kalends of Winter he is entitled to have a cape, and at the Kalends of March or February a mantle.

It is right for him to divide between the Lord and the cynghellor.

He is entitled to all the opened meat there may be in a dead-house, and the opened butter, and the lower stone of the quern, and the green flax, and the lowest layer of the corn, and the hens and the cats, and the fuel-axe, and the headland of the growing corn, or (if there is no headland) the margins. He is entitled to have from every house to which he comes on the King's errands a loaf and its enllyn.

His spear is three ells in length, two behind him and one before.

Additional Officers

From the booty which is taken in a strange country he is entitled to a bull, or a beast which has not been yoked, or a first-calf heifer.

When the serjeant dies, all his goods belong to the King.

If the serjeant is insulted while he is seated during a case, he is not entitled to have anything save a sieve-full of oats and an eggshell. His sarhaed, according to some, is as much as the sarhaed of the owner of the land on which he is insulted, and so also his galanas. Others say that his sarhaed is three kine and three score pence; his worth is three kine and three score kine.

The Porter

Fifth is the porter. He is entitled to his land free, and his house within the gate. He is entitled to have his sustenance always from the court, and a dish when the King is there.

He is entitled to a handful of every gift that comes through the gate, that is, of berries and eggs and haddock. From every load of firewood that comes through the gate he is entitled to a stick which he can draw out without holding up the horse, and with his hand on the gate.

> And though he may not be able to draw out any stick, he will still get a stick, but not the biggest.　*Cyfn.*

He is entitled to fourpence for every prisoner on whom he closes the gate.

It is right for him to take off the skins of the animals which are slaughtered in the kitchen, and he is entitled to a penny for every one of them. From the booty of pigs that comes through the gate he is entitled to a pig which he can lift by its bristles with one hand until its feet are as high as his knee. He is entitled to any docked beast that comes through the gate.

It is right for him to be serjeant in the maerdref, and he is entitled to fourpence from every amobr which comes from there. It is right for him to summon the men of the maerdref to work, and he is entitled to a fee from every dirwy or camlwrw which falls on them. He is entitled to his errands free in all the court, and is entitled to the leftovers from the cheese which he toasts. It is right for him to put the court in order, by having straw supplied and the fire lit.

His protection is to keep the person who commits the offence until the captain of the household goes to his lodging through the gate, and it is right for the captain of the household to take him to safety. His sarhaed is six kine and six score pence; his worth is six kine and six score kine.

The Watchman
Sixth is the watchman. He is entitled to his land free, and his food in attendance, and his footwear, and a loaf and its enllyn for his breakfast.

> The watchman must be a bonheddig of the country, for trust is put in him by the King. *Cyfn.*

It is not right for him to watch save from when they go to sleep until day; and he again is entitled to sleep in the daytime and not to do anything save for a fee. Some say that he is entitled to the eyes of the animals that are slaughtered in the court; and he is entitled to his clothing, in capes and hose. If he is found sleeping when he ought to be watching, he is bound to pay a camlwrw to the King, unless he is beaten; and though he should be beaten he is not entitled to have his sarhaed.

His protection is from when he begins to blow his horn at night when watching until the gate is opened on the morrow. His sarhaed is six kine and six score pence; his worth is six kine and six score kine.

The Fueller
Seventh is the fueller. He is entitled to his land free, and his food in attendance when the King is there, and his footwear.

Additional Officers
37

When gathering fuel he is entitled to what he needs from the court, and if he loses any of that, it is right for him to pay for it. It is right for him to keep the fuel-horse, and to take its fodder every night from the court, and to ride on it when he goes to gather fuel; and if it is lost while in his care, it is right for him to pay for it.

It is not right for him to break down the fuel from the state in which he loads it onto the horse, after he comes home. He is entitled to the necks of the livestock slaughtered in the court; the reason he is so entitled is that they are cut up with his axe.

His protection is as far as he can throw his axe or his hedging-bill. His sarhaed is six kine and six score pence; his worth is six kine and six score kine.

The Bakeress

Eighth is the bakeress. She is entitled to her food from the court, and her clothes, and a dish when the King is there, and at the end of baking, a cake from each kind of flour which she bakes; and to her bed in the food-house.

It is not right for her to stand up for anyone while she is baking.

Her protection is as far as she can throw her scraper. Her sarhaed, if she is married, is a third of her husband's sarhaed, both for her and for every woman; if she is not married, half her brother's sarhaed. Her worth, whether she is married or not, half her brother's worth.

The Court Smith

Ninth is the court smith. He is entitled to his land free, and his food in attendance, and a dish when the King is there.

It is right for him to fulfil all the court's needs free, except for three things; those are the rim of a coulter, and the head of a spear, and the socket of a fuel-axe;

38   The Law of Hywel Dda

for each of those three things he is entitled to payment for his work.

It is right for him to fulfil the needs of the officers of
the court free; it is right for them at every present-
ation to honour him.

He is entitled to the amobrau of the daughters of the
other smiths. He is entitled to the ceinion: the
ceinion are the first liquor that comes to the hall.

His place in the court is at the end of the bench,
next to the priest of the household. His protection is
from when he begins to do his work in the morning
until he finishes that night. His sarhaed is six kine
and six score pence; his worth is six kine and six score
kine.

The Pencerdd

Tenth is the pencerdd. He is entitled to his land free.
His place is at one side of the court justice.

It is right for him to start the song, first of God, and
secondly of the Lord to whom the court belongs, or of
another.

No one is entitled to solicit except a pencerdd, and
from what he and his companions gain together he is
entitled to have two shares.

> When a bard solicits a monarch, let him sing one song;
> when he solicits a breyr, let him sing three songs;
> when he solicits a villein, let him sing until he is
> tired.   *Cyfn.*

He is entitled to twenty-four pence from every
cerddor after he leaves his instruction.

> Every harp pencerdd is entitled to twenty-four
> pence from the young cerddorion who want to
> give up the horsehair harp and be competent
> cerddorion and to solicit.   *Dw.*

He is entitled to twenty-four pence from every
woman who sleeps with a man, if he has not
previously had the payment from her.

Additional Officers 39

> He shall have a neithior boon (to wit, twenty-four pence) from every maiden when she marries; he shall not, however, have anything at the neithior of a woman from whom he has had goods previously, at her neithior when she was a maiden. *Cyfn.*

He is entitled to the amobr of the daughters of the cerddorion.

> This is a pencerdd, the bard when he wins a chair. No bard can solicit for anything within his pencerdd area, without his permission, unless he is a bard from a strange country. Even if the King forbids the giving of goods within his realm until the end of a period, the pencerdd will be free of the law. *Cyfn.*

His lodging is with the edling. His protection is from when he begins the first song in the court until he ends the last. His sarhaed is six kine and six score pence; his worth is six kine and six score kine.

The Laundress

Seventh is the laundress. She is entitled to her food from the court, and a dish when the King is there, and her clothes; and on the day that she washes for the Queen she is entitled to a present from her. Her protection is as far as she can throw her dolly. She has the same sarhaed and worth as the bakeress.

6. Miscellanea

Above we have treated of the officers who belong to the court and those by use and those by custom, and their status and their entitlement. Here we treat of other things.

The three indispensables of a king are his priest, for blessing the food and singing mass; and the court justice, for resolving doubtful things; and his bodyguard, for his necessities. The three indispensables of a goodman: his harp, and his brycan, and his cauldron. The three indispensables of a villein: his trough, and his threshold, and his firestone.

The Law of Hywel Dda

Three things which it is right for the King not to share with anyone: his treasure, and his falcon, and his thief.

The three nets of a king: his stud of horses, and his herd of cows, and his herd of pigs; if a person loses an animal and it is found among the animals of the King, he is entitled to fourpence for each one that he finds. The three nets of a goodman: his stud and his herd of cows and his herd of pigs; where he finds a person's animal among his animals, he is entitled to fourpence. The three nets of a villein: his herd of cows and his herd of pigs and his winter-house from Mayday to August: if he finds a stray animal in any of these he is entitled to have fourpence for information.

The King has three horns: it is right for them to be buffalo horn and of the same value: the horn from which the King drinks, and his social horn, and the chief huntsman's horn; and the value of every one of them is a pound.

There are three legal harps: the King's harp and a pencerdd's harp and a goodman's harp. The value of the first two is six score pence, with twenty-four pence for their tuning-horn; a goodman's harp, three score, with twelve pence for its tuning-horn.

Three things a villein is not entitled to sell without his lord's leave: a destrier and honey and pigs; and if he sells them, let him be liable to dirwy, and the transfer rescinded; and if his lord does not buy them, let him sell whither he will. Three arts a villein's son is not entitled to learn without his lord's leave (and though he should learn them, the lord is entitled to retake them, except for clerkship after he takes orders): those are clerkship and smithcraft and bardism.

The eight packhorses of the King: the sea, and waste, and a needy person from another country, and a thief; a man suddenly dead leaving no son, a dead man for whom he gets ebediw, an offender from whom he gets dirwy or camlwrw.

Miscellanea 41

Whosoever says an uncouth word against the King, let him pay him a double camlwrw.

Wheresoever the priest and the steward and the court judge are found, there will be the status of the court.

The King is entitled to take his host out of the country only once in the year. But it is right for them to go within his own realm when he likes. The King is entitled to a man with a horse and an axe from each villein townland, to make a camp for the King; and it is right for them to be at his cost.

There are nine houses which it is right for the King's villeins to make: hall, chamber, food-house, stable, porch, barn, kiln, latrine, dormitory or sleep-house.

All goods without an owner are King's waste.

Three things it is right for a king not to share with another person: gold treasure and silver, and buffalo horns, and clothing which has gold edgings.

It is right that there should be double camlwrw in court and in church. Whosoever commits an offence in a mother church, let him pay her fourteen pounds, one half to the abbot if he is a literate divine, and the other among the priests and the clas. If an offence is committed in the churchyard, it is worth seven pounds; and those are shared in the same way as the others. Whosoever commits an offence in another church, let him pay seven pounds, one half to the priests and the other to the parsons.

And so ends the Court Book.

> Thus far by the permission of God we have treated of the laws of a court; now by the help of the glorious Lord Jesus Christ we will set out the laws of a country. *Cyfn.*

Book II
THE LAWS OF THE COUNTRY

1. The Laws of Women

HERE we begin the laws of women.

First of them is: if it happens that a woman has bestowers, it is right for her to be subject to her agweddi until the end of seven years; and though three nights should be wanting from the seventh year and they separate, it is right for them to share everything in two halves.

It belongs to the woman to divide and to the man to choose. The pigs for the man and the sheep for the woman; if there are only the one kind, sharing in two halves, but if there are sheep and goats, the sheep for the man and the goats for the woman; if there are only the one kind, they are shared. Of the sons, two thirds to the father and one to the mother: the eldest and the youngest to the father and the middle to the mother.

The equipment is shared like this. All the milk vessels, except one pail, go to the woman; all the dishes, except one dish, go to the woman; all the vessels for drink go to the man. The woman is entitled to a car and yoke to take her equipment from the house. The man is entitled to the riddle, the woman is entitled to the fine sieve. The man is entitled to the upper stone of the quern and the woman to the lower. The bedclothes which are over them to the woman, and those which are under them to the man until he takes a wife. After he takes a wife they belong to the woman, and if the wife who comes to the man sleeps on them, let her pay the woman from whom he separated her wynebwerth.

To the man belong the cauldron and the brycan and the pillows of the cross-bed, and the coulter and the fuel axe and the auger and the crane, and all the reaping-hooks except one for the woman. To the woman belong the pan and the trivet and the broad axe and the hedging-bill and the ploughshare, and all the flax and the linseed, and the wool and the luxury-bag, except for gold and silver; if there is any of those, it is shared. This is the luxury-bag: the purses and what is in them, except gold and silver, if any. If there are woven materials, they are shared; the balls of yarn for the sons (if any): if there are no sons, they are shared.

The man is entitled to the barn and to what corn there is above ground and below ground. The man is entitled to all the hens, and to one of the cats, with the rest for the woman. The food is thus shared: to the woman belongs the opened meat and what is in salt; and after it is hung up it belongs to the man. To the woman belong the opened vessels of butter and the opened cheese. To the woman belongs as much as she can carry of flour by the strength of her hands and her knees from the larder to the house.

To each of them belong their own clothes, except their mantles, and the mantles are shared.

If the man has a special right, let him show his right before the sharing, and after he has had his right, let him share as we said above.

Their debts let them pay in two halves.

And if they separate before the end of the seventh year, let him pay her agweddi and her dowry, and her cowyll if she was given as a maiden; what survives of these is what she gets. And if she leaves her husband before the seventh year, she loses all that, except her cowyll and her wynebwerth in discharge of her gowyn. If her husband is leprous or of stinking breath or cannot copulate with his wife: if because of one of these three things she leaves her husband, she is entitled to get the whole of what is hers.

If by death they separate, she is entitled to have everything, except the corn. No wife in the world is entitled to have any of the corn, except a woman of weight. If they separate by living and dying, let the sick one divide, with the parish priest, and let the healthy one choose. No one is entitled to bequeath anything save the Church's daered and his debts; and

The Laws of Women

if he should bequeath, the son can break the bequest, and that is called an uncouth son. Whosoever again shall break a legal bequest, to wit daered and debts, will be excommunicate like a publican.

If in life they separate, let her stay with what is hers in the house until the end of nine days and nine nights, to know whether their parting is legal. And if their parting is proper, let her goods go before her, and after the last penny let her go herself.

The sarhaed of a married woman, a third of her husband's sarhaed; if she is not married, half the sarhaed of her brother. Her galanas, whether single or married, half her brother's galanas.

> If it happens that people suppose that the status of a woman who is taken clandestinely, or a woman who is slept with from three nights on, does not follow their husbands' status, because their kin did not bestow them, and they suppose that their status is according to their kin and their sarhaed according to their brothers' status, law says that after she becomes entitled to agweddi from him she cannot leave him if she does not want to lose her agweddi, and that he cannot eject her if he does not want to pay her agweddi (and this is the agweddi of each of those two women: three steers whose horns are as long as their ears), and accordingly law says that it is right for those women that their status and their sarhaed should be according to their husbands' status. *Dw.*

If a man takes another wife after separating from the first, the first will be free. If it happens that a man separates from a woman, and the latter takes another man, and the first man regrets separating from his wife, and that he overtakes her with one foot in the bed and the other outside the bed, the first man is entitled to have the woman.

The Law of Hywel Dda

If it happens that a woman commits a gross offence, whether giving a kiss or allowing fondling or copulation with her, that is sarhaed to her husband. If intercourse with her happens, that sarhaed is augmented by one half, for it derives from kin-feud. If fondling of her happens, let him pay sarhaed without augmentation. If there is a kiss, let him pay two-thirds sarhaed, since there is no full act.

If a man denies being found between her two thighs, let the man give the oath of fifty men and the woman the same number of women. If he denies fondling her, let the man give the oath of fourteen men and the woman the same number of women, from among their relatives. If he denies giving a kiss, let the man give the oath of seven men and the woman the oath of seven women, from among their closest relatives, father and mother and brothers and sisters.

> Here are the three cases in which a man is not entitled to compensation from his wife though they be admitted: for fondling her when playing rhaffan, or in a carouse, or if a man from afar from a strange country should fondle her before knowing the law of the country. *Col.*

> A man can freely leave his wife if she acts manifestly with another man; and she shall have no compensation except the three things which are not taken from a wife; and the paramour shall pay his sarhaed to the legal husband. *Bleg.*

> Goronwy ap Moriddig used to say that a man was not bound to pay anything to another man for lying with his wife while she approved the act; and if the act is manifest, the wife is bound to pay his sarhaed to her husband, or her husband may freely repudiate her.
> *Bleg.*

Whosoever takes a maiden clandestinely, if before he has connection with her the maiden asks 'What will you give me?' and he specifies what he will give, by his faith, then though he should try to deny it, if

The Laws of Women 49

the maiden charges it she is to be believed, for in that she is one of the nine tongued ones; and it is for this reason that she is to be believed, that there are no wedding-guests.

> A woman who is taken clandestinely, and who does not make a contract in the presence of witnesses for receiving her full right, gets according to the men of Gwynedd only three steers. According to the men of the South she used formerly to get her agweddi in full like a woman given by her kin. *Bleg.*

If a maiden is given to a man and is found to be corrupted, but the man suffers her in his bed until the morrow, he cannot on the morrow take away any of her entitlement. If immediately after he finds her to be corrupted he rises to the wedding-guests with his penis erect, and testifies to them that he found her corrupted, and he does not sleep with her until the morrow, she is not entitled on the morrow to anything from him. If it happens that her breasts and pubic hair have developed and she has menstruated, then law says that no one knows what she is, whether maiden or woman, because the signs of childbearing have appeared on her; and therefore law allows her to be vindicated by the oath of seven persons from among her mother and father and brothers and sisters. If she does not want to be vindicated, let her shift be cut off as high as her groin, and let there be put into her hand a yearling steer with its tail greased, and if she can hold it by its tail, let her take it for her share of her agweddi; and if she cannot hold it, let her be without anything.

Whosoever gives a woman to a man, it is for him to pay her amobr, or else let him take sureties from her for paying it. And if she gives herself, let her pay her amobr, for she herself was her bestower. If a man takes a woman clandestinely, and comes with her to a goodman's house to sleep with her, and the goodman

50   *The Law of Hywel Dda*

does not take surety for her amobr, let him pay it himself.

If it happens that a man takes a woman clandestinely, let her expectation, until the end of seven years, be three steers whose horns are as long as their ears. Since she has lost her status, let her be of that status until the end of seven years. If she has a dowry, let it be unconsumed until the end of seven years; if she allows it to be consumed, she will not be compensated for what teeth and side consume. If she reaches three nights from the end of the seventh year, there will be a sharing in two halves with her as with a wife having bestowers.

A wife, whether she be bestowed or taken clandestinely, does not remain of the status of her agweddi save for seven years, and since she is not agweddïol from the end of seven years on, therefore let them share in two halves.

Whosoever sleeps three nights with a woman from when the fire is covered until it is uncovered on the morrow, and from then on wants to leave her, let him pay her a steer worth twenty pence and another worth thirty pence and another worth forty pence. And if he takes her to house and home and she is with him until the end of seven years, he is bound to share with her from then on as with a wife with bestowers.

There are three legal agweddïau: the agweddi of a king's daughter, twenty-four pounds (and her cowyll eight pounds); the agweddi of a goodman's daughter, three pounds (and her cowyll a pound); the agweddi of a villein's daughter, a pound (and her cowyll six score pence).

> Seven pounds is the gobr of a king's daughter, and it is paid to the mother. And the husband pays her cowyll, for it is land which he pays to her.   *Cyfn.*

If it happens that a person makes pregnant a woman of bush and brake, it is right for him to maintain the child; for the law says that though she may lose the

The Laws of Women   51

man, it is not right for her to suffer want from him or because of him, though she gets no benefit; and therefore it is right for the man to rear the child. If it happens that a man separates from his wife when she is pregnant, let the time from when he separates from her until she is delivered count as half a year of the rearing of the child; and after the child is born it is for her to rear it again until the end of the year. Whether she wants to or not, it is necessary for her to rear it in return for goods from the man. This is the measure of the goods: a cow in milk, and a smock worth four-pence, and a pan worth a penny, and a car-load of the best corn that grows on the father's land; and that is for her for rearing it for a year. And she herself after that rears it for half a year, and from then on she cannot be compelled to rear it except for her own share. And from then until the end of fourteen years, two thirds from the father and one third from the mother; and from the end of fourteen years on it is proper for the father to take him to his lord, and for him to do homage to him. And from then on let him be at the lord's maintenance.

If it happens that a woman says of a man that he raped her and the man denies it, let him give the oath of fifty men without aliens and without designated men. If it happens that she makes a legal charge, let her take the man's member in her left hand, with her right hand on the relic, and let her swear by the relic that that member had connexion with her by force and that blemish and sarhaed were done to her and to her kin and to her lord. Some of the justices do not allow denial against that: the law however says that it is right to allow denial as we have said above.

If it happens that a man admits raping a woman, let him pay twelve kine as dirwy to the King, and her amobr to her lord, (and if she is a maiden, her cowyll), and her agweddi at the highest rate to which she is entitled, and her wynebwerth, and her dilysrwydd.

And if she is a married woman, her sarhaed augmented by a half.

> There is in the law of Hywel no castration of a man for raping a woman. *Bleg.*

> If two women are walking through any place and there is no one with them, and two men come upon them and copulate with them, no compensation is made to them; if, however, there is one person with them, however small (unless it is a carried child), they lose none of their right. *Cyfn.*

> If a woman travels alone, and a man comes to her and rapes her, if the man denies let him give the oath of fifty men, three of them being under vows that they will not take a wife and will not eat meat and will not ride horses ever. If he does not want to deny, let him pay the woman her endowment and her dilystod, and a dirwy and a silver rod to the King in the manner which is right. If the man cannot pay, let his testicles be taken. If there were two women, let him give one testicle to one and the other to the other if he lies with them both. *Cyfn.*

> If it happens that a maiden goes clandestinely with a man against the will of her father and her mother and her lord, they can take her back against her will. Her father is not bound to pay amobr for her. If she is a woman and has previously been with a man, she cannot be taken against her will; and since she cannot, let her amobr be claimed from where she dwells.

> If it happens that a man wants a woman, let him give a surety for her agweddi, and let him take a surety from her father and mother that she will not cause him shame by her body, and that she will not be offensive towards him, which is the custom of the Welshwomen. *Col.*

> If it happens that a woman says shameful words to her husband, such as wishing a blemish on his beard or dirt in his teeth, or calling him a cur, law judges the payment of a camlwrw to her

The Laws of Women   53

husband for every one of them, for every woman's husband is her Lord; or if he prefers it, let him strike her three blows with a rod as long as a man's forearm and as thick as a long finger, in any place except the head.   *Dw.*

If a woman leaves her husband's bed without a reason, let her pay him three kine camlwrw before being taken to him again.   *Bleg.*

The three privy things of a wife: her cowyll and her gowyn and her sarhaed. This is the reason those three are called three privy things, that they are three things proper to a wife and that they cannot be taken from her for any reason. This is her cowyll, the thing that she gets for her virginity. This is her sarhaed, every beating which her husband gives her, except for three things; these are the three for which he is entitled to beat her: for giving away a thing which she is not entitled to give; and for her being found with a man under deception; and for wishing a blemish on his beard. And if for her being found with a man he beats her, he shall have no compensation save that, for there is no right to compensation and vengeance for the same offence. This is her gowyn: if she finds her husband with another woman, let him pay her six score pence on the first occasion; for the second, a pound; if she finds him the third time, she can separate from him without losing any of what is hers.

If it happens that a woman takes the wynebwerth to which she is entitled from her husband three times and she does not separate from him at the third time, she is not entitled to wynebwerth from then on.   *Col.*

If it happens that a woman suffers her husband's being found with another more than three times without claiming her wynebwerth from him, she is not entitled to have it from then on, for she is a shameful woman.   *Col.*

54   *The Law of Hywel Dda*

It is right that the goods which she receives for these three things should be apart from her husband.

> Everything of the goods which we said above were to be got, the wife can set those goods aside for her issue, and when she separates from him she is not bound to share them with him, and though she should die he is not entitled to them.   *Dw.*

The King's wife can give away without his leave the third of the casual acquisitions which comes from the King. An uchelwr's wife can give away her mantle and her shift and her shoes and her headkerchief and her food and her drink and the store of her larder, and can lend all her equipment. A villein's wife cannot give away anything save her headcloth, nor lend anything save her sieve, and that only so that her call from the dunghill to bring it back can be heard.

The three stays of a wife: when she is slept with, it is right for her not to start from there until the ninth day;

> this is the reason that she is not bound to go, for the sake of getting used to her husband and to his bed;   *Dw.*

and when she separates from her husband, it is right for her not to start until the ninth day, and then after the last penny let her go; and when her husband dies, it is right for her not to start until the ninth day, and then after the last penny let her go.

> A woman who says that she is pregnant when her husband dies is entitled to stay in her house until it is known whether she is pregnant; and if she is not pregnant, let her pay three kine camlwrw to the King, and let her leave the house and the land for the heir.   *Cyfn.*

In three ways amobr becomes due for a woman: by gift and transfer, although she be not slept with; and the second, by sleeping openly, although there be

The Laws of Women 55

neither gift nor transfer; and the third, by her pregnancy.

The amobr of a maer cynghellor's daughter, a pound.

The amobr of a maer's daughter, six score pence.

The amobr of an aillt's daughter, three score pence.

The amobr of an alien's daughter, twenty-four pence.

The amobr of a chief-of-kindred's daughter, a pound.

The amobr of an uchelwr's daughter, six score pence.

The amobr of every chief officer's daughter, according to some, a pound; according to others, six score pence.

The amobr of other officers' daughters, according to some, six score pence; according to others, three score.

The amobr of a slave's daughter, twelve pence:
> if she is servient, twenty-four pence.
> The amobr of a woman from another country, twenty-four pence, whatsoever be her status in her own country.
> The amobr of an innate bonheddig's daughter, twenty-four pence; others say, as much as the ebediw of her father when he was on the land.
> > *Col.*

If it happens that a maiden is raped and from that rape she becomes pregnant, and that she does not know who the father is, and the lord claims amobr and she says that there is no right to it from her (for she was raped and no woman who is raped is bound to pay amobr): the reason is, law says there that her amobr is extinguished because he could not keep her from rape when he was bound to keep her. Moreover, if she is doubted for what she says, only her own oath will be given that what she says is true.

The son of such a woman will have his status adjudged according to his mother's kin until it is known who his father is.

If it happens that a man says that a woman is

56   The Law of Hywel Dda

pregnant by him, with the woman denying and
the man admitting and the lord claiming amobr:
let the man who admits pay, since there is no
denial of a vouchee for him.   *Dw.*

If it happens that a daughter is denied by a
kindred, and after that she is given to a husband,
and there is a dispute about her amobr, law says
that it is the King who is entitled to it, since
there is no other owner who is entitled to it; and
that is King's waste. And if the mother is a
Welshwoman, her amobr will be as much as the
amobr of an innate bonheddig's daughter, that
is, eighty pence; and if the mother is an alien
woman, her amobr will be as much as the amobr
of an alien woman, that is, twenty-four pence.
And the ebediw of a son who is denied goes in the
same way unless he rises so that his ebediw is
increased.   *Dw.*

If it happens that a woman is given to a man
and her amobr is paid, and after that she is taken
to another father, and the lord of the father to
whom she was taken claims her amobr in respect
of the marriage which she completed before she
came to the new father whom she has—for she is
the daughter of his man and he has not had her
amobr: he is not entitled to it, for three reasons;
because there is right only to one amobr from a
woman; second is because she has not married
since she came to that new father; and the third
reason is, whatever she did in the family group in
which she formerly was, no claim or surclaim
will follow her in the other family group to
which she has come. If she did not pay the amobr
to the lord who was over her former father, let
her pay to the lord who is over the new father.
                                                Dw.

If it happens that a servient slave is made pregnant,
it is right for him who made her pregnant to give a

The Laws of Women 57

woman as good as her to serve in her place until she is delivered, and to rear the child after she is delivered, without hindrance to him whom she serves; and if she dies in giving birth, let him pay her value to her lord.

The ebediw of a woman having a cell is sixteen pence.

If it happens that an alien woman is going through a country and then dies, let her pay sixteen pence for her death-clod to him to whom the ground belongs.

If it happens that a man separates from a wife, and he takes another woman, the wife from whom he separated is validly free, since no man is entitled to have two wives.

Every woman is entitled to go the way she will, for it is not right for her to be car-returning, and there is no right to anything from her save her amobr, and one amobr at that, for a woman has no ebediw save her amobr; therefore, as it is right that a man should pay only one ebediw, in the same way it is right that a woman should pay only one amobr, since she has no ebediw save her amobr.

A woman is not admissible as surety or testifier in relation to a man.

If it happens that a woman is seen coming from one side of a grove and a man on the other, or coming from an empty house, or under one mantle, if they deny it, the oath of fifty women for the woman, and as many men for the man.

If it happens that a Welshwoman is given to an alien, her sarhaed will follow the alien's status until the alien dies, and after the alien dies until she takes another husband, since her status does not return again to her kin.

58   *The Law of Hywel Dda*

If it happens that a Welshwoman is given to an alien and they have children, the children will be entitled to patrimony by mother-right, except that they will not be entitled to a share of the status toft until the third person—unless the alien is a chieftain, who will be entitled to his share of the whole without delay. For the sons of such women there is a right to cattle of dark ancestry: those cattle are called cattle of dark ancestry because it is not the father's kin that pays them, but the mother's kin.

A woman is not entitled to buy or sell unless she is *priod*; if she is *priod*, however, she is entitled to buy and sell.

There are three women whose sons are entitled to mother-right according to law: the son of a Welshwoman who is given to an alien; and the son of a woman given as a hostage into a country of strange speech, if she becomes pregnant after being given as a hostage by her kin and her lord; and a woman whom an alien rapes.

If it happens that a maiden is given to a man, and her cowyll is not claimed before she rises from bed on the morrow, he is not bound to answer for it from then on. If it happens to a maiden that she does not appropriate her cowyll before she rises from bed on the morrow, it is right for her cowyll from then on to be in common between them.

A daughter is entitled to only as much as half what her brother gets of her father's goods, and she is bound to pay for galanas only as much as half what a brother pays, and that on behalf of her children. If she has no children and she swears that she will not have any in future, she is not bound to pay anything; and if she has any, and they have reached legal age, let them pay for themselves from then on. No woman in the world is bound to pay a shaft penny, whether she be old or young.

The Laws of Women 59

If it happens that a woman says of a man that he cannot have connexion with her, and because of that seeks to separate from him, law orders her to be tested. This is how testing is done: a freshly-laundered white sheet is spread under them, and the man goes to her on it to have her; and when his will comes he ejaculates on the sheet; if it is seen on it, it is a quota for him, and she cannot separate from him for that cause. If he cannot do it at all, she can separate from him, and take the whole of what is hers.

If it happens that a maiden says that a man has raped her and the man denies it, and the maiden says that if he has not raped her she is a maiden: the law says that it is proper to test whether she is a maiden or not a maiden, for her plea is that she is a maiden. It is right that the edling should test her, and if he finds her to be a maiden, the man will be free and she will not lose her status.

If a married woman is raped, there is no obligation to pay amobr for her, for she paid it when she married.

If it happens that a woman lays a son legally to a man, even though the man denies him, the law says that after she has once laid him legally she is not entitled to lay him to another man, for he will not be car-returning from him to whom he was first laid.

If it happens that a woman is given to a man and her goods are named, and all the goods are received up to the last penny but that penny is not received, we say that the man can separate from her and that he will get none of what is hers; and that is called one penny which draws a hundred. No surety is needed for the validity of goods which accompany a woman as endowment.

A wife is entitled to a third of her husband's sarhaed, whether it was by killing him that sarhaed was done to him or in some other way.

60   *The Law of Hywel Dda*

A woman has no right to female compurgators, whether for theft or for homicide or for surety, but to male compurgators.

Law says that a woman is not entitled to cowyll after she begins to menstruate, unless her closest relatives vindicate her, that is to say her mother and father and brothers and sisters to the number of seven. And it is right that she should menstruate from fourteen years of age on, and from then until the end of forty years it is right for her to rear children; that is, for fifty-four years it is right that she should be in her youth, and from then on she ceases to conceive.

If it happens that a maiden is given to a man and he has not slept with her, and wrong is done to her, according to her husband's status will compensation be made to her, and not according to her brother's status; and she is called a maiden-wife. And if she is raped, it is right that her cowyll be paid to her.

If it happens that a wife is accused of having a man, on the first occasion, the oath of seven women from her; on the second occasion, the oath of fourteen women; on the third, the oath of forty women.

If it happens that a woman kills a man, she is entitled to receive a shaft penny; and she is the person who takes it and does not pay it.

Every female lord is entitled to the amobr of her realm. The dung-maer's wife is entitled to the amobr of the women of the maerdref.

A harlot has no status. Though she be raped, she is not entitled to receive compensation; if she suffers sarhaed, let her sarhaed be paid according to her brother's status, and her galanas if she is killed.

Every damage which a woman does, let her kin pay for her as for a man if she is not married; if she is

The Laws of Women

married, let her and her husband pay the dirwy and the camlwrw.

The three unclaimable things of a man: his horse and arms; and what comes to him from his land; and what comes to him as wynebwerth from his wife; he is not bound to share any of those with his wife. The three unclaimable things of a woman are her three privy things, and those she does not share with her husband.

The three shames of a maiden: when her father says 'O maiden, you have been given to a man'; second is when she first goes to bed to her husband; third is when she rises from bed and comes among people. For gift is amobr paid; for her virginity her cowyll; for her shame her agweddi. *Col.*

And so ends the Law of Women.

2. The Nine Tongued-ones

Here begin the Laws of the Country; first is the Nine Tongued-ones.

There are nine persons each of whom is believed when giving evidence on oath. *Bleg.*

Those are these: a lord between two men of his; a priest between two monks of his; a father between two sons of his. If one of those above-named does not want to put the decision in the mouth of the three tongued-ones while the other does want to, law orders that it be put in their mouth.

Fourth is a justice on his judgment. If it happens that a person of the one party of those between whom there was litigation denies a judgment while the other asserts it, the justice's word is then the final word as to his judgment.

Fifth is a surety on his suretyship. If there is an admitted surety, and one says that the suretyship is

The Law of Hywel Dda

for a large thing and the other that it is for a small thing: since the surety is admitted, he is to be believed as to what he was given for; and since he is admitted he cannot be denied.

Sixth is a donor as to his gift. This is how it is: if it happens that a man gives a thing and two men are saying 'It was to me', 'It was to me that it was given', his word is the final word as to where he gave it.

Seventh is a maiden as to her virginity: if it happens that a man takes a maiden clandestinely, and after taking her to a waste place and before he has connexion with her she asks 'What will you give me?' and he specifies how much he will give her and afterwards regrets it, though he should deny it, and she affirms it, her word is then the final word.

> A maiden as to her maidenhood. If the man to whom she is given says that she was not a maiden, in order to take away her right and her entitlement, or if she is raped and the man who raped her says that she was not a maiden, the maiden's evidence is to be believed against him. *Cyfn.*

Eighth is a hamlet's herdsman: if it happens that a person's beast is killed by the stock of other owners, for that the herdsman's word is the final word as to which steer killed it.

Ninth is a thief at the gibbet as to his fellow-thieves. If it happens that he says that a person was a fellow-thief of his, and he is being put to death for that theft, and he affirms it by the death to which God went and to which he is going, then his word is the final word.

> Also to be believed is a contract-man on the contract; and so also to be believed is an informer who makes a sufficient information; and a donor is believed as to the goods which he gives; and then it is said 'There is no gift unless willingly'. *Cyfn.*

The Nine Tongued-ones 63

3. Injury to Animals

If it happens that a person breaks the foot of an animal which is not his, or its thigh, or gives it a wound from which the animal may suffer wasting, and the animal is clean, so that its flesh can be eaten, it is proper for the person who wounded it to take the animal to him for medical care until it is healthy, since it is not right for the owner of the animal to labour for the illegality of him who did him wrong. And if it was a milch animal or a plough-ox which he wounded, let there be given to its owner a similar one as good as it, to make such use of it as he would make of his own; and if the animal dies, let the substitute remain validly in its place; if it lives and is seen to be healthy and of full value, let everyone take his own as before.

If it happens that the animal dies on the spot when wounded, let it be offered to him who wounded it, and if he does not want it, let the owner make use of it. If the other says 'You use it, and I will pay you for it as law says', what the law says is that from St John's Day to the New Year the meat and hide are worth two thirds of the whole, with a third for the life, for then is the time for slaughter. From the New Year to St John's Day again, two thirds for the life and one third for the meat and hide, for every animal is carrion at that time.

If it happens that the person who wounded it refuses the dead animal, let the owner do what he likes with it, and in addition to that he shall have its full value.

4. Surety and Contract

Surety (Mach)
Concerning a claim of surety and principal debtor. If it happens that a person gives a surety to another for a thing, it is proper for him to release the surety. For one of three reasons a surety will be free: either by paying on his behalf, or by gaging, or by denying a surety.

64   The Law of Hywel Dda

If he wants to deny it, thus it is denied. The two parties and the surety come to the justice, and it is for the justice to ask the two parties to admit whether the man is a surety or not. 'A surety,' says the claimant. 'No surety,' says the principal debtor. Then it is proper for the justice to ask the surety 'Are you a surety?' 'I am,' says the surety. 'Complete denial', says the principal debtor, 'that you are a surety from me for that or for anything.' 'God knows,' says the surety, 'as best it is right for a surety to assert that he is a surety will I assert that I am a surety.' 'God knows,' says the principal debtor, 'as best it is right for a principal debtor to deny a surety will I deny you.'

Then it is proper for the justice to examine in what form it is right to deny a surety. What the law there says is that as there is only the one tongue of the surety to charge against him, there is required only the one tongue of the principal debtor to deny him. 'Yes,' says the principal debtor, 'I will deny you.' Then it is proper for the justice to take the relic in his hand and say 'The protection of God before you, and the protection of the Pope of Rome, and the protection of your Lord, do not go to a false oath.' If he goes to the oath, let him swear to God first, and to the relic which is in the justice's hand, that he is not a surety from him, either for what he says or for anything. If the surety does not counterswear against him, let the principal debtor be free of the claim for the denial which he effected, and let the surety pay the whole of the debt to the claimant.

If the surety counterswears against the principal debtor, let him counterswear while the principal debtor is putting his lips to the relic after swearing; and this is how he counterswears: 'By the relic which is there, I am a surety from you for what I said, and falsely have you sworn; and by the counterswearing which I have performed against you I claim judgment from the justice.' And then it is proper for the justice to go out to judge a judgment. What the law sees there

Surety and Contract 65

is the oath of the principal debtor as one of seven to deny it: six men with himself as seventh, four of them from his father's side and two from his mother's side, and himself as seventh. And it is right for those men to be so nearly related to him that it is right for them to pay galanas with him and to take it.

The date for that compurgation is a week from the forthcoming Sunday; and the place in which that compurgation is given is the church which has his holy water and mass bread; and the time at which that compurgation is taken, between the Benedicamus and the giving of the mass bread. And if he gets the compurgation it is the quota for him. If he does not get the compurgation, let him pay the claim; and if the Lord wants to prosecute him for perjury, let him prosecute.

Whatsoever surety counterswears against the principal debtor, let him be free from the claim and from the suretyship, for he has performed the characteristics of a surety. Whatsoever surety does not counterswear against the principal debtor, let him pay the claim himself, since he did not perform the characteristics of a surety and what he was bound to do. When a surety admits to the justice that he is a surety, it is proper for the claimant to attest that he admitted it, lest he should again withdraw.

> He who denies suretyship, let him give his oath as one of seven in like manner. And if his kin are not in the same country with him, let him give his own oath above seven consecrated altars in the same cantred as himself, for so briduw is denied. *Cyfn.*

If it happens to a surety that he does not remember whether he is a surety or not, it is proper to give him the delay to which he is entitled for reminding himself. That delay is three days, and if he does not remember within those three days that he is a surety and does not deny that he is a surety, let him pay the whole of the debt. *Dw.*

The Law of Hywel Dda

If it happens that a person takes a surety from another, it is proper to give a date for the thing to which there is a right; and when the date comes, it is proper for him himself to ask the principal debtor first, and if the principal debtor refuses him, let him come to his surety and claim on his surety, and say that the principal debtor has refused him. If what the surety says is to deny that he is a surety, let him come to the justice, and let the claimant claim against him before the justice. And if the surety wants to deny and the claimant does not counterswear against him, the surety will be free from the claim by the denial which he has effected. If what the claimant does is to counterswear against the surety and to call for judgment, it is proper for the justice to adjudge on him the oath and the denial as we said above.

> If there is between debtor and creditor a set day for paying the debt, he is bound to wait for that day. Whosoever claims a debt by plaint before the due date, it is right for him to be without it for as long as that after the date. *Bleg.*

If it happens that a person takes a surety from another for a thing, and that the two parties come together, the claimant and the surety and the principal debtor, and that the claimant claims against the surety and says that he is surety for a large thing, and the principal debtor answers and says that he is surety for a small thing, without denying the suretyship, it is then proper for the justice to adjudge that it is in the surety's return what he is surety for, whether for a large thing or for a small thing, by the surety's oath, since he is an admitted surety.

> If it happens that there is an admitted surety for a debt, and the claimant says that it is for three score pence and the defendant says that it is for twenty pence, while the surety says that he is surety for a pound and the claimant testifies that the surety admitted to being surety for a pound: law judges that the defendant is not bound to pay

Surety and Contract   67

anything save what he admitted, since the surety did not admit the measure which the claimant asserted. And if the surety has that wherewith he may compel, let him compel; and if not, let him himself pay to the claimant what he admitted he was surety for; and if the surety returns less than the measure, let the defendant pay what he admitted, since the surety did not admit either of the two other measures.

If it happens that there is an admitted debt with two sureties for it, and the claimant says that the debt is three score pence and the defendant says that it is twenty pence, and the return is put in the mouth of the sureties; and one of them returns that he is for three score and the other admits that he is for twenty: law says that, where two persons agree and put the return in the mouth of a number of persons and those persons do not agree on a return, they have returned nothing, since the two parties agreed only on what the returners would be in agreement to return as between the two parties. And if they want a delay for memory, let them take it; and if they do not want it, let there be paid to the claimant the twenty which the defendant admits; and it is not because the surety returns it that it is paid to him, but because the defendant admits that he is entitled to it from him.   *Dw.*

If it happens that a person takes many sureties for a thing and the principal debtor wants to deny them, as many as we said above for denying a surety are needed for denying each of them. Some of the justices want to deny them with one set of seven men though they should be twenty-four sureties; the law however says that that is not proper and not competent.

If it happens that a person takes many sureties for a thing and wants to deny them, it is right for him to deny every one of them as one of seven

68   *The Law of Hywel Dda*

men. If moreover he wants to deny them, he can
deny them with the same seven men if he likes,
for it is no bar to them that they have sworn
before.   *Col.*

If it happens that a person denies surety and he
gets no compurgators to deny with him save his
brothers, and the claimant puts it to the law that
there is no right save to two thirds from the
father's kin and one third from the mother's
kin: law judges that the seven brothers are entitled to deny surety; the reason is, that there is no
bar to a surety's compurgator save that it is right
for him to pay galanas with him and to take it,
and the brothers can give their oath that it is
right for them to pay galanas and to take it with
each of them.   *Dw.*

If it happens that a person supposes that a surety is
free from his suretyship by paying part of the debt,
without paying the whole, the law says that he will
not be free, and that it is right for him to be a surety for
the last penny as for the first.

If it happens that there is an admitted surety for a
thing, and there is refusal to pay by the principal
debtor, it is proper for the surety to give a legal gage: a
legal gage is one third better than the payment. If it
happens that the giving of a gage is obstructed, it is for
the surety to convey the gage with him to safety, and
he is bound to receive the first cudgel-blow if there is
fighting; and if he does not do that, let him pay the
debt himself.

If it happens that the surety seeks to take a gage
without the principal debtor, he is not entitled to take
it unless there has been refusal in his presence. If he
has seen refusal to the claimant before that, he can
give a gage from the principal debtor to the claimant
in his absence.

If the principal debtor allows the surety to give a
gage of a pound instead of one penny, and before the

Surety and Contract 69

due date of the gage the gage is lost, the law does not say that he is entitled to anything back except a half-penny, for the third part of a legal penny is a half-penny. If it happens that a person gives the value of a pound instead of one penny as gage, and the gage falls forfeit, there will not be restored to the principal debtor as much as one farthing, for he himself corrupted the status of his gage.

Whosoever gages a gage, and supposes that as there is no surety for it, the gage is invalid: the law says that that gage will fall forfeit and that it is valid.

If it happens that the surety gives a large thing as a gage for a small thing, law is that the claimant should take what is given him, in spite of its size, as gage; and though he should lose it before the due date, the claimant will not restore more than a third to the surety who gave it to him. The surety, however, will compensate the principal debtor fully for it, since he took it illegally.

If it happens that there is a surety for twelve pence, and the principal debtor has to his name nothing save a horse worth ten pounds, and the claimant comes with the surety to exact the twelve pence; and the principal debtor says 'I have nothing with which I can pay you, save my horse, and that I will not pay you and will not gage to you', the surety is not entitled to take a gage from him and the claimant is not entitled to take the surety's gage; but they should both go to the Lord and report to the Lord that there is nothing there save a large thing, and there is no right to take a large thing for a small thing. Then it is proper for the Lord to give the surety leave to give the large thing as gage for the small thing, lest the claimant should suffer loss.

If it happens that a person gives a surety for a debt to another, and that he has nothing save joint goods, and that the surety supposes that he is entitled to gage those, law judges that there is no right to gage them; a Lord however can be a stone in place of an icicle and authorise the surety to divide the goods and to gage part of the principal debtor's share for his suretyship.   *Dw.*

If it happens that a surety allows a gage to be taken from him and regrets it, let that be instead of payment for him who took it, since he is not a surety from then on.   *Dw.*

If it happens that a person calls on his surety to come and enforce payment of what is his for him, and the surety prefers to gage from his own, rather than enforcing against the other: whether he releases or not, let him pay the debt himself.
          Dw.

If it happens that a person gives a surety for a debt to another, and after giving the surety goes into protection against the debt, the law says that he is not entitled to protection against that, and that the surety is entitled to give his gage to the claimant, or else that he should deny his suretyship.

It is not right for anyone to take a surety for a fixed day; for if he does not claim it on that day, it becomes a time when he has no surety.

It is not right for anyone to take a debtor-surety, for they are two pleas, and he is allowed only to choose his plea. If he chooses suretyship there is no principal debtor; if he chooses debtorship there is no surety; and accordingly no person can stand as debtor-surety.

Whosoever buys goods from another and is himself surety for the price, and dies before paying and leaves his goods with friends, the claimant is entitled to payment from those goods, for the goods belonged to the dead man who was debtor-surety to him. It is right for him to swear, as one of seven persons most nearly related to him, on the payer's grave if he can find it, and on a consecrated altar if he cannot, that he sold the goods to him and that he was debtor-surety to him for the price of the goods.   *Bleg.*

Surety and Contract 71

A surety is not entitled to take a gage from the principal debtor when he is on his lord's errands, or on his own errands, or when he is feeble. And the claimant is not entitled to take the surety's gage during the same period.

If it happens that a person takes a surety for goods, and after that the principal debtor is exiled, whether by reason of homicide or by reason of theft, or for other illegalities for which he is not entitled to be in the country, and the claimant seeks the goods from the surety: what the law there sees is that it is proper to share the loss between them in two halves, the surety paying half to the claimant, for it is unfair for the surety to pay the whole when he is innocent, and it is no fairer for the claimant to lose the whole because he trusted in the surety. And that is one of the three places where law shares in two halves. If it happens that the principal debtor comes back to the country again, they are entitled to exact the goods from him, and then it is proper for the surety to have half the goods. And that is the place where the surety is an exactor of goods for himself.

If it happens that there is a surety for a debt, and before the due date of the debt the surety dies and leaves a son, it is right for the son to stand to his father's obligations. Some say that if the son does not want to stand to the suretyship, it is right that he should make denial by law over his father's grave. The law says nevertheless that it is not right: for the wise say that worldly law does not pursue any person (whether it is to heaven that he goes or to hell) save until he leaves the earth. This is the reason for it: though there be law between persons and each other on this earth, there is no law between angels and each other, and there is no law between devils and each other, save the will of God. And accordingly there is for a person who leaves this earth no law, but the concord of one or other of those. And accordingly it is proper for the son of that dead surety to serve law for his father as his father would serve if he were alive; and if he has no son, it is right for the Lord to stand instead of a son of his; and if it is necessary to exact, it is right for him to exact as the surety would exact if he were alive.

If it happens that a person takes a surety from another for a thing, and before the due date of the debt the principal debtor dies, it is right for the surety to exact from the principal debtor's son as from the principal debtor. If it happens that he has no son, let the Lord stand instead of a son of his, and let him pay on his behalf or let him deny; and if he wants to deny, let him deny as would the man to whom he became a son for the sake of his goods. And as he preferred becoming that man's son for the sake of his goods to being a Lord, let him be of the status of the man to whom he became a son for the sake of his goods, and let him deny the suretyship as one of seven; and it is right that those men should belong, not to the kin of the principal debtor but to that of the Lord, for the principal debtor's kin are not related to the Lord even though the Lord is denying the surety. When denial falls on a son for his father's suretyship, it is not right for anyone of his mother's kin to deny anything on behalf of his father.

There are three vain suretyships. One of them is when a person buys something from another for money and takes a surety for the thing, and no surety is taken for the money, and the owner of the money regrets the bargain. Since he does not want to enjoy the surety which he has for the thing he took, and the other has no surety for the money to enforce the bargain for him, the surety is vain on one side because the owner does not want it.

The second is, if it happens that a person gives a surety to another for something invalid as though it were valid, and the owner of the property comes to

Surety and Contract

73

invalidate it, it is proper for the owner of the property to have what is his although a surety was given for it, since it was not right to give it; and it is not right to move it from the hand in which it is until a substitute as good as it comes from the warrantor. If it happens that the warrantor says that it is right for him to pay only as much as he received for the thing (whatsoever kind of thing it may be), the law says that it is right for him to pay the legal value of the thing, whatsoever kind of thing it may be. And because the surety cannot maintain the suretyship for which he became a surety it is called a vain surety. As for the invalid property of which we spoke above, let the Lord follow up whomsoever falls into wrong in relation to the movement of the property.

Third is, the surety of a woman is not a surety. That is, a woman is not entitled to be a surety, as women cannot deny a surety, and she is not entitled to compurgators for her denial. The law says however that the surety which a woman gives is a surety, for whosoever can invalidate property, law says that it is free to him to validate it; and since a woman can invalidate property, the law says that a surety is needed from her and that the surety which she gives is a surety. And since it is a man that she is denying, she is entitled to men in support of her to deny a surety.

If it happens that a woman gives a briduw for a thing and legally denies it, the law says that it is women that deny it with her.

> Three blemishes of suretyship: one is to deny it; second is false returning; third is that he cannot enforce it.   Dw.

Three buckle suretyships there are. First of them is, if a person buys a thing from another and asks for a surety for the property from him who sold it: 'I will give it,' says the person, and puts his hand in the surety's hand, and the person who is to take the suretyship does not

The Law of Hywel Dda

come to take it from the surety's hand and to put his hand in the surety's hand, but stretches his hand out towards the surety, and the surety towards him, and it is supposed that that is enough: law says that that suretyship is of no force on the day it is needed, because there was no skill to take it; though he may be a surety from him who gave him by one hand's joining the other, he is not a surety to him who took him, since the hand did not join the other, and accordingly it is a buckle suretyship.

The second buckle suretyship is: if it happens that a person buys a thing from another and asks for a surety for that thing, and the person who is selling that thing says 'I will give a surety', and stretches out his hand towards the surety and the surety stretches out his hand towards him, but neither of them puts his hand into the other's hand, and afterwards the surety gives his hand to him who bought the property and becomes a surety to him, law says that he is a surety to the man who took him legally and that he is not a surety from the man who did not give him legally and there is nowhere he can enforce his suretyship; let him himself fall into the trouble which comes from the suretyship.

Third buckle suretyship: if it happens that a person takes a surety for another in his absence for a thing, and the giver of the surety comes and puts the suretyship in the hand of the surety and names it for the person who is not there, and puts his hand into the surety's hand as would be legal; and the surety comes to the proctor, who is in the place of the person to take the suretyship for him, and gives the suretyship to him with the hands in each other, and the surety names also the one who is not there, that he is surety to him: law says of this that that suretyship is of no force. This is why: though the hands of all those who

Surety and Contract 75

were in the suretyship have met, it was not named for the proctor who took it, accordingly he is not entitled to either the suretyship or the claim. If the surety had named the suretyship for him, he would himself have had to pay the price. The man for whom the suretyship was named, and who was not in the place, is not entitled to it since he did not take the suretyship from the surety's hand as would be right for him to do, and accordingly it is of no force; and accordingly these are called three buckle suretyships.

This is the meaning of their being so called: the nature of a buckle is to bind firmly until it is opposed, and when it is pulled in the opposite direction it releases the bond, and accordingly the bond itself is not secure; and such are these suretyships: if they are opposed they do not stand and are of no force. *Dw.*

Some say that a gage does not fall forfeit from the hand of a surety until after a year and a day. The law says that a gage falls forfeit at its due date from the hand of three persons; those three persons are, a Lord, a surety, and the owner of the property. This is the reason, since a Lord will be surety for all admitted property for which there is no surety, and accordingly the gage falls forfeit from his hand or from that of his servants. From the hand of a Lord or from the hand of a surety no surety is needed for the validity of a gage, for they do not deny that it was given, and it is right for them to be sureties for the validity of that gage for ever. From the owner of the property it is right to take a surety for the validity of the gage, lest he should again deny it, either for greed of the property or for other property which he had not given.

It is not right for anyone to say that he will not become a surety for another, if he is such a man that he is entitled to become a surety. Many persons are not entitled to become surety or to give a surety (this is the reason, as they are not entitled to deny a surety they are not entitled to give a surety): to wit, a monk, and a hermit, and a person of foreign speech, and a scholar from a school, and every person who cannot serve law without the leave of another.

If it happens that a person is a surety and the claim is cited for that, and he becomes leprous or a monk or of a character on account of which he does not suppose he is bound to answer, we say that he is bound to fulfil what he promised while he is alive—and that is one of the places where it is not right for the son to stand in the father's place. The reason it is not right is that he did not leave any of his property to him save by will.

Dw.

If it happens that a person gives a surety for a debt, and the due date falls in the three special feasts, Christmas, or Easter, or Whitsun, though he should claim he will suffer only a postponement. If he starts a claim on Christmas Day, he will not have an answer till the day after New Year's Day. If it is Easter Day, the Tuesday after Low Sunday. If it is Whit Sunday, the Tuesday after the next Sunday to Whitsun. And those three weeks are called by their status blank days.

There is no need to take a surety for the validity of money, nor for interchangeable trinkets, to wit, for a brooch, and a knife, and a belt, nor weapons either.

If it happens that a surety and a principal debtor meet on a bridge of a single tree, he is not entitled to refuse to do one of three things, either to pay, or to gage, or to seek law. And he is not entitled to move his toe to his heel without doing one of those three things. If he refuses to do any of them, let the surety give his gage to the claimant; if he prefers it, let him seek immediate law.

Surety and Contract

It is not right to give a delay for aid in a claim of surety and principal debtor, for it is right for it to be immediate. If it happens that a claimant refuses law before a justice, let the surety be free and let the claimant be deprived of his claim, since his claim lasts only while the surety lasts. If the principal debtor refuses law and the surety is an admitted surety and the claim is fresh, let the surety exact for the claimant the whole of his debt.

> If it happens that a claim of surety and principal debtor comes before a justice and that the surety and the claimant and the principal debtor are in the place, and that the claimant makes his claim and the defendant replies 'God knows,' says he, 'I am not bound to answer you today; this is the reason: it is after midday, and it is not right to start law after midday', and then the claimant says 'God knows,' says he, 'this is a claim of surety and principal debtor, and I rely on the law that where surety and claimant and defendant are before a justice, that is immediate law': law then says, wherever the law is imprisoned in time (as after midday or blank days or law falling on a Sunday or on a feast day, or law for land and earth at harvest or in spring), that the prison of time is superior to a claim of surety and principal debtor; and since it cannot be done at those times it is proper to delay it. *Dw.*

If it befalls two persons that there is litigation between them and one of them calls for surety for law, and the other says that he is not bound to give a surety for law but is entitled to a delay for aid, and the claimant says 'God knows,' says he, 'I am entitled to a surety: he is entitled to a surety who is entitled to nothing'; 'God knows,' says the other, 'he is no surety who is a surety for nothing, and from me you are not entitled to anything, for it is admitted by you yourself that you are not entitled': the law says that

The Law of Hywel Dda

he is not entitled to a surety for law, since the other pleaded a delay for aid, and if he gave the surety there would be immediate law, since there is no delay in a claim of surety and principal debtor.

Briduw

If it happens that a person gives a briduw for a thing, let him pay or deny as law says. This is what law says, that if there is no counterswearing against him, his own oath is enough. If there is counterswearing against him, let him call for judgment. What the law sees for him is his oath to deny, as one of seven: four from his father's kin and two from his mother's kin, with himself as seventh. The due date of that compurgation is a week from the forthcoming Sunday. And if he gets the compurgation, that is the quota; if the compurgation fails the person, a camlwrw to the King, and let the Church follow him up, and let him pay the debt in full.

If it happens that a person takes a briduw from another, and says that it is for twenty-four pence, and the other says that there is a briduw for sixpence, what the law says is that it is right for him to have the return as to what the briduw is for, whether for twenty-four or for six pence, since he does not deny the briduw; all this on his oath. Though it be said that it is a briduw, the law says that there is no briduw until the hands meet each other, and that there is no surety and no gorfodog until the three hands meet together.

It is right for the Church and the King to enforce a briduw, for God was taken instead of a surety, and accordingly it is for the Church to forbid him for a briduw and for the King to enforce it. For it is right to take a briduw from every person who is baptised, both from man and from woman; accordingly both man and woman are entitled to give it, even down to a seven-year-old boy who goes under the parish priest's hand.

Surety and Contract 79

> Whosoever claims property by promise, let him
> claim by briduw. *Dw.*

Amod
Whosoever makes a legal amod with another, let the
two amod-makers come together and let them state
their amod as they wish to make it, and let them put it
into the hand of the amodwyr to maintain the amod
in the form in which they promised it.

If it happens that a person makes an amod and does
not want to keep it, and that he does not deny the
amod, it is for the Lord to compel him to keep it as
returned by the amodwyr. If it happens that a person
wants to deny an amod, with another charging it
against him and himself denying it alone, the law says
that there is required from him only his own oath to
deny it, unless there is counterswearing against him.
If there is counterswearing against him, let him call
for judgment; and this is what is adjudged to him: his
oath as one of seven to deny it—and all this as a surety
is denied, with the delay allowed for compurgation of
a surety. If it happens there that someone wants to bar
one of those compurgators, there is no bar to him save
that he does not belong to his kin, so that he is not
entitled to be a compurgator for him. Thus is he
entitled to be a compurgator for him: by his being so
near that it is right for him to pay galanas with him
and to take it for him, on the compurgator's oath that
the relationship is true.

If it happens that a person makes an amod with
another without amodwyr, but with his hand in the
other's, and the other wants to deny it, there is
required from him only his own oath to deny it. If it
happens that a person enters into a promise with
another for a thing in the presence of witnesses, and
he again wants to deny it, the law says that he is not
entitled to deny it until the witnesses fail. If it
happens that a person enters into a promise with
another, without witnesses on the spot, that is not an

amod, and as it is not an amod, let him deny it by his own oath.

No one is entitled to make an amod for another, since an amod lasts only for the lifetime of the person who makes it. A father is not entitled to promise an amod for his son save by the son's leave, nor can the son make an amod to burden the father while the father is alive.

An amod breaks a rule of law. Though an amod be made contrary to law, it is necessary to keep it.

An amod is stronger than law.   *Cyfn.*

Some say of an amod that it can never be dissolved; this is the reason, that an amod is like a vow, and for every vow (though it be broken) it is proper to return to it and to keep it anew: so he who breaks an amod and repents, and calls for his amod, indemnifying him with whom he broke his amod, is entitled (say some) to have his amod and his place again. The law nevertheless says, whatsoever person repudiates a legal thing, however much he binds himself to the thing (whether it be an amod or another thing), has no claim to the amod again, since he broke the amod and to break an amod is to repudiate it. The person with whom the amod was broken can fulfil the amod, since he did not break the amod and did not repudiate it; and accordingly he is entitled to his amod again and his place.

Dw.

If a person makes two amodau with one person for one thing, it is right for him to keep the later one. If a person makes two amodau with two persons for one thing, it is right for him to keep the earlier one.   *S.*

Bail
Whosoever takes another on bail, let him fall into every liability under which the person he took may be. If he wants to be indemnified by the person for

Surety and Contract

whom he undertook to answer, let him take sureties from that person for his possible loss; and if he does not take them, though he is bound to make compensation because of his bail for the person, the person is not bound to make any compensation to him, since he did not enter into any promise with him. If the bailsman takes sureties from the principal offender for indemnification, there will be no protection for the latter against those sureties.

If it happens that a person takes another on bail for a fixed term, and before the term the principal offender flees from the bailsman, let the bailsman pay in full for him. If it happens that a person promises to become bailsman for something for another, it lies in his mouth to say what he became bailsman for, whether for little or for much; since he himself was trusted.

> A person will not be free from his bailsmanship until the end of a year and a day, unless he limits it to less when he becomes bailsman. *Col.*

> Whosoever is bailsman surety for another will not be released until the end of a year and a day, and will not be troubled within that period for the offence which the other commits, since he is as though bound in the case until he knows whether the wrongdoer will stand to law or not before the term. *Bleg.*

5. Church Protection

Three things from which there is no right to protection, when they are admitted: bailsmanship and suretyship and conquest. If it happens that the parsons of the church say that they can give protection against any one of these three, it lies in the mouth of the King (the man who gave them that sanctuary) to return in what way he gave them that sanctuary; and if he gave it against himself, let them keep what he gives them.

82 The Law of Hywel Dda

It is right for all owners of church land to come to each new king who may come, to declare to him their status and their entitlement; the reason that they declare them to him is lest the King be deceived. And after they declare their status to him, if the King sees that their status is proper, let the King invest them with their status and sanctuary.

If it happens that a person commits illegality and seeks sanctuary from that illegality, and that while he is in that sanctuary a claim is brought against him: it is not right for the abbots or the priests to escort him until he makes compensation for the primary illegality. If no claim is made against him, let them escort him to the place to which they are entitled to escort him. If it happens that a man does wrong worth a penny when in sanctuary, and a claim is made against him for the illegality which he committed in sanctuary, he is not entitled to be defended by the protection under which he did wrong, unless he renews it by another protection in another church.

Whosoever takes sanctuary, it is right for him to go about in the churchyard and the enclosure without relics on him, while his livestock go with the livestock of the clas and the abbots as far as the farthest point to which they go while able to return to their cattle-pen. If it happens that a person has relics on him and that he does wrong under the relics, he is not entitled to have protection or defence from those relics, for he has not deserved them.

The measure of an enclosure is a legal acre in length, with its end at the churchyard, and surrounding the churchyard.

> Whosoever betrays a lord and finds protection and wants to make compensation as law says, the law judges that he should lose his patrimony though his life be saved because of the protection which he found. If it happens that a person does a pennyworth of wrong while he is under protect-

Church Protection 83

ion with a relic on him, it is right for him to suffer total confiscation in spite of that protection, unless he finds protection anew; the reason is, that from the protection which he found he is entitled to no protection. If it happens that a person has a relic on him and weapons in his hand, and seeks to make use of them, he is not entitled to the protection of the relic; if he chooses the relic, let him abandon the weapons and leave them where he will not lose them. *Dw.*

If it happens that there is a church which says that it is entitled to maintain a person in its sanctuary for seven years without making compensation, or for a longer period; and that the Lord who is over the country opposes it in this and says that it has not that status from him: the church must have legal witnesses who will maintain that status, and if it has them let its status be allowed to it without hindrance. And if it does not have them, let the church escort him as it is best entitled to do, or else let him make compensation for the illegality which he committed.

6. Land Law

Procedure in an Action for Land
At two periods law is open for land and earth, and at two closed. From the ninth day from the Winter Kalends it is open until the ninth day of February; from the ninth day of February it is closed until the ninth day of May. From the ninth day of May law is open until the ninth day of August; from the ninth day of August law is closed until the ninth day after the Winter Kalends. And the reason that law is closed at Harvest and Springtime is that the earth is cultivated at those two periods, lest ploughing be hindered in Springtime and lest reaping be hindered at Harvest. The reason that law is closed for nine days after the Winter Kalends and open for nine days after St Bride's

84   *The Law of Hywel Dda*

Day is lest the law should be closed on a single day;
and in the same way closed for nine days after May
Day and open for nine days after August lest law be
opened on a single day also.

Whosoever wants to start a claim for land and
earth, let him start when he likes from the ninth day
from the Winter Kalends onwards, or from the ninth
day of May; for it is at those periods that law is open
for land and earth. If it happens that a claimant wants
to claim land and earth, let him come at those periods
to the Lord to ask for a day for hearing his claim, and
that on the land. On that day let him state his claim;
and he is not entitled to have an answer on that day,
for it is a sudden claim against the occupiers, and
therefore the occupiers are entitled to a delay for aid.
And then it is proper for the justices to hear them, and
to ask where their aid is. If they say that their aid is in
their own commote, let them be given a delay of three
days; if it is in the next commote, nine days; if it is in
the third commote, or there is ebb and flow between
them and their aid, then if the delay is adjudged before
midday, the date will be a fortnight from that day; if it
is after midday, a fortnight from the morrow: the
reason for that is, that there is not a full day, and it is
not proper to render a part of a day instead of a day.

And at that adjudged date it is proper for all to come
to the land, both them and their aid. And then it is
proper to make two parties and to sit legally. This is
how they sit legally: the King, or the man who is in
his place, sits with his back to the sun or the weather
(lest the weather should disturb his face), with the
court justice or the commote justice (whichever is the
senior) sitting in front of him, with the other justice
or justices who may be present on his left hand, and
the priest (if any) or priests, on his right hand; and
next to the King his two elders, with his goodmen
from there on, on either side of him. From there a
gangway for the justices, opposite them, for them to

Procedure in an Action for Land 85

proceed to their judgment seat. The claimant's cyngaws with his left hand to the gangway, with the claimant next to him in the middle and his canllaw on the other side of him, and the serjeant standing behind the cyngaws. The other party on the other side of the gangway: the defendant's cyngaws with his right hand to the gangway, with the defendant next to him in the middle and his canllaw on the other side of him, and the serjeant behind the latter.

Goodman	Goodman	Elder	King	Elder	Goodman	Goodman
	Priest	Priest	Court Justice	Commote Justice		
Def-endant's Canllaw	Defendant	Def-endant's Cyngaws		Claim-ant's Cyngaws	Claimant	Claim-ant's Canllaw
Serjeant				Serjeant		

When they have sat thus, let surety be taken for law. Sureties for land and earth will be pledges in the form of living persons, two or more from each party; and those pledges go into the control of the Lord. After that, concord is proclaimed, that is, silence in the field. Whosoever breaks that concord will pay three kine camlwrw, or nine score pence, and the words spoken after the proclamation of silence will be useless to him who spoke them and to the case in support of which they were spoken.

After being legally seated as we have said above, it is then proper for the justice to say to the two parties 'Plead now by law.' And then it is proper for the justice to ask the claimant 'Who is your cyngaws and who is your canllaw?' and then it is proper for the claimant to name them. And then it is proper for the justice to ask the claimant whether he will put loss or gain in their mouth, and then it is proper for the claimant to speak; 'I will,' says he. And then it is proper for the justice to ask the cyngaws and the canllaw whether they will stand by him in what he is putting upon them; and then it is proper for them to say 'We will.'

86 *The Law of Hywel Dda*

After that it is proper for the justice to ask the defendant 'Who is your cyngaws and who is your can-llaw?' and then it is proper for him to name them. And then it is proper for the justice to ask him whether he will put loss or gain in their mouth, and then it is proper for him to speak; 'I will,' says he.

> And then it is proper for the justice to ask them whether they will stand by him; and then it is proper for them to say 'We will.'   *Col.*

And then it is proper for the justice to say to the claimant 'Make now your claim', and then it is proper for the claimant to begin to claim. Here is what it is proper for the claimant to say: to declare that he is true proprietor of this land and earth, and if there is anyone who doubts whether he is true proprietor, that he has those who will maintain his proprietorship by kindred and descent, to the number which is sufficient in law; and that he was illegally ejected from his proprietary holding, and if there is anyone who doubts it, that he has enough who know that he was illegally ejected. And what he puts on the law is that he is entitled to come back legally to the place from which he was illegally ejected. If it happens that there are some who are surprised that maintainers and knowers are offered by the same party, the law says that it can be done until the defendant's answer is heard.

> If it is laid against him that he has two warranties, maintainers and knowers, and it is said that there is no right to them in the same claim, 'God knows,' says the claimant, 'wherever I am doubted for as much as I have said, I want maintainers where they are right and knowers where they are right, that what I have said is true; and I put it to the law that I am entitled to it.' Law says that there is in that only one warranty and one claim, and that it is best when there is most to confirm the claim and that

Procedure in an Action for Land 87

he is entitled to what he says where he is doubted.   *BG.*

Says the defendant, 'It is I who am true proprietor by kindred and descent, and what I am occupying is my own and my proprietorship, as best I am entitled to occupy it; and if there is anyone who doubts that, I have enough who will maintain that what I say is true. As for you, if you have been here, you went from here legally; and if there is anyone who doubts that, I have enough who know it.' The law says that though the defendant may have answered before the claimant makes his claim against him, the answer is void until he hears the claim, and that then he should give answer.

And after their two sets of pleadings have been completed as we said above, let the justice ask them whether what they have said is enough and let him ask them whether they want to better their pleadings. And if there is anyone who wants to, let it be allowed him, and if not, let the justice take the two sets of pleadings and state them. And after he has stated them, let the justices go out, together with the priests, with the serjeant with them to guard them so that people shall not come to listen to them. If it happens that a person comes to listen to them, it is right for him to pay three kine camlwrw to the King, and if the King is present it is right for him to pay a double camlwrw for that. And then after they have sat, it is proper for the priest to pray God that God will show them the right and for them to sing their paternoster; and after the paternoster it is proper for the justice to state the two sets of pleadings a second time.

And if it happens that a word of inquiry is needed, let two be sent to ask for it. And if the party which is asked for a word of inquiry needs to consult together, let them go to consult with the leave of the justice. And those who go will be the team who were at the

88 *The Law of Hywel Dda*

pleadings and no more, with a servant of the Lord accompanying them to guard them so that no one shall come to advise them; and if anyone comes to them and advises them, let him pay a camlwrw to the King and let the advice be void. Thereafter let those two come to the justices and let them declare to the justices what their decision is.

If it happens that there is no need for a word of inquiry, it is proper to leave them their pleas and to send two to ask them who their knowers and their maintainers are, and where they are. If they say that they are on the spot, let them be enjoyed. If they say that they are in the same commote as themselves, let a delay of three days be given them. If they say that they are in the next commote, let a delay of nine days be given them. If they say that they are in another country, or that there is ebb and flow between themselves and them, a fortnight's delay from that day if it is before midday; if it is after midday, a fortnight from the morrow.

> If it happens that there is litigation between two persons and that the claimant claims before the justice and the defendant says 'I am not bound to make law today: it is after midday and it is not right to invoke law or to make it after midday', 'God knows,' says he, 'it is not midday, and since it is not midday I put it to law that it is right in law to answer'; law then says that it is right for the justice who judges the case, and the priest if any, to judge whether it is midday or not midday. And whichever of the two parties doubts them, let him be put to the relics that it is to his mind most likely that it is midday or that it is not midday; and if it is not midday let law be allowed between them and if it is midday let the law be postponed until the morrow. *Dw.*

And that day will be the day of loss and gain, and the pledges are to be in the King's prison until that day;

Procedure in an Action for Land 89

and everyone is ordered to bring his materials to the land on that day. Though this be not agreed by the two parties, it is the adjudged law-day.

On the third day, after they come face to face it is proper for everyone to sit in his place as he sat on the earlier day; and if some of those who were at the pleading have died, let others be put in their place. And after sitting, then it is proper for the claimant to offer his testifiers and his maintainers and his materials and to say that he is ready with his materials as he promised. And then it is proper for the defendant to respond, and the answer he gives is to say that he too is ready with his materials as he promised. And then it is proper for the King to order that the pledges be shown on the spot, for they are the sureties. And then, after the pledges have been shown, the serjeant is ordered to proclaim silence in the field; and then it is proper for the justice to say 'Disturbance will be punished': that is three kine camlwrw and the word spoken to be void.

And then it is proper for the claimant to put it in the justices' mouth that it was he who first promised his testifiers and his maintainers and that he is entitled to enjoy them first. And then it is proper for the justices to order him to bring his maintainers and his testifiers for them to be enjoyed. And then it is proper for him to bring them around him and to show them; those he will show are those which he promised on the earlier day. It is not right for the defendant to object to any of them until he knows what they will say, since he does not know that what they will say will not be good for him; and any one of them to whom he objects before knowing what he will say, let him stand. And the defendant can ask whether they have such status that they are entitled to be testifiers; and if they have, let them come forward. The reason that he can ask that is because an alien cannot be a knower against a patrimonial Welshman, nor a woman against a man; and in addition there are many persons who cannot be

90 The Law of Hywel Dda

knowers or maintainers because of status; and therefore it does not prejudice the defendant to say that.

If it happens that the defendant has promised better
testifiers than those which the claimant had promised, whether from their being of better status or from
their being more numerous, and he wants to rely on
that, it is proper to show them; and after he has shown
his testifiers it is not proper for the claimant to object
to them. Then it is proper for the justice to ask the
claimant, 'What is the status of your testifiers?'; and
then it is proper for the claimant to state the status of
his testifiers, whether they are meiri or cyngellorion
or monks or teachers or priests or clerks or laymen of
status. When the justice has asked the claimant the
status of his testifiers, then it is proper for the justice
to ask the defendant the status of his testifiers, and
then it is proper for the defendant to state the best
status that his testifiers have. Then it is proper for the
justice to declare the two status which the two parties
there have stated for their testifiers.

Then it is proper for the justice to ask the knowers
whether they will stand to what is being put in their
mouth. Here are all the knowers saying that they will
stand. Here are both the parties doubting each other's
knowers, that they will not take it to the bitter end
though they say it by word of mouth. It is proper for
the justices to put them to the relics, and after putting
them to the relics it is proper for them to go out to
examine what they see as most proper according to
what they have heard. And if they see that the testifiers of one set are better than the others, let them
disjudge those whose testifiers are the worse. If it
happens that the testifiers are equally good, let the
defendant be disjudged, since he promised testifiers
who would be better than the other had, and did not
get them. And then it is proper for the justice to
adjudge that the claimant should come to the land
with the status which he had when he was unlawfully
moved from it.

Procedure in an Action for Land 91

And after that it is proper for the justices to test the maintainers to see whether each set of them will return that the party which he supports is a proprietor; the maintainers of both sets say that they are proprietors, and if they are doubted, it is proper to put them to the relics, and he whose maintainers withdraw from their oath, let him lose the land. If their maintainers stand for both parties, that is equality; and where there is equality there will be two halves.

Though it be adjudged to him that he should come to the land, the man who was there before him will not move on his account if he can get for him a standard plot in the same place, with equally good land for both, as he will not be ejected from there; but it is not right to pay land without status instead of land to which a status is attached, such as the office of cynghellor, or the office of maer, or an immunity.

And then it is proper for the justices to come to their place of judgment. And then it is proper for them to take security for abiding by the judgment, and to take surety for their fee. And then it is proper for the justices to declare the two sets of pleadings, and after that to declare the judgment. And then it is right for the King to release the pledges from their prison. The measure of the justices' fee for land and earth, twenty-four pence; and of that, two men's share for the court justice; and he is not entitled to more, whether he is in court or not.

If it happens that a non-proprietor has maintainers for his being in occupation of land and earth as second man or as third, and that a proprietor claims against him and has maintainers for his proprietorship, the non-proprietor will move away before him. If it happens that he claims by reason of being second man or third and that a proprietor is sitting against him, the proprietor will not move before him from the land. A proprietor displaces a third man. A third man dis-

92 · The Law of Hywel Dda

places a patrimonial: this is a patrimonial—a son whom his father leaves after him on the land. A patrimonial displaces an incomer: this is an incomer—a man who comes of himself to land, and of whose kin no-one has been on the land before him. And so their status proceeds according to their priority of occupation.

The King's fee from land which carries no office, six score pence; from land which carries an office, such as the office of chief falconer or steward or cynghellor or standard-bearer, or maer, a pound; from land which carries two offices, a pound and six score pence: this is from the measure of a shareland. The captain of the household is entitled to twenty pence from every pound which comes to the King for cases of land and earth, out of the King's share; and likewise tenpence to the steward.

After land and earth have been adjudged to a person, he cannot be refused a sharing thereafter when he wants it; whether the season be closed or not, sharing is legal for him at all times. And he is not bound to take acquired land instead of proprietorship, and if he takes it and loses it by law, there is no duty to regain it for him, since he took the invalid instead of the valid.

It is not right for a joint holder of land to render to another land which carries no office, instead of land which carries an office, unless the other himself wants it; and if he takes it, let him lose the status.

Whatsoever claimant puts up testifiers on the day of loss or gain, with the defendant putting up others against him: what the law says is that it is not right to deprive him or any of them of his warrantor until his warrantor fails him. And then it is proper to ask them who their warrantor is, and their testifiers, and where they are: and if they are on the spot let the claimant's be taken first, and if they are not on the spot let a delay

Procedure in an Action for Land 93

be given to them according to where they are, as law says. And if the claimant's testifiers are not on the spot, let the defendant's be taken; the reason for that is that it is not right to hold up readiness for unreadiness. If the claimant's are on the spot, it is proper to show them to the justices and to set them apart.

And then it is proper for the justices to take the testimony of the first into whose mouth it was put when enjoying them, and to ask him whether what the claimant says is true or not true; and to set the protection of God before him, that he shall not say false testimony; and as to that he says that what the claimant was saying is true. Let the defendant then think how he wants to defeat the testifiers, whether by his having more competent ones, who will be more easily believed, or by objecting to them. If he chooses to object to them and they escape from his objection, there is no right to enjoy his testifiers after that, but the unobjectionable ones shall be enjoyed. If he chooses to depend on his testifiers' being better, let the best ones be enjoyed and let there be judgment according to the best ones; if they are equally good, let the claim be adjudged to the claimant, since the defendant promised that his testifiers would be better than the others; if he had promised that they would be equally good, it would be equality and a sharing in two halves.

If the defendant wants to object to testifiers, let him object like this: when the testifier speaks his mind after the justice has asked him, let the claimant say 'Though you say it by word of mouth, you will not take it to the bitter end.' And if the testifier takes it to the bitter end and swears to it, let him counterswear against him, that he has sworn falsely, 'and withal your word is no word against me'. And then it is proper for him to set against him one of the three legal points, either land-feud, or enmity, or nearer kin to the claimant than to himself.

94   *The Law of Hywel Dda*

Three kinds of objection there are in the law of
Hywel according to the Book of the White
House, to wit objection for offence, objection for
nature, and objection for act. By reason of
offence there are these objections: that an ex-
communicated person cannot be a testifier if he
admits that he is such or if it can be proved
against him; that he cannot be a testifier if he
admits, or if it can be proved against him, that he
has earlier been a thief or that he has made compensation for his theft although he has not been
judged; and a person can never be a testifier who
swears falsely in testimony or in another place, if
he admits it or it can be proved against him—and
that is according to the three systems of law,
although he may have done his penance.

And there are found in the law of Hywel as
many objections as that by reason of nature:
those are, nearer kin, and a woman against a
man, and an alien against a Welshman. By
reason of act there are in the law of Hywel these
objections: those are land-feud and blood-feud
and woman-feud, and those last count as one
objection, for woman-feud is of the essence of
enmity of kindred.   *Col.*

And if the testifier does not deny what is charged
against him, let him be rejected; and if he denies it, let
him stand unless the defendant charges it against him
by other testifiers, those testifiers being on the spot.
And if they are not on the spot, let the claimant's
testifiers stand, for there is no right to a delay for a
testifier against another testifier. And if the claimant
gets two testifiers or three who stand, or more as we
have said above, let the claim be adjudged to him.
Some say that woman-feud is a fourth ground of
objection; the law however says that it is of the
essence of enmity of kindred and is one of the three.

If it happens that both parties put their case in the

mouth of testifiers and that neither objects to the other's testifiers, let it be judged according to the testifiers who are of best status and most competent and most numerous. If it happens that they are equally good, let that which is disputed be adjudged in two halves; and that is the law of equality.

It is right for maintainers to swear the same kind of oath as the principal swears before them in every point, and that they do not swear for hate nor for love nor for reward nor for value, nor for anything save to maintain truth. There is no right to object to a maintainer if he is of status, for he charges no ill against anyone, but keeps for the owner what is his.

It is right for an attestor to swear that what he confirms is true, and that he does not swear for hate nor for love; and as an attestor charges ill against a person that person can object to him.

> An attestor is a person called to witness the statement made in his presence. *BG.*

It is right for a designated compurgator to swear that the oath of the person with whom he swears is clean; and if one man from among the designated compurgators fails, the whole compurgation fails. It is right for an other compurgator to swear that it is to his mind most likely that what he swears is true; and though a third of the ordinary compurgation fail, it is right to judge according to the two-thirds.

> If it happens that a person names testifiers, let him bring those whom he promised or let him fail. *Col.*

If he promises a particular number of testifiers, let him fulfil or fail. If he promises what will be a quota in law, two or three are enough, though more would be better. The testimony of one person is not testimony.

> In the law of Rome will be found that where the number of testifiers is not named, two testifiers are

96   *The Law of Hywel Dda*

enough. This law says that the testimony of one testifier is not complete.   *Bleg.*

If it happens that a person on the day of loss or gain
seeks a postponement because his vouchee or his
testifiers are sick or about other business, the law
says that that will not help him, since he did not get
the thing which he promised.

If it happens that the day of loss or gain falls in the
close season for law concerning land and earth, or in a
blank time, some say that it is right to renew it again
at the open season. The law however says that there is
nothing which postpones a day of loss and gain save
one thing: that is, that the justice does not remember
the judgment for it; and if he is doubted, let him be
put to the relics. And then a delay is given to the
justice, to remind himself and to discuss with others
whose discretion is older than his; the delay is nine
days, and on the ninth day let him declare the judgment to the two parties, without pleadings.

If it happens that the due date is hindered, whether
by death or by another fate, or by the contempt of the
claimant in not coming to hear the judgment, let the
defendant be in control and occupation from then on.

If it happens that a person, when there is a claim in
sessions for land and earth, says that he will not do
right, and the claimant calls the Lord and his justices
and his goodmen to witness that he did not deny the
claim and that he is an oppressor, and the claimant
calls for judgment; then it is proper, if the person
submits to judgment on the spot, that he should be
disjudged from his occupation in perpetuity. If he
leaves the place illegally, he will be disjudged for the
life of the Lord to whom that judgment seat belongs,
for there is no room in a country for him who will not
do justice.

Whatsoever defendant has a cyngaws and a canllaw
standing with him, being himself the third, and then

Procedure in an Action for Land   97

seeks a delay for aid, is not entitled to have it, for
those persons are his lawful aid. It is not right that a
cyngaws and a canllaw should stand with him for a
claim of less than the value of three score pence, or for
land and earth, and a horse and a steer.

Fixing boundaries is free at all times.

If it happens that a person begins to sue at sessions and the defendant is ready to answer: if after
that the claimant is silent for a year and a day
about his claim and lets it sleep, the law is closed
between him and his claim, and it will never be
heard.   *Col.*

If a kin-stock is disjudged from land and earth
and some of the kin-stock are in a strange
country and they are not awaited for the law,
they are entitled to law when they come; and if
they do not ask for law until after a year and a day
from when they come to their country, law will
be closed from then on because thickset hedges
have come between them and their entitlement
and it is a superannuated claim.   *Dw.*

If it happens to a person that a Lord will not allow
right for land and earth or for something else, law
judges that however long he may be without it it
will not be a superannuated claim even though
the person and his claim be in the same country,
and that it is a claim when it is brought.   *Dw.*

Law for church land is not closed at any time
between themselves, for it does not belong to our law.
If they sue us or we sue them, then if the season is
restricted, law will be closed between them.

If it happens that a person says on the first day on
which he claims land and earth that that is the
day of loss or gain, and that if there is anyone
who doubts that, he has enough who know it, and
that the defendant answers and says 'I put it in

98   *The Law of Hywel Dda*

the mouth of the justice and the Lord that there has never been a claim against me for this until today; I put it on the law that there could not be a claim on me in the absence of those men': then it is more proper to believe the Lord and the justice than his knowers and that everything done in their absence is void.   *Dw.*

There are three dead testimonies. One is, if a person claims land, and says that he is entitled to it and that his ancestors were on that land before him and left ditches or other works on the land, and if there were anyone who doubted it that he had maintainers who would be enough in law to maintain it; and that when it was desired to test the maintainers they returned that they had heard from their ancestors that it was the others' ancestors who made that stone work or the ditches or banks, that is taken as testimony. Second is, if it happens that a person claims land by kindred and descent and puts that in the mouth of maintainers, and that the maintainers say that they heard from their ancestors that that was true, and did not see it, yet that is taken in place of testimony. Third is, if a person claims land and the defendant answers him and says that it was adjudged by law to his father and his grandfather, and puts that in the mouth of knowers, and the knowers stand by him that they heard that from their ancestors before them and that they did not see it adjudged, that is a quota.   *Dw.*

Sharing of Land
It is free at all times to share land (unless the right to the share is denied), though the season be closed.

Thus it is right for brothers to share land amongst them: four acres to each toft—and after that Bleddyn ap Cynfyn changed it to twelve acres for the uchelwr

Sharing of Land 99

and eight for the aillt and four for the godaeog; and yet it is soundest that the toft is four acres.

The measure of the legal acre: four feet in the length of the short yoke, eight in the mid-yoke, twelve in the armpit yoke, sixteen in the long yoke; a rod as long as the latter in the caller's hand, with his other hand on the middle peg, and as far as he reaches with it on either side of him is the width of the acre, and thirty times the rod is its length. Others say a rod as long as the tallest man in the townland with his hand stretched above his head, handled in the same way as the other.

If there are no houses, it is right for the youngest son to divide the whole patrimony, and for the eldest to choose and then from eldest to next eldest down to the youngest. If there are houses, it is right for the second-youngest brother to divide the tofts (for he is the bottom rung in that case) and for the youngest to choose from the tofts; and after that he divides the whole patrimony and they choose from the eldest to the youngest; and that sharing holds for the life of the brothers.

> When brothers share their patrimony amongst them, the youngest gets the special croft and eight acres, and all the buildings; and the cauldron and the fuel-axe and the coulter (for the father cannot give them or bequeath them except to the youngest son, and though they should be gaged they never fall forfeit). Thereupon let every brother take a croft and eight acres; and the youngest son divides, and choice goes from eldest to next eldest.   *Cyfn.*

And after the brothers are dead the first cousins are entitled to divide equally if they want to. This is how they are entitled: it is right for the youngest son's heir to divide equally, and for the eldest son's heir to choose, and so from eldest to next eldest down to the youngest. And it is right for that sharing to be among them during their lifetime.

The Law of Hywel Dda

And if the second cousins do not like the sharing which their fathers had, they are entitled to equalise, like the first cousins; and after that distribution, no one is entitled to equalise or to change.

It is for gwely-land that it is as we have said. For geldable land, however, there is no right to sharing among brothers, but it is right for maer and cynghellor to divide it, and to give all in the townland as good as each other. And it is because of that that it is called reckon land. And there will be no extinguished acre in reckon land, but if there is such an acre in it, maer and cynghellor share it out in common to all as good as each other.

> The law of reckon land is that one man's share of the land shall not be more than another's, and therefore it does not extinguish, for everyone is an entitled person in relation to it.   *Dw.*

And no one is bound to leave his legal toft if he can find its equal in other land.

> It is right to maintain every man of a reckon townland in his toft if it can be done without expelling another.   *Col.*

> One son who need not wait for his father's death for his patrimony is the son of a man of a reckon townland, for his father shares his acre with him no more than does the farthest man in the townland. Law sees that it is proper for the youngest son to wait for his father's death, for it is in his place that he will sit by entitlement.
> *Dw.*

And as we have said above for the other, so it is right for the dung maer to do for the land of the maerdref, leaving everyone in his toft as best he can.

Regalities

It is not right for any land to be kingless. If it is abbey land, if there are any laymen he [the King] is entitled to dirwy and camlwrw and amobr and ebediw and theft and hosting. If it is bishop's land he is entitled to hosting and theft. If it is hospital land he is entitled to theft and fighting. And accordingly there is no land without him.

When the bishop dies the King is entitled to all his goods (for all goods without an owner are king's waste) except the vestments of the church and its ornaments and what belongs to it.

There are three enthroned ones who can conduct their chapter by their own law where they do not hinder the King's law; those are, a bishop, and an abbot, and a master of hospitallers.

Dadannudd

Three kinds of dadannudd there are: dadannudd of tillage and ploughing; dadannudd of car; and dadannudd of bale and burden. And it is not proper to uncover those dadanhuddau save by the son for the place where his father was before that, since there is no right to dadannudd by kindred and descent.

Whosoever has dadannudd adjudged to him by tillage and ploughing, he is entitled to sit there until he may turn his back on the stack, without answering, and shall then answer; and on the ninth day from that Winter Kalends law. Whosoever has dadannudd adjudged to him from his having been on that land with car and habitation and a hearth, for himself or for his father before him, he is entitled to be there without answering until the ninth day, and shall then give answer; and at the end of the second ninth day law. Whosoever has dadannudd adjudged to him from his having been with his bale and burden (either himself or his father before him) inhabiting a hearth on the land, he is entitled to be there three nights and

102 The Law of Hywel Dda

three days without answering, and shall then give answer; and at the end of the ninth day law.

And these dadanhuddau it is not right to adjudge to any one unless there has previously been grant and investiture of the land to him by a Lord.

A person is not entitled to claim dadannudd except of a hearth which was covered by him or by his father before him. A person is not entitled to claim dadannudd of land because his grandfather or great-grandfather was on the land, unless he will claim by kindred and descent.

If it happens that a person claims land by dadannudd of tillage and ploughing and house and home, let him come onto the land at a time when law is open for land and earth, and let him say that he, or his father before him, has been sitting on that land and earth by investiture of a Lord, and has had tillage and ploughing and house and home for a year and years, and that he was unlawfully ejected from there, 'and if there is any who doubts that, I have enough who will maintain that it was as long as that', and if there is any who doubts that he was unlawfully ejected, that he has enough who know it, and puts it to the law that he is entitled to uncover the hearth which he or his father before him covered up. The defendant answers him, 'God knows,' says he, 'if you were here, you went from here lawfully, and if you doubt that, I have enough who know it; and moreover, I am a proprietor seated on my proprietary holding, and if there is any who doubts that, I have enough who will maintain that what I have said is true; and I put it to the law that a person who once goes lawfully from land and earth is not entitled to be car-returning to it by law.' And then it is proper for the claimant to speak: 'God knows,' says he, 'as to my having been here for as long as I said, and

Dadannudd 103

my being unlawfully ejected from here, I put up maintainers and knowers that what I said was true, and did that before you did; and I put it to the law that since I put them up before you did I am entitled to enjoy them first.' And then it is proper to let him enjoy them first; and if they stand let there be adjudged to him as much land as he claims, to sit on, and to make tillage and ploughing on, without any beside him of the men who opposed him; and so he will be, until he turns his back on the stack at the harvest next following; and then he gives an answer, and on the ninth day of the Winter Kalends law. And then if the defendant can prove that he is a proprietor let a non-proprietor move away before him. And if the two parties are equally entitled, let them share in two halves and let them both sit there.   *BG.*

If it happens that a person claims land and earth by dadannudd of tillage and ploughing, let him come onto the land and say that he was seated on this land for a year and years through the investiture of a Lord, and had tillage and ploughing of it, and that he was unlawfully ejected from it; and if there is anyone who doubts this of him, he has enough who know that what he has said is true. And then the defendant answers: 'God knows,' says he, 'if you were here as long as you say, and if you were unlawfully ejected from here, you made a claim here by dadannudd and won it; and after you won it you were cast out from here as a person entitled casts out a person not entitled, by justice and law; and if you doubt that, I have enough who know that it is true as far as I have said.' If the claimant does not deny that, let the defendant attest that against him, and let him call for judgment and say that he has not denied his having previously had dadannudd;

and let him put it to the law that he is not entitled to two dadanhuddau for the same land. And then it is proper to disjudge the claimant perpetually from that dadannudd. If the claimant denies that he previously had dadannudd, let his knowers be allowed to the defendant, and if they stand let the claimant be disjudged perpetually. *BG.*

Claims by Proprietary Right

Whosoever wants to claim land by kindred and descent, let him show his pedigree as far as the stock from which he derives; and if he is there as fourth man he is a proprietor, for it is as fourth man that a person becomes a proprietor. And not so does a person drop from proprietorship to being an alien; for law says that if it happens that a person is in another country (either because of banishment or because of blood-feud or from other necessities) so that he cannot fairly reach his country—the law says that his proprietorship is not extinguished until the ninth person, whensoever he may come to ask for it. And unless others are proprietors seated on the land against him, he is entitled to the whole of what he left; and if others are proprietors against him the law of equality is right between them, with a sharing, since a proprietor is not entitled to advantage over another.

If the ninth person comes to ask for land, his proprietorship is extinguished, and he gives a shriek because he is passing from proprietor to non-proprietor. And then the law hears that shriek and gives him an allowance, that is to say, as much as each one of their number who are seated against him; and that is called *Diasbad uwch Annwfn*. And though that shriek be given thereafter, it will never be heard; and others say that the ninth person is not entitled to give that shriek, but that he has passed from proprietor to non-proprietor.

Claims by Proprietary Right　　　105

It is not right to hear any of the following three claims in a close season of law for land and earth: those are a claim of proprietorship and a claim of dadannudd and a claim of contention.

If it is by contention that a person chooses his claim, there can be no contention save by two persons who are seated on the same land together; and if one of them wishes to contend with the other, let him on the day when he overtakes justice say that he is wholly proprietor of this land and earth; and let him say that there is an unlawful oppressor of him and let him name the oppressor, 'and if there is anyone who doubts that I am true proprietor of the whole of this land, I have enough who will maintain it; and if there is any one who doubts that he is an oppressor and unentitled, I have enough who know it; and therefore today I want to throw off the oppressor from me, and I call for my entitlement and put it to the law that I am entitled.'

If the defendant denies that, it is proper to allow the claimant his knowers; if the defendant admits it, it is proper to allow the claimant his claim. If the defendant says 'God knows, it is I who am proprietor of this land and earth, and it is a sign of that that I am occupying my proprietary holding; and if there is any one who doubts that what I say is true, I have enough who will maintain my proprietorship and my occupation as it is right for a person entitled to maintain his proprietorship and occupation; and I put it to the law that I am better entitled to hold my proprietorship and my occupation than you are to hold that which is not in your occupation and which it is not right should be so; and therefore I want to enjoy my maintainers first, and I am entitled to that'—then it is proper for the claimant to say 'God knows, I said first that I was proprietor and entitled to the whole of this land and that you were an oppressor; and though you could take my land by force, you could not cause me not to be an entitled proprietor; and for my proprietorship and my entitlement I put up maintainers, with knowers to your being an oppressor; and that I did first, and to the law I put it that I am entitled to enjoy them first.' The law says that wherever a person says that he is an entitled one for land and earth, though a person may lose the fruits of his entitlement he has not lost his entitlement; and that he is entitled to bring maintainers for his entitlement, and to do that first—and after that to enjoy the defendant's maintainers. And if both sets of them stand, let the disputed matter be adjudged in two halves and it will be an equal claim; and let him among them whose warranty does not stand lose his claim wholly. If each of them seeks to defeat the other by maintainers and the maintainers of each of them stand by him, let each of them remain in occupation. If the maintainers of one fail, let his plea fail him. The law says that it is more proper that the fruits should follow the entitlement than that the entitlement should follow the fruits.

If it happens that there is contention between two persons for land and earth and the claimant says that he is a proprietor and that the other is an oppressor, and if anyone doubts it that he has enough who will maintain it; and that the defendant answers and says 'God knows, if you have been a proprietor here, now you are not, and your claim is a superannuated claim: here am I, and I have sat on this land a year and years, with house and home and tillage and ploughing and without violence and harm, in the same country as you, so that there is a thickset hedge between you and your right; and if you doubt that, I have enough who know; and I put it to the law that since you put up with my being here as long as that, you are not an entitled one so as ever to refuse me this land': if the claimant denies it, let the defendant be allowed his knowers. If the claimant admits it, let the defendant have the claim.   *BG.*

Women and Land

According to the men of Gwynedd a woman is not entitled to have patrimony, since she is not entitled to two status in one hand, that is, her husband's patrimony and her own. And since she is not entitled to patrimony, it is not right that she should be given save where her sons will be entitled to patrimony.

> As a brother is entitled heir to his patrimony, so his sister is entitled heir to her endowment (through which she may get a wedded husband entitled to land), to wit, from her father or his heirs, if she abides by the advice of her parents and her co-heirs. If an owner of land has no other heir than a daughter, the daughter will be heir of all the land   *Bleg.*

Some say that the sons of no woman are entitled to patrimony by mother-right save those of one woman, that is, a woman whom her father and brothers give to an alien. Others say that though her kindred give her to an alien, if those persons do not give her, her sons are not entitled to mother-right. The law however says that there are three women whose sons are entitled to patrimony by mother-right. One of them is a woman whom her kindred give legally to an alien. Second is a woman whom an alien admittedly rapes, if she has a son from that rape; the law says that since she has not lost her status her son does not lose his entitlement by mother-right. Third is a woman whom her kindred give into hostageship in an alien land, and who in that hostageship has a son by an alien; that son is entitled to patrimony by mother-right. There is no woman who gives herself to an alien whose sons are entitled to mother-right.

Some say of the sons of such women that though they are patrimonials they are not proprietors. The law says that a proprietor does not move from before a non-proprietor and that a proprietor moves from before the sons of such women (whether from part or from the whole); and therefore the law allows that these are proprietors. The law nevertheless says that if there is office or status from the land, he does not get that until the third man, for the status of a proprietor previously occupying land is better than that of one newly arrived, and that it is as third man that the latter will have sufficient occupancy—unless it so befalls that a Welshwoman has a son legally by an alien chieftain, and to that one the law allows his office and his status immediately.

An innate man of Powys is not entitled to mother-right in Gwynedd, nor one of Gwynedd in Powys; and so also for Deheubarth.

If it happens that a person claims land and earth by mother-right, let him come onto the land at a time when law is open, and let him say that he is an alien's son by an entitled Welshwoman; and let him say that his mother was given legally by her kindred to his father, and that he was made an alien, and that if there is any one who doubts that, he has enough who know it: 'and therefore I put it to the law that since they made me an alien, I am entitled to come to them as a patrimonial today; for this day is a day of loss and gain between me and them'. If the defendant admits it, let it be adjudged for the claimant that he is a patrimonial with his uncles, with as much for him as for one of the uncles, except for the status toft and that if there is office from the land he does not get it until the third person, and that he cannot be chief of kindred until the third person.

Women and Land 109

If the defendant denies it, let the claimant be allowed his knowers, and if they stand by him let the claim be his, and if they do not stand let him lose his claim in perpetuity.

If it happens that the defendant speaks in answer to him: 'God knows,' says he, 'though you say that you are an alien, your father was a patrimonial in another place, and if you doubt that, I have enough who know it; and I put it to the law that I gave my sister to a patrimonial and that the son of a patrimonial does not return to me': if the claimant does not object otherwise to that, let his knowers be adjudged to the defendant, and if they stand by him let the claimant be disjudged. If the claimant speaks: 'God knows,' says he, 'for so much as I said I offered knowers that what I said was true, if I was doubted; and I put it to the law that it is not right for knowers to arise against mine until it is known whether mine will stand or not, since what I said was doubted'—it is proper to adjudge him his knowers, and that none be enjoyed against him, since he was doubted.

If it happens that a person claims land and earth by mother-right and says that his mother was legally given to his father and that his father was an alien, and he wants patrimony on that day, and that the defendant then answers: 'God knows,' says he, 'though your father may have been an alien, he has already claimed mother-right in such-and-such place and he has had it by justice and law and become a patrimonial there; and if there is any one who doubts it I have enough who know it, and I put it to the law that since you have become a legal patrimonial in another place you are not entitled to an answer for another patrimony'—and then it is proper to allow the defendant his knowers if the claimant makes denial. If he does not deny it, it is better, and let him be disjudged from mother-right in perpetuity. *BG.*

Whosoever claims land, if he traces his pedigree by the distaff more than three times he will lose his claim. *Cyfn.*

Miscellanea on Land

The father is not entitled to use his son's entitlement to land and earth save in his own lifetime, any more than the son is entitled to despoil his father in his lifetime for land; so the father is not entitled to despoil the son for land, and though he should despoil him the son will recover it, except in one case—where there is agreement by father and brothers and first cousins and second cousins and Lord for paying land as blood-land; and that the son cannot recover, since peace was bought with it for the son as for the father; for those persons are the degrees without whose consent land cannot be used. And although such a person may have no land, yet he will not be an alien, but an innate bonheddig. An innate bonheddig is a person whose complete stock is in Wales, both from mother and from father.

The law for an innate bonheddig, when he takes land in another country, is that he will have the status of the land. *Dw.*

Church law says that no son is entitled to patrimony save the father's eldest son by the wedded wife. The law of Hywel adjudges it to the youngest son as to the eldest, and judges that the father's sin and his illegality should not be set against the son for his patrimony.

A person's coming to land is not valid save by the judgment of the law, or by the investiture of a Lord.

Some say that if a person is killed for land, his heirs are entitled to the land as blood-land after that. The

Miscellanea on Land   111

law says that none is blood-land save what is legally paid over after the homicide has nothing to his name which he can pay, either from shaft penny or from anything else; and it judges that there is no right to kill any person save the homicide who does not pay in full. And it is right to share that land among them as it is right to share the galanas.

Whosoever suffers his land to be enjoyed for a year and a day without violence and harm, being in the same country with him who is seated on it, the law says that he is not entitled to an answer thereafter, but that his claim is withered and is a superannuated claim. This is violence and harm: burning houses and breaking ploughs.

> This is violence: burning houses and breaking ploughs. This is harm: complaint to a Lord, for there is no right to complain for land save to a Lord.   *Col.*

> If it happens that a person does violence or harm against another for land and earth, let him do it on the land and earth for which his claim is; and if he does it on other land which he is not claiming, let him pay for what he does, for he is not entitled to devastate anything save the land which he is claiming. This is violence: burning houses and breaking ploughs. Harm is frequent complaint to country and Lord until he gets justice in a year and years: his right is not extinguished, however long he is without it.

> For a claim for money and livestock and all other goods there is no right to do violence, but harm and claiming every year; and if he is a year and a day without claiming what is his (being in the same country as his claim), it is an extinguished claim from then on, and superannuated.   *Dw.*

> Whosoever holds land for three men's lifetimes in the same country as those entitled (the life of father

and grandfather and great-grandfather) without claim and without surclaim, without burning houses and without breaking ploughs, they will never be answered for that land, since law has closed between them.

Cyfn.

Law does not close between a person and his entitled land in a lesser period than three ancestors' lifetimes on each side, and that in peace. This is three ancestors' lifetimes: nine score years, three score years in each lifetime.

S.

Law does not close for Lord's land in a lesser period than one hundred years.

Col.

Whosoever suffers his patrimony to be given in his presence to another, without obstruction and without prohibition, he will not get it while he lives.

Cyfn.

Whosoever owns land alongside the shore, he owns the same breadth of the shore as of the land, and let him make a weir on it if he wants to. But if the sea casts something onto the land or onto the shore, it will belong to the King, for the sea is the King's packhorse.

If a ship breaks up on the land of a monarch, it belongs to the monarch, and if a ship breaks up on a bishop's land, it is shared in two halves between the King and the bishop.

Cyfn.

If it happens that a ship breaks up before she has paid her toll, her goods belong to the King, and it is not right for her to be without paying toll except for three flows and three ebbs; and though she should break up after paying her toll, there is no right to any of their goods from them, for they will have the status of king's aliens from then on; and though she should remain there at anchor for ever, it is not right to drive her away and it is not right to take any gage from her save what she has unlawfully put into the proprietor's land, and that is the anchor as gage for the toll.

Dw.

Miscellanea on Land

A mill and a weir and an orchard are called the three precious things of a kindred, and there is no right to share these or to alienate them, but their fruits are shared to those who are entitled to them.

It is not right to share hamlet land by tofts, but by quillets. And if there are buildings on it, the youngest son is no more entitled to them than the eldest, but they are shared by chambers.

> There are three kinds of purchase of land: first is the fee for protection; second is goods given for adding to land or to its status; third is lawful labour applied to the land by which the land is improved. *Cyfn.*

> If a person seeks a share of land from his relatives after being long in exile, let him give them six score pence as fee for protection, if they allow it to him without plaint. *Bleg.*

No one is entitled to retain possession of quillets in right of his manuring save for one year, since it is right to manure them every year.

For fallowing there is a right to plough for two years. For rotten dung, the same indeed.

> This is rotten dung: where livestock are wont to lie without a fold. *S.*

Scrub land, the same indeed.

> He who cuts scrub from another person's land, by his leave, gets it for the first year free, and for the second year for payment; and the third year the owner gets it free. *Cyfn.*

For folded manure, three years' ploughing. For carried manure, it is right to plough for four years. For wooded land, the same indeed.

> He who removes trees by leave of the owner of the land is entitled to it for five years free, and the sixth year the owner is entitled to it free. *Cyfn.*

For manured fallow, also four years.

It is not right for one brother to be woodman to another, but let him render him woodland as good as what he has cleared. And if he does not find woodland as good, let him render old field as good as the wood-land; and if he does not find old field, let him for four years plough what he cleared of trees, and from then on let him leave as good to his brother from it as to himself.

No one is entitled to sell land or to gage it without the leave of a Lord, but let him lease it every year if he wants to. Men who are under abbots and men who are under a bishop are entitled to gage their land if they want to, by their leave.

7. Aliens

The law says that uchelwyr are entitled to maintain lordship over their aliens as the King is entitled to maintain lordship over his aliens. And just as aliens become proprietors as fourth man after being put on king's waste, so uchelwyr's aliens become propriet-ors as fourth man, if they occupy land under them as long as that. And from then on they are not entitled to depart from the uchelwyr, for they are proprietors under them, and they are not entitled to two pro-prietorships, one in the country from which they come and one here. After they are proprietors their tofts will be left to them according to what they are entitled to, and their land save that as arable land between them.

> If it happens that an alien comes and does homage to the King and the King gives him land, and that he occupies the land for his lifetime, and his son after him, and his grandson and his great-grandson and his fourth-man, the latter will be a proprietor, and it is right that he should from then on have, not the status of an alien, but the status of the land which he occupies and the status of a Welshman.
>
> If it happens that that great-grandson gives his daughter to an alien after that, that daughter's son will be entitled to mother-right with the children of that great-grandson; and there would

Aliens   115

be no entitlement to mother-right arising from
the first alien, nor from his son, nor from his
grandson, since they were not proprietors; and it
is because the great-grandson is a proprietor that
there is an entitlement arising from him, and
from every proprietor; and it is until the alien
rises to proprietor that he has the status of a
king's alien.   *Dw.*

Is there any case in which it is right for a son to be
by law lord over his own father? There is: if it happens
that an uchelwr gives his daughter to his own alien,
and that they have male children and after that the
uchelwr dies and the alien's sons get mother-right to
their grandfather's land: they will be lords over their
father.   *J.*

If it happens that an alien comes to Wales and
does homage to an uchelwr, and from him goes
to another, and that he moves on, both himself
and his son and his grandson and his great-
grandson and his great-great-grandson, from
uchelwr to uchelwr without their settling in one
place more than another, let them have the
status of aliens for ever while they are thus
without settling, save like that. If it happens that
an alien does homage to an uchelwr and is with
him until death, and that the alien's son is with
the uchelwr's son, and the alien's grandson with
the uchelwr's grandson, and the alien's great-
grandson with the uchelwr's great-grandson,
then the uchelwr's great-grandson will be proprietor over the alien's great-grandson and that
great-grandson's heir over the heir of the alien's
great-grandson, in perpetuity; and from then on
they are not entitled ever to go to the country
from which they come, away from their lord
proprietor, since they have missed the time at
which they were entitled to go if they wanted to
go.

The Law of Hywel Dda

If it happens that a patrimonial bonheddig goes into the service of an uchelwr and is with him for a period, and he is killed while in the uchelwr's service, the uchelwr is entitled to three kine of the corpse for him; and others of the books say that it is six kine of the corpse for him. And he is entitled to depart from the uchelwr when he likes, but leaving to the uchelwr what he is entitled to, as the *Book of Hywel* says; and he is said to be a carllawedrog; a carllawedrog is a person who is car-starting when he likes: *llawedrog* is in old Welsh *tomog*, and so he is called *cartomog*.   *Dw.*

If the aliens want to depart from their lords before they are proprietors, it is right for them to leave half their goods to their lords. And if they come from this island they are not entitled to stay in any place on this side of Offa's Dyke. And if they come from overseas, they are not entitled to stay here, save until the first wind by which they can go to their own country; and if they stay, let them return to their bondage as before. Others say that they are not bound to go until the third wind. And if the uchelwr sends them away before they are proprietors, against their will, he is not entitled to any of their goods.

If it happens that an alien wants to depart from his lord and supposes that he is entitled to a delay by law before going to the country from which he comes, we say that he is not entitled to it, save until he finishes the sharing of his last penny, and that he is then a starting man if he comes from this island; if from overseas, he is entitled to a delay until the first wind by which he can go to the country from which he comes.   *Dw.*

Whatsoever alien parts from his lord and stays without leave in his own commote for longer than three nights and three days without

Aliens 117

going to the place where it is right for him to go, law says that it is right for him to lose all his goods. *Dw.*

If it happens that an alien goes to the country from which he comes, and stays there for a year and a day, though he should come back, the man with whom he previously was has no more claim on him by law than another, unless the alien himself wants it. *Dw.*

No one can set an alien free, save for his own lifetime, unless he goes to the country from which he comes. *Dw.*

If it happens that an alien takes on himself orders, or membership of a hospital, or another form, without a lord's leave, law judges that that does not free him from his lord's bondage, though the Church is entitled to prosecute the disrespect. *Dw.*

An alien is not entitled to take a wife without his lord's consent, and if he takes a wife let the lord avenge himself on him. If he chooses a Welshwoman and has children, they will belong to the higher lord if their mother comes from the King's land. *Dw.*

If it happens that an alien seeks to leave his lord, and that he has a wife under agweddi who wants her argyfrau not to be shared, some of the books say that she is entitled to separate from her husband, taking what is hers and being set free. Proper law judges that she is not entitled to separate from her husband unless for illegality, and that it is not illegality for him to give his lord what he is entitled to, and that the lord is entitled to share in two halves with his man what the latter has to his name. *Dw.*

The Law of Hywel Dda

Every alien who shares his goods with his lord in two halves is entitled to a share of the buildings; the reason is, because he is entitled to half of everything.   *Dw.*

It is right for a free man to answer on behalf of his alien for every claim for which he is not liable to lose his tongue and life and limbs, since it is not right for anyone to lose tongue and life and limbs through another's tongue.   *Cyfn.*

If it happens to an uchelwr's alien that theft is charged against him, and it falls out that he is a sale thief, and that the uchelwr does not redeem him and does not acquit him, and that he can redeem himself or acquit himself in some other way, we say that the uchelwr is not entitled to have him, but that he is a king's alien.   *Dw.*

If it happens that an alien commits theft, and that before he is suspected of the theft he departs from the lord with whom he was when he committed the theft, and does homage to another; and the owner of the goods then comes and charges him with the goods as stolen, and he pleads denial: it is proper to adjudge his lord's oath to acquit him. What the lord says is that he is not bound to acquit him, save for the theft which he may have committed after he came to him; it is proper nevertheless for the alien to fall under the law of theft unless he finds a lord who will acquit him.   *Dw.*

If it happens that a servient comes to an uchelwr's house and takes land from him and keeps house, and pays twnc and gwestfa to his Lord, his worth will be half the worth of a king's alien and he will be the alien of an uchelwr of status from then on.   *Dw.*

If it happens that a person claims an alien and says that he is his authentic alien, and that if

Aliens

there should be any who doubt that of him he would have enough who knew it, and the alien then replies: 'God knows,'. says he, 'I am not your alien though I may be an alien'—it is proper to adjudge the proof to the claimant, and if the proof succeeds for him, let him take the alien as his own. And if the alien says 'I am not bound to answer you for that; this is the reason: I am an entitled bonheddig, and if there is anyone who doubts that of me, I have enough who know it; and I put it to the law that an entitled bonheddig is not bound to anwer for alienage of his own body', it is proper to allow him his plea, and the proof is his; and the kind of men who prove it with him are other boneddigion who are his relatives, since he says that he is a bonheddig: and that is called repellent law. This is repellent law: where the defendant takes the proof away from the claimant to be his own, that is like turning the law into its opposite, and therefore is it called repellent law.   *Dw.*

There are three kinds of homage: the lath of a gwasafwr and an aswynwr and a resident. If it happens that a patrimonial becomes the man of another patrimonial and builds on the land immediately, and that he regrets it and wants to depart from him, it is right for him to pay him six score pence, and that is called the lath of a gwasafwr. The second is, if it happens that a patrimonial becomes the man of another patrimonial and wants to go from him to his own patrimony, it is right for him to pay him three score pence, and he is called an aswynwr. Third is, if it happens that a patrimonial is a resident with another for a year and a day without interruption, and in service, and he wants to depart from him, let him pay him thirty pence: and he is called a resident.   *Dw.*

8. Royal Rights and Administration

Before the crown of London and the sceptre were taken by the English, Dyfnwal Moelmud was king over this island. And he was son to the Earl of Cornwall by the daughter of the King of Lloegr; and after the paternal line of that kingship was extinguished, he gained it by the distaff, as he was the King's grandson. And that man was a wise man of authority, and it was that man who first made good laws in this island; and the laws which he made lasted until the age of Hywel the Good. And after that Hywel made new laws and did away with those of Dyfnwal. Nevertheless Hywel did not change the measures of lands in this island from what Dyfnwal had left, for he was the best of measurers. He measured this island from the headland of Blathaon in Pictland to the headland of Penwith in Cornwall, that is nine hundred miles—and that is the length of this island; and from Grugyll in Anglesey to Shoreham on the shore of the Channel, five hundred miles—and that is the breadth of this island.

The reason that he measured it was in order to know its tribute and its mileage and its journeys by days. And this measure Dyfnwal measured from the barleycorn. Three lengths of the barleycorn in the inch; three inches in the palmbreadth; three palmbreadths in the foot; three feet in the step; three steps in the leap. Three leaps in the land: a land in newer Welsh is a selion; and a thousand lands is the mile. And this measure is still used here.

And then they made the measure of the legal acre from the barleycorn. Three lengths of the barleycorn in the inch; three inches in the palmbreadth; three palmbreadths in the foot. Four feet in the short yoke, eight in the mid-yoke, twelve in the armpit yoke, sixteen in the long yoke; a rod as long as the long yoke in the caller's hand, with the middle peg of that yoke in his other hand, and as far as he reaches with it, with

Royal Rights and Administration   121

his arm stretched out, is the two limits, that is, the width of the legal acre; and thirty times the rod is its length.

It is right that there be four such acres in the toft; four tofts in every shareland; four sharelands in every holding; four holdings in every townland; four townlands in every maenol; twelve maenolydd and two townlands in every commote. It is right for the two townlands to be for the king's need, one of them as maerdref and the other as king's waste and shieling-land for him. And as much as all we said above in the other commote, and that makes a total of five score townlands, and that is properly the cantred. It is right for ten times ten to be in a hundred and counting does not go beyond ten.

This is the number of acres that it is right should be in the cantred: four legal acres in every toft: sixteen in every shareland; sixty-four in every holding; two hundred and fifty-six in the townland; one thousand and twenty-four acres in every maenol; twelve thousand two hundred and eighty-eight acres in the twelve maenolydd. It is right that there should be five hundred and twelve acres in the two townlands which belong to the court; and that is, when all the acres in the commote come together, twelve thousand eight hundred; and as much as all that in the other commote: that is a total of acres in the cantred of twenty-five thousand six hundred, no more and no less.

Of the twelve maenolydd that it is right should be in the commote, four of them have eilltion to support hounds and horses and circuit and billeting; one is for the office of cynghellor and one for that of maer; and the other six have free uchelwyr. And from those eight the King is entitled to a gwestfa every year, and that is one pound from each of them; and it is divided into three score pence for every townland of the four which are in the maenol; and so from quarter to

122   *The Law of Hywel Dda*

quarter it is shared out until every acre of the toft takes its share. And that is called the twnc pound, and it is right for the usher to exact it. (And as much as all that from the other commote, and so the cantred will be complete.)

Maer and Cynghellor

It is right for meiri and cyngellorion to organise the country and conduct its sessions; and they are entitled to half of every thing against the King, except for three things, that is, the worth of land, and the worth of a thief, and the worth of a corpse. It is right for the cynghellor to divide between himself and the King, and for the King to choose. It is right for the maer to divide between himself and the cynghellor, and for the cynghellor to choose. The maer and cynghellor are entitled to have two servants with them to do their errands, with two others for the King; and they are entitled to take a circuit, as two of four, round the King's eilltion, twice a year. And they are entitled to half the ebediw of the eilltion and half their daughters' amobr.

It is right for the maer and cynghellor to dispose the King's eilltion on their legal acre when one of them dies, and to keep the King's waste and to swear for it when necessary; and if the King uses it, it is right for them to have their office from it.

> If it happens that the maer cannot maintain his house, let him take to him the villein he chooses, for a year from one May Day to the next, and let him enjoy the villein's milk in summer and his corn at harvest and his pigs in winter. And when the villein departs from him, let him leave him four grown pigs and a boar, and all the rest of his livestock, with four acres of winter tillage and eight acres of spring tillage. And the second year and the third year let him do likewise, but not with the same villein; and thereafter let him support himself from his own, for three years more. After that let the King relieve him, if he

Royal Rights and Administration 123

will, by giving him a villein in the same way as
before. *Cyfn.*

It is the cynghellor's function to hold the sessions
of the King in his presence and in his absence. It is for
him to set a cross and a prohibition for every case.
The cynghellor sits at the King's left at the three
special feasts, if the King is holding court within his
cyngelloriaeth. He receives a gold ring and a harp and
a throwboard from the King when he enters on his
office. In the age of Hywel the Good a third of the
villeins' living and dying came to the maer and the
cynghellor: and of that the maer took two-thirds and
the cynghellor a third; and the maer divided and the
cynghellor chose. *Cyfn.*

It is not right that either maer or cynghellor be chief
of kindred, but one of the uchelwyr of the country.
There is no right to the office of chief of kindred by
mother-right. The chief of kindred is entitled to
twenty-four pence from every man who takes a kinswoman of his to wife, for she herself pays her amobr;
and he is entitled to twenty-four pence from every boy
whom he receives into the kindred. And it is right for
him to intervene with his kinsman in every need
which comes upon him.

A chief of kindred does not himself pay his ebediw,
for he who is chief of kindred after him pays it. The
son will not be chief of kindred next after the father,
for the office of chief of kindred is limited to a lifetime. *Cyfn.*

There is no entrenched fee for an uchelwr at
sessions, save what the Lord wants to give.

As for the maenol from which twnc is paid, the Lord
is not entitled to either its honey or its fish, for there
is a right to mead from it; and together with the mead
there is a right to twenty-four pence from every
maenol, and that is called the supper money; and as
the twnc pound is shared, so is that shared.

There is no right to impose on free maenolydd
either maer or cynghellor or circuit or billeting or

The Law of Hywel Dda

pages or anything save what we have said above, except for the great circuit of the household in winter.

Hostings

The King is not entitled to have from his country any hostings outside its limits save once in each year, and he is not entitled to be in that save for a fortnight and a month. In his own country it is free for him when he likes. Everyone is bound to do work on the King's castles when he wants it, except for the men of the maerdref.

King's Villeins

The King's eilltion are not bound to support him, nor to support the household; and as they are not bound to support him they are not entitled to their honey or their fish, but are to give them to the King's court. And he is entitled, if he likes, to make weirs on their waters and to destroy their swarms.

It is right that one of the eilltion should be dung maer.

They are bound to give packhorses to the King for his hostings, and bound to honour the Queen once a year with food and drink, and are bound to support the hounds, and the huntsmen, and the falconers, and the pages, each of them once a year. And if there are aliens from another country in the King's realm, whether as his men, or waiting for a wind, or on other things, he is entitled, if he likes, to billet them on his eilltion. According to some, those aliens are entitled to have whatever goods they show when they come to the aillt's house when they leave it, and if he loses anything, to have it paid for to them, except for three things which it is right for them to keep with themselves day and night, that is to say their breeches and their swords and their gloves; and if they get bread and one enllyn they are not entitled to ask for more except on the first night.

Royal Rights and Administration   125

For their horses the villeins do not answer except at night, for they pay for them if they are lost at night.
Cyfn.

The King's eilltion are bound to make seven buildings for the King, that is to say, a hall and a foodhouse, and a kitchen and a sleephouse and a stable and a porch and a latrine.

The King is entitled to a man with an axe from every villein townland to make encampments for him in his hostings.

The Dung Maer

The dung maer is not entitled to hold sessions save for the men of the maerdref; but he receives goods of the King from the meiri and the cyngellorion, and it is right for him to give twenty-four pence to the usher when he is invested with the office of maer. It is right for the servants of the maer and cynghellor to bring the goods to the dung maer.

It is right for the dung maer to organise the court within, and to organise what concerns it in ploughing and sowing and care of the King's livestock and his shielings and other things which may be necessary. And it is right for him to punish the men of the maerdref for their illegalities; and to their dirwy and their camlwrw and their ebediw he is entitled. And to the amobr of their daughters his wife is entitled. It is right for the porter to exact the amobr and ebediw of those persons, with fourpence for himself from each one of them; the dung maer is entitled to fourpence from the porter when he is invested with his office. It is right for him to swear for the board land of the court and its shieling land if necessary, and to defend both them and what appertains to them.

The men of the maerdref are bound to make a kiln and a barn for the King and to repair them when necessary. It is right for them to pay the twnc of their land into the dung maer's hand, and they are bound to

126   *The Law of Hywel Dda*

support him twice a year; and they are bound to thresh and to dry and to reap and to harrow, and to mow hay and to gather straw and fuel as many times as the King comes to the court. And it is right for them to honour the King when he is in the court according to their ability, whether with sheep or with lambs, or with kids, or with butter, or with cheese or with milk.

If an uchelwr puts his son to fosterage with the aillt of a lord, with his consent or with his acquiescence for a year and a day, that son will be entitled after that to a son's share of the aillt's land and of his goods.

From every free maenol the King is entitled to a vat of mead, nine fistbreadths in diagonal length; and if mead is not had, two of bragget; and if bragget is not had, four of beer.

Boundaries

From whomsoever shall break the boundary between two townlands by ploughing it the King is entitled to the oxen which ploughed it, and the plough-frame and the irons, and the worth of the ploughman's right foot and the worth of the caller's left hand, with fourpence to the owner of the land, and the boundary to be restored as it was.

Whosoever ploughs land without permission, let him pay fourpence to him to whom the land belongs, and a penny for every furrow ploughed, with a surreption fee for the King.

> If it happens that there is a dispute between two parties about land and earth, and the land is prohibited until it is freed from dispute, and in spite of the prohibition one of the persons makes use of the land (whether by building or ploughing), law says that the punishment for that is the same as for breaking a boundary.

Royal Rights and Administration   127

And if it is ploughing that happens, this is the punishment: the eight oxen and the plough-frame and the irons and the worth of the plough-man's right foot and the caller's left hand, and that to the Lord. If it is building or other use that he makes, the building or use which he makes will belong to the Lord, since the land was in the Lord's hand when they were done, and there was no occupier of it save the Lord; with nine score pence camlwrw, and the land of its former status.   *Dw.*

If it happens that there is fixing of boundaries for land between two men of equal status, and the one sets the boundary there and the other here, and both parties swear, that is one of the three places where law shares in two halves.

There are three stays of boundary: status and proprietorship and prior occupation. A person whose status is lower than one of these cannot set boundaries against them.   *Dw.*

If it happens that there is fixing of boundaries between two owners of two maenolydd, whether they are abbots or they are bishops, setting the boundary belongs to the higher in status of them. If they are equally high, setting the boundary belongs to him who has prior occupation of his bishop-land or his abbot-land, on his oath by his crozier and his gospel, the crozier and the gospel being on the spot when they are sworn by.   *Dw.*

If it happens that there is fixing of boundaries between two persons, and that the claimant says that he has status to set the boundary, unless the defendant doubts him, let him go and show the boundary; if the defendant doubts him, let there be law between them for their primary status, and if his status is adjudged to him, let him afterwards show the boundary.   *Dw.*

The Law of Hywel Dda

Whosoever removes a boundary stone which is notorious between two townlands, let him pay six score pence to the owner of the land, and a camlwrw to the King; and similarly for a road which marks a boundary alongside the road.

Food Renders

This is the measure of the King's gwestfa from a free maenol in winter-time: a horse-load of the best flour that grows on the land, and a meat steer; and a vat's quota of mead (nine fistbreadths in length diagonally, and the same in breadth); and seven thraves of single-bound oats as horse-fodder; and a three-year-old pig, and a salt flitch with fat three fingers' breadth thick; and a vessel of butter three fistbreadths deep without the heap, and three wide. And if this cannot be had, a pound in its stead, and that is called the twnc pound; and twenty-four pence for the King's servants. If the mead cannot be had, two quotas of bragget; if bragget cannot be had, four of beer. And that comes from every free maenol of the King's. This is how that pound is divided: six score pence for the bread, and three score for the drink, and three score for the enllyn.

From the bond maenolydd there is a right to two food-gifts every year. In winter, a three-year-old pig, and a vessel of butter three fistbreadths long and three wide, and a vat's quota of bragget (nine fistbreadths in length diagonally); and a thrave of single-bound oats as horse-fodder; and twenty-six loaves of the best bread that grows on the land: if it is wheat land, six of them of fine flour, and if it is not wheat land, six of them of groats (four of them for the hall and two for the chamber)—being as broad as from the elbow to the wrist, and so thick that they do not bend when held by the edges; with a person to light the fire in the hall that night, or a penny for him who lights it for him.

Royal Rights and Administration 129

The measure of the summer food-gift is a three-year-old wether; and a mass of butter as broad as the broadest dish in the townland and so thick that there are two bare fistbreadths in it; and twenty-six loaves of the kind of bread mentioned above, with all the milking beasts belonging to the owners in the townland gathered together and milked once in the day (and let them not be milked save that once), so that a cheese be made from that milk; without brew, without horse-fodder, without anything to light a fire.

The maer and cynghellor are entitled to a circuit once every year around the King's eilltion, with two servants accompanying each of them, and the cynghellor choosing the house. And they are not entitled to a circuit in summer.

> It is not right to pay twnc from reckon-land; this is the reason it is not right, because there is no right to cwynos from it. There is a right to a circuit of hounds and horses and to billeting on the land of a reckon townland, and it is because of that that there is no right to support of the lord from it. Dw.

> From a townland with the office of maer or cynghellor, mead is paid. From a free townland without office, bragget is paid. From a villein townland, beer is paid. Cyfn.

9. Family Law

Some are doubtful about the pregnancy of a woman, as to what the right for it is, if it is destroyed, whether wynebwerth or galanas. The law says that it is galanas to which there is a right in respect of it. This is the reason: for the first three months it will be white, and then there will be one-third galanas for it; and for the second three months it will be red, and there will be two-thirds galanas for it. And in the last three months

130   The Law of Hywel Dda

it will be complete in limbs and life, and there will be
full galanas for it.

Some say that it is not more proper to pay the
galanas of a man for it than that of a woman, since it is
not known what it is, whether man or woman. The
law says that it is most proper to judge according to
the higher thing, and that there is a man's galanas for
it, and that until it is baptised. And this is the reason:
it is right to name by his name every person whose
galanas is claimed, whether it be a man or a woman,
and no one can be named by his name until baptised;
and therefore it is necessary that it be of the status of
the foetus until baptised.

From then on, until it is seven years old it is right
for its father to swear and to pay on its behalf, except
that he is not bound to pay either dirwy or camlwrw
to the King for it; since the King is not entitled to anything for inadvertence, and the child has no judgement. He is, however, bound to indemnify the victim
from what is his. From the end of its seventh year, it is
for the child itself to swear for its acts, and for its
father to pay; for then it goes under the priest's hand
and takes God's yoke upon it.

Sons

From when the son is born until he is fourteen years
old, it is right for him to be at his father's platter, with
his father as lord over him. And no punishment of
him is right save his father's. And he is not entitled to
a single penny of his goods in that period, save what
his father controls. And it is not right that there be a
dead-house for him, though he should die in that
period, but all the goods that are in his possession will
be his father's, since his father is bound in that period
to answer for him in respect of everything.

> A boy is entitled to a guardian for him until he is
> fourteen years old—his father if he is alive; and if his
> father is not alive, it is for the lord to give him a

Family Law 131

guardian, to act on his behalf to claim compensation
for him, and to make compensation on his behalf.

Cyfn.

If it happens that the father dies in the first year that
he is born, the son himself enters into his father's
status. It is not right to pay ebediw for a son until he is
fourteen years old if his father is alive. After he enters
into the father's status he will pay it.

At the end of the fourteenth year, it is right for the
father to take his son to the lord and to commend him
to him. And then it is right for him to do homage to
the lord, and to be dependent on his lord's status; and
it is for him himself to answer on his own behalf to
every claim that is made against him, and it is for him
to control his goods. And his father is from then on no
more entitled to strike him than a stranger; and if he
strikes him, and the son complains of him, he will be
liable to dirwy and will make compensation to the
son for his sarhaed.

If a son dies, from fourteen years of age on, and he
has no heir, his goods will all belong to the lord, who
will be entitled to be in the place of a son to him, and
his house will be a dead-house. And from that age on
he will be of the same status as an innate bonheddig,
for he has no status except his bonedd, and he does not
ascend to his father's status until his father dies; and
no one will be a knight until he ascends.

The worth of an innate bonheddig is three kine and
three score kine; his sarhaed is three kine and three
score pence. If he is a man of the bodyguard, his worth
will be four kine and four score kine; his sarhaed is
four kine and four score pence.

Daughters

A daughter, after she is baptised, until she is seven
years old, is not entitled to take an oath. From when
she is born until she is twelve years old it is right for
her to be at her father's platter. From twelve years old
on, her breasts and pubic hair develop and she men-

132 *The Law of Hywel Dda*

struates, and she is then of age to be given to a husband; and from then on, even if she does not take a husband she is entitled to control what is hers, and it is not right for her to be at her father's platter unless he himself wishes it. And the father is not bound to pay amobr for his daughter unless he is himself her bestower, for every bestower of a woman is bound to pay her amobr unless he takes sureties for paying it from him to whom she is given. If it happens that a woman is taken clandestinely from her father's house to another house, and there slept with, the man of that house is bound to pay her amobr, unless he takes sureties from the man who took her clandestinely.

At twelve years old it is right for a woman to menstruate, as we have said above. And from twelve to fourteen years old it is right that she should not become pregnant, and from fourteen until she is forty it is right for her to conceive, and from then on galanas does not fall on her and she gives no oath that she will not have children, since it is undoubted that she will not.

Affiliation

Whosoever wants to deny a son legally, it is not for him to deny him until he has first been legally laid to him, for no one need answer irregularly, since everything is irregular which is not according to law. Whatsoever woman wants to lay a son legally, thus it is for her to lay him: she and the son come to the church where his burial-place is, and she comes as far as the altar and puts her right hand on the altar and the relics, and her left hand on the son's head, and so swears, to God first, and to that altar and to the good relics which are on it, and to the son's baptism, 'that no father created this son in a mother's heart save' (such-and-such man, naming him) 'in my heart'. And so it is right to lay a son to a Welshman.

Family Law

And thus it is right to lay a son to an alien: to come to the church in which he takes his holy water and his mass bread, and then to lay him to him as said above.

Then it is proper for the father to do one of two things, either to accept his son legally or to deny him legally. If he wants to deny him, it is proper for him to come to the church which we mentioned above, and there to put his right hand on the altar and the relics which are on it, and his left hand on the son's head, and so swear, to God first, and to that altar and the good relics which are on it, and to the man who separated him from the creation of father and mother, that he never created that son in a woman's heart and that there is no drop of his blood in him but what comes from Adam.

If it happens that he seeks a delay for his oath, he is not entitled to a delay till the morrow. If it happens that she seeks a delay for seeking relics, she is not entitled to a delay save for three days, since she is not entitled to seek relics save in her own commote.

If it happens that a father denies a son from kindred after he is laid to him, he cannot afterwards ever get a father. This is the reason, that his mother laid him legally to the father who denied him, and therefore she can never lay him to another father for a second time. As for the father who legally denied him, he will never be car-returning to him again, since law does not undo what it does. That son now will have status according to his mother's kin; and if he kills a man, the mother's kin pays two-thirds of the galanas, with one third from himself, the homicide; and if he is killed, the mother's kin is entitled to have two-thirds of his galanas. And that is one of the three dire losses of a kindred.

Another is, if it were to happen that a man killed another, and the homicide's kin gave surety for the galanas, and before the kin paid the galanas the homicide's mother laid him to another father: the law says that it is for the kin which gave surety for the galanas to pay it, for two reasons: because he committed the offence while he was of their status, and because it is right that those who gave surety should pay. A third is, if a Welshwoman is given to an alien and she has a son by the alien, and he kills a person, two-thirds of the galanas fall on the mother's kin and the third on the homicide; and that is because there is no father's kin to pay it. And those are called secured cattle, because it is necessary to give surety for those cattle, since all payments were formerly made in cattle.

The two sons we have mentioned above are of the same status and the same worth and the same sarhaed as an innate bonheddig.

There can be a son by clamour and a son by sufferance. This is a son by clamour: a son of whom a woman says that he is a man's son, by word of mouth without taking it to the bitter end; he can be denied at will. A son by sufferance is a son whom a woman lays legally, and whom the man suffers for a year and a day without denying him; from then on he can never be denied. And if it happens that he commits an offence, he cannot be denied in the strait since he was not denied in the clear, for he is a son by sufferance.

> The three dire losses of a kindred: one is, if it happens that a doubted son commits an offence, and because of that offence it is sought to deny him when they had not previously denied him, law does not allow him to be denied until the kindred compensate for that offence. The second is, if it happens that the doubted son is killed, though he was suffered he was not accepted and there is no right to his galanas; this is the reason it is not paid: since they did not accept him legally in his presence, law does not judge that they get goods from his death. Third is, if it happens that a person kills another and galanas comes from that and that he and the kin give

surety for the galanas, and before the date for payment he is laid to another father, what law says is that they are bound to pay the galanas except for his share, and therefore it is said 'He paid who gave surety.' *Dw.*

Even though the King should be the father of an alien woman's son, if he denies him, the son will be an alien. If an alien denies the son of a Welshwoman, the son will be an innate bonheddig, since every son is of his mother's status after he is denied.

A father can deny his son the day after he pays compensation for his offence for him, if he wants to. If it happens that a father gives goods for rearing a son, he is not entitled to deny him from then on, for to give goods for rearing him is one of the three acceptances of a son.

In three ways a son cannot be denied by a kindred: one is, by his being begotten in the legitimate bed and reared on the man's goods for a year and a day without rejection. The second is, giving goods for rearing him even though he be the son of a woman of bush and brake. The third is, accepting him legally in the mother church as law says. *Dw.*

If it happens that a dumb woman has a son, it is not necessary to deny him nor to accept him, since she does not say that he is theirs. After the mother is dead the son can intervene and say that he is a son of the kindred, and after that he must be denied or accepted. *Dw.*

There is no right to take a son from a dead man nor to lay him to a dead man: this is how there is no right, whatsoever son a man accepts legally in his lifetime law does not allow to be taken from him when he is dead; and the son whom a man rejects in his lifetime there is no right to lay to him when he is dead. Whatsoever son has not been rejected or accepted, law allows the kindred to do about him what they are entitled to.   Dw.

If it happens that the father has died, the chief of kindred can deny him as one of seven, in the same manner as the father would deny if alive, and in the same church with seven men with him from among the best men of the kindred, by their oath that his oath is clean. If there is no chief of kindred, twenty-one men from among the best men of the kindred deny him; according to the men of Powys fifty men deny a son from kindred.

No one into whose hand a son's land would fall can deny him: one brother cannot deny another; and if there are no brothers, the first cousin cannot, and if there are no first cousins the second cousins cannot deny him, lest they deny him for his acre; and no one is entitled to deny him who will be entitled to his patrimony after that.

An alien's sons can all deny each other, as the acre of none of them falls into the hand of another.   Dw.

If it happens that some of the kindred of a son deny him and others accept him, by their oath that it is not for fee or for value that they accept him, it is more proper to believe those who accept him, since it is most usual to deny a son for the sake of his patrimony. Every brother can deny his sister, unless in one place, that is, when the goods of her mother or her father are shared. If it is sought to deny her for the sake of her share of the goods, it cannot be done. And likewise every alien can deny his brother or his sister, unless it be against sharing their mother's or their father's goods with them, or against making compensation for their offence.

Thus it is right to accept a son into kindred. The father himself can accept him after the mother has laid him legally to him. If there is no father, the chief

Family Law 137

of kindred can accept him, as one of seven, those men being from among the best men of the kindred. This is how he is accepted: the chief of kindred takes the son's two hands between his own two hands, and gives him a kiss, for a kiss is a sign of kinship. And after that he puts the son's right hand into the hand of the eldest of the other men, who gives him a kiss— and so on from hand to hand down to the last man. If there is no chief of kindred, twenty-one men, from among the best men of the kindred, act; and the man who is in the Lord's place takes the son by his right hand and puts it into the hand of the eldest of those men, who gives him a kiss and takes him by the right hand, and puts it into the hand of the second eldest man, who also gives him a kiss,—and so on from hand to hand down to the last man. (According to the men of Powys, if there is neither father nor chief of kindred, fifty men accept him and deny him.)

> In three ways a son is laid to a man. One is for a woman of bush and brake, if she is pregnant, when she comes to her full time let her call her parish priest to her and swear to him, 'May I be delivered of a snake from this pregnancy if any father created it in a mother but the man to whom I lay it', naming him. Second is, it is for a chief of kindred and seven hands of the kindred with him to lay him. Third is, if there is no chief of kindred, the oath of fifty men of his kindred lay him; and the son himself swears first, for the mother's oath is legal only on the laying named above. *Cyfn.*

> When a son is denied by a kindred, it is for the eldest son of the man whose son he is said to be to swear first before the kindred. *Cyfn.*

Book III

THE JUSTICES' TEST BOOK

PROLOGUE

Whosoever wants to take up justiceship, thus it is proper for him: to know this book so that it is worthy for him to take justiceship: and when his teacher sees that he is worthy, let him send him to the Court Justice, and it is for the Court Justice to test him; and if he finds him worthy, it is for him to send him to the Lord and it is for the Lord to grant him justiceship, so that the judgment which he judges from then on shall be accepted as properly judged. And it is for him to give twenty-four pence to the Court Justice as his fee.

If it happens from then on that he judges a false judgment, he is not entitled to his tongue, unless he redeems it for its legal value. If it happens that there are pledges with him and that he is in the right, he is entitled to wynebwerth from him who pledged with him, with a camlwrw for the Lord. A justice is not bound to accept a pledge after he leaves his place of judgment, unless he himself so chooses; and he is not bound to accept one from a layman unless he promises a better judgment from another justice than the one which he judged.

And this book was gathered together by Iorwerth ap Madog from the book of Cyfnerth ap Morgenau and the book of Gwair ap Rhufawn and the book of Goronwy ap Moriddig and the old book of the White House, and besides that from the best books that he found also in Gwynedd and Powys and Deheubarth. And this book is called 'The Test Book', that is to say the Three Columns of Law, and the Value of Wild and Tame, and what pertains to that.   *C.*

It is at twenty-five years of age (and that according to law) that a person can be made a justice, for it is then that he will have a beard and

142   *The Law of Hywel Dda*

that his discretion will be steady, and that it will be fair for him to judge everybody in general, both the old persons and the young ones.   *Dw.*

If the King wishes to appoint anyone unskilled and unprepared in law as a court judge, it is right for him to be in the court in the King's company, inquiring and listening to justices who come from the country to the court; and learning laws and practices and customs and the ordinances of the King which pertain to authority, and above all the three columns of law and the value of all tame animals, and other, wild, ones of which persons make use; and listening to claimants and defendants in cases; and being with justices at their giving of judgments; and listening to arguments, if they send to the King what they are doubtful about, which they want clarified by him. Let him do that throughout the whole year. Thereafter it is right for the King's chaplain to take him to church, and with him the twelve special court officers, to mass; and after mass and offering by everyone, let the chaplain cause him to swear on the relic and the altar, and by the elements that are put on the altar, that he will never give a false judgment knowingly, either for anyone's entreaty or for value or for love or for hatred of anyone. After that let them come to the King, and let them tell him what they have done. And then it is right for the King to give him office, if he is satisfied with him, and to install him in a seat appropriate to him, and then it is right to give him idle trinkets: a throwboard from the King and a gold ring from the Queen; and let him not give nor sell those ever.

It is not right for anyone to be judge save him who is taught like that, or who is learned in law and will swear like him that he will not judge falsely in his lifetime.   *Bleg.*

Here begins the Test Book, that is to say the *Three Columns of Law* and the Value of Wild and Tame and what pertains to them.

1. Homicide

First is the Nine Abetments of Homicide, that is to say: first is pointing out the person who will be killed to him who will kill him, and he is called red-tongued; second is giving counsel to the person who kills the other, to kill him; third is agreeing with him and approving him. For each of those three points, the oath of a hundred men denies it; if he admits it, let him pay nine score pence.

Fourth is being an onlooker; fifth is companionship with the person who kills the other; sixth is going to the townland where the person who will be killed is, with him who will kill him. For each of these three, the oath of two hundred men, or twice nine score pence if it is admitted.

Seventh is, helping the person who kills the other, and that is called aid to violence; eighth is to hold the person who will be killed, until he who will kill him comes; ninth is to see the person killed in his presence, without protecting him. For each of these three, if it is denied, the oath of three hundred men, or thrice nine score pence if it is admitted.

Some say that the money which we have specified above comes to the kindred. The law says that it goes to the Lord, and that if there is denial, there is no right save to denial (and this is the reason that there is no right: because denial plus payment is not proper; and though it be admitted, the kin are entitled to nothing, for there is no principal offence in it). He, however, is entitled to it, for to commit the above-named abetments is wrong; he is entitled to a camlwrw for each of them according to the extent of the abetment, one trebled, another doubled, another single. There is no right to a dirwy for abetting homicide, but only to camlwrw.

There is a right to dirwy for fighting. This is fighting: assault and battery, and blood, and wound: the three things are fighting, and therefore dirwy is proper for them. This is the measure of the dirwy: twelve kine or three pounds. The measure of a camlwrw is three kine or nine score pence. There are three dirwy pennies: a dirwy for theft, and a dirwy for violence, and a dirwy for fighting; and save for those, every offence which a person commits attracts camlwrw; and for every camlwrw let what we have said above apply.

Whosoever has the principal offence of homicide laid against him, let the kindred pursue him. And first for the Lord: what he gets of his spoil or that of his kin on the original day that the person is killed or he hears of his being killed will be valid for the Lord, and if he does not get that, full galanas follows him.

The legal measure of galanas is three times the sarhaed of the person killed, according to his status. Others say that for the person whose sarhaed is three kine and three score pence, the worth is three kine and three score kine; and similarly as every person's status rises.

Galanas is shared like this. The first third falls on the homicide and on the mother and father and brothers and sisters with him; since those persons would take a third of the galanas with him if it were being paid to them, let them pay with him in that way. And then they share in three thirds: a third on the mother and father, and a third on the brothers and sisters, and a third on the homicide. If the homicide dies, let those persons pay a third of the galanas in full. Of the brothers' and sisters' third, two pence on a brother and one on a sister. Of the third which falls on the father and on the mother, two pence on the father and one on the mother. If all the persons we have named above should be dead, the homicide himself will pay that. If some are dead and others alive, let them contribute equally to pay that third, so that none of that third is spoilt so as not to be paid to the kin which is entitled to it, and to the Lord.

Homicide 145

If it happens that the homicide has nothing which he can pay, it is proper to give him a shaft penny in assistance; and thus it will be paid to him—from the seventh person on, and these are those seven persons: brother and first cousin and second cousin and third cousin and fourth cousin and fifth cousin and nephew son of a fifth cousin; and since kinship cannot be counted from there on, let them pay him a shaft penny.

This is how that is exacted: the Lord provides a servant to go with the homicide to take a relic with them, and where a person meets them, from the seventh degree on, let them require from him an oath that he does not derive from the four kindreds from which the homicide derives. If he does not give the oath, let him pay a shaft penny; and if he gives it he pays nothing.

A woman does not pay a shaft penny, for she has no shaft save her distaff; and a cleric does not pay it.

A woman does not pay galanas if she gives her oath that she will never have children; and a boy does not pay it before he is fourteen years old.

Col.

A stock inquiry is rightly this, that is to say: when a kinsman is denying the homicide the payment of a share of galanas, and asking 'Where is the stock where I separated from you?'; and then it is proper for the homicide to show him the stock according to his kinship as we have written above. In addition it is proper that there should be enough from among their fellow-kinsmen to maintain that what the homicide says is true. This is the reason that the fellow-kinsmen are good: because it is not right for strangers to bring into kindred or to separate from kinship.

Dw.

146 The Law of Hywel Dda

If it happens that he has not the whole payment, either from the shaft penny or from his own goods, and, though only one penny be wanting, he is killed for that one by his enemies, they have committed no illegality, since the complete cannot come from the incomplete. And though he should be killed, neither the goods we have named above, nor he himself, will be compensated for to his kindred; and therefore the law calls what we have named above a cold case of galanas.

> Three dire losses of a kindred: one is a homicide after the kindred pay for him their share (that is to say, the two-thirds) and he himself pays up to the last penny, and for that one he is killed by his enemies, it is legal to kill him for that one penny; and because the kindred lose their man and their goods it is so called. Second is, after the kindred pay their share of the galanas and the homicide has nothing which he can pay for the one-third, and he is banished to another country and is killed in that country, then they have lost their kinsman and their goods. Third is, if a man is charged with killing another, and does not deny it although he is innocent, and he is killed because he did not deny it, the killing is legal; and it is because their kinsman was killed when he was innocent that the loss is dire. *Dw.*

There is no right to kill anyone for another, save a homicide, whether for a share of the galanas or for anything else; for if the kindred discharge the homicide, there is no claim against them. And they are not bound to pay unless a Lord enforces it, and therefore there is an enforcing third for the Lord.

> No one is entitled to charge galanas save those for whom it is right to take it and to pay it.
> *Dw.*

Homicide 147

Women and clerics pay it, unless they deny that they will ever have children. And it is for this that they pay, on behalf of their children; and those are the persons who pay galanas and do not take it.

And the two-thirds falls on the kindred; and that is divided into three thirds, and of those, the two-thirds on the father's kindred and the third on the mother's kindred. And so let them take the oldest men of the kindreds, and let them set a third on mother-kin and two-thirds on father-kin. Of what remains in the gwely without going onto the kindreds, let two pence go on the brother and a penny on the sister. And so the galanas proceeds from third to third as far as the nephew, son of a fifth cousin; and that is where the father pays the galanas and the son does not pay it; and here is the reason: the son's kinship cannot be traced to the homicide, though the father's kinship can be traced to him. And if it happens that the homicide pays his share, there is no right to kill him, even if the kindred do not pay their share; and likewise there is no right to enforce against the kindred even if he does not pay it.

If it happens that a Lord and kindred are exacting galanas, and the other kindred calls for a delay by law, the law says that there is a right to a delay of a fortnight for each lordship in which the kindred are, for gathering the kindreds together to give an answer and to arrange the galanas.

No one is killed without first suffering sarhaed; that sarhaed, however, is not augmented for him. If the man is married, let the wife be given a third of her husband's sarhaed, and the two-thirds are put in with the galanas. After that let the galanas be divided into three parts, and let the third part go to the Lord as enforcing third. Let the two-thirds again be divided into three thirds, with one of those thirds for the family, to wit for the father and mother and the brothers and sisters, if any. (Married women and

148 The Law of Hywel Dda

clerics are not entitled to a share of the galanas, since they are not avengers; their children, however, if any, are entitled to one.) Let the two-thirds again be divided into three parts, and let a third of that two-thirds go to the mother's kindred; and after that let the oldest men of the kindreds go and let them apply thirds, a third to mother-kin and two-thirds to father-kin; and of what remains among them let them themselves distribute equally as they see to be proper for the share that remains among them, as far as the seventh person.

It is right for the eldest son of the person killed to indicate his father's heir and his gwely, and to be present when the galanas is received and when it is shared.   *Col.*

The delay for galanas is a fortnight for each lordship in which the kindreds are, for summoning them together to organise the payment, and another like period for enforcing the payment and bringing them together to pay it. It is proper to pay galanas at three dates and in three thirds: two dates for the father's kindred and one for the mother's kindred, since two thirds fall on the father's kindred. At the first date for the father's kindred to pay one of their thirds, they are entitled to the oath of a hundred men, from the best men of the other kindred, that their kinsman is forgiven; and at the second date when they pay a third they are entitled to the oath of another hundred men from the other kindred that their kinsman is forgiven; and at the third date it is right for the mother's kindred to pay their third, and then they are entitled against the other kindred to the oath of a hundred men that their kinsman is forgiven, and it is right that there should be perpetual reconciliation between them on that day, and perpetual concord between them.   *E.*

Homicide

The oath of three hundred men comes by law to deny the principal offence of blood and wound and killing of a person; and therefore the oath of three hundred men is proper for his forgiveness and as concord between the kindreds that we named above. To deny killing by fury, the oath of six hundred men: since his galanas and his penance are double, his denial will accordingly be double.   *EC.*

Whosoever denies homicide and its abetments entirely gives the oath of fifty men.   *Bleg.*

It is thus that the galanas of one in dispersion is shared. If it should happen that an innate bonheddig from Powys is in Gwynedd, or from Gwynedd in Powys, and galanas falls on him, and that his gwely kindred are not in the country with him, but yet there are many kinsmen of his there, it is proper for him to pay galanas and to bring them with him. And that is not shared by either mother-kin or father-kin, but according to the number of those of his kindred whom he has in the country. This then is how it is shared, in thirds: first, a third on him, together with his children, if any, and his mother and father, if they are there; and the two-thirds is shared among the kindred, and is shared thus: as much on a brother as on two first-cousins, and as much on a sister as on two second-cousins; and so sharing goes on as far as the seventh person. And no shaft penny comes from such as this.

What kindred soever pay galanas with the homicide, the like on the part of the person killed receive it, from the great-great-great-great-grandfather to the fifth cousin.

Thus are named the degrees of kindred for which it is right to pay galanas or to take payment: the first degree of the nine is the father and mother of the homicide or the slain; second is a grandfather; third, great-grandfather; fourth, brothers and sisters; fifth,

first cousin; sixth, second cousin; seventh, third
cousins; eighth, fourth cousins; ninth, fifth cousins.
The members of those degrees are: nephews and
uncles of the homicide or the slain. A nephew is the
son of a brother or sister or first cousin (male or
female) or second cousin. An uncle is the brother of a
father or mother or grandfather or grandmother or
great-grandfather or great-grandmother.

This is the share of each of all those: whosoever is
nearer to the homicide or the slain by one degree than
the other, he will pay or receive twice as much as the
other; and so it is for everyone in the degrees and their
members.

It is not right for the children of the homicide or the
slain to pay any of the galanas payment or to receive
it; for the share of the homicide, who pays more than
any one other, stands for himself and his children;
and the care for them also belongs to him. The care
for the children of the slain belongs to his closest
relatives and his fellow-heirs, who take a third of the
galanas and the whole payment of sarhaed.   *Bleg.*

If a kinsman of the homicide is a churchman bound
by sacred orders or by religion, or is leprous, or dumb,
or insane, he does not pay and he does not receive
anything by way of galanas. There is no right to take
vengeance on one of those for galanas, and they are
not entitled to avenge him who is killed, and they
cannot be compelled in any way to pay or to receive
anything for galanas.   *Bleg.*

If it happens that a person makes an ambush or
a rout, let him pay twelve kine doubly to the
Lord, and double worth and double penance.
       Col.

He who denies ambush or murder or public rout,
let him give the oath of fifty men without slave and
without alien. There cannot be a public rout of less
than nine men.   *Cyfn.*

Whosoever is in the place where a person is
killed, though his hand did the other no harm,
let him pay three kine of violence, with the oath
of a hundred men to deny blood and wound and

Homicide 151

loss of life. If it happens that a person is charged with killing a person in a battle, and he wants to deny it, let the oath of fifty men be given to deny it, with half a pound for the Lord. *Col.*

If a person kills another with arms which are not his, it is right for him to whom the arms belong to pay a third of the galanas. If the owner of the arms set on the arms the protection of his Lord and his goodmen, that no one should do wrong with them, and that in the presence of the Lord and his goodmen as he could prove by attestators, though persons should be killed with the arms after that, he should pay nothing in respect of the arms. *Col.*

If it happens that a person kills another with poison, he pays double galanas, for it is furious; or else let his life be forfeit for one galanas, and his manner of death will be at the will of the Lord, whether by hanging or burning; if he denies it, let him give the denial for killing a corpse, redoubled; that is, the oath of six hundred men. The persons who make poison in order that others be killed with it are at the option of the Lord, whether they are banished or put to death; if they deny it, let them give the oath of six hundred men. *E.*

If it happens that an insane person kills a sane person, let his kindred pay on his behalf as on behalf of a sane person, for it is right for his kindred to keep him so that he does not do wrong. If it happens that a sane person kills an insane one, let him pay his galanas like the galanas of a sane person. *Dw.*

If it happens that a person has rabies and he bites another person with his teeth, and from that bite the person dies, the kindred of the rabid

person will not pay for him, for it was by the
nature of the disease that the other lost his life.
Dw.

If it happens that an animal kills a bonheddig
person, and the kindred seek galanas for him,
they are not entitled to it, but only to the
homicide, for a kindred are not bound to pay
galanas on behalf of their kinsman's animal, and
one person cannot pay galanas.   *Dw.*

If it happens that the principal offence of
homicide is laid against a dead man, there is no
right to lay it, since the son does not stand in his
father's place, since the innocent kindred is not
entitled to kill the son; and therefore there is no
right to claim against a dead man, because the
son is not bound to stand in his father's place.
Dw.

If it happens that a homicide dies, or is killed
by a person from a kindred not entitled to kill
him, before paying his share of the galanas, law
says that it is his father who pays on his behalf,
since it would be the father who would take it if
he were killed.   *Col.*

If it happens that a woman kills a person, let
her be a homicide like a man; and she is entitled
to a shaft penny if she has not goods which she
can pay, and that is the one person who receives a
shaft penny and does not pay it.   *Dw.*

If it happens that an alien's son by a bonheddig
woman kills a person, and his father and mother
are alive, and that galanas falls on him, let the
two-thirds fall on the mother and the third on the
father, for it is right for her to be in the place of a
father to him.   *Dw.*

Special Cases of Liability

If it happens that a person gives another a fright, and that from that fright the person loses his life, let it be examined on what account the fright was given, whether on account of the person or on account of something else; and if it was on account of the person, let his galanas be paid, and if on account of something else, though he died from seeing it in his presence, there will be no compensation. *Dw.*

If it happens that a person throws at either an animal or something else, and if that throw rebounds to strike a person, and from that blow he meets his death, and it is desired to lay either galanas or sarhaed for it: law says that there is no disgrace in that, for it was inadvertence. It is proper to pay galanas if the person dies; if the person lives he is entitled only to be indemnified for his hurt and his blood. This is the reason that there is no disgrace in it: because there is neither assault nor battery on the person hurt though there was on the thing thrown at, and therefore law does not give judgment for both causes.

If it happens that a person pierces another with an arrow, and in that flight it goes through another person, it is proper to pay the galanas of both of them, and it is not proper to pay sarhaed save to the first of them. *Dw.*

If it happens that a person fells a tree, and when the tree falls it kills a person, and he who felled the tree did not warn the person killed, let him pay his galanas; and if he warned him, he will pay nothing. *Dw.*

Measure of Galanas and Sarhaed

The galanas of the King of Aberffraw is his sarhaed three times. The galanas of the King's wife, and his son, and his captain of the house-

154   *The Law of Hywel Dda*

hold, and his edling, and his nephew, one third of
the King's galanas, without gold and without
silver; and the sarhaed of each of those is one
third of his sarhaed.   *Col.*

Thus we treat of the sarhaedau: first of the sarhaed of
the King of Aberffraw. What the law looked at was
what is sarhaed both to him and to everybody, and
what the law saw was that nothing is sarhaed to
anyone save one of three things in particular: causing
him shame in respect of his wife, or killing his
messenger, or breaking his protection. This is how
compensation is made to him for his wife: a gold plate
for him, as broad as his face and as thick as the nail of a
ploughman who has been a ploughman nine years;
and a gold rod as long as himself and as thick as his
little finger, and a hundred cows for every cantred
that he has, with a white bull with red ears for every
hundred cows among them; and if they are coloured
cows, a coloured bull for every hundred cows among
them. And this is augmented to be greater by a half.
The two other sarhaedau are not augmented, but the
compensation we have stated above is for them.

If it happens that a man from another country does
sarhaed to him, his sarhaed is three score and three
pounds; and that is his own sovereign tribute to the
King of London when he receives his land from him;
and save for that he is never entitled to anything from
him save dogs and falcons and horses.

In three ways sarhaed is done to the Queen: by
breaking her protection, or by striking her, or by
snatching something from her hand. A third of the
King's compensation (except for gold) is paid to her;
and of the same sarhaed as her are the captain of the
household and the edling and the King's son: the
sarhaed of each of those is a third of the King's
sarhaed. Her worth is her sarhaed three times, and so
is the worth of each of the persons we have named
above. The sarhaed of the King's daughter is half her

Homicide: Measure of Galanas and Sarhaed   155

brother's sarhaed until she marries; after she marries, her sarhaed is a third of her husband's sarhaed, both for her and for every woman. In three ways every person in the world suffers sarhaed: by striking, and battery, and by violence to him; and if it is a man, to lie with his wife is sarhaed to him; and though it be a woman, if she finds a woman with her husband, it is sarhaed to her; and so no-one escapes without a way to suffer sarhaed.

The sarhaed of the steward and the chief of kindred and the cynghellor: nine kine and nine score pence; their worth is nine kine and nine score kine, augmented. The worth of an uchelwr and every person who has an office from a Lord, six kine and six score kine, augmented; their sarhaed is six kine and six score pence. Every man of the bodyguard without office, his sarhaed is four kine and four score pence. Every innate bonheddig and every king's alien, his sarhaed is three kine and three score pence; and their worth is three kine and three score kine. Every uchelwr's alien has half the sarhaed of a king's alien and half his worth.

> The galanas of an uchelwr, if he is chief of kindred, nine kine and nine score kine, three times augmented . . . The galanas of his alien or his member, i.e. his kinsman, six kine and six score kine, three times augmented . . . *Col.*

> The galanas of a king's aillt, three kine and three score kine; his sarhaed, three kine and three score pence; and likewise for an alien. The worth of an aillt's alien, half the worth of an uchelwr's alien; his sarhaed, half the sarhaed of an uchelwr's alien.   *Col.*

The sarhaed of a slave, twelve pence: six for a smock and three for breeches and one for a rope and one for a hedging-bill and one for brogues. His worth is a pound if he comes from this island; if he is from overseas, his worth will be six score pence and a pound.

The Law of Hywel Dda

The sarhaed of a slave woman, if she is servient and does not go either to the spade or to quern, twenty-four pence. *Col.*

Every person who is killed or suffers sarhaed, except an alien, has his sarhaed and his galanas augmented: what is augmented is the scores of pence which are set with the cows; and the cows in the sarhaedau are not augmented. *Col.*

Whosoever admits doing sarhaed to any one of those we have said above, let him pay him his sarhaed as we have said. Whosoever denies sarhaed, there are three points which it is proper for him to deny: that he did not do either shame or sarhaed to him, nor to his kindred, nor to his Lord. This is why it is denied as against the Lord, against a dirwy to the Lord, and against paying him his sarhaed, and against the vengeance of the kindred. Why is it denied against the kindred, when the kindred does not get any of the sarhaed which is paid to him? Here is the reason: when their kinsman suffers sarhaed, it is disgrace to them, and it is legal for them to avenge their disgrace; and therefore it is proper to deny, as against them, that their kinsman suffered sarhaed. If his sarhaed is paid to him, the kindred is undisgraced; and where there is no disgrace there is no claim.

The sarhaed of a single woman, before she marries, is half her brother's sarhaed. The sarhaed of every woman, after she marries, is one third of the sarhaed of the last husband she has publicly had. The galanas of every woman always goes to her kindred.

2. Theft

The nine abetments of theft: first is among them, showing the thing which will be stolen. The second is agreeing to the theft. Third is giving provisions to the thief. Fourth is going in his company and carrying the provisions. Fifth is going with him and breaking the

Theft 157

place in which the stolen property is. Sixth is being an adviser for the thief and receiving him. Seventh is travelling by day or night with the thief. Eighth is taking a share of the stolen property. Ninth is taking value from the thief and concealing it for him.

For each of these there comes a dirwy, if it is admitted and was concealed by him before that. This is the measure of the dirwy: twelve kine or three pounds, and that goes to the Lord. They are not bound to pay anything to him who owns the goods, since they are not principal offenders. If they cannot find this dirwy, the Lord can banish them on account of it; he can take three pence instead of the three pounds if he likes, and the law will be fair. And if they can find the payment, it is not right for them to be banished men, nor liable to be despoiled. If the abetments we have named above are denied, their denial is as great as the denial of principal offenders.

Thus is theft denied in the law of Hywel. The oath of twelve men for a horse, and for three score pence, since that is the horse of least value in law; half of those being designated men and the other half being such men as may be got from among competent men. And it is right for those men to derive, two-thirds from the father's kindred, and one third from the mother's kindred, and so near to him that it is right for them to pay galanas with him and to take it. To deny a horse's burden, and a steer (for a horse can carry a steer as its burden), six men are required of him, with himself as the seventh, half of them being designated men. To deny a pig, or a sheep, or a back-burden, his oath as one of five (two of them being designated men and two being other competent men, together with himself); and then the compurgation will be shared in two halves between the two kindreds, since four men cannot be divided into thirds.

These compurgations do not apply save after a legal charge. This is a legal charge: the oath of the owner that the theft which he charges is true against that person; for nothing is a charge save the owner's charge. When the owner of stolen goods accuses another of theft by word of mouth and does not take it to the bitter end, law adjudges only the oath of the defendant to deny it. Though a person who is not owner charges theft on relics, it is not law to give more than the defendant's oath to deny it, for no one save an owner is entitled to charge theft. At the present time it is the custom to take for every theft, both great and small, the oath of twelve men, half of them being designated men.

Though the compurgation should fail for a person accused of one of the abetments above named by us, he will fall only under dirwy, unless it is desired to prosecute him for perjury. Though the compurgation should fail for the principal offender, however great the theft alleged against him, it is not right for his life to be forfeit if he can pay seven pounds. And even if he cannot, it is right, not that his life be forfeit, but that he be banished, since there is no right to put to death anyone in whose hand nothing is taken,

> unless he admits theft himself when it is charged against him before the law, that theft being of greater value than fourpence. Others say that his life is forfeit if he does not get his compurgation.
>
> Whosoever is banished by judgment of the law, it is proper for him to be a starting man on the morrow, and from then on, one day for every cantred which the Lord has who banished him, and so to be a banished man by law.   *Col.*

Whosoever catches a thief with the stolen property in his hand, and releases him, whether for kinship or for value, if he admits it let him pay seven pounds; for though the thief's life would be forfeit, law does not judge his life to be forfeit. If he cannot pay, let him be banished like a thief.

Theft   159

Whosoever is banished by judgment of law, and is found in the country after the delay given to him to stay in the land, let his life be forfeit unless he finds one who will buy him, since he has no right to his country during the life of the Lord who banishes him, unless he is reconciled with him.

Whosoever has stolen property traced to his house, and cannot deny it, let him be liable to be despoiled, and if there is nothing to despoil, let him be banished. Whosoever has stolen property found in his house, or in the curtilage of his house, in which he has his residence, though he may have that which will save his body from the theft, yet it is for him to keep his house from theft; and therefore the law judges it a foul house, with himself and what he has, except for deposits, if any; since the owner of the deposit is not bound to keep the house from theft, he will not suffer loss of what is his. There is not in law any place where there is a right to extortionate spoliation, except one place; that one place is for killing a corpse.

Whosoever wishes to make a sufficient information, let him go to the Lord and say that theft has been committed by a person against whom he does not dare to allege it, either because of his gentility or because of his wealth. Then it is proper for the Lord to call the priest to him and tell him what has been said to him, and to send the priest with him to the church door; and then it is proper for the priest to set God's cross before him lest he should swear falsely, and if he wishes to swear, let him swear first at the church door, with the second oath in the chancel and the third on the altar. And thereafter let the priest come to the Lord and say that he has received the whole; and then it is for the Lord to swear that he has had a sufficient information, when he claims against the person at the session, and against that nothing is possible. His life will not be forfeit though sufficient information has been received, but he will be a sale thief; and if he cannot find his price, he is banished like

160 *The Law of Hywel Dda*

a thief. Other forms of law wish to allow him denial against the Lord's charge as against another owner's charge, and that is what the men of Gwynedd most believe in.

> An informant is entitled to the tenth penny of the goods of which he informs. *Dw.*

> If it is said against a person that stolen property was seen with him in broad daylight, and another presents against him that he was seen, let him who is accused give the oath of twenty-four men, such that an equal number come from each commote of the same cantred, and the presentor can do nothing against him; and that law is called 'bitter denial against sufficient information'.

> This is how it is right to present theft legally: that the person was seen between when the day grew light and when dusk fell, having the stolen property with him, and that the presentor should swear, as one of four men of the same status as himself, at the gate of the churchyard, and at the church door, and above the sacred altar. *Cyfn.*

If it happens that a person finds the flesh of an animal which is not his, either with dogs or in another's cache, and takes it without leave, he will be liable to dirwy as far as it proceeds, whether by gift, or by sale, or by sharing, to the hundredth hand; and therefore it is called *cyhyryn canastr*; and it does not go farther than the hundredth hand.

> These things are of the same status as theft in hand: if a person is walking, and livestock or dead property is found travelling with him or before him, that is as good as theft in hand. The second is, if stolen property is found under the same roof and the same under-thatch as himself, that too is as good as theft in hand. Third is to find stolen property in a person's hand or on his back or thrown to the ground away from him. For each of these three, the person must seek a legal plea to cast the theft from him, or else he will be an admitted thief. *Dw.*

Theft   161

Whosoever wishes to attach stolen property in
another's hand, let him come to the thing which he
attaches, and ask 'Who is in possession of this?' If
there is no one who acknowledges it, let him take
leave to take what is his, and after he has had leave let
him go his way to the justice, and as the justice
indicates let him swear to it and let him take what is
his. And if it happens that, when he is attaching what
is his, there comes a possessor who opposes him, let
him then ask 'Who is in possession of this?' It is
proper for the possessor to say that it is he who is in
possession. Then it is proper for the claimant to say 'It
is wrong for you to have possession of what is mine.'
And then it is proper for the defendant to say 'Total
denial that there is any of what is yours here. And as
there is none, what separated you from your lost
property and when did you separate from your lost
property?' This is the reason it is good to know that:
there are six ways in which a person's goods go from
him, and for three of them it is possible to swear and
for the other three it is not possible. These are the
three for which it is not possible: deposit, or loan, or
hire, or a favour: for it is not proper to claim against
anyone save him to whom it went by these three
ways. For the other three it is proper to swear: one of
them is theft, and the second is loss by laxity, and the
third, surreption. This is the reason he can swear:
because no other hand received it from his hand,
therefore he can swear to it in the place where he sees
what is his.

Whosoever wishes to swear to what is his, thus it is
for him to swear to it. If it is a dead thing to which he
is swearing, let him swear with the left hand on the
thing to which he is swearing, and the right hand on
the relic. If it is an animal to which he is swearing, let
him swear with his left hand on the right ear of the
animal and the right hand on the relic; and the right
hand of the defendant on the left ear of the animal;
and so let the claimant swear that there was no owner

162 The Law of Hywel Dda

of it who had power either to sell it or buy it save himself, and in addition to that, that it did not leave him either by gift or by loan, or on deposit, nor was it sold or given, but taken from him by theft or surreption, or lost. And let him name the day or night of the week when it was lost, and name the week of the month, and name the month of the season, and name the season of the year.

For an animal there are three pleas: birth and rearing; and keeping before loss; and voucher to warranty. For a dead thing there are only two: keeping before loss, and voucher to warranty. If he seeks his plea by birth and rearing, let him do thus: let him put it in the mouth of maintainers that its mother was his, and that it was born and reared with him, and that it never left his ownership and his possession till today. And this is the kind of maintainers which it is right for him to have: a neighbour above and another below; and this is the kind of men that those are: a man of higher status and a man of lower status than him. And if he gets it, that is a quota for him.

If he chooses his plea by keeping before loss, let the man swear to it in the way we said above; and after he has sworn to it, let the other say that he had it either a week or a month or a season longer than the other had it, and that he has such maintainers as we have just said above who will maintain for a week or a fortnight or more before he lost what was his; and if he gets that, that is a quota for him.

If he pleads voucher to warranty, let him say 'Who avows or warrants this?' And if he is on the spot, let his warrantor take the stolen property to himself and let the other be free. And if it happens that the warrantor takes it, let the claimant swear to it in his hand; and it is for him, if he likes, to seek another warrantor, or let him fall himself.

It is not proper that attachment and swearing should be followed by compurgation, but by voucher to warranty or keeping before loss or birth and

Theft   163

rearing. If it happens that stolen property is taken
with a person, and he says that he is innocent of the
theft, but that it was thrust on him against his will by
another person, and was taken in his hand, and the
person nevertheless says that it was stolen: it is
proper then to adjudge compurgation on him for that;
and that is the one place in which compurgation is
adjudged after attachment and swearing.

And so the stolen property can proceed from hand
to hand as long as he finds on the spot anyone who will
take it from him. If he finds no one on the spot who
will take it, and he vouches a warrantor in another
place, let him be given the delay to which he is
entitled, to seek his warrantor. This is the delay: if he
is in the same commote, three days; if he is in another
place, a fortnight; and so it proceeds as far as the third
hand, and in the third hand immediate law. And if the
third hand finds on the spot someone who will take it
from him, it is allowed him, provided that law be not
postponed for him from that day forth.

> If it happens that a person swears to stolen
> property in the hand of another person, who puts
> it in the mouth of a warrantor for him, who
> comes but does not take it from him, whether it
> was by gift or by loan or by exchange with a
> surety for it, and that he does not accept that, lest
> he lose his case, law says then that he is entitled
> to prove against his warrantor that it came from
> him, whether by surety or by testifiers. This is
> the reason for that: though it be sworn to as theft
> in the first hand, it is not by way of theft that he
> casts that thing on his warrantor, and therefore
> he is entitled to enjoy his surety or his knowers
> against him.   Dw.

> If it happens that stolen property is attached in
> a person's hand, and when the stolen property is
> sworn to, he vouches to warranty a priest or
> another man in orders or a religious, and the

latter comes to take the stolen property from the hand of the person from whom it was claimed, it is not right for him to submit to it, since it is not right for him to submit to law when he has relics on him (the relics being the degrees or orders, or the religious habit for another); and since they cannot cast off their relics and submit to the Lord's law and take on the thief's status, therefore the law does not allow them to be warrantors for the stolen property, for it is not proper to draw law from the Lord's throne to the bishop's chapter.   *Dw.*

Whosoever puts warranty in the mouth of another, if his warrantor fails him, let him be an admitted thief according to the amount of the stolen property taken with him. In the law of Hywel, he is a sale thief up to the value of fourpence, and from there on his life is forfeit. Others say that for every four-footed animal which is stolen, whether lamb or kid or piglet, his life is forfeit; nevertheless it is safer to say from fourpence.

For everything which has no legal value, sworn appraisal is allowed according to the law of Hywel. Rhys ap Gruffudd, the suzerain of Deheubarth, by agreement with his country laid down sworn appraisal for every beast, to wit, that the owner should swear that the beast was worth the value he put on it, and that he would get that for it.   *Bleg.*

If it happens that a person swears to property in the hands of another person as being stolen, and that the thing has no legal value and because of that the defendant thief seeks, although the thing is worth much, to appraise it at little (since there is no right to put anyone to death save for the value of fourpence or more): then it is proper for the owner of the property to swear to it a second time. This is how he swears to it: that he would get so much for it, and that he would not

Theft 165

give less than that; and if the sworn appraisal is more than fourpence, let the thief's life be forfeit for that property as if it had a legal value; and if the sworn appraisal is less than fourpence, let him be a sale thief. *Dw.*

The thief who is to be sold, his value is seven pounds. From one whose life is forfeit there is no right to any of his goods, since there is no right to both compensation and vengeance; provided that the victim be repaid his goods. And this is the reason that he is bound to pay the victim: because it is not right for him to leave behind him any debt owing from him.

In the law of Hywel there was payment and second payment for stolen property; and thereafter Bleddyn ap Cynfyn changed it, so that it was enough to pay the person his loss according to his sworn appraisal. Let his own goods go as he wishes, if he has no children; if he has children he is not entitled to bequeath anything except the church's daered, and his debts.

It is not right to destroy a thief who is put on sureties. *Cyfn.*

If it happens that a man commits theft and is condemned to death for that theft, and the Lord supposes that he is entitled to his goods and also to put him to death, he is not entitled; and he is not entitled to the goods of his wife or his sons under fourteen years of age, nor anything of which he was lord. There is no right to take for that theft anything save his life, and he is lord of his wife, and of his sons and of their goods as long as it is right for them to be at his platter. *Dw.*

The Lord is not entitled to the ebediw of the person whom he himself puts to death. Whatsoever death befalls him in another country, if he himself has not put him to death, the Lord is entitled to his ebediw. There is no galanas for a thief, and there is no bar between two kindreds by his being put to death. The

166   *The Law of Hywel Dda*

law says of marauders from another country, who
share in thirds with their own Lord, that it is right
that they should be sale thieves; and if they are killed
there is a right to galanas for them

—and it is right to set it as a bar between the two
kindreds.   *Col.*

Betrayers of a Lord, and furious thieves, and all persons
whose lives are forfeit by judgment of law: there is no
right to galanas for them.

Furious men, if they deny their fury, their denial is
double the denial of other theft. This is fury: spoiling
the property both for himself and for him to whom it
belongs.

Three persons who are not entitled to be buried
in consecrated ground: a thief put to death for the
theft, and the betrayer of a Lord, and a furious
man put to death for his fury.   *Dw.*

This is theft: everything done which is denied.

Theft is moving from its place that which is taken.
Bleg.

This is surreption: everything taken in absence which
is not denied. This is robbery: everything taken in
presence against the will. This is 'against the will':
everything which is taken to the evil and to the
disgrace of the other. This is misapprehension: everything which is taken in mistake for another thing; for
misapprehension there is no right to dirwy or camlwrw or anything save indemnifying the person for
his goods.

It is not right to put a slave to death for his first
offence, if six score pence are obtained for him,
nor for the second if a pound is obtained, or if his
lord acquits him of each of the above; and for the
third a limb is cut off. Some say that from the
third theft on it is right to put him to death;
others say that it is right only to cut off a limb for

Theft 167

each theft that he commits. The value of a slave from this island, a pound; if he is from overseas, six score pence and a pound—that is, if he is stolen and admitted. *Dw.*

If it happens that a slave is killed (what slave soever it be, whether servient or another slave) or is stolen, the oath of twenty-four men is proper to deny it, half of them being designated men; for it is right for every theft that half the compurgators should be designated men. *Dw.*

It is not right to put a slave to death if his lord redeems him, and if nothing is found in his hand, his lord can acquit him; and because of that, it is the custom to let lords acquit their alien servants. Aliens from overseas or from another country, who are weak, it is not right to put to death for food or anything, but he who owns the goods is to be compensated. They are free until the end of three nights and three days.

Three thieves who escape from admitted theft: a needy one who travels through three townlands, with nine houses in each townland, without getting alms which will save him, or hospitality, though he be caught with stolen provisions he will be free by law; and a woman for joint theft with her wedded husband; and the thief of a bird, except that he must pay the legal value of the bird to its owner. *Bleg.*

For a dog or for a bird, or for the like, there is no right to dirwy or the death penalty, but a camlwrw to the Lord and compensation to the owners for their goods.

If it happens that a person rescues property from a thief in another lordship, he who rescued it shall have a third of the rescue fee, with two-thirds to the Lord. *Col.*

No one forfeits his life for robbery; this is the reason: since the sarhaed of him who is robbed is compensated according to his status, and his goods are restored to him, with dirwy for the Lord.

168 *The Law of Hywel Dda*

If it happens that a person is asked to answer for the act of his servant because he has done a wrong while on his food and drink, we say that except for theft there is no right to claim for a person's act on another's food. If it happens that a person claims against his servant if he causes loss to him, whether by burning a kiln or by hurting a steer or by another matter, we say that there is no right save to his oath that he did not handle it save as well as his own. *Dw.*

If it happens that a cleric commits theft, and it is adjudged that his orders be taken from him according to the law of the synod, law judges that his life is not forfeit for that act, since there is no right to two penalties for the same cause. *Dw.*

If it happens that theft is charged against another person and compurgation is adjudged for him, and that before the date of the compurgation comes, the person dies leaving goods, and that the Lord wants the goods because he did not get the compurgation, law says that the Lord is entitled to the goods up to seven pounds, since he would be entitled to that if he did not get the compurgation (and that would also be the person's debt if he did not get it); and if he has more goods than seven pounds, let him leave them to his children to pay his debts and his daered. If it happens that he has no goods and the Lord then wants to claim against the person's son for the debt, since he did not get the compurgation and the compurgation was a debt of the father, law says that for theft there is no right to adjudge a compurgation against anyone save him whom the owner charges, and since the owner charged nothing against the son, therefore the son is not bound to answer for the father's compurgation. *Dw.*

Theft

> If it happens that a cow is stolen and she rears progeny with the person who stole her, and the owner hears where she is, either she or her progeny, he is entitled only to herself, and if she does not exist he is entitled to nothing, since treasure does not arise under deprivation. *Dw.*

3. Fire

The nine abetments of fire: first is giving counsel to burn the house. The second is assenting to burning it. Third is going because of the burning. Fourth is carrying the cresset. Fifth is striking fire. Sixth is seeking fuel. Seventh is blowing the fire until it catches. Eighth is giving the fire to him who burns it. Ninth is seeing it burning.

Whosoever wishes to deny any one of these, let him give the oath of fifty men to deny it; and if it is said that he burnt it by stealth, one half of them shall be designated men and the other undesignated men; or else let him pay in full. Others say that no compurgation in the world for stealth is more than twelve men, and that it is twelve men that deny stealth, one half being designated men and the other undesignated men: and so burning by stealth is denied, since the status of the stealth is greater than that of the burning.

> If a thief is found burning a house by stealth and is caught, let his life be forfeit. *Cyfn.*

Whosoever burns a house, which burns another, let him pay for the house to which he set fire, and so let it be paid from house to house as far as the fire travels. Whosoever gives another fire to burn with, and admits it, let him pay one-third of its act.

> He who strikes fire, or blows it until it catches, or gives fire to him who burns with it, pays half the loss which the fire causes, and the other half falls on him who puts the fire to what is burnt. And that is the full act of burning. And if no one is an abettor with him,

let him himself pay all the loss that comes from that
burning, unless he can acquit himself by compurgation of country.   *Bleg.*

Whosoever lights a fire in a house which is not his,
his act binds him until the end of three nights and
three days.

He who lends a house and fire to another, if the latter
lights a fire three times in it, shall have full payment
from him if it burns.   *Cyfn.*

Whosoever leaves fire in a kiln, though it be with
another that it burns, if he does not take security from
him who dries in it after him, let him pay one-third of
the act of that fire.

Whosoever takes fire from a house without permission, let him himself pay both for his act and for
his surreption. Whosoever asks for fire from a house,
after it is given to him it is for him to pay for its act.
Whosoever asks for the loan of fire, let the fire come
without claim and without surclaim against it.

Three fires for which compensation is not made: a
March muirburn; and the fire of a hamlet smithy
which is seven fathoms from the houses and has a roof
of shingles or tiles or turf; and the fire of a hamlet bath
which is seven fathoms from the houses.

Whosoever takes something to him on deposit, or
has it left for keeping, let him pay for it if it is burnt, as
in the past.

If it happens that a house within a townland
catches fire, let it pay for the two nearest houses
which first took the fire, and let them pay from the
nearest to the next nearest as is right for them.

Galanas does not follow fire, but only the act of the
hand itself.

Whosoever makes muirburn at any other time save
in March, let him himself pay for its act.

Weaving women who take the webs or balls of yarn
of others to themselves, howsoever they are lost it is
right for them to pay for them, since it is right for
them to keep them from all loss.

There is no damage done by a person's fire to another person's flesh, without the person's act associated with it, for which compensation is made.

If it happens that pigs come to a house and scatter the fire so that the house burns, and the pigs escape, it is for the owner of the pigs to pay for the house to him to whom it belongs. If the pigs are burnt it is equal between them and they are two irresponsible things; and therefore where there is equality in law there is no compensation but they are set against each other.

Let no one take fire without leave, and if he does take it, let him pay a camlwrw to the Lord, even though he does nothing with it. Let no one give fire without knowing what is to be done with it; and if he gives it, let him pay for a third of its act.

If it happens to a person carrying fire that the fire flies from him, let him pay for its act, unless he can throw a share of it off onto the fire.

If it happens that a person goes to dry in another's kiln, he will be bound until the end of three nights and three days.

> Three things which a person can take without another's leave: water not in another person's vessel, and a stone not in a piece of work, and fire from a hollow tree.　　　　　　　　　　　*Dw.*

And so end the Three Columns of Law.

4. The Value of Wild and Tame

Horses

The pregnancy of a mare, fourpence until the fourteenth day after the foal is born. On the morrow, twenty-four pence until a year is up, and if it is taken on corn, its compensation is as great as its dam's. And if it gets one day of the second year, it rises by another twenty-four, to be forty-eight; and so it remains until the third year. And then it goes to sixty, and it is right that it should be bridle-tame; and then it is proper to give it the training which is right for it, whether it be destrier, or palfrey, or working horse.

A destrier does not lose its value or its status in spite of grazing out during three seasons, which are these: from the middle of April to the middle of May, and the whole of October. And if it goes into a stall, though it be only for three nights and three days, its value is a pound. A palfrey's value is six score pence. The value of a rouncey or sumpter horse is six score pence. A working horse which draws a car and a harrow, its value is three score pence. A wild horse's value is three score pence.

The value of a stallion's two testes is as much as the value of two mares, with himself as a third: that is to say, nine score pence.

In relation to the properties of a horse, it is right to be under liability for three diseases: for the staggers for three dewfalls, for the strangles for three moons, and for the glanders for a year; and for restiveness until it is ridden in a crowd of persons and horses through their midst; and if it is not restive there, let him who sells it be free; and if it is restive let a third of its value be returned, leaving the transfer as before, since it is not proper to undo the transfer.

> He who sells a horse, let him warrant its grazing and drinking water and that it is not restive, and if it is restive let him who sold it choose whether to take his horse back or to return one-third of the value to the other. *Cyfn.*

> A dung horse or a dung mare is of the same value and the same increase as a steer, except for their properties. The properties of a dung horse or dung mare are to carry a load and to draw a car uphill and downhill, without irregularity. *Cyfn.*

The value of a horse's foot is its value in full; one third of its value for its eye, and one third for the other eye. Every harm to a horse is a third of its value, as for its ear and the flesh of its tail. Whosoever cuts the hair

The Value of Wild and Tame 173

of a horse's tail, let him put the horse in a place where it will not be seen, and let him give the owner another horse to do what it would do, until the tail hair of his own horse is as it formerly was at its best. The value of its mane is the same as that of its bridle; its halter and forelock are of the same value.

A destrier which is fattened for six weeks over a manger is worth a pound. A destrier grazing in the open and a greyhound without its collar lose their status. A destrier's tail hair is worth twenty-four pence if it is cut outside the flesh; if however any of the flesh is cut, then the whole value of the destrier is paid and the destrier is the valid property of him who damaged it. A destrier's eye and ear are each worth twenty-four pence. *Cyfn.*

If it is wholly blinded, its whole value is paid. *Bleg.*

A rouncey is worth six score pence. A rouncey's tail hair is worth twelve pence if it is cut outside the flesh; if however any of the flesh is cut, then the whole value of the rouncey is paid and it is the valid property of him who damaged it. A rouncey's eye and ear are each worth twelve pence. A palfrey is worth a mark; its limbs are of the same value as a rouncey's limbs. *Cyfn.*

A sumpter-horse's legal value is four score pence. If its tail hair is cut, twenty-four pence; if the flesh is cut, it loses its whole value. Its eye and ear, twenty-four pence; if it wholly loses its eyes, the whole of its value falls away.

He who denies killing a destrier or a palfrey by stealth, let him give the oath of twenty-four men.

A stud mare is worth six score pence. Her tail and eye are each worth six pence. *Cyfn.*

A legal stud is fifty mares. *Cyfn.*

Whosoever borrows a horse from another, and rubs the hair from his back, let him pay fourpence. If the skin is broken as far as the flesh, eightpence. If the flesh is cut to the bone, he pays sixteen pence.

Whosoever takes a horse without its owner's leave,

174 The Law of Hywel Dda

he pays fourpence for mounting and fourpence for every shareland he rides, and nothing is due for dismounting, since that is proper. The above is the owner's compensation, with a camlwrw to the Lord.

Whosoever hires a horse, though the horse should die with him, there falls on him only his own oath that he did as well by him as by his own horse, with payment of the hire. If it happens that a person hires a horse and agrees how far he will take him, if he goes beyond that let him pay one third of the profit if he gets exchanged goods, or if he gets other goods without exchange one third of that, to the horse's owner, and the surreption-fine to the Lord.

If it happens that a horse is lamed while borrowed, or some other hurt is done by accident to it, let another horse be given in its place, to do with it as would be done with the other; and if it remains damaged, let that horse remain in its place.

Four horseshoes and their set of nails are worth two-pence.

If a horse is sold with a fault in it, not being outside the skin, unless it is one of the three natural diseases, no compensation will be paid, but only his oath that he did not know of it.

> It is for him who buys to look for outward harm. *Cyfn.*

> If it happens that a person buys an animal from another, and after buying it comes to know that teeth are missing, and seeks compensation, law judges that there is no compensation, for it is harm outside the skin; for law says that wheresoever neither flesh nor skin is broken, it is harm outside the skin. *Dw.*

The value of a filly foal is fourpence until the end of fourteen days; and from then until a year is up, sixteen pence; from the end of a year until the end of two years, her value is thirty-two pence; and at three years old her value is three score, and then she is of

The Value of Wild and Tame

working age. The value of her mane is the same as that of her halter, that is to say, a penny. Her properties are, to draw a car uphill and downhill, and to carry a cross-load, and to bear foals; and if she is not so, in a case of buying let a third of her value be repaid.

Neat Cattle

For a small calf, from the night it is born until the Winter Kalends, sixpence; from the Winter Kalends on, two pence each season until the August when it is right for it to conceive, and on the ninth day of that August it rises by fourpence for its calf. And from then on two pence are added to it each season until the ninth day of May, and on the ninth of May it is right for it to calve. Then it rises to forty pence (and it is right for the calf to walk nine paces and to draw a stream from its four teats; the value of the calf is fourpence until the Winter Kalends; and from then on it is of the same value as every one): sixteen pence for its milk, and four pence for the calf. And from then on it rises by two pence each season until the middle of March, and then it is right for it to calve and its lactation money is added to it to bring it to its full value; and then its value is three score. And so it stays until the fifth calf, and that is its prime; after that it is to be appraised.

The value of its ear and its horn and its tail and its eye, fourpence. The value of its teat, fourpence every year that it lives, or a white ewe with its white lamb which it can hide from a May shower with its wool, to be paid once for all. Others say that however much is wanting from the vessel of milk, so much of the value of the milk shall be returned to him who owns the cow: if half the milk, half its value; if a third of the milk, a third of its value; and that is the best style.

If the cow is always bulling, thirty pence every year while she lives.

If there is contention about the milk, let her be

176 *The Law of Hywel Dda*

examined on the ninth day of May, and taken to a fit place where no beast has been before, and let him who owns her milk her, leaving nothing for the calf, and let it be put in the measuring vessel twice in the day. That is the quota, if it is full; and if it is not so, it is made up with oatmeal until St Curig's Day; from St Curig's Day to Michaelmas with barley meal; from Michaelmas to the Winter Kalends with rye meal. This is the measure of the vessel: three inches in width at the bottom, and six in the middle, and nine at the mouth; and nine inches in length diagonally. (If it happens that there is a dispute about a large thumb and a small one, it is right for the justice to resolve it with his thumb.)

If it happens that an in-calf cow is bought, and the calf is lost, he must give the oath of the herdsman and the woman who milked her that he did not cause the loss of her properties.

A male yearling has the same progress as a female yearling. As it is proper to raise her value until she takes the bull, so his value is raised until he is put under the yoke in February. And from then until the end of a year, two pence every season until the ninth day of February, and then he is raised by fourpence. And from then until he is working for the third time two pence come to him every season and then his legal value will be complete; and then he remains in his prime until he is working for the sixth time, and from then on he is appraised. And at his first working he is put to the plough on the ninth day of February, and if he ploughs until noon from the morning, let him who sells him be free; and if he does not plough against his yoke-fellow, thirty pence every year is the value of his properties. This is his yoke-fellow: one of the same age and the same size, to be put against him; and he is tested on the ninth day of February every year both on furrow and on sward; and if he ploughs on the one side, whether on furrow or on sward, and

The Value of Wild and Tame   177

does not plough on the other side, he pays fifteen pence every year while he lives.

A calf's tail is worth a penny for the first year; in the second year, twopence, in the third year threepence, in the fourth year fourpence: and so it remains.

Whosoever sells a yearling to another, it is proper for him to be liable for the three cattle diseases and in addition for scab until St Patrick's Day (he to whom they come is bound to keep them on pasture and in healthy houses where there has been no scab for seven years past) and for the staggers for three dewfalls.

> An ox is in his prime only from his second year of working to his ninth, and a cow only from her second calf to her sixth calf; and though they go on beyond that, their legal value is not reduced while they live.
>
> If the stock of a hamlet kill a steer, and it is not known which of them killed it, let the steer's owner bring a relic to the townland, and let them give an oath of ignorance, and then let them pay according to the number of steers; and if there is a polled steer the share of two steers falls on him. And that law is called 'Utter payment after utter swearing'. If it is admitted that a particular steer killed the other, let the owner pay.   *Cyfn.*

The value of an ox is three score pence; if it dies between St John's Day and the New Year, forty pence for the meat and hide, and twenty pence for the life. And of the forty pence for the meat and hide, eightpence for the hide and thirty-two pence for the meat; and of that, five-pence halfpenny for each quarter (that is, twenty-two pence), and for the head and the back and the feet and the bowels and everything inside it, tenpence. And so for every clean animal whose meat is eaten. After the hide is separated from the meat, the value of the mis-cellanea is as much as the value of two of its quarters, except for a pig because it has no hide.

When the pig's life is separated from the meat, then the value of its miscellanea is as much as the value of one of its flitches. *Dw.*

The value of a steer's tooth or the tooth of a dung horse is fourpence. *Cyfn.*

The value of a hamlet bull is another bull which can serve, with a cow before and a cow behind. *Cyfn.*

There are three animals whose properties are more than their legal value: a stallion, and a hamlet bull, and a herd boar: for the breed is lost if they are lost. *Cyfn.*

A legal herd of cattle is twenty-four cows. *Cyfn.*

Pigs

The value of a piglet from the night it is born until it goes grubbing, a penny. While it is sucking from then on, twopence. The length it is right for it to be sucking, three months; and from then on until the pigs go to the woods, it will be a pigling and its value is fourpence. And from St John's Day when the pigs go to the woods until the New Year its value is fifteen pence. From the New Year until St John's Day at the end of a year, fourpence added to it, and then thirty pence under the trees like its mother.

An autumn piglet has no legal value until the end of a year; at a year old it takes the value of a grown pig. *Cyfn.*

A wild pig is of the same value and the same increase as a domestic pig. *Cyfn.*

For as long as this it is right to preserve woods: from St John's Day when the pigs go under the trees until the fifteenth day after the New Year, and during that time there is a right to pannage if a person finds another person's pigs in his wood, even though he should find only three head. Others say ten head: the one is law, and the other

The Value of Wild and Tame

is custom, namely ten head; and the pigs are entitled to be in the woods during that time, after pannage has been levied for them. *Dw.*

On the fifth day before Michaelmas the King is entitled to forbid his woods, until the end of the fifteenth day after Epiphany; and of the pigs taken in the wood the King has the tenth head until the end of the ninth day, and from then on the King has his will about them. *Cyfn.*

The properties of a sow are that she is not always on heat and that she does not eat her piglets, and that she is guaranteed against quinsy for three nights and three days; and if she eats her piglets or is always on heat, one third of her value is repaid and the exchange remains as before. The value of her litter is as much as her own value, even though there should be only one piglet. The value of a boar is as much as the value of three pigs. If he is castrated and dies, his two testes are worth two pigs, with one on account of himself.

The value of a herd boar, another boar which can serve, with a sow before it and another behind it. *Cyfn.*

If pigs kill a person, let their owner pay his galanas or let him deny the pigs. *Cyfn.*

Sheep and Goats
For a lamb from the night it is born until the Winter Kalends, a penny; from the Winter Kalends until the end of a year, it is worth twopence; and then two pence more are added to it, so that there are four pence for it.

The properties of a sheep are that she should have milk and a lamb, and should be guaranteed against liver fluke until May Day, until she has three times had her fill of the new dock-leaves. For her properties, three pence or a dry sheep. For her milk twopence and for her lamb a penny. For her eye and her ear and her tail and her horn and her teat, for each of them a penny.

> A sheep's tooth and her eye are each worth a legal penny. *Cyfn.*

The ram is worth two sheep. If he is castrated and dies, he is worth three sheep, one for each of his testes, and one in respect of the body itself.

Goats have the same progress as that, except that a dry yearling has no properties save being dry; but a goat-heifer has, for her value is half that of a goat: one penny for her milk and a halfpenny for her kid.

> A goat's tooth and her eye are each worth a curt penny. *Cyfn.*

Cats

The value of a cat, fourpence. The value of a kitten from the night it is born until it opens its eyes, a legal penny; and from then until it kills mice, two legal pence; and after it kills mice, four legal pence, and at that it remains for ever. Her properties are to see and hear and kill mice, and that her claws are not broken, and to rear kittens; and if she is bought, and any of those is wanting, a third of her value is to be returned.

Every clean animal in the world, its properties are half its value. Every unclean animal, its properties are a third of its value, since its milk is useless.

> The value of a cat which guards a king's barn, if killed or stolen: her head is set down on a clean level floor, and her tail is raised up, and wheat grains are poured over her until they hide the end of her tail. That will be her value; if the grain is not obtained, a milking ewe with her lamb and her wool. *Bleg.*

The Value of Wild and Tame   181

Poultry
The value of a goose, a penny; the value of a gander, as much as the value of two geese. The value of a brood goose, as much as the value of her nest; this is what it is right that there should be in her nest, twenty-four chicks. This is the value of each chick: a halfpenny or a sheaf of barley; and that is its value until the female lays eggs and until the male treads; and after that it is worth a penny, and the brood goose is worth eight-pence at that time.

As for a hen, it is worth a penny; a cock is worth two hens. For every chick, a sheaf of oats or a farthing until it can fly; and after it can fly it is worth a halfpenny until it lays eggs or crows. And after it lays or crows, it is worth a penny.

Dogs
The King's staghound is worth a pound when skilled; six score pence when unskilled; sixty pence when a year old; thirty pence in its kennel; fifteen pence from when it is born until it opens its eyes. The King's greyhound, if it is skilled, six score pence; when unskilled, sixty pence; when a year old, thirty pence; in its kennel, fifteen pence; from when it is born until it opens its eyes, sevenpence halfpenny.

An uchelwr's staghound is of value as much as half the value of a king's staghound; an uchelwr's grey-hound is of value as much as half the value of a king's greyhound. A king's pet dog is worth a pound; an uchelwr's pet dog, a pound; a free man's pet dog, six score pence. An aillt's pet dog, fourpence, the same value as his dunghill cur: whatsoever dog an aillt has, it is of the same progress as his dunghill cur. A dunghill cur, to whomsoever it belongs, (even if it belongs to the King), its value is fourpence. A herd-dog, however, which guards the stock and goes before them in the morning and comes home behind them at

182   *The Law of Hywel Dda*

night, is worth the most important beast of the stock he guards.

One animal which goes from fourpence to a pound in one day is a staghound: if it belongs to a villein in the morning it is worth fourpence, and if it is given to the King that day it is worth a pound.   *Cyfn.*

He who puts out the eye of a king's staghound or cuts its tail, let him pay four legal pence for each cow of the dog's value.

A guard dog, if it is killed more than nine paces from the door, is not paid for. If it is killed within the nine paces, it is worth twenty-four pence.   *Cyfn.*

A scenting-hound has no legal value, since there was no such dog in Hywel Dda's age. Everything for which there is no legal value in writing has its value by sworn appraisal.   *Bleg.*

There is no dirwy or camlwrw for a dog though it be stolen. The oath of one person is enough to deny a dog, since it is a back-burden and an inedible beast. If a dog attacks any person to try to tear him, even though the person should kill the dog with a weapon in his hand, he does not pay either dirwy or camlwrw for him. If a dog bites any person until blood flows, let the dog's owner pay for the person's blood, but if the person torn, however, kills the dog without moving from there, he will get only sixteen pence. For a habituated.dog which tears a person three times, if the owner does not kill it, law is that it be tied to its owner's foot, two spans away from him, and so killed; and then let him pay three kine camlwrw to the King. The evil that a rabid dog does is not compensated, since there is no control over it. Though a dog be stolen, the law of theft is not applied for it.   *Cyfn.*

Hawks and Falcons

A falcon's nest is worth a pound. As a red chick the falcon is worth six score pence. After being mewed, when it is white, if it belongs to a king it is worth a pound. If it belongs to an uchelwr it is worth six score

The Value of Wild and Tame 183

pence if it is mewed and white. If it is a chick it is worth sixty pence. A tiercel, if it is a falcon, twenty-four pence. A sparrowhawk's nest is worth twenty-four pence. A sparrowhawk before going into mew, twelve pence; and after going, twenty-four pence.

Whether it be a sparrowhawk or a falcon or any bird in the world, if it belongs to a villein it is of the same value as a hen: it is worth a penny.

A goshawk's nest is worth six score pence. A goshawk before mewing and while it is in mew is worth three score pence; if it is white after mew, it is worth six score pence.   *Cyfn.*

The properties of every female bird are to lay and to brood; the properties of every male bird are to sing and to tread.

There will be neither dirwy nor camlwrw for any winged one, though it be stolen, but only payment of its legal value to its owner if it is not itself recovered.
                                                              Cyfn.

Bees

The lineage of bees is from Paradise, and it was because of man's sin that they came from there and that God gave them his grace; and therefore mass cannot be sung without the wax.   *Cyfn.*

The value of an old colony, twenty-four pence. The value of the first swarm, sixteen pence; the value of the bull-swarm, twelve pence. A swarm from the first swarm is worth twelve pence: a swarm from the bull-swarm is worth eight pence. If it happens that a swarm goes out after August, it is worth fourpence, and that is called a wing-swarm. So they are until the Winter Kalends; from the Winter Kalends on, they will be old colonies and are worth twenty-four pence. But a wing-swarm does not become an old colony until May Day, and then it does, and is worth twenty-four pence. The value of the queen bee, twenty-four pence.

184   *The Law of Hywel Dda*

Three free huntings are, a swarm of bees on a branch, and a fox, and an otter, since they have no habitation, as they are always on the move.

A beehive is worth two shillings. A clustered swarm in the woods, two shillings. If a clustered swarm is stolen, and the tree in which it is is cut, the value of the tree and the value of the clustered swarm are paid to the owner of the land.   *Bleg.*

Any swarm is worth only fourpence until it has been in flight and steady for three days: a day to seek a place to move, and the second to move, and the third to rest.

He who finds a swarm on a branch on another person's land shall have fourpence from the owner of the land if the latter wants the swarm.   *Cyfn.*

On the ninth day before August every swarm reaches the status of a queen-colony and is then worth twenty-four pence—except for a wing-swarm, since that does not take the status of a queen-colony until the following May Day, and then it is worth twenty-four pence like the others.   *Cyfn.*

Deer and Hunting

Of the value of a hart: from the Winter Kalends to St John's Day it is worth three score pence, with nine score pence camlwrw for it; and from St John's Day on until the Winter Kalends next following, twelve legal joints are added to it, and every one of these is worth sixty pence and is added to the stag. These are those joints: its two chaps, and its two pipes, and its tongue, and its breast, and its heart, and its liver, and its two loins, and its haunches, and its stomach, and its intestine, and its rectum. For each of those a camlwrw is due; this is the total of that: four kine short of two score.

Whosoever makes use of a king's champion-hart, let him pay three kine camlwrw to the King.   *Cyfn.*

There will be no status joints in a king's hart save from St Curig's Day to the Kalends of December, and

The Value of Wild and Tame 185

it will be a champion-hart only while the status joints are in it. *Cyfn.*

If a king's hart is killed and hidden, a dirwy shall be paid for it. If anyone knifes it without hiding it, there is a liability to camlwrw, but in the manner aforesaid. *Bleg.*

The King is free to hunt in every place in his country. *Bleg.*

If a free man has a staghound hunt, let him wait in the morning until the King's huntsmen have loosed their hounds three times, and then let him loose his. *Cyfn.*

If it happens that the King's hounds follow a hart and kill it on another person's land, whatsoever kind of person the land belongs to, let him take the King's hounds and his hart, and let him keep it until midday without skinning it, if it was killed in the morning; and if the huntsmen have not come by then, let him skin the hart and let him keep the hounds and the skin and feed the hounds and take them home. If it is killed at midday, let him leave it till after nones without skinning it; if after nones, let it be left till after vespers. If after vespers, let it be left till the morrow, and let a mantle be spread over it that night. If they do not come on the morrow, let him use the meat and feed the hounds, and let him keep the skin and the stomach for the huntsmen. If they come before the meat is used, let the land quarter be given to him and let them use the meat as they will; the hindquarter to every owner of the intestines and the forequarter to every owner of stomach. If it happens that hounds are loosed on a hart and it is killed, whosoever the hounds belong to, he to whom the land belongs is entitled to the hindquarter.

Whosoever kills a hart on another person's land, let him give a quarter to the owner of the land, unless it is a king's hart, since there is no land quarter in a king's hart. *Cyfn.*

Whosoever finds a clean beast lying dead on another's land, a quarter belongs to him, and the meat, save for that, to him to whom the land belongs. Whosoever finds an unclean beast lying dead on another's land, he shall have a penny, and the beast goes to him to whom the land belongs; and for wild animals that is not obtained. Whosoever finds a clustered swarm shall have a penny or the wax, and the swarm goes to him to whom the land belongs. Whosoever sets a snare on another's land without his leave, let him pay him four pence for opening the land and four pence for closing it, with what may be in the snare; and a camlwrw to the Lord.

If it happens that a person goes hunting and looses his hounds on an animal, then if idle hounds meet it and kill it, the animal will belong to the first hounds, which started it, unless the idle hounds belong to the King. It is not right for any animal to be accredited to the huntsman and the hounds which started it save while the huntsman is following it and has not turned his face towards home and has not abandoned the hunt; after that, if idle hounds kill the animal he is entitled to nothing.

If it happens that a wayfarer aims a blow at an animal from the road, whether with an arrow or with another thing, it is proper for him to pursue it until he takes it, but it is not proper for him to aim at it or pursue it unless he hits it from the road.   *Dw.*

If a wayfarer sees a beast in a king's forest from the road, let him aim a blow at it if he likes; and if he hits it, let him pursue it while he sees it, but from when it goes out of his sight let him leave it alone.   *Cyfn.*

If it happens that a person supposes that it is not free for a person generally to hunt the fish of the sea, there is a right to it while they are alive; and when they are dead and are cast up on land they

The Value of Wild and Tame   187

belong to the King, but if the King does not take
them for as long as three high tides and three
ebbs come by them, they will be casual acquisitions for him who finds them. The dead fish in the
sea all belong to the King.   *Dw.*

There are three free huntings for a villein:
snare, springe, gin.   *Dw.*

A roebuck is of the same value as a he-goat, and a
roe as a goat, and a fawn as a kid.

A stag is of the same value and the same increase as an
ox, and a hind as a cow. A roe is of the same value and
the same increase as a goat, and likewise a roebuck as
a he-goat.   *Cyfn.*

Other Animals

For a badger Hywel Dda's justices could not set a legal
value, for in a year when there was quinsy among the
pigs it would take the status of a dog, and in a year
when there was rabies among the dogs it would take
the status of a pig. For a hare no legal value was set,
since one month it will be male and another month
female.   *Cyfn.*

A wolf and a fox and various others which do nothing but harm have no legal value set on them: it is
free for everyone to kill them.   *Cyfn.*

The value of the King's tame hart is a pound. The
value of every tamed animal of a king or queen is a
pound. The value of every tamed animal of a breyr or
his wife or his daughter, six score pence. The value of
a villein's tamed animal, a curt penny.   *Bleg.*

No one is bound to pay for the act of a tamed
animal. This is a tamed animal, one which is
brought from being a wild beast to being tame,
such as a fawn or a fox or such a wild animal as
that.   *Dw.*

The value of a beaver, six score pence. The value of
a marten is twenty-four pence.   *Bleg.*

188   *The Law of Hywel Dda*

Skins

The skin of an ox, eightpence; the skin of a hart, eightpence; the skin of a cow, sevenpence; the skin of a hind, sevenpence; the skins of a sheep and a goat and a roebuck and a roe, a penny for each of them; the skin of a fox, eightpence; the skin of an otter, eightpence; the skin of a wolf, eightpence; the skin of a marten, twenty-four pence; the skin of a beaver, three score pence.

> The skin of an ermine is worth twelve pence.   *Cyfn.*

> Three beasts to whose value the King is entitled, wherever they are killed: a beaver and a marten and an ermine, since the ornamentations of the King's clothing are made from their skins.   *Cyfn.*

5. Trees

The value of an oak, six score pence. If it is twin-forked, sixty pence for each stem, if they are equally thick, and even though they are not, if they are of the same growth. The value of a cross-branch which reaches the heart of the tree, thirty pence; beyond that, it is a bough and has no legal value, except for a camlwrw to the King. For making a hole in it, twenty-four pence; and all that goes to the owners of the woodland, with a camlwrw to the King. A scrub oak which bears no fruit, fourpence. The value of a hazel grove, twenty-four pence; if one hazel is taken from the hazel grove, fourpence.

Every tree which bears fruit, except oaks and apple-trees, is of the same value as a hazel grove. A graft, fourpence until the next Winter Kalends after it is grafted; from then on it is increased by two pence each season until it bears fruit. After it bears fruit it is worth sixty pence; and therefore it is of the same progress as a cow's calf. A sour-apple tree, until fruit grows on it, is worth fourpence; after fruit grows on it, it is worth thirty pence.

Trees

189

A sweet-apple tree is worth three score pence. *Cyfn.*

Every apple-tree in the orchard has its legal value. *Dw.*

Every tree which is planted for shelter is worth twenty-four pence to its owner, whether he plants it in gardens or as shelter for his house. Every tree which does not bear fruit, except a yew, is worth fourpence —such as an ash or an alder or a willow. Every branch which reaches the heart of one of the minor trees we have mentioned above, is worth a penny. The value of the trees goes to the owners of the woodland. The value of a yew, thirty pence.

A holy yew is worth a pound. *Cyfn.*

A woodland yew is worth fifteen pence. A thorn-bush is worth sevenpence halfpenny. Every tree beyond that is worth fourpence, except a beech; that is worth six score pence.

He who fells an oak on the King's highway, let him pay three kine camlwrw to the King, and the value of the oak; and let him clear the road for the King; and when the King comes by, let him cover the stump of the tree with cloth of one colour. *Cyfn.*

If other trees are cut in a person's woodland without his leave, apart from the three timbers which are free to every builder on open land or those which have no legal value, a penny is paid to the owner of the woodland for the load of two oxen or the load of a horse, and a camlwrw to the Lord. If he denies it, the compurgation for theft falls on him, and that law applies to every man for his woodland. *Bleg.*

Every builder on open land is entitled to have three timbers from him to whom the woodland belongs, whether the woodlander will or no: a roof-tree and two roof-forks. *Cyfn.*

If a tree falls across a river and snares are set on the tree, the owner of the land on which the stump of the tree is is entitled to the windfall, no matter in what direction the river turns the top of the tree. *Cyfn.*

There is no right to dirwy or death sentence for a wild animal, or for a tree without labour done

190   *The Law of Hywel Dda*

on it; this is a tree without labour done on it: a
tree after its stock and its top are cut from it,
whether it be green or dry.   *Dw.*

And so ends the Test Book. Here Iorwerth ap Madog
ap Rhawd saw that it would be useful to write the
value of houses and equipment, and about joint
ploughing and corn damage, in association with the
Test Book.

6. Houses

First of them is, whosoever destroys the King's hall,
either by fire or by another thing, let him pay him
sixty pence for every fork which supports it (it is right
that there be six columns in it), and four score for its
roof, and six score for each of the minor houses in it.

An uchelwr's hall, twenty pence for every fork
which supports its roof (that is, six columns) and
sixty pence for its roof, with two score for each of the
minor houses.

An aillt's house, tenpence for every fork which
supports its roof (that is, four forks) and twenty pence
for its roof, and thirty pence for every one of the minor
houses. Those are these: his larder and his cowhouse
and his barn and his kiln and the sheepcote and the
pigsty and his summer house and his harvest house.

> The value of a winter house: the roof-tree is worth
> fifty pence and every fork which supports the roof-
> tree is worth thirty. The benches and the end-
> benches and the fireback-stones and the doors and
> the porches and the lintels and the thresholds and the
> side-posts: four legal pence is the value of every one of
> them. He who lays bare a winter house pays a third of
> its value.
>
> The value of a harvest house: it is worth twenty-
> four pence if there is an auger hole in it, and if there is
> not, it is worth twelve pence. A summer house is
> worth twelve pence. The fork of a summer house or a
> harvest house is worth two legal pence. A door-
> hurdle is worth two legal pence.   *Cyfn.*

Houses 191

Whosoever damages houses illegally, thus he makes compensation: fourpence for every big timber within it, and for every one of the doors fourpence; for the door-frames and the bars and for the beams and the threshold, fourpence for every one of them. For every pole and rod and rail, a penny; the weatherpoles and the rafters, a penny for every one of them. A binder, a penny; a thatch-spar, a penny; for each of them is a rod. For the roof of the house and its under-thatch, one third of the value of the house, and of that a third for the under-thatch.

> A king's barn is worth six score pence; a breyr's barn is worth three score. The barn of a king's villein is worth thirty. *Cyfn.*

> A king's piped kiln is worth half a pound if there is a house over it. A breyr's piped kiln, if there is a legal house over it, is worth three score pence. The piped kiln of a king's villein is worth thirty pence if there is a legal house over it. The piped kiln of a breyr's villein is worth twenty-four pence if there is a legal house over it. Every kiln which is not a piped kiln is half the others above according to the status of their owners. *Cyfn.*

7. Equipment

The King's brycan, six score pence; a pillow, twenty-four pence. A king's boiler, six score pence; a king's meat-fork, twenty-four pence. A king's crane, six score pence. A king's cauldron, sixty pence; its meat-fork, twelve pence. A king's harp, six score pence; its tuning-horn, twenty-four pence. The pencerdd's harp, six score pence; its tuning-horn, twenty-four pence. A king's throwboard, six score pence.

> The King's throwboard is worth six score pence, and that is shared thus: sixty pence for the white forces, and sixty pence for the king and his forces; and this is how that is shared: thirty

pence for the king and thirty pence for his forces, and that again is shared out for the separate men at three pence and three farthings for every man, and as much likewise for each of the white forces. This is the reason that thirty pence are set for the king, that he plays against eight men. And for an uchelwr's throwboard, half of that.   *Dw.*

The horn from which a king drinks, a pound; a starting-horn, a pound; a chief huntsman's horn, a pound: and it is right for all three of them to be of buffalo horn. Every precious thing of a king's, such as his cups and rings, its value is a pound, since it is not right for him to appraise on oath.

An uchelwr's brycan, sixty pence; an uchelwr's pillow, twenty-four pence. His cauldron, three score pence; its meat-fork, twelve pence. An uchelwr's harp, sixty pence; its tuning-horn, twelve pence. His throwboard, if it is of whalebone, sixty pence; if it is of hart's antler, twenty-four pence; if it is of steer's horn, twelve pence; if it is of wood, fourpence.

A vat made of boards, if it belongs to a king, twenty-four pence; if to an uchelwr, twelve pence; if to an aillt, sixpence. Every vat made of a single timber, fourpence.

A sack, fourpence; a winnowing sheet, fourpence. A churn, twopence; a cask, twopence. A jar, a penny. A trough, a penny, without augmentation: this is the reason, because it has no lid. A foot-trough, a penny; an iron pan, a penny. A wooden liquor-cup, fourpence. A yew pail, fourpence; a yew bucket, two-pence. A willow pail, twopence; a white pail, a penny; a willow bucket, a penny.

A broad axe, fourpence; a fuel axe, twopence; a small axe, a penny. A drill, twopence; a medium auger, a penny; a gimlet, a halfpenny. A reaping-hook, a penny; shears, a penny; an iron shovel, a penny; a hoe, twopence. A hedging-bill, a penny. An adze, a penny; a hook-knife, a penny; a drawknife, a

Equipment 193

halfpenny; a cropper, a halfpenny; an awl, a halfpenny; a plane, a penny; a saw, a halfpenny.

An iron lock, a penny; a wooden lock, a halfpenny.

A water cup, a farthing; a weeding-hook, an arrow, a turning-lathe, a spindle, a skein-winder, a twisting-frame, a flail, a scraper, a mallet, a spatula, a wooden shovel, a fork, a rake; a sheaf of oats, a hank of flax, a hen's chick; a cow spancel, a ruler, a guiding thong, a mirror, a butter-vessel, wooden tongs, a wooden fetter, a bowl: a farthing for each of these.

A chest, sworn appraisal; a brass vessel, a trivet, a griddle; a skiff and its appurtenances; a tun, a hammer; a scenting-hound; an earthen cruse; a steer after it has passed its prime; a barrel, a costrel; a breastplate, a cap of mail, a helmet, a crest, a gilt or silvered belt, a ring, a bracelet, a brooch; a throw-board board: all that we have said above, and everything which has no legal value, sworn appraisal.

A bag, twopence. A meat-dish, twopence. An other dish, a penny. A sieve, a penny; a riddle, a penny. A comb, a penny. A polishing stone, a halfpenny. A platter, a halfpenny; a baking sheet, a halfpenny.

A hair rope of twelve ells, twopence; an elm-bark rope of twelve ells, a penny.

The collar of a king's greyhound, eightpence. The collar of a goodman's greyhound, fourpence. The leash of a king's greyhound, fourpence. The leash of a goodman's greyhound, twopence. The leash of a tracker dog, eightpence.

A manure-shed, fourpence. A manuring basket, a penny. A barrow, a penny. A gauntlet, twenty-four pence. A handcuff, fourpence.

A sewin net, twenty-four pence; a grayling net, sixteen pence; a young-salmon net, eightpence; a drag-net, fourpence. A sewin, twopence.

A car, twopence; a pack-saddle, a penny; a stool, twopence; a wort-trough, a penny.

A weaving-woman's frame, twenty-four pence; the reeds and the plates, eightpence; the heddles,

194 The Law of Hywel Dda

eightpence; the harnesses, eightpence; the beams and the wheels and the treadles, eightpence.

A smith's implements, six score pence. A large anvil, sixty pence; a bicorne, twelve pence; bellows, eightpence; pincers, fourpence; a sledge-hammer, fourpence; a bender, fourpence; a nail-maker, fourpence; a furrower, fourpence; a vice, fourpence; a hoofrasp, fourpence; an iron file, fourpence. A grindstone, fourpence.

A quern-house, a legal pound; for every stone in it, sixty pence; for the ironwork, sixty pence; for the woodwork, thirty pence; for the house, thirty pence. A hand-quern, twenty-four pence; for each of its stones, twopence; for the furniture, a penny; for the quern-shed, fourpence.

A spear, fourpence; a bow and twelve arrows, fourpence; a battle-axe, twopence. A sword, if it is ground on the stone, twelve pence; if it is dark-blue-bladed, sixteen pence; if it is white-bladed, twenty-four pence.

> A sword which has gold or silver on its hilt is worth twenty-four pence; a sword without gold and without silver on it is worth twelve pence. *Cyfn.*

A shield, eightpence; if it has blue enamel or gold enamel, twenty-four pence.

> A shield whose wood is coloured is worth twelve pence. *Cyfn.*

A saddle, eightpence.

> A gold-enamelled saddle is worth twenty-four pence. A saddle whose wood is coloured is worth twelve pence. *Cyfn.*

A gilt bridle, eightpence; other bridles (of tin, and black-stained, and of brass), fourpence; a silvered bridle, sixpence. Gilt spurs, fourpence; silvered spurs, twopence; other spurs (of brass and tin and black-stained), one penny. Some reckon the two stirrups and the three girths as going with the saddle; others allow a legal value for them. That is this: a stirrup, if

Equipment 195

gilt, eightpence; if silvered, sixpence; if of tin or brass or black-stained, fourpence. A breast-girth has the same progress as a stirrup; the two girths, twopence. A horse-cloth, fourpence. A felt saddle-cloth, a penny; a linen saddle-cloth, two pence. A horse-brass, a penny.

Long hose, eightpence; a pair of hose, sixpence; a pair of kneeboots, fourpence. Felt boots, fourpence; thonged shoes, twopence; buskins, a penny. A belt, a penny.

A dirk, a penny; a larder knife, a penny; a dagger, twopence. A whetstone for the belt, a penny. A cresset, a penny. A breeches-belt, a penny. A thrave of mixed corn, eightpence; a thrave of oats, fourpence. Two fold-hurdles, a penny. An iron fetter, a penny. A distaff, a farthing. A corn-measure, a farthing. A sounding-horn, whoever it belongs to, twopence.

Some say of clothes that it is sworn appraisal which applies to them. Others say that it is this arrangement which applies to them, to wit: A dark-blue mantle, twenty-four pence; every town-made garment, twenty-four pence; every town-made cape, twenty-four pence; every home-made garment, eightpence. A shirt and breeches, twenty-four pence. A quilt, sworn appraisal; a blanket, eightpence; a sheet, eightpence. A headkerchief, eightpence; a neck-kerchief, four-pence; a headcloth, a penny. A king's robe, a pound; the Queen's robe, a pound. If it is an uchelwr's, six score pence; if it belongs to his wife, six score pence. An aillt's cloak, sixty pence; his wife's cloak, sixty pence. The cloak of a villein or his wife, thirty pence. A cushion, fourpence.

A day's ploughing in winter, twopence; a day's ploughing in spring, a penny. A plough-head, a penny; wheels, a penny; the stilts and beam, a penny. Every yoke and its yoke-bows, a penny; a yoke-bow, a farthing. A cleaning-stick, a penny; a goad, a penny; a harrow, a penny; a thorn-hurdle, a penny.

A ploughshare, two legal pence; a coulter is worth four legal pence.   *Bleg.*

Everything else in the world for which there is no legal value is subject to sworn appraisal.

8. The Human Body

This is about the value of the nine members of equal rank. Those are these: the two hands, and the two eyes, and the two lips, and the two feet, and the nose: the value of each of these separately is six kine and six score pence. The value of the ear if it is cut off, two kine and two score pence. If it closes so that it does not hear, six kine and six score pence. The value of the two testes is as much as the value of the nine members of equal rank. The value of the tongue is as much as the value of all those, since it defends them.

All the members of a person when reckoned together are worth eighty-eight pounds.   *Cyfn.*

The value of a toe, a cow and twenty pence; the value of the big toe, two kine and two score pence. The value of a finger, a cow and twenty pence; the value of the thumb, two kine and two score pence. The value of its nail, thirty pence. The value of the upper joint of the finger, twenty-six pence and a halfpenny and a third of a halfpenny. The value of the middle joint, thirty-three pence and two-thirds of a halfpenny. The value of the lower joint, eighty pence; and that is the value of the finger.

The value of every one of the teeth, a cow and twenty pence; the value of every one of the canine teeth, two kine and two score pence, for they are the herdsmen of the teeth.

A front tooth is worth twenty-four pence with three augmentations, and when a front tooth is paid for, the value of a conspicuous scar is paid with it. A back tooth is worth fifty pence.   *Cyfn.*

The Human Body

The value of the trunk itself is as much as all that; this is the trunk: the head, and the body, and the penis; since the life can be therein, therefore it is of the same value as all that.

Three kinds of blood which are not compensated: blood from teeth, and blood from the nose, and blood from a scab. Dirwy is paid to the Lord for them, and nothing is paid to him to whom they belong, since they are released blood; his sarhaed is, however, paid to him.

> Three stays of blood: blood as far as the cheek, and blood as far as the breast, and blood as far as the ground. For the third, if it is charged there is a right, for making the earth bloody by it; and for each of them there is a right if it is sued: what is right is a dirwy for each of them.   *Dw.*

The three dangerous wounds of a person: a blow to the head reaching the brain, and a blow to the body reaching the bowels, and breaking one of the four posts. For each of these he who is wounded shall have three pounds from him who wounds him. This is the measure of the medication: a pound without food, or nine score pence with his food, and his blood-clothes. Medication with tent, twenty-four pence; medication with red ointment, twelve pence; medication with herbs, fourpence. The physician's food daily is worth a penny; his light every night is worth a penny.

There are three conspicuous scars: one on a face and another on a hand and a third on a foot: thirty pence on the foot, sixty pence on the hand, six score pence on his face. Every hidden scar, fourpence. The skull, fourpence. Every broken bone, twenty pence, unless there is a dispute about its smallness; and if there is a dispute, let the physician take a brass bowl, and let him set his elbow on the ground with his hand above the bowl, and if its sound is heard, fourpence, and if it is not heard there is no right to anything.

198   *The Law of Hywel Dda*

> Law says that the members of every person are of the
> same value as every other's; that if the King's
> member is cut off, it is of the same value as the
> villein's member. Nevertheless the value of a king's
> or a breyr's sarhaed is greater than a villein's sarhaed
> if his member is cut off.   *Bleg.*

The value of hair uprooted, a penny for every finger
which grasps it to pull it out, and twopence for the
thumb.

> The value of a person's eyelid as far as the lashes are
> on it: every lash is worth a legal penny; if any of the
> lid is broken, the value of a conspicuous scar is paid
> there.   *Cyfn.*

The value of free blood, twenty-four pence. The
value of slave blood, sixteen pence. Every person's
sarhaed is paid to him according to his status.

> The value of a person's blood is twenty-four pence,
> since it is not worthy that the value of human blood
> should be as high as the value of God's blood. Though
> he was true man, he was true God and did not sin in
> his flesh.   *Cyfn.*

> If it happens that a person gives another a box on
> the ear and does not deny it, let him pay his
> sarhaed according to his status, and twenty-four
> pence for the box.   *Dw.*

> A blow received from inadvertence is not sarhaed;
> it is proper, however, to compensate for the damage,
> to wit blood and wound and conspicuous scar, if any.
>   *Cyfn.*

9. Joint Ploughing

Whosoever wishes to make a joint-ploughing
contract, it is proper for him to undertake to remain
with it, and that his hand should meet the other; and
after they have done that, to keep it until the loop is
finished. The loop is twelve acres. This is the
measure of the acre: three barleycorn lengths in the
inch; three inches in the palmbreadth; three palm-

Joint Ploughing

breadths in the foot. Four feet in the short yoke; eight feet in the mid-yoke; twelve feet in the armpit yoke; sixteen feet in the long yoke. And a rod as long as the latter in the caller's hand, the caller being in front of the oxen with the peg of the long yoke in his hand: as far as he can reach with the length of his arm and his rod on either side of him are the two limits of the land; and that is the width of the acre, and thirty times the rod is its length.

The first acre for the ploughman; the second for the irons; the third for the prime furrow-ox and the fourth for the prime sward-ox, so that the yoke is not broken; and the fifth for the caller. And so it proceeds from best to next best, except that the yoke is not broken between them, to the last; and after that the acre for the woodwork; that is called *cyfair casnad* and comes once a year.

> No one in a villein townland is entitled to plough until everyone in the townland has found a joint-ploughing. *Cyfn.*

If it happens that they want to separate after the loop ends, they can separate if they want to, unless there is a contract which binds them.

If it happens that collars are closed on oxen, and one of the oxen dies (no matter what cause takes it), it is proper for it to have its acre. If its owner is suspected of having caused harm to the ox, let him be put to the relics that the harm did not come to it from him either by its food or by its attendance. And that one is called 'the black ox's acre'.

Though a joint-ploughing contract be made for an ox, if it does not come to the work, to have the collar closed on it, so that it does not plough either a turn or two, it is not entitled to have anything. If it happens that an ox is sick, whether by a wound or by something else, it is proper for the owner to support the end of the yoke.

The Law of Hywel Dda

If it happens that a person wants to sell an ox from the joint-ploughing into which it has been contracted, he is not entitled to sell it until the joint-ploughing expires, nor to traffic it. And if he does so, though it be one day before having his acre, he loses his acre; or, if it is after having his acre, he is to support the end of the yoke.

It is for everyone to bring his contribution to plough, whether he has an ox or irons or other things. After everything has come to them, it is for the ploughman and the caller to keep everything fault-less, and to do as well for them as for their own. It is right for the caller to close the oxen in so that it is not too confined for them, and to call them so that they do not break their heart. And if any ill comes to them during that period, it is for him to pay for them, or his oath that nothing came to them from his wrongdoing. It is not right for the ploughman to cast at the oxen, lest they be hurt; and if he hurts them let him pay or deny. It is right for the ploughman to help the caller to yoke the oxen; and it is not right for him to loose any save the two short-yoked oxen. After the joint-ploughing finishes, it is for everyone to fetch his contribution home to himself. A cleanser and a harrowing-horse do not belong to joint-ploughing. No one is entitled to lay an extra burden on another's ox unless by contract or free will.

If it happens that there is a dispute about bad ploughing, let the ploughman's acre be inspected, with the depth of its tilth and its length and breadth, and according to that one be it done as well for every-one as for every other. If it happens that there is a dispute between two joint-ploughing partners about wild rough land and other, cultivated, land and the one wants the rough land ploughed and the other does not want it; unless a contract term withholds it from him, it is proper for him to plough for the other the land which he has. If it happens that there is a dispute about ploughing afar off and other ploughing near at

Joint Ploughing 201

hand, between two joint-ploughing partners: the law says that they are not bound to go to a place so that the oxen cannot reach their tying-posts and their team when weak as when strong, within the commote.

Oxen which are in a joint-ploughing cannot be bequeathed without the consent of the partners, since no one is entitled to bequeath anything save what he controls, and he does not control that. For oxen which are in joint-ploughing there is no right either to gage them or to distrain on them, since no one is entitled to gage anything save what is under his control, and those are not so.

Whosoever makes a joint-ploughing contract, and after that contracts for joint-ploughing with another, the law says that it is right that those oxen be in the first joint-ploughing; and though he should make a hundred joint-ploughing contracts after that, he is bound to support the end of the yoke everywhere he has made a contract. Whosoever makes a joint-ploughing contract, and does not come readily to plough, whether it be one day or two that he fails to come, the law says that, whether he comes of his own will or under compulsion, he is not entitled to anything of what is ploughed without him.

There is no right to put either horses or mares or cows to the plough, and if they are put, though mares and cows abort there will be no compensation, and though horses be hurt, there will be no compensation; and moreover the law does not say that they are entitled to a single acre unless it is contracted for.

If it happens that a person puts an ox into joint-ploughing and the ox is stolen, the law says that he is not bound to support the end of the yoke and that he is not entitled to have the acre. If it happens that a person puts an ox into joint-ploughing and that the person prefers to put another in its place, the law says that he is not entitled to move it without the leave of the partners. There is no right to move oxen which are put into joint-ploughing on the furrow to the sward, without the leave of their owner.

It is not right for anyone to take on ploughmanship who does not know how to make the plough and to set the irons, for it is right for him to make the plough from the first nail to the last. Whomsoever the irons belong to, let him put them in order without hindrance to the ploughmen, and they are not bound to help. It is right for the caller to provide the yoke-bows and draught-ropes of withes, and if it is a long team, the little rings and the pegs of the bows.

> Whosoever breaks a joint-ploughing contract which he makes voluntarily, let him pay three kine camlwrw to the King, and all the ploughing to the partners. *Cyfn.*

10. Corn Damage

It is right for every owner of corn to keep his corn, and every owner of stock to keep his stock, within and without; and therefore it is proper for everyone to take animals on his corn. This is how it is proper to hold them: on winter tilth, for money payment until St Bride's Day, and from then on for compensation for damage; on spring tilth, from St Bride's Day until May Day for money payment, and from May Day for compensation for damage.

At all times, in order to release stock from pound, there is no right save to money. This is how there is a right: a penny for a horse, and a halfpenny for a steer.

> For every folded steer, a halfpenny by day and a penny by night. For every horse which has a fetter or hobble on it, a penny by day and twopence by night; if it is unrestricted, a halfpenny by day and a penny by night. If the taker unhobbles it when he takes it on the corn, let him pay three kine camlwrw to the King; let him however put both loops on the same foot and he will lose nothing. *Cyfn.*

Corn Damage

A colt or a filly from the fourteenth day after it is born, a penny for it as for its dam. A calf from when it is born until the Winter Kalends, to be confined until the same time next day. Lambs and kids, to be confined until the same time next day, while they are sucking; or to be mixed with their dams. This is how long it is right for them to be sucking: until May Day; and from then on they are of the same status on corn as their dams. For pigs and sheep and goats and geese and hens there is a right to the second choice from them. Small piglets, from when they can turn a piece of dung over with their snouts, are of the same status on corn as their dams.

In the law there used to be a right to a pig from the pigs; or from the small livestock we have named above, though there might be only three head of them, there was a right to one. This was the reason for that: he to whom they belonged would get pigs, and a pig would remain with the owner of the corn. There was no right to take a pig from two, since the pigs' owner would not get pigs if one of them remained behind. From that it was changed to one out of fifteen head of pigs; and from thirty head of sheep, a sheep; and from goats and geese and hens, one out of every thirty likewise. If it happens that pigs to that number are not taken on the corn, according to some of the justices, fourpence is paid for five head of pigs; others say that a penny is due for every one of them; and for every five head of goats and sheep, a penny.

> From the legal herd of pigs let him take the pig he likes, except for the three special beasts, and keep it until the same time next day; and then let him offer it to its owner; and if he does not redeem it for its legal value, let the taker make his own use of it. This is the legal herd of pigs: twelve head and a boar. *Cyfn.*

For geese then and for hens, if so many as to give a right to one of them are not taken on the corn, an egg from every one of them. There is no right to take hens on corn save in the fortnight after it is sown, before it

204   The Law of Hywel Dda

sprouts; and from then until there is grain in the corn
there is no right to take them.

> He who finds geese in his corn, let him cut a stick as
> long as from his elbow to the tip of his little finger and
> as thick as he likes, and let him kill the geese in the
> corn with the stick; and for what he kills outside the
> corn let him pay. As for geese which are found damag-
> ing corn in a rickyard or in a barn, let a withe be
> twisted round their necks and let them be left there
> until they die.   *Cyfn.*

As for all fodder with which a person provisions
himself, let everyone keep his fodder, and let the livestock be free. This is fodder: corn after it is moved
from the land where it grows, and an orchard, and
cabbages, and flax after being reaped (or in a garden
unreaped), and dry hay, and the thatch of houses and
their under-thatch, and leeks, and everything which
is pertinent to a garden. Let him make a fence round
his garden, so strong that stock cannot break it; and if
he does not, though it should be broken he will not be
compensated, except for hens and geese; this is the
reason: since they cannot be kept out, for they can fly.

> He who finds a hen in his flax-garden, or in his barn,
> let him hold her until her owner redeems her by a
> hen's egg; and if he takes the cock, let him cut one of
> his claws and set him free, or let him take a hen's egg
> for every hen in the house. To him who takes a cat
> mousing in his flax-garden, let the owner pay for the
> damage.   *Cyfn.*

It is right for barns to be open from when the first
sheaf goes into them, to let the wind into them, until
the Winter Kalends, and if they are damaged during
that time, compensation and payment are made for
them to the owner. From the Winter Kalends on, let
the barns be closed as is right. This is how it is right:
so strongly that there are three wattling-rods on the
coping, and a board on the doorway, with three bonds
on the board (two behind and one in front). And if that
is broken, let both the barn and the corn be compen-

Corn Damage

sated for. This is how compensation is made: a sound sheaf instead of a damaged one.

If it happens that a person finds livestock on his corn and there is a dispute whether they were found, let it be left to the oath of the taker.

> If a person takes livestock on his corn and there is an argument between the taker and the owner, it is right for the taker to swear to finding the foremost and the hindmost on the corn. *Cyfn.*

If it happens that corn is damaged and that the livestock are not overtaken on the corn, let it be for the owner's oath to clear them, since there can be no testimony against an animal; though everyone says that they were seen, it is of no effect. There is no right to a fore-oath about corn, since it is of no effect even if it is allowed, if the owner of the animal denies it.

> If corn is damaged for any person beside a hamlet, and no single beast can be taken on it, let him take the relic and come to the townland, and if they swear an oath of ignorance, let them pay for the corn according to number of head of steers; and that law is called 'It is paid after a befouled oath'. *Cyfn.*

If it happens that a horse is found damaging corn at the reach of its neck over a hedge, it is not proper to take it, but only to compensate the damage, if it is not cleared. If it happens that a horse or other animal is found with its two forefeet on the corn, there is no right to take it, since it was not completely on the corn, and the complete cannot be made from the incomplete; and if the owner does not clear it, compensation for damage. If it happens that a person tethers a mare beside corn, and the foal damages the corn and cannot be caught, let the mare be taken from where she is and taken into the house; and let the foal be held in the house and the mare put back in her place as before: and that is the wild one which the tame one catches, and this does not return against him as illegality.

The Law of Hywel Dda

If it happens that a person chases livestock from his corn and in that chase they break their necks or are hurt, he is not bound to pay for them if he chased them legally. This is how he is entitled to chase them: while they are on his own land and his corn. If he has dogs with him and the dogs kill the stock, it is right for him to pay for the act of his animal. If it happens that he chases and that the neighbours' dogs come to him to the chase, and those dogs kill the stock, it is proper for everyone to keep his animal from doing wrong, and therefore let each of them pay for his own dogs; and if he chases them beyond his own boundary, let him pay a camlwrw, and the livestock to the owner.   *Dw.*

The taker need not release calves and lambs and kids (except of his own free will) until the same time next day, since no beast will die from being confined until the same time next day. There is no right to take bulls from Midsummer to August, whether on corn or on grass, since in that period the mature cows are bulling; nor from August until the first feast of St Mary, since the heifers are then bulling. It is not proper to take at any time a bull following a bulling cow. It is not proper to take at any time a boar following a sow. There is no right to take rams and he-goats from Michaelmas to the Winter Kalends. There is no right to take stallions from the middle of April to the middle of June. There is no right to take a darting colt following its dam. There is no right to take pigs on corn (unless they are found in a barn or on a meadow) from St John's Day until the New Year.

Whosoever wants a meadow, let him keep it from St Patrick's Day until the Winter Kalends. This is a meadow: land without use save for hay, with a bank round it. This is why it is kept until the Winter Kalends: because it is right to mow it twice in the year. Whosoever finds livestock on a meadow of that

Corn Damage 207

kind, let him take them from it as from corn. If it
happens that he finds them on it, and does not overtake them on it, though it be admitted there is no
right to compensation for damage to grass.

> Meadows are forbidden to pigs because they damage
> the land. He who finds pigs on his meadow or on his
> corn before it is ripe, let him take four legal pence
> from the owner of the pigs. If they damage ripe corn,
> let their damage be paid for. *Cyfn.*

Whosoever makes a fence round his corn, let him
take animals on the grass which is within it as on the
corn, since there is no right to pasture there. No one
except a Lord is entitled to enclose more than two
plots of grass for himself, namely a paddock and a
meadow; and if he wants to enclose other grass let
him take a cross from the Lord, and that will keep it.

Thus it is right to hold livestock: wild ones in a fold
out-of-doors, and tame ones confined indoors or out-
of-doors as desired. And if there be two persons'
stock, let them not be mixed; and if there be different
kinds, let them not be mixed; and if they are put
together, let all of them be tied. Pigs it is not proper to
tie, but to confine. Hens and geese it is proper to tie
when they are held.

> If a person takes livestock unfamiliar to each other on
> his corn or on his hay, and they fight in their confine-
> ment and a beast kills another, it is for the owner of
> the livestock to pay for the beast which is killed, and
> the taker will be free. *Cyfn.*

If it happens that a person calls for a gage for his
corn damage, with a date for the gage to fall forfeit, no
one is bound to give it save with the date for a gage for
corn; and a gage for corn does not fall forfeit until the
Winter Kalends. Whosoever is entitled to corn
(whether by contract, or for damage by livestock at
harvest, or by having bought it) and does not claim it
until the Winter Kalends, he is not entitled to it there-

208 The Law of Hywel Dda

after. This is the reason that he is not entitled to it: because it has become a season when it is not proper to claim it, since it is not proper to claim the corn of one year in the other.

Whosoever takes livestock, and when he has taken them they cause harm: whatsoever harm they cause the taker is bound to pay for, since it is right for the stock to return home without claim and without surclaim upon them, save for paying the taker his loss. Whatsoever person takes livestock, though he lets them out to graze he does not lose his status by reason of doing better than he was bound to. Whosoever takes livestock, if they break out for home, nothing is due for them, since there is no right to two takings for one damage. Whosoever takes livestock and refuses a legal gage in order to insist on money, if the stock die he shall pay for them. Whosoever takes many livestock, and keeps one of them, thinking that he is entitled to it in respect of the act of them all, and releases the rest to go away, he is entitled only to what comes in respect of that one beast. Whosoever takes small livestock, whether a goat or a sheep or a pig, let the taker choose either to count until the beast itself comes, or to have a penny for a sheep or a goat when it has been taken five times; and a penny for a pig when it is caught, or to await the count until the beast comes in full.

Whosoever comes to release livestock for others, it is proper for the taker to ask him whether he will stand on their behalf in all things; and if he will not, he is not bound to release them to him, and though the stock die with him so, they will not be paid for. If he will stand in all things, let a gage be taken from him, with a surety for its validity, and if it happens that an owner comes to invalidate the gage, he is entitled to have from what is that owner's something as good as it in its place, before that other leaves him. The gage which the wife gages the husband is not

Corn Damage — 209

entitled to invalidate, nor likewise the wife for the husband's gage.

Whosoever has great damage done to his corn and finds livestock on it and wants compensation from those stock for the whole damage, he is not entitled save to be paid according to the oath of the stock's owner for what they damaged, whether it be much or little; and it is right for the two pieces of land to be of the same kind and their tilth of the same age; and that is called compensation for damage. Thus it is right to ask for it: before the Winter Kalends.

Whosoever moves his corn from the stubble to the grassland and makes his stack on the grassland, though it be damaged there it will not be compensated. Flax which is outside gardens is under the same law as corn.

There is no single person who by status is entitled not to compensate for damage. No one is entitled to milk milch stock or to make any use of them while they are held, without the leave of the taker, even though they are his. The taker is not bound to seek out the owner of the livestock, and he is not entitled to conceal them; and if he conceals them, let him pay if they die or if they get lost by his default.

> He who gets full compensation for his damaged corn from the owner of livestock is not entitled either to payment or to take livestock on that straw after that.
> *Cyfn.*

And so ends concerning Corn Damage.

210 *The Law of Hywel Dda*

How to use the Source References

The references in the Table of Source References are not in the same form as those at the end of the indented passages in the translation, because their purpose is different. The reference in the translation tells the reader at a glance what kind of text/source the passage comes from: a *Ior* manuscript, but not the main text (*B,C,E,G*); the *Colan* 'revised edition' of the Iorwerth Redaction (*Col*); the 'Book of Case Law' (*Dw*); the Blegywryd Redaction (*Bleg*); the Cyfnerth Redaction (*Cyfn*); or material found in the 'tail' of a later manuscript (*J, S*).

The reference in the Table leads to the original Welsh form of the passage translated. With one exception, the references are all to the latest printed edition of the source. This means that *Cyfn* and *B,C,E,* and *G* do not appear in the Table: for *Cyfn* the references are to WML, and for the four *Ior* manuscripts to AL. The three references to *S* in the text are a special case: for one, the source is a transcript in an unpublished thesis; for another, the printed edition (LHDd) of another manuscript which has the same passage, and for the third, AL.

SOURCE REFERENCES

The main text (Ior) is that of *Llyfr Iorwerth* (ed. A. R. Wiliam; Cardiff, 1960); references are to the numbered sections, and (where necessary) to the unnumbered sentences within sections. The other sources are:

AL   *Ancient Laws and Institutes of Wales* (ed. A. Owen, 1841); most references are to Book, chapter, and section (and where necessary to unnumbered sentences within sections) of the second volume (the second part of the single-volume folio edition), but AL i.216 refers to a page of volume 1. See also VC.

Bleg   *Cyfreithiau Hywel Dda yn ôl Llyfr Blegywryd* (ed. S. J. Williams and J. E. Powell; Cardiff, 1942, 1961); references are to page and line.

Col   *Llyfr Colan* (ed. D. Jenkins; Cardiff, 1963); references are to numbered sentences.

Dw   *Damweiniau Colan* (ed. D. Jenkins; Aberystwyth, 1973); references are to numbered sentences.

J   *Cyfreithiau Hywel Dda o Lawysgrif Coleg yr Iesu, Rhydychen LVII* (ed. M. Richards, Cardiff, 1957); references are to page and line.

LHDd   *The Laws of Howel Dda* (Llanstephan MS. 116; ed. T. Lewis; London, 1912): references are to page and line.

S   Christine James, 'Golygiad o BL Add 22356 o Gyfraith Hywel . . .', unpublished Ph.D. thesis, University of Wales, 1984; the reference is to a numbered sentence.

VC   'Venedotian Code' in AL (see above), vol.1; references are to Book, chapter, and section.

WML   *Welsh Medieval Law* (ed. A. W. Wade-Evans; Oxford, 1909): references are to page and line.

212 The Law of Hywel Dda

1.1-27	Ior 1	30.12-24	Ior 26
5.1-16	Ior 2	30.25-31.2	Ior 27
5.17-6.2	Ior 3/1-5	31.3-14	Ior 28
6.3-7	WML 3.7-11,	31.15-28	Ior 29
	Bleg 4.1-5	31.29-32.3	Ior 30
6.8-18	Ior 3/6-8	32.4-29	Ior 31
6.19-7.25	Ior 4	32.30-33.7	Ior 32/1-4
7.26-8.10	Ior 5	33.8-9	WML 26.20-22
8.11-28	Bleg 6.1-15	33.10-11	Ior 32/5
8.29-10.14	Ior 6/1-22	33.12-31	Ior 33/1-12
10.15-27	Dw 192-4	33.32-3	WML 33.4-5
10.28-11.24	Ior 6/23-30	33.34-7	WML 33.7-10
11.25-12.4	Ior 7/1-9	34.1-5	Ior 33/13-15
12.5-10	Bleg 13.15-20	34.6-35.13	Ior 34
12.11-23	Ior 7/10-14	35.14-24	Ior 35/1-4
12.24-13.39	Ior 8/1-21	35.25-6	WML 32.7-8
14.1-4	WML 14.1-5	35.27-36.13	Ior 35/5-14
14.5-25	Ior 8/22-4	36.14-17	Ior 36/1
14.26-15.18	Ior 9/1-12	36.18-19	WML 32.19-20
15.19-28	WML 17.14-23	36.20-33	Ior 36/2-6
15.29-33	WML 18.15-19	36.34-37.15	Ior 37
15.34-16.6	Ior 9/13-19	37.16-29	Ior 38
16.7-9	WML 18.4-6	37.30-38.14	Ior 39
16.10-12	WML 18.21-3	38.15-23	Ior 40/1-4
16.13-38	Ior 10/1-9	38.24-7	WML 22.19-22
17.1-2	WML 15.15-16	38.28-9	Ior 40/5
17.3-6	Ior 10/10,11	38.30-33	Dw 77
17.7-9	WML 15.23-5	38.34-6	Ior 40/6
17.10-32	Ior 10/12-21	39.1-5	WML 33.16-
17.33-6	WML 17.10-13		20
18.1-19.9	Ior 11	39.6-7	Ior 40/7
19.10-30	Ior 12/1-9	39.8-13	WML 33.20-25
19.31-2	WML 22.13-15	39.14-17	Ior 40/8-10
19.33-5	Ior 12/10	39.18-24	Ior 41
20.1-32	Ior 13	39.25-40.34	Ior 42
20.33-21.20	Ior 14	40.35-41.30	Ior 43
21.21-35	Ior 15/1-6	41.31-4	WML 36.21-4
21.36-8	WML 20.10-12	45.1-46.21	Ior 44
22.1-23.18	Ior 15/7-23	46.22-47.9	Ior 45
23.19-24.2	Ior 16	47.10-13	Ior 46/1,2
24.3-21	Ior 17/1-5	47.14-30	Dw 471
24.22	WML 25.14-15	47.31-48.18	Ior 46/3-11
24.23-25.5	Ior 17/6-14	48.19-24	Col 22
25.6-29	Ior 18	48.25-9	Bleg 61.10-13
25.30-26.24	Ior 19	48.30-35	Bleg 67.1-5
26.25-27.12	Ior 20	48.36-49.4	Ior 47/1
27.13-38	Ior 21	49.5-10	Bleg 63.10-14
28.1-29	Ior 22	49.11-31	Ior 47/2-5
28.30-29.10	Ior 23	49.32-50.32	Ior 48
29.11-30	Ior 24	50.33-5	WML 89.18-20
29.31-30.11	Ior 25	50.36-51.22	Ior 49

Source References   213

51.23-52.2	Ior 50/1-4	70.5-8	Dw 363
52.3-4	Bleg 63.31-2	70.9-14	Dw 324
52.5-10	WML 95.20-96.5	70.15-20	Ior 62/14
		70.21-8	Ior 63/1,2
52.11-19	WML 97.12-21	70.29-38	Bleg 41.16-25
52.19-21	WML 315.19-20	71.1-5	Ior 63/3
52.22-35	Col 63-6	71.6-72.26	Ior 64
52.36-53.5	Dw 411	72.27-73.29	Ior 65
53.6-8	Bleg 61.20-22	73.30-32	Dw 407
53.9-27	Ior 51/1-4	73.33-75.18	Dw 462-8
53.28-32	Col 24	75.19-76.6	Ior 66/1-7
53.33-7	Col 67	76.7-16	Dw 117,118
54.1-2	Ior 51/5	76.17-37	Ior 66/8-16
54.3-8	Dw 183	77.1-9	Ior 67/1-3
54.9-20	Ior 51/6-9	77.10-28	Dw 485
54.21-3	Dw 177/3	77.29-78.4	Ior 67/4
54.24-8	Ior 51/9	78.5-38	Ior 68
54.29-34	WML 95.14-19	79.1-2	Dw 387
54.35-55.15	Ior 51/10,11	79.3-80.10	Ior 69
55.16-23	Col 17-19	80.11	WML 89.13
55.24-56.4	Dw 124-7	80.12-29	Dw 437.438
56.5-18	Dw 314-17	80.30-33	LHDd 63.29-31
56.19-36	Dw 424,425		
56.37-57.29	Ior 52	80.34-81.17	Ior 70
57.30-58.37	Ior 53	81.18-20	Col 146
59.1-33	Ior 54	81.21-6	Bleg 41.26-31
59.34-61.9	Ior 55/1-15	81.27-82.32	Ior 71/1-11
61.10-16	Col 42-5	82.33-83.10	Dw 199-201
61.17	Ior 55/16	83.11-21	Ior 71/12,13
61.18-20	Ior 56/1,2	83.22-84.25	Ior 72
61.21-2	Bleg 37.29-30	84.26-85.9	Ior 73/1-6
61.23-62.15	Ior 56/2-7	85.10-16	Ior 73/11
62.16-21	WML 41.8-13	85.17-26	Ior 73/7-10
62.22-31	Ior 56/8,9	85.27-86.6	Ior 74/1-11
62.32-6	WML 41.19-23	86.7-9	Col 459
63.1-30	Ior 57	86.10-12	Ior 74/12,13
63.31-64.13	Ior 58	86.12-27	Ior 75/1-3
64.14-38	Ior 59	86.28-87.2	AL VII.i.10/4,5
64.38-65.26	Ior 60	87.3-14	Ior 75/4-6
65.27-31	WML 85.7-11	87.15-88.20	Ior 76/1-14
65.32-9	Dw 321,322	88.21-36	Dw 484
66.1-16	Ior 61/1-4	88.37-89.3	Ior 76/15,16
66.17-21	Bleg 39.25-9	89.4-91.25	Ior 77
66.22-32	Ior 61/5	91.25-92.28	Ior 78
66.33-67.28	Dw 402-5	92.29-93.38	Ior 79/1-12
67.29-35	Ior 61/6,7	94.1-25	Col 528-31
67.36-68.4	Col 89,90	94.26-34	Ior 79/13-16
68.5-16	Dw 325	94.35-95.17	Ior 80/1-6
68.17-21	Ior 61/8	95.18-19	AL VII.i.13
68.22-69.34	Ior 62/1-13	95.20-27	Ior 80/7
69.35-70.4	Dw 344	95.28-30	Col 544

214 The Law of Hywel Dda

95.31-4	Ior 81/1-3
95.35-96.2	Bleg 37.26-8
96.3-97.6	Ior 81/4-12
97.7-12	Col 558
97.13-21	Dw 291
97.22-7	Dw 373
97.28-31	Ior 81/13,14
97.32-98.7	Dw 369
98.8-31	Dw 339-42
98.32-4	Ior 81/15
98.35-99.22	Ior 82/1-7
99.23-31	WML 50.5-13
99.32-100.4	Ior 82/8-10
100.5-13	Ior 83/1-3
100.14-17	Dw 216
100.18-19	Ior 83/3
100.20-22	Col 592
100.23-30	Dw 305, 306
100.31-101.16	Ior 83/4-10
101.17-102.5	Ior 84
102.6-103.18	AL VII.i.26/3, 4;27
103.19-104.8	AL VII.i.29
104.9-105.4	Ior 85
105.5-107.6	AL VII.i.22,23
107.7-13	Ior 86/1,2
107.14-20	Bleg 75.19-25
107.21-108.20	Ior 86/3-11
108.21-110.3	AL VII.i.24,25
110.4-6	WML 51.13-15
110.7-23	Ior 87/1-4
110.24-6	Dw 410
110.27-111.14	Ior 87/5-11
111.15-18	Col 613,614
111.19-36	Dw 495-8
111.37-112.5	WML 50.23-51.3
112.6-10	AL XI.v.48
112.11-12	Col 576
112.13-16	WML 51.11-13
112.17-22	Ior 88/1
112.23-6	WML 114.11-13
112.27-39	Dw 357
113.1-8	Ior 88/2,3
113.9-12	WML 53.2-6
113.13-16	Bleg 78.8-10
113.17-21	Ior 88/4,5
113.22-3	S 2334
113.24	Ior 88/5
113.25-8	WML 62.12-15

113.29-31	Ior 88/5
113.32-4	WML 62.4-6
113.35-114.10	Ior 88/5-9
114.11-24	Ior 89/1-3
114.25-115.8	Dw 476,477
115.9-15	J 91.4-8
115.16-116.13	Dw 478-82
116.14-25	Ior 89/4-7
116.26-34	Dw 274
116.35-117.3	Dw 292
117.4-9	Dw 275
117.10-12	Dw 382
117.13-18	Dw 370
117.19-24	Dw 337,338
117.25-35	Dw 355,356
118.1-4	Dw 328
118.5-9	WML 111.20-112.2
118.10-16	Dw 235
118.17-29	Dw 428,429
118.30-35	Dw 453
118.36-119.21	Dw 458-60
119.22-38	Dw 158-61
120.1-122.5	Ior 90
122.6-26	Ior 91/1-5
122.27-123.2	WML 28.14-29.1
123.3-14	WML 29.5-16
123.15-24	Ior 91/6-8
123.25-9	WML 100.6-11
123.30-31	Ior 91/9
123.32-124.10	Ior 92
124.11-36	Ior 93/1-6
125.1-3	WML 99.2-4
125.4-10	Ior 93/7,8
125.11-126.16	Ior 94
126.17-28	Ior 95/1,2
126.9-127.11	Dw 473-5
127.12-16	Ior 95/3
127.17-20	Dw 140,141
127.21-9	Dw 454,455
127.30-37	Dw 499
128.1-5	Ior 95/4
128.6-129.16	Ior 96
129.17-23	Dw 213,214
129.24-7	WML 56.10-13
129.28-130.23	Ior 97
130.24-34	Ior 98/1
130.35-131.3	WML 293.19-23
131.4-32	Ior 98/2-9

Source References

131.33-132.21	Ior 99	152.24-8	Dw 309
132.22-133.28	Ior 100	152.29-34	Dw 313
133.28-134.14	Ior 101	153.1-10	Dw 130
134.15-24	Ior 102/1-6	153.11-28	Dw 169-72
134.25-135.5	Dw 149-51	153.29-33	Dw 246
135.6-16	Ior 102/7-10	153.34-154.4	Col 304,305
135.17-24	Dw 152-4	154.5-155.22	Ior 110/1-15
135.25-30	Dw 268,269	155.23-27	Col 318,320
135.31-136.2	Dw 358,359	155.28-33	Col 323-6
136.3-18	Ior 102/11-15	155.34-8	Ior 110/16,17
136.19-21	Dw 354	156.1-3	Col 331
136.22-34	Ior 102/16-19	156.4-8	Col 333
136.35-137.18	Ior 103	156.9-30	Ior 110/18-25
137.19-30	WML 129.6-16	156.31-158.23	Ior 111
137.31-3	WML 143.3-5	158.24-32	Col 358-60
141.1-35	AL i.216.23-218.13	158.33-159.20	Ior 112
		159.21-160.4	Ior 113/1-8
141.36-142.3	Dw 420	160.5-6	Dw 255
142.4-36	Bleg 16.16-17.18	160.7-21	WML 100.14-101.5
142.37-144.8	Ior 104	160.22-8	Ior 113/9
144.9-20	Ior 105	160.29-40	Dw 445-8
144.21-145.9	Ior 106/1-8	161.1-162.8	Ior 113/10-20
145.10-24	Col 268-71	162.9-163.20	Ior 114
145.25-36	Dw 82-5	163.21-34	Dw 298,299
146.1-10	Ior 106/12,13	163.35-164.12	Dw 472
146.11-27	Dw 300-302	164.13-21	Ior 115/1-3
146.28-33	Ior 106/14	164.22-8	Bleg 93.23-4; 154.11-15
146.34-5	Dw 308		
147.1-4	Ior 106/15	164.29-165.5	Dw 304
147.5-28	Ior 107	165.6-19	Ior 115/4-7
147.29-148.11	Ior 108	165.20-21	WML 117.14-15
148.12-15	Col 273		
148.16-38	VC III.i.16	165.22-31	Dw 443,444
149.1-9	VC III.i.17	165.32-166.4	Ior 115/8-10
149.10-11	Bleg 30.29-30	166.5-6	Col 396
149.12-29	Ior 109	166.7-13	Ior 115/11,12
149.30-150.21	Bleg 31.28-32.25	166.14-17	Dw 286
		166.18	Ior 115/13
150.22-9	Bleg 32.27-33.3	166.19	Bleg 135.12-13
		166.20-29	Ior 115/14-16
150.30-33	Col 277	166.30-167.4	Dw 276-8
150.34-7	WML 46.19-22	167.5-10	Dw 452
150.38-151.4	Col 278, 279	167.11-19	Ior 115/17-19
151.5-14	Col 292, 293	167.20-27	Bleg 122.26-32
151.15-26	AL IV.iii.12,13		
151.27-33	Dw 2,3	167.28-30	Ior 115/20
151.34-152.3	Dw 6	167.31-4	Col 410
152.4-9	Dw 20	167.35-8	Ior 115/21
152.10-17	Dw 240	168.1-10	Dw 250,251
152.18-23	Col 291	168.11-15	Dw 372

216 The Law of Hywel Dda

168.16-37	Dw 503,504
169.1-6	Dw 113
169.7-25	Ior 116
169.25-6	WML 104.1-2
169.27-31	Ior 117/1,2
169.32-170.3	Bleg 34.11-18
170.4-6	Ior 117/3
170.7-9	WML 103.15-18
170.10-19	Ior 117/4-7
170.20-31	Ior 118
170.32-171.3	Ior 119
171.4-21	Ior 120/1-6
171.22-5	Dw 163
171.26	Ior 120/7
171.27-172.11	Ior 121
172.11-15	Ior 122/3,4
172.16-24	Ior 123/1,2
172.25-9	WML 69.11-15
172.30-34	WML 68.10-14
172.35-8	Ior 123/3,4
172.38-173.6	Ior 124/1,2
173.7-15	WML 67.19-68.2
173.16	Bleg 91.16-17
173.17-24	WML 68.2-10
173.25-9	Ior 126/4
173.30-33	WML 68.22-69.2
173.34	WML 301.17
173.35-174.24	Ior 124/3-13
174.25	WML 69.10-11
174.26-32	Dw 331
174.33-175.5	Ior 125
175.6-176.18	Ior 127
176.19-177.11	Ior 128
177.12-24	WML 74.7-20
177.25-178.3	Dw 415-19
178.4-5	WML 74.20-21
178.6-7	WML 78.4-6
178.8-11	WML 140.13-16
178.12	WML 301.17-18
178.13-23	Ior 129/1-3
178.24-6	WML 76.16-19
178.27-8	WML 77.13-14
178.29-179.3	Dw 142-4
179.4-9	WML 110.12-18
179.10-19	Ior 129/4-7
179.20-22	WML 78.6-8
179.23-4	WML 77.2-3
179.25-180.3	Ior 130/1-4
180.4-5	WML 75.6-7
180.6-12	Ior 130/5,6
180.13-14	WML 75.16-18
180.15-26	Ior 131
180.27-32	Bleg 94.8-14
181.1-15	Ior 132
181.16-182.2	Ior 133
182.3-6	WML 64.17-20
182.7-12	WML 35.3-8
182.13-16	Bleg 54.7-11
182.17-34	WML 82.13-83.5
182.35-183.8	Ior 134
183.9-12	WML 79.13-15
183.13-19	WML 79.19-24
183.20-24	WML 81.1-4
183.25-184.3	Ior 135
184.4-8	Bleg 55.18-21
184.9-15	WML 81.12-18
184.16-21	WML 81.21-6
184.22-34	Ior 136/1-4
184.35-36	WML 35.11-12
184.37-185.2	WML 35.19-22
185.3-6	Bleg 51.30-52.3
185.7-8	Bleg 51.1
185.9-12	WML 36.11-14
185.13-34	Ior 136/5-9
185.35-8	WML 36.14-17
186.1-13	Ior 137/1-4
186.14-30	Dw 22-4
186.31-4	WML 36.17-20
186.35-187.5	Dw 233,234
187.6-7	Dw 423
187.8-9	Ior 137/5
187.10-13	WML 77.10-13
187.14-21	WML 77.15-78.2
187.22-4	WML 78.8-11
187.25-9	Bleg 52.6-10
187.30-34	Dw 217
187.35-6	Bleg 52.28-9
188.1-9	Ior 137/6
188.10	WML 98.16-17
188.11-14	WML 131.4-7
188.15-36	Ior 138/1-9
189.1	WML 104.12-13
189.2-3	Dw 147

189.4-12	Ior 138/10-13
189.13	WML 104.8
189.14-22	WML 104.14-105.2
189.23-30	Bleg 98.21-7
189.31-4	WML 117.7-9
189.35-8	WML 105.2-5
189.39-190.3	Dw 164
190.4	Ior 138/14
190.4-24	Ior 139/1-4
190.25-37	WML 101.16-102.8
191.1-11	Ior 139/5-7
191.12-14	WML 102.9-12
191.15-23	WML 102.19-103.7
191.24-32	Ior 140/1-12
191.33-192.7	Dw 412-4
192.8-194.2	Ior 140/13-133
194.3-19	Ior 141/1-21
194.20-22	WML 105.6-9
194.23-4	Ior 141/22
194.25-6	WML 105.10-11
194.27	Ior 142/1
194.28-30	WML 300.20-21
194.31-195.10	Ior 142/2-20
195.11-17	Ior 143
195.18-32	Ior 144
195.33-8	Ior 145/1-11
196.1-2	Bleg 97.12-14
196.3-4	Ior 145/12
196.5-15	Ior 146/1-6
196.16-17	WML 42.7-9
196.18-31	Ior 146/7-16
196.32-5	WML 42.17-20
197.1-4	Ior 146/17,18
197.5-10	Ior 147/1,2
197.11-16	Dw 138,139
197.17-37	Ior 147/3-13
198.1-6	Bleg 57.15-19
198.7-9	Ior 147/14
198.10-13	WML 43.4-7
198.14-16	Ior 147/15-17
198.17-21	WML 42.21-5
198.22-5	Dw 334
198.26-9	WML 112.4-7
198.30-199.17	Ior 148/1-6
199.18-20	WML 108.4-6
199.21-4	Ior 148/7
199.25-200.7	Ior 149
200.8-27	Ior 150
200.28-201.4	Ior 151
201.5-202.2	Ior 152
202.3-11	Ior 153
202.12-15	WML 117.20-22
202.16-28	Ior 154/1-5
202.29-36	WML 83.8-15
203.1-29	Ior 154/6-15
203.30-35	WML 83.15-21
203.36-204.2	Ior 154/16,17
204.3-10	WML 84-3-10
204.11-22	Ior 155/1-3
204.23-9	WML 84.10-16
204.30-205.2	Ior 155/4-8
205.3-5	Ior 156/1
205.6-9	WML 295.2-4
205.10-16	Ior 156/1-3
205.17-22	WML 84.19-24
205.23-38	Ior 156/4-6
206.1-15	Dw 173?6
206.16-32	Ior 156/7-14
206.33-207.4	Ior 157/1-4
207.5-9	WML 117.23-118.3
207.10-16	Ior 157/5,6
207.17-24	Ior 158/1-3
207.25-9	WML 84.24-85.3
207.30-208.27	Ior 158/4-12
208.28-209.2	Ior 159
209.3-24	Ior 160/1-8
209.25-8	WML 118.16-19
209.29	Ior 160/9

NOTES

Prologue

All the complete manuscripts of the three Redactions begin with a version of the Prologue about Hywel's assembly, but no two manuscripts agree exactly, though some differ from each other only slightly. The version printed in the text now seems to be the oldest, and certainly has fewer additions than the later versions: of the variants shown by different manuscripts of the Iorwerth Redaction only one seems likely to be significant. MSS. *B* and *D* alone name Whitland ('the White House on Taf') as the meeting-place of the assembly; since these manuscripts belong to different branches of the tradition, it seems likely that the reference was in the archetype of the Redaction and was removed in a sub-archetype, perhaps because a reference to Dyfed was unacceptable in Gwynedd. The lost Llanforda manuscript of the Iorwerth Redaction (*Ll*), written in Merioneth early in the fourteenth century (so that it falls between *B* and *D* in time) placed the assembly at the White House in Dyfed (*e Ty Gwyn en Devet*: 14 BBCS 100, 101).

The other Redactions, especially in their later manuscripts, add more detail, most of it improbable and some of it demonstrably impossible. In its most extreme form the Prologue names a drafting committee of twelve wise laymen, with the cleric Blegywryd, Archdeacon of Llandaf and Doctor of both Canon and Civil law, as secretary; when the committee's work had been confirmed, Hywel went to Rome with a company which included Archdeacon Blegywryd and the bishops of St Davids, Bangor, and St Asaph, and there had the law recognised by Pope Anastasius as consistent with the law of God.

The development of the Prologue was examined in detail in 1928 by J. G. Edwards (*Hywel Dda and the Welsh Lawbooks*, reprinted, CLP 135-60): it had already been pointed out that most of the men named as the drafting committee were known as jurists of a later age. Edwards later showed (1 WHR Sp. No. 1-17) that an earlier identification of Blegywryd with a particular person of that name who apparently lived in the tenth century was unsound; it has also been shown that there is no evidence that the name of Blegywryd was associated with Welsh law before the thirteenth century (Emanuel, (1963) 20 BBCS 256-60). Hence the

220   *The Law of Hywel Dda*

suggestion sometimes made, that the Blegywryd Redaction has a specially close relation with the original work of Hywel, is not acceptable: names like 'the Book of Blegywryd' must never be understood as implying a special relation between the text and any particular Blegywryd.

1.2 prince of all Wales. As *prince* (W. *tywysog*) is the word in all the manuscripts except the late *D*, it was probably that of the Iorwerth archetype, though *D* and the other Redactions have *king* (W. *brenin*); the use of *prince* is anachronistic for Hywel, but appropriate to the period of the Redaction: see 'Kings, Lords, and Princes', 26 BBCS 451-62, and Glossary, s.v. *arglwydd*.

1.2-3 saw the Welsh misusing the laws. This clause is awkwardly misplaced in MS. *B*; it is here placed in its position according to the other manuscripts.

1.12 holy. W. *glân*, literally 'clean', but the usual word for 'holy' as applied to Scripture, matrimony, etc. Other manuscripts have *iawn*, 'proper, right', or *cyfiawn*, 'just, righteous'.

1.14 examined. A compromise between the 'looked at' (W. *edrychasant*) and 'considered' (W. *ystyriasant*) of different manuscripts.

Book I: THE LAWS OF COURT

The other Redactions introduce the subject more impressively, as in *Cyfn*, following the account of the promulgation of the lawbook, 'And first they dealt with laws of court, since they were the most important and since they pertained to the King and the Queen and the twenty-four officers who accompany them . . .' (WML 1.24-2.3). The Laws of Court are much more orderly in *Ior* than in the other Redactions, in which the sections do not even correspond to the lists of officers given at this point: see also the introductory note to c.5 below. The list in *Ior* differs from those of the other Redactions mainly because the Queen's Officers have increased in number from five to eight and have been set out as a separate group: this seems to reflect the enhanced status likely to have been given to the wife of Llywelyn the Great, Joan, daughter of King John of England.

Notes: The Laws of Court

1. The Court's Members

5.4 priest. MS. *D* adds 'of the household', but the priest, though called 'priest of the household' at 11.26, was certainly a stay-at-home officer in thirteenth-century Gwynedd, as the account of his functions shows.

chief falconer. W. *penhebogydd*, see the Glossary s.v. *falcon*. Other manuscripts, and the other Redactions, have *hebogydd*, 'falconer'.

5.4-5 court judge. W. *brawdwr llys*, the name used in *Bleg* and *Cyfn*; in the section dealing with him (16.13-17.36) he is called by the usual *Ior* name *ynad*, 'justice': see the Glossary s.v. *ynad*.

5.14-15 woollen clothing. W. *brethynwisg*: 'cloth raiment' might be a better translation of the word, which to a modern ear suggests woven material.

2. The Royal Family

The King and Queen (5.18-6.18)

5.28-9 misuse of his wife. W. *camarferu*; *Cyfn* has 'obstructing his wife' (*rhwystro*, WML 2.20); one *Bleg* manuscript explains *camarferu* as 'lying with her' (*bot genthi*, J.2.27).

5.30-6.2 The translation gives all the items found in any of the manuscripts: the bulls are named only in MSS. *B* and *D*, and the gold plate is omitted from MS. *B*. The other Redactions suggest that *Ior* may have lost something more, since they make the gold plate a cover for a gold cup which can hold the King's quota of drink, though the rod given by them is of silver. *Bleg* gives the full sarhaed to any king having 'an especial seat such as Dinefwr under the King of Deheubarth or Aberffraw under the King of Gwynedd' (3.26-9), and restricts other kings to cattle; *Cyfn* seems to allow gold to all kings: WML 2.23-3.7. The royal sarhaed is set out again in the Test Book section on sarhaed: see 154.12-20n.

6.1 seven years. MSS. *B* and *D* have 'nine years', as has MS. *B* at 154.14; the other Redactions have 'seven years', and our translation follows the general consensus.

6.6 Argoel. It is not certain where this was, but it was probably near the two farms '*Sarn Agol* and *Cwm Agol* between Dryslwyn and Grongaer, some three and a half miles in a direct line from Dinefwr' (*B Bleg* 122, summar-

222   *The Law of Hywel Dda*

ising earlier work). It is hardly likely that this compensation
was ever paid to any ruler of Dinefwr, but Walter Map has a
tale which parodies it. When a jealous Welsh king learnt
that a young man had dreamt of sleeping with the queen,
his claim for compensation was referred to a learned judge,
who ruled that for a shadow insult the King was entitled to
a shadow compensation. If the offence had been real, the
King would have taken 1000 kine; it was therefore ordered
that the offender should 'set 1000 kine in the king's sight
on the bank of the lake of Behthen, in a row in the sunlight,
that the reflection of each may be seen in the water, and
that the reflections shall belong to the king, and the kine to
him who owned them before' (*Walter Map's 'De Nugis
Curialium'*, tr. M. R. James; Cymmrodorion Record Series,
London, 1923), 101-2.

6.14-15 The words 'on horseback, to wit the twenty-four
officers' have been lost in MS. *B*. It is not clear who the
twelve guests would be: they would no doubt include those
who were not officers of the court but were allotted specific
places in the hall; see 7.26-8.28n.

The Edling (6.19-7.25)

The word *edling* is borrowed from the Anglo-Saxon *ætheling*; 'heir-apparent' translates W. *gwrthrychiad*, an older
word with Irish parallels: it seems to imply a looking-forward
by the heir or a looking-up to him: see Binchy, 3 *Celtica*
221-8, *Kingship* 26ff; Charles-Edwards, 9 *Celtica* 180-90
(where it is suggested that in the provision of *Cyfn*, *Bleg*,
and the Latin texts, that the edling sat on the opposite side
of the fire from the King in the hall, the 'fire symbolized the
kingship': ibid. 187). The AS *ætheling* (which contains the
root meaning 'noble') meant 'a close relative of the king',
thus corresponding to the wider meaning here given to
edling; it has been suggested that the narrower meaning
was developed in AS before the word was borrowed into
Welsh, but there is no evidence that the narrower meaning
ever developed in English (see Dumville, (1979) 8 *Anglo-
Saxon England* 1-33) and it seems more likely that it developed in Welsh in the thirteenth century, when Llywelyn
the Great designated his younger son Dafydd (by Joan) as
his successor.

6.23 nephew, W. *nai*. In Wales, the English 'nephew' is
used for the son of a first (or perhaps remoter) cousin; this

Notes: The Royal Family   223

usage agrees with the definition of *nai* in *Cyfn*: 'A nephew
is the son of a brother or sister or a male or female first cousin
or second cousin' (WML 38.23-5) and the reference to a
'nephew son of a fifth cousin' at 145.6-7. In the present
passage *nai* has perhaps the narrow meaning of 'nephew' in
English usage.

6.25 host, W. *osb*, from Lat. *hospes*. The word might
mean 'guest, visitor', as suggested at AL i.9 n.c. and GML
s.v.; but it seems more consonant with the atmosphere of
the court of Gwynedd that the *osb* should be a local notable
(perhaps a mediatised lord) who as leader of the community
welcomes the King.

6.30 offering, W. *offrwm*. This suggests the gift to the
church, and is the reading of MS. *B* alone; the other manuscripts have *ffrwyn*, 'bridle'. The other Redactions charge
all the edling's expenses to the King, but name neither
bridle nor offering.

7.9 the latter himself. The Welsh of the various
manuscripts is confused and ambiguous; the translation
gives what seems to be the most reasonable interpretation.

7.20 villein-land. MS. *B* has *byleyntref*, 'villein townland',
but there seems to be no need to assume the acquisition of a
whole townland, and the reading of the other manuscripts
has been preferred.

The Order of the Court (7.26-8.28)

This section, taken with the references in the supplement
to the Justices' Test Book (190.10-14), makes it possible to
visualise the 'normal' royal hall in which the festive court
was held. It is of course clear that the hall is not at the King's
principal seat, but is the royal headquarters in a part of the
realm which is being visited by the King and his entourage
in their progress. Like other Welsh houses, the hall was of
cruck construction: it had a cruck couple at each end and
one in the middle, with a roof-tree supported by the crucks.
(It has often been said that the hall had aisles between the
cruck columns and the walls, but aisled houses are almost
unknown in Wales and there is nothing in the lawbooks to
support the view.) In surviving British medieval halls, the
dais at one end is the place of dignity, but Mr Peter Smith
has kindly informed me that there is evidence from Germany
for halls in which the middle of the hall was the place of
dignity, and in the Welsh lawbooks the middle couple was

224   The Law of Hywel Dda

the focus of the hall—literally, since the fire was there, and figuratively, since the King sat near it. It divided the hall into upper precinct (*uch cyntedd*) and lower precinct (*is cyntedd*), but the division was not one of dignity, for the officer of highest dignity, the captain of the household, had his place in the lower precinct. There must have been a more elaborate division than the bare cruck columns: there seems to have been a screen (W. *celfi*, literally 'furnishings, apparatus') projecting from the column on either side and giving some protection from draughts. The word translated 'bar' is W. *corf* (which occurs in the compound *corflan*, 'enclosure': see the notes to II.5 and 82.22), whose exact meaning is uncertain; here it seems to designate the screens (regarded as a division or barrier) rather than the columns as has sometimes been suggested.

The text does not give a complete seating-plan for the banquet; nor do the other Redactions. A few persons are named as having chairs: this may imply that the others sat on benches, but what is important is where they sat, not what they sat on. *Cyfn*, after placing the edling, the court justice, the priest, and the pencerdd in relation to the King, adds 'Thereafter no-one has an authentic [W. *dilys*] place in the hall' (WML 4.6-11); *Bleg* (5.21-3) gives the first place on the King's left to 'some one bonheddig who has status by heredity to sit beside him'.

7.32-3 physician, W. *meddyg*, correcting the *medyd* of MS. *B* in the light of the other manuscripts and of the reference at 24.8-9.

3. The King's Officers

The Captain of the Household (8.30-11.24)

8.37-9.1 Apart from this statement, there is no trace in *Ior* of this change, which cannot in any case have had much practical effect, since steward and captain had little opportunity for any clash of authority when each had his sphere in the hall, as the detailed rules show. The Latin texts (Lat D 316.31-3, Lat E 436.2-3) add to this statement, giving the vacant place among the twenty-four officers to the pencerdd, but *Ior* makes no change in the latter's position: see the Glossary s.v. *pencerdd*, and 38.16-39.17nn.

9.32 for cases related to. If these words, added from MS. *A*, are omitted, the captain seems to be entitled (like the Queen,

Notes: The King's Officers 225

see 5.19-20) to a share of all goods received by the King in respect of land.

9.34 the first year he rides. The wording may mean no more than 'the first year of his membership', but there may also be an implication that the new recruit has become a knight (W. *marchog*, lit. 'horseman'): cf. 131.20-27n.

10.14 chief huntsman. Other manuscripts name the chief falconer as the third, but the fuller triad justifies the reading of MS. *B*: cf. 23.1-2.

10.38 For a definition of the four columns (or posts), see 24.22n.

11.23 As the word *ebediw* (containing the root meaning 'horse' found in Latin *equus* and W. *ebol*, 'colt', *ebran* 'fodder') indicates, this payment was originally, like the Germanic heriot, a return to the lord of martial equipment provided for the vassal: D. Howells, (1973-4) 8/9 SC 48-67 at p.50. By the thirteenth century the ordinary man's ebediw was a money payment related to his holding of land, and payment in kind was regarded as anomalous; like the edling (6.35), the captain of the household paid in kind because of his close relationship to the King, not because of his office.

The Priest of the Household (11.26-12.23)

11.31-2 *Cyfn*, *Bleg*, and the Latin texts lodge the priest in the chaplain's house: *ty y caplan* in WML 9.19-20; the Latin versions (A 113.22-3, B 197.6, C 281.3-4) suggest that this should be translated 'his chaplain's house', but *ty caplan y tref*, 'the townland chaplain's house', (*Bleg* 9.25-6) is quite plain: Lat D 321.13-14, *domus capellani ville*.

12.13 It is not clear what is meant by 'service' (W. *gweini*) here; some payment due to the church is evidently in question, and the rule is concerned with the competing claims of the priest of the household and other clergy.

The Steward (12.24-14.25)

13.8 Other manuscripts confine the right to money coming from 'cases on land and earth'; *Cyfn* and *Bleg* do not mention the right.

13.18-20 Cf. the passage from *Bleg*, 8.11-19.

13.34-7 Other manuscripts give the skin 'between the middle of February and the end of the spring'; *Cyfn* (WML 12.18-20) and *Bleg* (11.19-22) give it between mid-February and the

226   *The Law of Hywel Dda*

end of the first week in May. As the names of the months show, the Welsh summer consisted of May, June, and July; so the first week in May can be regarded as a period of grace beyond the strict end of spring.

The Chief Falconer (14.26-16.12)

14.30-31 *Cyfn* (WML 17.23) gives an even more distinguished place to the falconer: on the left of the cynghellor, who sits at the King's left hand on the three special feasts (WML 29.7-10).

14.35 Other manuscripts have 'against weakness to his birds' (*rhag gwander i'w adar*); AL translates MS. *B*.

15.7 The other manuscripts omit 'wild'; *Cyfn* (WML 18.19-20) and *Bleg* (14.13-14) give the falconer the hearts of all animals killed in the kitchen (*Cyfn*) or court (*Bleg*), but do not mention lungs.

15.19-27 A similar passage in *Bleg* (13.24-14.10) is interrupted by rules for the falconer's drink.

15.35-7 Other manuscripts have 'the last place where he loosed his hawk at a bird'; *Cyfn* (WML 5.5-6) and *Bleg* (6.23-4) specify the furthest point of his hunting, *Bleg* adding 'during the day'.

The Court Justice (16.13-17.36)

16.20,21 pillow (W. *clustog*); cushion (W. *gobennydd*). In modern Welsh the meanings would be reversed, but both words must originally have had the modern sense of pillow, being derived from *clust*, 'ear', and *pen*, 'head'.

16.37 wicket (W. *wyccet; guychet, wychet, wicket* in other manuscripts), an English or French borrowing. Neither the word, nor the rule which involves it, is found in *Bleg* or *Cyfn*.

17.21-4 The second measure of the court justice's protection agrees in substance with that given in *Cyfn* (WML 5.8-10) and *Bleg* (6.25-8). The different measures are perhaps to be understood as applying in different circumstances: the first in the festive court, the second in the justice's tribunal.

17.25-9 Legal procedure for challenging a judge's decision is dealt with more fully in *Bleg* (98.28-107.8; translated by Melville Richards at B *Bleg* 95.4-101.10); the litigant and the judge were required to support their respective opinions by showing that they were recorded in lawbooks, and 'if the

Notes: The King's Officers 227

contrary opinions are found in written law, the decision is laid on canonists who practise justice'. Reference of a case to canonists is recorded in the Duchy of Lancaster lordship of Kidwelly in 1510: PRO Just 1/1156, 6 (a reference for which I thank Mr J. Beverley Smith).

The Chief Groom (18.1-19.9)

18.14-17 The structure of the Welsh sentence is ambiguous: in the later manuscript *D* an addition to the wording makes it clear that the King waits on the bishop, not the bishop on the King.

18.20-23 The relation of king and fool in *King Lear* will serve to remind us that the position of the jester at court was anomalous: that is no doubt why the jester is nowhere mentioned as a court officer in the Welsh lawbooks. For comparisons with the contumelious treatment of the jester (W. *croesan*) see 35.6-8n; Anners and Jenkins, 1 WHR 325-33; Nerys Patterson, 16/17 SC 73-103; Rolf Stratmann, *Die Scheinbussen im mittelalterlichen Recht* (Frankfurt, Bern, Las Vegas, 1978). Patterson (p.91) takes the testicles to be the horse's; the Welsh text is ambiguous.

The Chamberlain (19.10-35)

19.27-8 *Cyfn* (WML 22.7-9) and *Bleg* (21.27-9) explain that the chamberlain has no authentic (W. *dilys*) place in the hall because of his functions in the chamber.

19.31-2 For cattle whose horns are as long as their ears, see Sheringham, (1982) 29 BBCS 691-708.

The Bard of the Household (20.1-32)

For the relation of the bard of the household (W. *bardd teilu*) to other bards, see the Glossary, s.v. *pencerdd*.

20.14-15 three songs of some other kind (W. *tri chanu o gerdd amgen*). This wording seems to be the Iorwerth version of an expression whose meaning had been lost; it appears in various forms, none of which has been satisfactorily explained, in manuscripts of the other Redactions.

20.23-4 *the Sovereignty of Britain* (W. *Unbeiniaeth Prydain*, perhaps better translated 'the Monarchy of Britain'). In the other Redactions, this was sung by the bard of the household before going to battle; to sing it at the sharing of the spoils of a raid was evidently a vestigial practice. For the editors of LW (p.36, note g), the song, referring as it surely did, to the

228   *The Law of Hywel Dda*

Welsh claim to sovereignty over the whole island, was appropriate to warfare against the English, and it has been suggested that the song in question was *Armes Prydain*.

20.29 The reference to the bard of the household travelling with other bards seems to indicate a change from the original pattern, in which it is to be expected that he would spend his whole time at the court or with the bodyguard on its expeditions.

The Usher (W. *gostegwr*, lit. 'silencer': 20.33-21.20)

21.7-8 Two interpretations of this sentence seem possible: (*a*) the usher follows the King when he is absent from his chief court; (*b*) the usher performs his function in the court as though the King were present, if the court assembles in the King's absence. The other Redactions give no help.

21.18 'that he proclaims' (not in *Ior* 14) is added from MS. *C*.

The Chief Huntsman (W. *pencynydd*, lit. 'head houndsman': 21.21-23.18)

21.38 when they take office. These words, not in the primary text of WML, are added from MS. *Mk*.

22.15-23.8 For further material on the hunting of deer, see 184.23-186.34; for 'legal joints', see 184.26-7n.

22.24-5 Kalends of December. Following *Ior* p.107, the *Calan Tachwedd* of all the manuscripts has been taken as an error for *Calan Rhagfyr*. *Calan Tachwedd* is in any case an unusual expression for what is normally *Calan Gaeaf*, 'the Winter Kalends'; the fact that the error was not corrected in any of the manuscripts suggests that the material was obsolete. In *Cyfn* (WML 19.3-5) the chief huntsman shows his equipment to the King on 9 December.

23.1-2 The other two were the Queen and the captain of the household, see 10.14n.

The Mead-brewer (23.19-24.2)

23.29-31 The butler was also entitled to the cover or fourpence: 25.12-14. *Cyfn* (WML 25.24-5) speaks of 'the wax which is removed from the mead vat'.

The Physician (24.3-25.5)

For further material on medical treatment see III.8. Though here translated 'physician', W. *meddyg* has the more gen-

Notes: The King's Officers 229

eral meaning of 'medical practitioner'. For a professional examination of medicine in the lawbooks, see John Cule, 'The Court Mediciner and Medicine in the Laws of Wales', (1966) 21 *Journal of the History of Medicine and Allied Sciences* 213-36, and for other evidence of medieval Welsh medicine, Morfydd E. Owen, 'Meddygon Myddfai, a preliminary survey of some medieval medical writing in Wales', (1975-6) 10/11 SC 210-33. Miss Owen is editing *The Physicians of Myddfai* for The Welsh Classics.

24.9 by the screen: W *egyt a'r keluy.*

24.18 dangerous wounds (W. *arberygl*). *Cyfn* (WML 25.8, 12, 13-14) requires the wounds to be so severe that the brain, the bowels, and the marrow respectively are seen; it uses the expression *gweli angheuol*, 'mortal wounds', as does *Bleg.* Cf. 197.17-27.

24.22 two arms: W. *dau fyriad. Byriad* perhaps means the upper arm: so Wade-Evans's translation 'humeri' at WML 170, following AL at GC I.xxiii.5; there is no evidence to decide the question. The definition in *Bleg* (26.22-3), which is differently worded, has *dwy vreich*: the corresponding passage in Lat D omits the definition, but *ascwrn y vreich* in the similar rule at *Bleg* 57.2 is *os brachii* at Lat D 339.5.

24.29-30 fourpence. *Ior* 17/8 corrects this to the 'eightpence' of MS. *E*, but there is not enough evidence in the texts to decide between the two readings: there is haplography in MS. *A* and a lacuna in MS. *C*. At 197.25-6 medication with herbs (without mention of swelling) is worth fourpence.

24.33 assurance: W. *tyllwedd*, essentially 'concord, peace': it is the word used for the concord proclaimed in court (85.21), and at *Col* 275 it is used for the perpetual concord which replaces the blood feud when compensation has been paid. At *Dw* 249 the same rule (using the same word *tyllwedd*) is expressed more generally, for all harm done to a human being or an animal by medical treatment.

The Butler (W. *trulliad*, cf. Genesis xl.1: 25.6-29)

25.12-14 Cf. the claim of the mead-brewer, 23.29-31.

25.19 'legal liquor' would be the entitlement of the 'normal' member of the court, as contrasted with those who were given a special allowance and those who were restricted because they must keep sober.

230   *The Law of Hywel Dda*

The Doorkeeper (25.30-26.24)

26.10-12 MSS. *A* and *E* provide that the porter holds the
offender until the captain of the household comes through
the gate, and that the captain takes him to safety. *Cyfn*
(WML 6.11-16) and *Bleg* (7.15-21) perhaps achieve the
same result: for them the porter receives the offender, and
the captain is not mentioned in the context of the doorkeeper, but they immediately state the porter's protection
as keeping an offender until the captain comes through
the gate. This corresponds to the porter's protection as
given at 36.8-11.

26.18-19 This must refer to the provision for some officers
to eat or drink outside the hall.

The Cook (26.25-27.12)

26.36 seasons: W. *ardymheru*. Comparison with the parallel rule for the Queen's cook (31.9) suggests that here the
word may mean 'cooks' (so GPC), but its use in the reference to herbs at 27.6-7 suggests the narrower meaning.

4. The Queen's Officers

The Queen's Steward (28.6-29)

28.8-10 Some of the manuscripts give precedence to the
Queen's gift of linen clothing to her officers; LW has silently
emended its text accordingly, though MS. *B* gives precedence to the King's gift.

28.12-13 Since the Queen's chamberlain waits on her outside the three special feasts, her steward must be understood
as waiting on her only at those feasts; LW has accordingly
added 'at the three special feasts'. It was usual for court
officers to perform their functions by deputy except on
special occasions: in 'Culhwch and Olwen' Glewlwyd
Gafaelfawr was Arthur's porter on New Year's Day and his
four deputies for the rest of the year.

28.13-14 a third of the dirwy: 'of the dirwy' is added from
the other manuscripts, being omitted in MS. *B* and in *Llyfr
Iorwerth*.

The Queen's Doorkeeper (30.26-31.2)

31.1-2 'with augmentation' is added from MS. *C*, here and
for the Queen's Cook at 31.13-14. Though MS. *C* alone seems
to have these additions, they are surely needed, for there is

Notes: The Queen's Officers   231

no reason to draw a distinction between these officers and the Queen's other officers.

The Queen's Cook (31.3-14)

31.9 prepares, W. *keweyrhyo*. MS. *C* has *ardymhero*: cf. the note to 26.36.

5. Additional Officers

Only in the Iorwerth Redaction are these additional officers brought together in an orderly chapter. In *Cyfn* and *Bleg* the groom of the rein and footholder are among the twenty-four primary court officers, but the other nine are not listed though there is some material about most of them; the baker-ess and the laundress are not mentioned in either Redaction, and the watchman is not mentioned in *Bleg*. In *Cyfn* the material about the Additional Officers appears at different points in different manuscripts, so that it must have been added to the original core of the Redaction; in *Bleg* the pass-ages about these officers seem to have been inserted among those about the twenty-four, in the archetype of the surviving manuscripts. Some of the Additional Officers are certainly local men, who would be present only when the court visited their locality: see the Glossary, s.v. *cynghellor, pencerdd*.

The Groom of the Rein (32.4-29)

32.23 his status and his right: W. *ei fraint a'i ddylyed*. This could be translated 'his privilege and his duty'; the terms in their context nicely illustrate the ambivalence of *dylyed*, but it seems at least clear that the justice was to adjudicate free on questions of both right and duty.

32.29 MS. *C* (in contrast to all the other manuscripts) apparently added 'with augmentation': a gap in that manu-script begins after the first word of the addition. There is some variation between the manuscripts in the measure of galanas for some of the Additional Officers.

The Footholder (32.30-33.11)

33.11 Other manuscripts add 'with augmentation'; there is too little evidence to decide which version is the original. It is hardly likely that a footholder carried out his physical duties at any thirteenth-century Welsh court, and the ref-erence to the office as passing in right of land (which is not to be found in *Cyfn* or *Bleg*) suggests that it had become an honorific sinecure.

232   The Law of Hywel Dda

The Dung Maer (W. *maer biswail*, see the Glossary, s.v.; 33.12-34.5)

33.15 court steward: W. *ystiwart llys*, not *distain* as would be expected. Stephenson (*Governance* 46 n.26) persuasively suggests that this 'court steward' was the usher rather than the distain.

33.29-30 cattle skins of the dung maer: W. *crwyn gwartheg y maer biswail*, which it would be natural to translate 'the skins of the dung maer's cattle'. In the context, however, it seems more likely that the reference is to the skins which the previous sentence allots to the dung maer: the point would then be that, whereas the chief huntsman (for instance) shared with the other huntsmen the skins to which he was entitled, the dung maer kept the whole of his allocation for himself.

34.3 food-house, W. *bwyty*. This was one of the buildings which villeins were required to build for the King: see 41.12-15, 125.4-7. It may have been the permanent home of the dung maer, for since he was a local man we should not expect him to need accommodation. *Cyfn* and *Bleg* do not name his lodging.

The Serjeant (34.6-35.13)

The name translates W. *rhingyll*, which is used in modern Welsh for a military or police sergeant. The *rhingyll* of the lawbooks is likewise an officer concerned with the maintenance of order and the enforcement of the commands of authority; his functions seem very similiar to those of the serjeants of the peace in northern and west-midland England (for which see R. Stewart-Brown, *The Serjeants of the Peace in medieval England and Wales*; Manchester, 1936), though when these officers appear under a Welsh name it is *cais* rather than *rhingyll*. This may be because in later medieval Wales the functions of the *rhingyll* became relatively more important: see the references indexed under *rhingyll* in W. Rees, *South Wales and the March* (Oxford, 1924) and R. A. Griffiths, *The Principality of Wales in the Later Middle Ages*, vol. i (Cardiff, 1972), and under various extensions and abbreviations of the anglicised form *ringild* in *Rec. Caern.* It seems certain that there would be serjeants in territorial divisions of a kingdom, so that the serjeant who is present at court as one of the officers by custom is probably the local officer rather than a court officer in permanent attendance

Notes: Additional Officers 233

on the King. The unpopularity of the serjeant is indicated by the triad of the Three Names of the Serjeant (*Tri Enw Rhingyll*), 'the cry of a country, and bad tidings the servant of the cynghellor, and rhingyll': *Bleg* 115.9-10. B *Bleg* 107.10-11.

34.20 ankles: W. *uffarnau*, Lat D *cavillas*. It is not easy to see how cows' legs could be used to make brogues: the passage was probably obscure in the thirteenth century and was copied although the right was obsolete. The corresponding passage in *Cyfn* does not mention brogues: 'The leg of every steer from the court belongs to him. And the length of them will be only to the *ucharnedd*' (MS. *Mk*, 24.4-5; the reading of WML 30.2 has lost some words). The reference to brogues may have been introduced in the archetype of *Bleg* 28.7-9.

34.22 mixed fabric: W. *tenllif*. Though the expression 'breeches without mixed fabric' seems awkward, it has been adopted because there is no evidence in favour of the meaning 'lining' (adopted by AL, LW, and B *Bleg*) except that of Davies's *Dict. Dupl.* of 1632: the Latin words often cited from AL are the editor's translation of the *tenllif* of the text. *Cyfn* (WML 30.3-5) and *Bleg* (28.10-12) give the serjeant the right to linen for making his breeches, and both provide that there shall not be *tenllif* in his breeches.

34.30 dead-house: W. *marwdy*; the meaning is slightly more technical than 'dead man's house', cf. 40.35-9n; but the translation 'escheat' sometimes used is misleading, since the whole of the property concerned is *marwdy*, though not all of it will necessarily escheat to the King: see 131.23. The present passage is concerned with the serjeant's share of the escheat: such allocations as that of the opened meat seem to be inconsistent with the rights of the wife on separation as set out in the Law of Women: 46.7-16. Cf. 40.35-9.

34.34 margins: W. *eirionynnau*. The word is also used for the lateral boundaries in the definition of the acre: 121.1, 199.7, there translated 'limits'. It does not appear how wide the margins to which the serjeant would be entitled would be.

35.6-8 As Stephen Williams pointed out (*Bleg* p.177-8), the serjeant was not free to sit during a case, so that he was entitled only to a derisory compensation which compared him to a sitting hen: cf. 18.20-23n, and Glossary s.v. *maer biswail*.

234   *The Law of Hywel Dda*

35.8-13 The later MS. *D* gives the same six-unit values for the serjeant as for the other Additional Officers; the other Redactions give no values.

The Porter (35.14-36.13)

35.21 haddock: W. *penwaig.* In twentieth-century Gwynedd *penwaig* means 'herrings'; the place-name Porth Ysgadan in Llŷn suggests that an earlier word for herrings was *ysgadan*, the word still used in West and South Wales.

35.35 any docked beast: W. *y llwdn cwta.* The expression might mean 'the beast at the tail', i.e. the last in the queue; *Bleg* (24.21) gives the porter 'the last beast' and *Cyfn* (WML 32.13-15) a tailless steer if there is one, and also the last steer which comes to the gate. The translation 'docked beast' is not intended to imply any theory of how the beast became tailless.

The Fueller (W. *cynutai:* 36.34-37.15)

The usual translation 'woodman' is rejected because that word is needed for the *coedwr* mentioned in other contexts (113.36, 155.33-5n). The fueller was not a mere fuel-gatherer, though he was not (it seems) responsible for lighting the fire in the hall (128.35, 129.10-11).

The Court Smith (37.30-38.14)

37.35-6 three things. The different manuscripts have slightly differing lists, and the text is clearly corrupt. *Cyfn, Bleg,* and the Latin texts all agree that the three things for which the court smith must be paid are a cauldron, an axe, and a spear; but the *Ior* text seems to reflect something more archaic and even mystical. Comparison of the variants suggests that the original rule related to work on a cauldron, a coulter, and an axe, and that the spear-head was an addition which led to a confusion of the coulter with the cauldron. Cauldron, coulter, and axe had a special significance: they were the three things which must be left to the youngest son and which could be reclaimed by the kindred if gaged by the owner: WML 50.6-11, *Bleg* 74.23-6; the Latin texts therefore called them the Three Precious Things of a Kindred (*tri thlws cenedl,* Lat A 133.1, Lat D 387.5): ct. 189.2-3n. But in the original form of the rule, as in the manuscript versions of *Ior,* the work for which the court smith was entitled to payment was not the making of these things but special work on them: the *teddf* (usually understood as the

Notes: Additional Officers 235

socket for the handle) of the axe, the 'stirrup of the rim' (*gwarthafl cant*, following MS. A) of the cauldron, and some part of the coulter: the 'rim' of our text (W. *cant*) may mean the edge, so that the smith's service was to re-sharpen the worn edge; cf. 1 Samuel xiii.20.

The Pencerdd (see Glossary: 38.16-39.17)

38.21 solicit: W. *erchi*. V.C.I.xli.5 has the note 'Apparently to solicit a largess, or permission to address a poem to a patron'. This rule is one of the indications that the pencerdd was in essence a master of craftsmen.

38.24-7 This passage comes from the *Cyfn* section on the bard of the household; in the *Bleg* version the rule is applied specifically to the bard of the household, but it seems certain that the rule was originally one for all bards.

39.1 neithior. This is still the name for the marriage celebration in parts of Powys. The bards' right to a boon was a relic of their function in pre-Christian Celtic society as witnesses to the kindred's giving of the bride to her husband; it is not clear whether they were the wedding-guests (W. *neithiorwyr*) who had an important part to play under the Law of Women: see 49.4,15.

39.8 Other texts indicate that the chair was won by competition, but there is no evidence to show whether the chair was that of a post as pencerdd for a particular area, or was comparable with the chair at the modern National Eisteddfod. *Llawysgrif Hendregadredd* (ed. Morris-Jones and Parry-Williams, Cardiff, 1933), 180-81, prints verses composed by Cynddelw and Seisyll Bryffwrch in their contest for the office of pencerdd to Madog ap Maredudd of Powys (who died in 1160), but there is nothing to show whether or not these bards had already qualified as penceirddiaid.

39.14 *Ior* alone names the pencerdd's lodging; this suggests that the pencerdd had to travel a long way from his home to the court: see the Glossary s.v. *pencerdd*.

6. Miscellanea

This chapter brings together a mixed bag of fragments relating to the King and the court in one way or another, and thus gives an insight into the way the lawbooks were put together; some of the fragments appear elsewhere in the *Ior* manuscripts as well as in the other Redactions. The chapter

236   *The Law of Hywel Dda*

seems to show an exceptionally large number of words borrowed from the French.

39.36 threshold: W. *trotheu*. Other *Ior* manuscripts have *trwyddew*, 'awl, auger', but *Bleg* (109.1) and Lat D (370.31) have *trothyw*; the triad is not in WML but *Cyfn* MS. *Mk* has *trotheu* at 126.12-13.

firestone: W. *pentan*. In modern Welsh *pentan* has come to be used mainly for the iron hobs on either side of the fire (whence, no doubt, its use for the abutments of a bridge); the word must originally have referred to the fireproof stone which carried the fire safely in a wooden house. *Bleg*, Lat D, and *Cyfn* (MS. *Mk*) have *talbren*, which Richards translates 'backlog', explaining that it was of stone: B *Bleg* 102.22 and note at p.140.

40.2 treasure: W. *swllt*. In the version of this triad at 41.17-19, the expression is *eurswllt ac arian*, which could be translated 'gold treasure and silver (or money)' or 'gold and silver treasure'. *Swllt* is the Latin *solidus* and is the ordinary Welsh word for 'shilling'; here it should perhaps be understood as 'bullion'.

40.4 stud: W. *allwest*. The argument of *Bleg* 223 against AL's 'pasture' is strengthened by the fact that the *pascuum* of AL ii.774, 829 is the editor's gloss; all the Latin texts have the Welsh word. The goodman's stud is *gre* (Lat. *grex*), as is the stud at 173.34.

40.5 herd of cows: W. *cenfaint gwartheg*; *cenfaint*, now used only of pigs, is omitted from most of the manuscripts. *Gwartheg*, used in some modern dialects as the general word for neat cattle, is in others the normal plural of *buwch*, 'cow'; it is so understood here because it must have that meaning in the tractate on Joint Ploughing at 201.26, but see 58.8-9n, 134.8-9n.

40.12 winter-house: W. *gaeafdy*. Only MS. *B* has this reading, and at *Ior* 42/8 it is emended to the *hafdy* of MSS. *A*, *E*. But MS. *D* and *Cyfn*, *Bleg*, and the Latin texts support MS. *B*: the Welsh texts have *hendref*, as does Lat A (126.39); Lat B and Lat D have 'mansio hyemalis, id est, *hendref*'. The Latin texts make the point clearer by referring to the animal found as trespassing between May Day and the time of reaping: the villein's crops would be growing on the land of the *hendref* ('old settlement') while his animals were grazing the summer pasture on the hills.

Notes: Miscellanea 237

40.14-19 As found in *Ior*, this triad seems to need emendation, since it names the King's *corn cyweithas* as the second of his *tri chorn cyweithas*. The emendation adopted here follows the *Cyfn*, *Bleg*, and Latin texts: it drops the *cyweithas* from the *tri chorn*. The 'social horn' (*corn cyweithas*) is explained in Latin as 'cornu quod semper habet in comitatu suo' (Lat A 127.32, B 200.9, C 284.20, E 465.20); Lat D 370. 10-11 has 'cornu quod iugiter in commitatu suo defertur'. This 'horn of companionship' would surely be used to call for help from the King's companions.

40.29-34 As given in *Bleg* (108.17-22), the triad is more generous to the villein's son: after naming the three arts, it goes on 'for if the lord suffers it until a tonsure is given to the clerk, or until a smith goes into his smithy or a bard to his craft, (W. *wrth gerdd*), he cannot enslave them after that'.

40.35-9 The 'Eight Packhorses' were sources of casual income for the King: the list is found in slightly different words in *Cyfn* (perhaps borrowed from *Bleg*) and the Latin texts, which call them '*pynfeirch* que ad opus regis bona semper cumulant'. The 'man suddenly dead leaving no son' is 'dead-house' (W. *marwdy*) in *Cyfn* and *Bleg*; Lat D 377. 7-9 has 'mortuus subitanea morte preventus, de quo dicitur *marwdy*—regis est inde pars mortui solius de bonis eius omnibus, exceptis partibus uxoris et prolis, si fuerint'. See also 34.30n.

41.11 cost: W. *cost*, a borrowing from O.Fr. (or perhaps Middle English); the corresponding passage in *Cyfn* has the native word *traul* (WML 57.21-4, 59.9-12). So too *Bleg* (47.15-18), but there the *castra* of the Latin has been mistranslated as *cestyll*, 'castles', instead of the *lluestau*, 'camps' of *Cyfn*. *Cyfn* and *Bleg* have *taeog* and *taeoctref* where *Ior* has in this passage the borrowed *bilain* and its compound *bileindref*.

41.12-15 With this passage must be compared those at 125. 4-7,34-5. The first of the latter lists seven houses which the King's *eilltion* are bound to make, the second names two (a barn and a kiln) which the *maerdref* men are bound to make. Between them the two passages name all the houses of the present passage, save that the kitchen replaces the chamber; some of the words used are different. *Cyfn* (WML 57.18-21, 59.6-9) and *Bleg* (47.19-21) both have a list which differs from that of the present passage by substituting kitchen and

238   *The Law of Hywel Dda*

chapel for foodhouse and sleephouse, though with some verbal differences; their list differs from that of the Latin texts in having the chapel in place of the foodhouse (Lat. *penu*). Building obligations of this kind were imposed on tenants in marcher lordships: see e.g. P. Vinogradoff and F. Morgan, *Survey of the Honour of Denbigh* (London, 1914), 149, and G. P. Jones, *The Extent of Chirkland* (Liverpool, 1933), 60.

stable: W. *ystabl*; *marchdy* at 125.6

porch: W. *cynordy*. This item caused the copyists much trouble, and was evidently unfamiliar by the thirteenth century: the reading of Lat B 204.39-205.1, 'domus canum, id est, *kynordy*' was not adopted in Lat D (377.29) where *kynnordy* was left unexplained. The *kyuordy*, 'beer-house' of *Col* 672 seems most likely to be the original word: see the note at *Col* p.172.

latrine: W. *tŷ bychan* (a euphemism still used in virtually the same form) and *trefn fechan* in different manuscripts; *Col* 672 has *herechan*, a word not otherwise known, which GPC suggests may have resulted from a copyist's misreading of *trefn fechan*. *Bleg* and *Cyfn* have *peiriant*.

dormitory or sleephouse: W. *cerner neu hundy*. This passage and others parallel to it are the only substantive citations of *cerner* in GPC; the interpretation *hundy* perhaps needs closer examination, in view of the absence of any provision in the Laws of the Court for anyone to sleep in the *cerner*.

41.19 gold edgings: W. *wrlys aur*, *aur* being omitted in MS. B; *wrlys* represents the O.Fr. *orles*, and may correspond to the native *amaerwyau*, 188.13n. The King was entitled to all garments taken as booty which had *wrlys*, DwCol 196.

41.26-7 another church. The reading of MSS. *A, E* is preferred to that of MS. *B, sapel*, representing a French form for 'chapel'; the usual Welsh form is *capel*, which is the reading of MS. *D* here. At 12.22, 'chapels' translates *sapelau*.

41.30 priests, parsons. The words are in the singular in other manuscripts. The two words seem to point a contrast between the incumbent of the mother church and the subordinate who had charge of the subordinate church or chapel; both would no doubt usually be in priest's orders.

41.31-4 The passage in *Cyfn* continues 'and first the Three Columns of Law'; in *Ior* these form the first chapters of the Test Book (our Book III): see the Introduction.

Notes

Book II: THE LAWS OF THE COUNTRY

The order of chapters follows that of MS. *B*, LW, and (with one slight difference) AL, though it is hard to see why the editor of AL thought the order of MS. *B* more appropriate than that of his primary manuscript, in which our Chapter 2 precedes the Law of Women.

1. The Laws of Women

MS. *B* treats the Laws of the Country as beginning with our Chapter 2, and the Laws of Women as a separate entity; the tractate was perhaps an addition to the original nucleus of the Redaction. For detailed examination of the subject see *The Welsh Law of Women* (ed. D. Jenkins and M. E. Owen, Cardiff, 1980: hereafter WLW).

45.3-4 if . . . bestowers: i.e. if the woman has been given to the man by her kindred. This was the norm for marital union, and unions of other kinds had economic disadvantages for the woman, though all irregularity was removed if the union continued for seven years. Indeed, all unions were subject to the rule that during the first seven years the woman's share of the matrimonial property on separation would be her agweddi, whose amount was unrelated to the amount of the matrimonial property. The measure of the agweddi varied according to the circumstances of the union, being in some cases derisory: see 49.30n.

45.21 car and yoke: W. *carr ac iau*. The car would be a sledge (Mod. W. *car llusg*, lit. 'dragged car') and the yoke implies oxen to draw the car. It is not clear whether the woman would be entitled to cattle apart from this provision, for the tractate does not mention them. Donald Howells has argued that neat cattle would not form part of the matrimonial property: the man's cattle would be a fief from his lord: 8/9 SC 60-61. If the woman brought cattle as her dowry, they could be reclaimed by her kin because no surety was given for them: WLW 82-3.

45.29 let her pay: W. *taled*, which could mean 'let him pay': so translated in WLW 163.

45.32 cross-bed: W. *trawstyle*. The translation is used for the unusual Welsh word, which may well have no special sense; Wiliam (*Ior*, Index s.v.) has 'counterpane, coverlet'.

46.2 luxury-bag: W. *trythgwd*; purses: W. *llawgydau*. *Llawgwd* would be an obvious translation for 'handbag',

240   *The Law of Hywel Dda*

but the *llaw* may be the medieval Welsh word which means 'small': see PKM 271.

46.11-14 opened [meat, cheese]: W. [*cig, caws*] *bwlch*, lit. 'broken, gapped', i.e. that which has been cut into; we are concerned with 'preserved' provisions. See also 34.30n.

46.19-20 special right, right: the Welsh words are variants on *braint*, which in the lawbooks usually means 'status'; here the point is that the man could have an exclusive right to some part of what might appear to be matrimonial property, because it represented one of the 'unclaimable things' named at 61.3-6.

46.23-6 MS. *B* alone inserts 'and' before 'if she is given as a maiden'; this must be wrong, for the condition attaches to the right to cowyll, not to the following clause. Cowyll corresponds to the Germanic morning-gift, and could be claimed only by a virgin. 'Dowry' translates W. *argyfrau*: see 45.21n for the significance of the provision, and 117.25-37 for a special rule about the argyfrau of an alien's wife. In MSS. *B* and *D* the woman's claim is to wynebwerth and gowyn, but the reading of other manuscripts here translated is to be preferred: see 53.23-7 for the definition of gowyn, and cf. WLW 65-8.

46.35-6 woman of weight: W. *gwraig bwys*. There is no agreement on the meaning of the expression: Wiliam (*Ior* p. 109) suggests that it means a pregnant woman, who would be entitled to corn for rearing the child when born: 51.3-14, cf. WML 98.1-5.

46.38-47.4 This passage is doubly difficult. On the one hand it denies the dying man's right to make bequests so as to disinherit his sons, while it condemns as 'uncouth' the son who exercises his right to rescind such bequests; on the other hand it seems to run counter to the provisions which give the King (and the serjeant through him) a claim to goods from the estate of a dead man: see 34.29-34, 40.37. Both difficulties seem to arise from developments in society and state which altered practice and are reflected in the text, which has not been edited enough to be self-consistent. We have perhaps a vacillation between two systems of division: an older, in which the goods were divided into two parts, of which the wife took one while the husband was free to dispose of the other; and a newer, in which there were three parts, one for the wife, one for the sons, and one for

Notes: The Laws of Women 241

the dying man's disposal. The three-part division seems the newer, because it leaves the 'dead man's part' available for the state if the dead man has not disposed of it. The condemnation of the uncouth son must be understood as a moral judgment, not having any legal effect: there are parallels in law texts from England. The uncouth son, *mab anwar*, is 'believed to be a survival from common Celtic social ethics, in which the "un-warm" son was contrasted with the *mab gwâr* . . . whose warmth was made available to his parents in old age': WLW 85, citing Binchy, (1955) 3 *Celtica* 228-31. (The root of *gwâr* means 'warm', and in modern Welsh, though the derivative *gwareiddiad* may be translated 'civilisation', the basic adjective *gwâr* applies to the naturally civilised person who needs no civilising.) Other manuscripts allow for a payment to the lord, called ebediw or daered.

48.2 fondling: W. *gofysio*, for which MS. *D* substitutes the more definite *dodi bysedd ynddi*, 'putting fingers into her'; Lat D 345.24-5 has *pro palatione manuum in vulva, que dicitur gowys*, 'for placing of hands in the vulva, which is called *gofys*'.

48.5 kin-feud: W. *cenedlelyniaeth*. At an early date galanas between kins, which in classical law arose only from homicide, could arise from offences against women: see M. E. Owen, WLW 61-5.

49.2 tongued ones: see 62.9-15.

49.30 agweddi. MS. *B* has *argyfrau* (roughly 'dowry': see WLW 191), but the other manuscripts are clearly right, for the bride's kin would reclaim the argyfrau, as indicated above. The reading here adopted reflects an archaic feeling that any woman was entitled to agweddi on the termination of her union, though it might be a derisory agweddi as in this case: cf. the derisory sarhaed of the seated serjeant (35.6-8 and note) and the material cited in the note to 18. 20-23. The 'greased tail' procedure is applied in different circumstances according to different texts: see WLW, Index s.v. *greased tail*.

50.3-6 *Cyfn* (WML 89.21-5) and *Bleg* (62.4-8) give an eloping breyr's daughter six of these animals and a villein's daughter three. See also 19.31-2n.

50.11 three nights from the end of the seventh year. Different texts define the end of the agweddi period in different

242   *The Law of Hywel Dda*

ways, but this translation seems to give the most satisfactory sense, i.e. that the period was seven years less a 'tolerance' of three days: see WLW 117 n.14. It should be added that MS. *E* has emended 'seventh' to 'eighth', so that the period ends after seven years plus three days, which makes the text easier to understand but harder to believe.

50.27-32 There are variations in wording and substance between the manuscripts. MS. *B* alone has *taeog* for 'villein'; other manuscripts have *mab aillt*, as does the same triad at *DwCol* 285, where also 'goodman' is replaced by *uchelwr*. Two manuscripts give the villein's daughter a cowyll of eight score pence; in *Dw* 'the agweddi of an aillt's daughter is six score and a pound, and her cowyll a pound, as some say'. *Bleg* (60.23-8) and *Cyfn* (WML 90.2-7), where the material is not set out as a triad, give the breyr's daughter a cowyll of £1½ and the villein's daughter an agweddi of £1½; for their rules for the King's daughter see the next note.

50.33-5 In a similar passage *Bleg* (67.11-14) makes the gobr £6, and adds that the amount of the cowyll is what the husband thinks proper.

51.38 The payments to be made by the ravisher are worked out logically. There has been violence: so a dirwy is payable to the King. There has been admitted cohabitation: so the woman's amobr is payable to her lord. The rape has created a union which is terminated within seven years: so agweddi is payable to the woman; if she was a virgin she has lost her virginity, so that she is entitled to cowyll; and she has been insulted, so that she is entitled to wynebwerth. But it is not clear what *dilysrwydd* means in practice in this passage. For the word see the Glossary s.v. *llys*; here the idea seems to be 'that an unmarried girl is *dilys* only if she is a virgin, and the payment is a compensation for the loss of this *dilysrwydd*' (WLW 210), perhaps to be regarded as a solace to her injured feelings. At *DwCol* 122 the compensation for rape includes dilysrwydd but not agweddi; it could be argued that the payment of agweddi was evidence that the woman was *dilys* in the sense of being free to marry another man (see 57.13n), so that *dilysrwydd* could be an alternative name for agweddi.

52.1-2 In the light of other passages we should expect the sarhaed to be payable to the woman's husband, but only

Notes: The Laws of Women 243

the later manuscripts *G* and *D* (WLW 170) have a reading which makes this clear.

52.17 The main text of WML 97.18 has 'and her dirwy'; the translation here follows MS. *U.*

52.22-9 This passage from *Col* (63-5), which shows the influence of its Latin source, replaces the corresponding passage from *Ior* (50/5), which omits the references to amobr and is confusing over the unwillingness to give up the liaison; there is no manuscript authority for Aled Wiliam's emendation, which brings *Ior* into line with *Col* and the other Redactions.

52.34 offensive: W. *gygus*, derived from the noun *gwg* whose root is found also in *gowyn*: see 53.23-7 and WLW 65-8. It is impossible to tell whether it is the offensiveness or the giving of surety against it which is the custom.

53.9-27 This material early burst the bonds of the triad form: see WLW 65-8.

54.36 gift and transfer: W. *rhodd ac estyn*. The double expression seems to imply a separation between the kindred's agreement to give the girl as a wife and their handing her over: see WLW 215.

55.6 According to *Col* 15, the amobr of an alien's daughter was 24d., but 'according to custom [*defod*], 40d.' The other Redactions agree surprisingly closely with *Ior* in the measure of amobr (which they call *gobr*); this may indicate that the special social groups for whom a higher payment was due were no longer significant. For the villein (*aillt* in *Ior* and *Col*, *taeog* in *Cyfn*, *bilain* in *Bleg*), the amobr was still important, and the variations (*Ior* 60d. and 80d. in different manuscripts, *Col* 90d., *Cyfn* and *Bleg* 24d.) may well be significant.

55.16 As in other Western European societies, female slaves in Wales were of different classes. The servient slave is defined at 156.1-3 (cf. WLW 216) as one who goes neither to spade nor to quern.

55.20 innate bonheddig, W. *bonheddig canhwynol* (see Glossary s.v.). As the name implies, the bonheddig was the man of known stock. In the normal case, he would inherit land on the death of his father and would then become a breyr; and the texts do not seem to contemplate that he would have a marriageable daughter before becoming a breyr. The reference to 'when he was on the land' suggests that the present passage deals with the case of the bonheddig

244 The Law of Hywel Dda

who has lost his land without losing his status (see 110. 19-21); the view of the 'others' applies the general principle that a man's ebediw and his daughter's amobr were equal.

56.2-4 The reading of MS. *E*, 'canyt oes wat tros wayssaw' is preferred to that of *Col*, 'canyt oes gassaf'. The point seems to be that since the man asserts his responsibility for the alleged pregnancy, he cannot deny the liability for amobr which is the legal consequence.

57.6 a woman having a cell: W. *ystafellog o wraig*. *Ystafellog* is the adjective (used as noun) from *ystafell*, which is the lawbooks' word for the chamber in the court; here, however, it seems to mean a room occupied by a woman who was outside the pattern of kindreds, presumably an anchoress. Whereas the woman in the ordinary pattern of society has no ebediw save her amobr (57.18-19), the anchoress, who would never become liable to amobr, was charged with ebediw in respect of her cell. *Cyfn* (WML 100.4-6) and *Bleg* (49.25-27) both make the cell-woman's ebediw 12d. and specify an ebediw of 24d. for a man having a cell; in both, the passages follow others specifying ebediw in ecclesiastical contexts. *Bleg* (49.27-8) adds that the ebediw is paid to the lord of the land on which the cell stands.

57.13 validly free: W. *dilys*; cf. 51.38n.

57.16 car-returning: W. *karrdychuel*, where the -rr- indicates that the first element in the word is *car*, 'car', not *câr*, 'friend, relative'. Either element would be appropriate: the woman does not return to her kin, nor does she take back the car with the goods which she took with her to her husband; but the word may have been obscure to the thirteenth-century lawyers: see *Ior* p.110, *Bleg* p.230. On the rule that amobr was payable only once, see WLW 88-90; there are several references to the payment of amobr on a second marriage.

57.25-9 This paragraph is a formal triad, the Three Accusations of a Woman (*Tair Enllib Gwraig*) in *Col* (29), corresponding (but not exactly) to *Cyfn* (WML 127.7-11) and *Bleg* (111.24-8).

58.8-9 cattle of dark ancestry: W. *gwartheg dyfach*. This expression was clearly obscure in the thirteenth century, when it was understood as containing the word *mach*, 'surety', and variously explained. The present translation follows Charles-Edwards's analysis of *dyfach* as *du + ach*:

Notes: The Laws of Women   245

see WLW 205. The cattle in question will be those paid by a homicide's kin. See also 134.8-9n.

58.11-13 *Col* 33, 34 has 'A married woman is not entitled to buy and sell without her husband's leave; some say that she is entitled, if she is *priod*.' In Modern Welsh, *gwraig briod* is the ordinary expression for 'married woman', but in the present passage it must mean more than this: it seems most likely that the *gwraig briod* was the wife whose union had lasted seven years so that on separation she would take a half share of the marital property. The size of that share would be affected by her transactions, so that she had an economic interest in their success, whereas while she was still entitled to her agweddi her share would be unaffected by any loss or gain.

58.25 appropriate: W. *dyweto*; other manuscripts have *defnyddio*, but the meaning seems to be the same, i.e. that the bride names the goods which are to represent her cowyll, so that they can be identified and withdrawn from the common pool on a separation.

58.32-3 Cf. 132.14-21, 60.8-12n.

59.11-18 The corresponding text at *DwCol* 121-3 makes it clear that if the girl was found not to be a virgin, that was conclusive against the man, with the same financial consequences as in any case of rape; see 51.38n.

59.26-33 Though there was no legal requirement that a dowry should be provided for a bride, this passage shows that a marriage could be conditional on the dowry. MS. *B* has 'If . . . a woman is given to a man subject to her agweddi' (W. *adan e haguedy*); this hardly makes sense, and the consensus of the other manuscripts has been followed.

59.31 This provision should probably be read as 'No surety can be claimed . . .'; as there was no obligation to provide a dowry the wife's kin would not give a surety, since that would debar them from reclaiming the dowry if the union broke up: see the notes to 45.21 and 49.30 above, and cf. WLW 82 and n.65. 'Endowment' here translates W. *cynhysgaeth*, which is not a legal term of art.

60.8-12 This passage clearly gives the woman forty years of childbearing, which is consistent with the presumptions of modern English law; other manuscripts cut off the period at the age of forty, as does our text at 132.14-21; see WLW 71 n.7.

246   *The Law of Hywel Dda*

60.22 Most manuscripts add 'from then on for every accusation the oath of fifty women'.

60.33 damage: W. *cyflafan*, which in modern Welsh has a much stronger meaning ('outrage, massacre' in Spurrell's Dictionary). In the law texts its primary reference is to the harm caused to the victim of a wrongful act: so the first sentence of *Llyfr y Damweiniau* is 'Pob cyflafan a wnêl dyn o'i anfodd, diwyged o'i fodd', 'Every damage that a person does unwittingly let him compensate wittingly', *DwCol* 1. For other translations, see Glossary.

61.3-9 *Col* 40 and MS. *G* have illuminating variants on this triad. In MS. *G* the second item is what comes to him 'by way of daered of his land', which Charles-Edwards (WLW 179) translates 'in the way of land-rent': as the wife had no rights in the husband's land, she could not share in the financial yield from it if it was let for a rent. *Col* has 'those the man gets extra [*yn rhagor*] when there is separation' as the concluding clause, thus relating this provision to that of 46.19-20. For the whole subject see D. Howells, 'The Four Exclusive Possessions of a Man', (1973-4) 9/10 SC 48-67.

2. The Nine Tongued-Ones

This short tractate occurs in slightly different forms in *Bleg* (37.29-39.14, where it follows another short tractate on evidence) and *Cyfn* (WML 40.19-41.23, immediately after the Three Columns of Law). Its significance is that it lists exceptions to the rule (95.34) that the testimony of one person is not testimony.

61.23 *Cyfn* adds 'concerning a case which they admit was before him (where he had no interest in the case) and they are not agreed'; so too *Bleg*, in other words, with additional detail about procedure.

61.24 *Cyfn* and *Bleg* have the more satisfactory 'abbot' for 'priest'.

61.32 the justice's word is the final word: W. *gair yw gair yr ynad*, lit. 'the justice's word is a word', a frequent expression for a conclusive statement.

62.5-8 *Cyfn* has an entirely different case: 'A priest between two of his parishioners, on testimony attested to him'; so too *Bleg*, in different words. For the case of the donor, see 62.34-6.

Notes: The Nine Tongued-Ones 247

62.16-21 The case in *Ior* is that of 48.36-49.4; that in *Cyfn* is probably the original case, which has been modified in *Bleg*, according to which the girl's word as to her being a virgin is conclusive only if she is under twelve: 'if over twelve, she gives her oath as one of five of persons closest to her'.

62.31 *Cyfn* and *Bleg* add that the fellow-thief will not be put to death, but will be a 'sale thief': this should in any case follow from the fact that he was not taken with the stolen property.

3. Injury to Animals

63.5 clean: W. *glân. Col* has *llawn*, lit 'full', which suggests that the animal was required to be in good condition, but it is more probable that the qualification is that it should be of a kind used for food: cf. 177.34; 186.1.

63.13 validly: W. *yn ddilys*; the substitution would give the recipient a sufficient title to the substituted animal.

63.14-15 of full value: W. *telediw*; the word (whose root is *tâl*, 'payment') implies that the animal could be paid in discharge of a debt at the full standard legal value.

63.23-6 Cf. 177.25-178.3n; 184.35n.

4. Surety and Contract

The length and detail of this tractate in *Ior* are signs of the importance of contractual obligation in thirteenth-century Gwynedd, for though the traditional translation 'surety' is used for *mach*, the *mach* (pl. *meichiau*) as he appears in this tractate is not so much a surety in the modern sense as a figure whose intervention is necessary in order to make a transaction between two other parties into an effective contract. The later chapters of the tractate show that the classical lawyers found this procedure for establishing and enforcing a contract too cumbersome, and there is clear evidence that the *mach* was a survival from an earlier age, when courts and the state could not be counted on to enforce men's rights. The *mach* was in origin a private law-enforcement officer: he appears most prominently as enforcing a contract, but he appears also in at least two other contexts. The parties in law-suits are required to give *meichiau* to abide law; and in most cases of the transfer of property the

248   *The Law of Hywel Dda*

transferor gives a *mach* by way of guarantee: if the transferor later tries to re-take the property, the transferee can
call on the *mach* to protect his right to it—and (at least in
the theory of the lawbooks) he might have to do this by force.

65.4-6 For the relatives involved in the payment of galanas
see 144.21-38n, 147.5-18nn.

65.9-10 The normal man would take the oath in his parish
church. *DwCol* 501, 502 give rulings on two special cases:
court officers and other royal dependants took the oath in
the King's chapel, and a man who had no fixed home would
take it in the church of the parish in which he was found.

65.14-15 In spite of this reference to the Lord's prosecuting
for perjury, the lawbooks' comparative silence on the subject
suggests that it was left to the Church.

66.11 Some manuscripts here speak of the principal debtor
as counterswearing, but the sense clearly requires a reference to the claimant, as in our text.

66.15 *Ior* adds (after 'judgment') from MS. *E* 'on account
of the denial which he has performed [*digones*]'.

67.36-68.4 *Col* here states the opinion of 'some of the
justices' and presents a conclusive argument in support of
it. As the next paragraph (from the second part of MS. *Col*)
also shows, there was among the lawyers of the classical
period a tendency to unreasoning pedantry, which is
countered in MS. *Col* by reference to principle.

68.25 From the reference (at 69.2-4) to the repayment of a
halfpenny in respect of a lost gage, it appears that the gage
was required to be greater than the debt by one third of the
gage (*pace* the note at *Ior* p.113); this is still the norm as a
basis for secured loans.

68.33 The translation follows the reading of MS. *B:* all the
manuscript readings differ slightly and are perhaps the
result of attempts to emend a corrupt text. The point of the
rules seems to be that the surety must not take a gage unless
the debtor has been given an opportunity to pay or deny
liability. The refusal (W. *negyddiaeth*) which justifies taking
a gage is distinct from denial (W. *gwad*): refusal to pay seems
to imply that liability is admitted.

68.37-69.8 The point of these rules is that the debtor was
entitled to redeem the gage until the due date, but not thereafter. If the gage could not be produced when payment was

Notes: Surety and Contract   249

tendered, the debt was discharged and the debtor was entitled to be reimbursed for the 'security element' in the gage, i.e. for half the debt; and since he had voluntarily given as gage something too valuable, his claim to reimbursement was limited to the legal measure of the security element. Similarly, since the creditor was entitled to keep the gage if it was not redeemed at the due date, the debtor could not claim anything in respect of the extra value. The rules of 69.20-70.4 arise because of the obvious practical difficulties caused by these rules.

69.9-11 valid: W. *dilys*. The doubt is about the validity of the creditor's title; the rule is, in effect, that the gaging is itself sufficient guarantee of that title. If the debtor challenged the title, the creditor could presumably rely on the surety who took the gage from the debtor to prove the gaging and the forfeit: this suggests that there was no need to add 'admitted' (W. *addefedig*) from MS. *A* at *Ior* 62/9.

69.20 twelve pence: *Ior* adds (from MS. *E*) 'and the due date for the twelve pence comes'.

70.1-2 a stone in place of an icicle: W. *maen dros iaen*. This proverbial expression has caused difficulty to the translators, but as Ifor Williams pointed out (Bd iv.68, tr.) 'Ice is weaker than a stone, it does not bear so much weight. That is what a lord is, he is like a powerful stone to bear the weight lest the weak ones under him be crushed.' The present passage suggests that *iaen* should be understood as 'icicle' rather than 'sheet of ice', and *dros* as 'in place of' rather than 'over'; so too in *DwCol* 307, where the lord, as *maen dros iaen*, can secure the rights of a blind man to property which he cannot swear to because he cannot see it. It is as *maen dros iaen* that a lord has his place in the triad of the Three Powerful Ones of the World (*Tri Chadarn Byd, DwCol* 135): the others are the Fool (*drud*) who cannot be compelled to do anything against his will, and the Have-not (*diddim*) from whom nothing can be got because he has nothing.

70.21-2 for a fixed day: W. *yn unddyddiog*, lit. 'one-daily'; cf. 84.1, 4.

70.25, 26 plea: W. *arddelw*, for which see the Glossary. The classical law thus refused to recognise the 'self-surety', in contrast to *Bleg*, which may have adopted it under the influence of other systems in which it was well-known.

250 *The Law of Hywel Dda*

70.29-38 Richards (*B Bleg* 52-3) has correctly translated this passage, without comment on the unsatisfactory note at *Bleg* p.185. In the present translation 'most nearly related to him' represents an emendation of the text, which would give 'of nearest worth to him'; the Welsh is perhaps a mistranslation of a Latin text resembling Lat B 217.17 'cum sex viris probatis de proximis suis'. Lat D 369.11-12 is unequivocal, 'de septimo proximorum sibi'.

71.3 feeble: W. *gwan. Col* 102 is clearer, with *claf*, 'sick'.

72.21-3 Lord: the text has 'King' (*brenin*) three times where consistency requires our emendation to 'Lord'. This suggests that the passage is substantially older than the manuscript evidence for it, for there seems to have been 'some form of agreement among the leading princes to drop the title of king, an understanding which coincided with the assertion by Henry II of the principle of Anglo-Norman lordship over Wales' (T. Jones Pierce, *Medieval Welsh Society* (ed. J. Beverley Smith, Cardiff, 1972), 29; see also (1976) 26 BBCS 451-62).

72.36-73.15 This passage neatly illustrates the complexity of the institution of *mach*. In the case described, the surety guarantees the transaction for the transferee against the transferor; he does not guarantee the transferor's title, so that the true owner's title is not defeated. However, the transferee does not lose the property without compensation: the rule here given must be interpreted in the light of the law relating to theft: 162.9-12, 30-33. When the true owner claims the property by the procedure of *damdwng*, the transferee will plead voucher to warranty: that is, he will call on the transferor to warrant his title to the property. The transferor cannot do this, and the true owner is therefore entitled to his property. The transferee is of course entitled to compensation from the transferor, and according to this triad he is not bound to give the property up to the true owner until he receives the compensation: the wording of the triad in *Col* (112) makes it quite clear that the compensation comes from the transferor. *Col* also makes the meaning of the last clause clearer, by providing simply for a camlwrw for the Lord: it is payable by reason of the improper movement of the property from the transferor (who was not owner) to the transferee.

73.16 *Col* 113 has 'no woman is a surety unless she is a female lord' (W. *arglwyddes*). The female lord appears also

Notes: Surety and Contract   251

in the context of amobr, at 60.26; ct. 124.21 and see the note to that passage.

73.33 buckle sureties: W. *balog fechni*. MS. *Col* has *halauc uechny*, 'polluted surety', but the definition at *Dw* 468 shows that the manuscripts which have *balog fechni* are to be followed.

76.5 a scholar from a school: W. *ysgolhaig ysgol*; ct. the usual meaning of *ysgolhaig*, 'clerk (in holy orders)', at (e.g.) 1.6,7.

76.28 interchangeable trinkets: W. *tlysau treigledig*. For *tlysau*, see Glossary s.v. *tlws*; *treigledig* is rendered 'interchangeable' in the light of *Dw* 190, which explains that surety is not necessary 'because they cannot be followed [*erlyn*] to invalidate them': they cannot be identified. The practical result is that they are negotiable in the technical sense of modern law: the transferee gets a good title to them, even though his transferor may not have had a good title. *Dw* 189 adds *bwyd treigledig*, 'interchangeable food' to the list.

76.33 to seek law. *Col* 119 adds 'to deny the claim', and makes it clear that the gage given is the principal debtor's. The rule implies that submission to law was voluntary.

77.3 *Col* 120 names three causes which will delay a claim of suretyship: a claim of violence, and a claim of theft, and a claim of trumpet [*utgorn*]'; the versions of *Cyfn* (WML 85.20-23) and *Bleg* (40.26-8) expand the 'claim of trumpet' to 'from hearing the King's horn going to hostings', and *Dw* 486 names the third cause as the King's horn.

77.9 The various manuscripts of *Ior* all seem confused: the translation takes advantage of *Col* 122, 'let the surety exact the debt for the claimant without delay'.

77.29-78.4 This paragraph is concerned, not with suretyship for a transaction, but with suretyship in litigation; the text suggests that the imaginary defendant is deliberately confusing the two. *Col* 125 again clarifies the position by adding the sentence 'Since he has pleaded delay for aid, it is right for him (in order to seek a delay for aid) to give a surety for that law, since it is right to seek it through law.' The defendant, having claimed a delay for aid, is not required to give surety to abide law on his main claim: that comes at a later stage; he is, however, required to give surety that he will bring his aid to court to give answer. The quasi-proverb

252   *The Law of Hywel Dda*

quoted can be expanded to 'He is entitled to a surety [for law] who is entitled to nothing [when his claim has been tried]'.

Briduw (78.5-79.2)

Briduw, lit. 'the honour of God', corresponds to the pledge of faith found in so many systems. The brief references in *Cyfn* (WML 85.10-11) and *Bleg* (41.10-12) to denial by the defendant alone, by an oath repeated seven times on the altar, emphasise the religious basis of the form, which has been weakened in *Ior*. The requirement that the hands of the parties should meet is a sign of the assimilation to secular form.

78.14-18 The reading of the first passage in some manuscripts suggests that a camlwrw was paid to the Church as well as the King, but the second passage indicates that the Church's sanctions would be spiritual—if we follow LW's interpretation of 'forbid him for a briduw' as meaning excommunication of the offender.

Amod (79.3-80.33)

This is the normal word in the law texts for 'contract' in the widest sense: for its etymology, see Binchy, CLP 115. It is also used in the classical law in the narrower sense of this special form of contract, for which the fuller expression *amod ddeddfol*, 'legal contract', is used when it is necessary to make it clear that the narrower sense is intended. There is no reference to this form of contract in *Cyfn* or *Bleg*, and it may be a sign of its recent development that in the *Ior* manuscripts the word *amodwyr* is used both for the contracting parties ('amod-makers' in this translation) and for the persons called in to support the contract ('contract-men' at 62.32). These contract-men do not prove the existence of the contract: that proof depends on the oaths and counter-oaths of the contracting parties, and the function of the contract-men is to prove the terms agreed by the parties. Legal amod has for the parties the advantage over mach that it eliminates one set of oaths, those between mach and principal debtor. For the contract-men it has the advantage that they never become personally liable.

80.9-11 These brocards are notable as a sign of the developed character of the Welsh law. Corresponding statements are found in English and continental sources, but it can be

Notes: Surety and Contract 253

argued that the Welsh sources are the oldest, since the sentence from *Cyfn* uses the word *gwir* in the archaic sense of 'law': see 'The Medieval Welsh Idea of Law', (1981) 49 *Tijdschrift voor Rechtsgeschiedenis* 323-48 at pp. 340-42.

80.12-29 dissolved: W. *torri*. In this sophisticated paragraph, whose conclusion (expressed in terms of modern English law) is that breach of an amod amounts to repudiation, thus entitling the party not in breach to refuse performance, the word *torri*, lit. 'break', is used in two senses. Where translated 'break', it refers to the party's non-performance of his undertaking, but in this first use it refers to dissolution of the contract as a consequence of the failure to perform. 'Repudiate' translates *gwrthod* and *ymwrthod â*.

Bail (80.35-81.26)

81.7 principal offender: W. *llofrudd*, lit. 'red-handed'. The original application is to the principal offender in homicide, whence there has been an extension in the law texts to other offences. At 143.29; 144.9 the abstract *llofruddiaeth* means 'principal offence' but in modern Welsh the meaning of *llofruddiaeth* has narrowed to 'murder', as contrasted with manslaughter and non-culpable homicide.

81.10-13 This sentence has been emended in the light of *Col* 144. The reading of *Ior* 70/4, *dilysu o'r llofrudd y gorfodog*, is difficult: it seems to mean 'the principal offender renders the bailsman immune', but the consequence named makes it clear that this cannot be the meaning. *Col* has *ffo o'r dyn rhag ei orfodog*, 'the person flees from his bailsman'; perhaps the *Ior* reading is to be understood as 'renders the bailsman valid (i.e. operative)'. See also the Glossary, s.vv. *dilys*, *llys*.

5. Church Protection

In this chapter 'protection' and 'sanctuary' both translate W. *nawdd*: 'sanctuary' seems to imply protection in a particular place, whereas in some contexts *nawdd* is not confined in space. 'Sanctuary' also translates *noddfa*, which in some contexts in *Cyfn* and *Bleg* stands for the area called *corflan* (see 82.22n) in *Ior*. The whole chapter reflects the control exercised by the secular power in Gwynedd over the Church: there is nothing comparable in *Cyfn* and *Bleg*. For more detail, see Huw Pryce, 'Ecclesiastical Sanctuary in Thir-

254   *The Law of Hywel Dda*

teenth-Century Welsh Law', 5 *Journal of Legal History*, no. 3, pp. 1-13.

81.30 conquest: W. *goresgyn*. Like 'conquest' in the legal language of medieval England, *goresgyn* (which in modern Welsh has much the modern English meaning of 'conquest') has the meaning 'acquisition of land'; this may be the sense here.

82.11,13,14 escort: W. *hebrwng*. It is evidently contemplated that the offender will not remain indefinitely in sanctuary, but will be given safe-conduct to some other place, either to a place defined in a similar way to those mentioned in the rules for the protection offered by court officers, or to the boundary of the realm.

82.22 the churchyard and the enclosure: W. *y fynwent a'r corflan*. *Corflan* has usually been understood as *corfflan* and translated 'cemetery', but it seems safer to take the first element as *corf* and the whole word as meaning the enclosed ground which was associated with a church: see 82.31. *Col* 573 speaks of burying in the churchyard (*mynwent*); see also *Col* pp.155-6.

82.24 clas: the body of the community, who were not necessarily all clergy.

83.16-17 legal witnesses: W. *tystion deddfol*. As with *amod ddeddfol* (see 79.3-80.33n), the adjective seems to be added in order to make it clear that *tystion* is used in the narrower sense of attestators (persons called to witness) rather than the wider sense of testifiers in general. A church which had been granted especially large rights of sanctuary would be well advised to call persons to witness the grant.

6. Land Law

Much more space is given to the procedure in land cases in *Ior* than in *Cyfn* or *Bleg*, probably because the state was so much stronger in thirteenth-century Gwynedd than it had been earlier, or than it ever was elsewhere in Wales. The procedure described is formal and objective, as it was generally in medieval Europe; but in Welsh law trial by ordeal and trial by battle were not used: oaths and evidence were the materials of proof. There is no provision for testing the credibility of the individual swearer or testifier by cross-examination: if he has the prescribed qualifications and

Notes: Land Law   255

goes through the forms successfully, his contribution cannot be rejected. Nevertheless, these formal rules reflect a vigorous attempt to ensure a high probability that the truth will emerge: they aim at bringing before the court the evidence which is most likely to be true, while they leave to the court the function of deciding whether the parties have performed the objective feats required of them, or in some cases of balancing the weight of testimony (objectively measured) on either side.

84.15 a delay for aid: W. *oed wrth borth*: see Glossary, s.v. *porth*.

84.20 ebb and flow: W. *llanw a thrai*; as in the expression meaning 'a year and a day', the items are in reverse order in Welsh.

84.32-3 whichever is senior: W. *yr hynaf a fo*. It is surprising to find the possibility that the commote justice should take priority over the court justice: LW has *Judicum Commotae senior*, 'the senior of the judges of the commote'.

85.10-16 This diagram follows the next paragraph in most manuscripts, being added in a later hand in MS. *B*. Its form varies a little from manuscript to manuscript, and does not agree exactly with the text in any; as printed here it has been emended to agree with our text. A pictorial form of the diagram, from the fifteenth-century manuscript *S*, is shown in the frontispiece of this volume; the clothing there depicted reflects fifteenth-century conditions.

85.20 control: W. *meddiant*. *Col* 461 specifies that the sureties are to be 'in custody, i.e. prison'; for cases in which pledges (*obsides*) were offered, see *The Welsh Assize Roll* (ed. J. Conway Davies, Cardiff, 1940), 253, 257, 264-5.

85.25 case: W. *cyngaws*, for which see Glossary.

85.29 plead: W. *ymddywedwch*, lit. 'speak together', the imperative of the reflexive form of *dywedud*, 'to say, speak'. In *Col* 452-62 the order of proceedings seems more logical: (1) the parties name their cyngaws and canllaw; (2) the parties are called on to plead, and sureties for law are given; (3) the parties plead, i.e. they state their case. See also Glossary, s.v. *arddelw*.

86.27 *Col* 467 adds 'and then you have a proverb, "A fault in the mouth of a cyngaws" ', implying that the cyngaws who did not offer both kinds of testimony would be at fault.

256 *The Law of Hywel Dda*

The classical law clearly distinguished between three kinds of testifier: the attestator (W. *tyst*, also used in the wider sense of any kind of testifier: cf. 83.16-17n), a person called to witness to an act at the time of the act; the maintainer (W. *ceidwad*), who testified to a state of affairs; and the knower (*gwybyddiad*), who testified to an occurrence from his own knowledge. (The Irish parallel suggests that the form *gwybyddiad* is a re-formation from *gwyddiad*, in which the root is *gŵydd*, 'presence'; this does not affect the interpretation of the person's function.) The point of the present passage is that normally only one question would require an answer; here two questions may arise (the proprietorship and the ejection), and the claimant must answer both unless the defendant concedes his claim on either.

86.29 warranties: W. *arddelw*, for which see Glossary.

87.34 a word of inquiry: W. *gair cyfarch*. According to *Dw* 290, *gair cyfarch* means 'the justices' asking "Where is your warrantor or your aid?"', but this is in a different context, and the definition is inappropriate here, since the aid (cyngaws and canllaw) is already present and the call for the maintainers and knowers (who correspond to the warrantor) comes after the answer to the word of inquiry. A more probable explanation is that of AL IX.xvi.8,9 (ii. 244-6), which makes the word of inquiry necessary when a party has presented more than one argument. This would happen when it was not clear whether the two questions of proprietorship and ejection were still in dispute between the parties. It would also happen if the party himself, and also his cyngaws or canllaw or both, had made a plea: all three had the opportunity to present a plea, and the invitation to 'better' pleadings refers to this. In such a case, the word of inquiry would be a call on the party to choose one of the two or three pleas presented: *Dw* 483 makes it clear that it was for the party to choose the plea on which he would rely. In the present context the three-man team may need to consult together before the party answers; they must do this in private, and *Col* 477 adds that for this private consultation they should go as far as the justices go for theirs.

88.7 what their decision is: W. *eu cyngor*; 'they' are the parties to whom the inquiry was directed.

89.18-19 Disturbance will be punished: W. *cosb er anosteg*, lit. 'punishment for non-silence'.

Notes: Land Law 257

91.14 a standard plot: W. *tu a thâl*, lit. 'side and end', which seems to correspond to a traditional Irish scheme of sharing land 'in rectangular strips, the length being twice the breadth. The long side of the area is called *taeb*, "side", the short side is called *airchenn*, "fore-end".' (Eóin MacNeill, *Proceedings of the Royal Irish Academy*, xxxvi (sect. C), 287).

91.17 immunity: W. *rhyddid*, lit. 'freedom', presumably from services to the Lord.

92.10-11 office of . . . standard-bearer: W. *llumenyddiaeth*. This is added from other manuscripts: *Col* 512 has *llumanyaeth*. The office does not seem to be mentioned elsewhere, and it may well be a late innovation which would not have been mentioned in the archetype. From the name of *Gwely Hebogyddion* 'the falconers' gwely', in Dinlle (the townland from which Cyfnerth and Morgenau and Iorwerth ap Madog came, see CLP 123-33), it seems that land was reserved for the falconers in Arfon.

92.13 shareland: W. *rhandir*. This was (at least in name) a standard area of land: see 121.5-6n, 17-18. The reference here seems to imply that a holding of this size was the norm for which King's fee would be paid, so that he would claim larger fees for larger holdings and might accept smaller fees for smaller ones.

92.22 acquired land: W. *tir cynnif*. *Col* 515 has *annilys*, 'invalid', at this point as well as at the end of the rule. In spite of the notes at *Ior* p.118 and *Col* p.134, it seems best to understand *tir cynnif* as land acquired by the transferor otherwise than as patrimony—whether it was sold or given to him, reclaimed by him from the waste, or forcibly taken by him. In these cases there is a possibility that a proprietor will appear, to invalidate the transferor's title and hence to recover the land from the transferee; if that happens, the latter has no redress against the transferor, for it is his own carelessness in accepting 'invalid' land which has caused his loss. The background to the rule is a successful claim by the transferee to proprietorship: his success gives him an undivided share side by side with the sitting proprietor, and he then calls for a physical division: it is easy to see that the sitting proprietor might offer land bought or reclaimed by him, in order to keep his inherited land intact. The transferee would accept the offer at his peril.

92.29-30 on the day of loss or gain. This is the wording of

258 *The Law of Hywel Dda*

MSS. *A* and *E*, which is clearer than those of MS. *B* and *Col* 517.

94.1-25 A philosophic analysis of the grounds of objection (W. *llys*) to testifiers is found only in *Col* and Lat E (457.13-20). In the latter, the three classes of objection are *naturalis*, *generalis*, and *singularis*, corresponding respectively to the objections for nature, for offence, and for act. Both objection for nature and objection for offence are in fact general; they disqualify the testifier for all cases, whereas the objection for act is 'singular' in that it applies only to the testimony against specific persons. The allocation of the various grounds is not wholly satisfactory in either of the two versions, which seem to go back to a common source now lost. This may have been the 'Book of the White House', and was no doubt in Latin, for *Col* 565 reads 'If it be doubted whether all the objections introduced above are in the law of Hywel, let the Latin books be examined, and there they will be found.' The procedure and nomenclature of objection to testifiers, as recorded in *Cyfn* and *Bleg*, diverge substantially from the *Ior/Col* plan.

94.15 the three systems of law: W. *y tair cyfraith*. These were no doubt canon law, Roman law, and the law of Hywel.

94.22 The archaic text of the Nine Abetments of Galanas according to the men of Powys shows that woman-feud was originally recognised as a ground of galanas, as was 'land-feud': see 143.2n and WLW 61-5.

95.8 principal: W. *llofrudd*. The extension of meaning here is hardly logical, and *Col* 538 avoids the problem by speaking of 'him with whom he swears'.

95.9 for love: W. *er digasedd*; in conjunction with *er cas*, 'for hate', it seems better to understand the *di-* of *digasedd* as negative rather than reinforcing.

95.20 The translation follows the other manuscripts in preference to MS. *B*, which has wrongly inserted *tebygu* 'to suppose', thus making the designated compurgator's oath the same as the undesignated compurgator's. The designated compurgator (W. *rheithiwr nod*) is well known in medieval Europe: he is a compurgator designated by name in advance, not freely chosen by the principal when he comes to swear. There is nothing to show who named the designated compurgators in Welsh law: in other systems they might be chosen by the court or even by the opposing

Notes: Land Law 259

party. Designated compurgators in Anglo-Saxon law are discussed by L. J. Downer in *Leges Henrici Primi* (Oxford, 1972) 430-35. The silence of *Cyfn* and *Bleg* on designated compurgators suggests that their use in Wales was an innovation of the classical law.

95.35-96.2 This passage in *Bleg* leads in to a version of the Nine Tongued-ones (II.2), in which the name *tafodiog* is not used.

97.28-31 The text is emended from *Col*, as none of the *Ior* manuscripts distinguishes between the close and open season; 'restricted' translates *caeth*, lit. 'bond, enslaved', which may be a miscopying of *caeedig*, 'closed'.

97.32-98.7 The paragraph is concerned with proof that the procedure leading to the final day of loss or gain has been followed: it lays down that only the evidence of the court itself is admissible.

Sharing of Land (98.33-100.33)

99.1 four for the godaeog. *Ior* 82/2 gives the godaeog eight acres, following MS. *B*: the passage is missing from MSS. *A* and *C*, but *Col* and MS. *E* agree in giving the aillt a larger holding. Since *Col* uses the ordinary word *taeog*, it looks as though *godaeog* (which seems to occur only in this passage) were merely an elegant variant, perhaps introduced to point the contrast with *aillt*, which often seems to be synonymous with *taeog*: see the Glossary, s.v. *aillt*.

99.2 As the passage given below shows, *Cyfn* gave each participant eight acres; so too *Bleg* (74.21-8) in a passage which looks like a re-translation from a Latin translation of *Cyfn*.

99.3-9 The same rules for the size of the acre are repeated at 120.35-121.3 and 199.1-9, in other contexts. Since the Welsh foot measured nine inches (see 120.25-6 and 198.36-7), the long yoke was twelve English feet and the length of the acre 120 yards; if the caller's reach is taken as six English feet, the width of the acre will be twelve yards and its total measure 1440 square yards. This seems very small until it is remembered that the ploughing 'day', which was the nominal basis of the acre, ended at midday. The alternative measure given here would be even smaller, as would those of *Cyfn* (WML 54.12-15) and *Bleg* (71.13-15). Customary acres varied much, and those of Wales have often been studied, most recently by Colin A. Gresham, 101 *Arch.*

260   *The Law of Hywel Dda*

Camb. 118-22, and Brian Howells, (1967) 15 NLWJ 226-33.
For the significance of the four yokes and the 'middle peg',
see the notes to III.9 (pp.303-5).

99.18 The reading 'youngest' of MS. *E* has been preferred
to the 'eldest' of *Ior* 82/7, as more logical and more consistent with the other Redactions. If the eldest brother were
given first choice of toft, there would be no reason why the
youngest brother should not make the division as he did
when there were no houses. The youngest is given first
choice because he is the son most likely to have stayed at
home with his father: the special croft given by *Cyfn* is no
doubt the father's home, and the MS. *E* version gives the
youngest son the chance to choose this, where *Cyfn* and
Bleg allot it to him willy-nilly. Cf. 58.4.

99.25 buildings: W. *trefnau*, cf. *trefn fechan*, which alternates with *tŷ bychan* for 'latrine'. The Latin texts have
edificia, which gives *adail* in *Bleg*.

99.35, 100.2 The use of two different words for the re-
sharing by first cousins and that by second cousins has put
a strain on the translation. 'Divide equally' translates *cystadlu*, from *cystadl* (modern Welsh *cystal*), 'equally good';
in modern Welsh *cystadlu* means 'to compete'; 'equalise'
translates *cymheinio*, from *cymaint*, 'equally great'. The
process seems to have been the same in the two cases, and
the result to have been a redistribution per capita.

100.5 Gwely land (W. *tir gwelyog*) was land held by the
normal free tenure, under which it passed to the sons on
the holder's death. It took its name from the gwely, the
closest group of relatives (for which see 147.11n), and was
no doubt so called from its passing within the gwely on
inheritance. Geldable land (W. *tir cyllidus*) or reckon land
(W. *tir cyfrif*) was land held by the normal unfree tenure.
Since *cyllid* has come to be used in modern Welsh for
'finance', *cyllidus* suggests at first that the land concerned
was subject to cash payments; this is wholly improbable, and
it seems more likely that the adjective implies a liability to
payments in kind, as contrasted with the primary obligation
of military service owed by free land: *cyllidus* (used as a
noun) occurs as an alternative to *taeog*, 'villein', in some
contexts. When the 'geldable' townland was considered, it
was natural to think of it as one in which the occupiers were
reckoned or counted in order to determine their shares:

Notes: Land Law 261

from *tref gyfrif*, 'reckon townland', the verbal adjective spread to *tir cyfrif*.

100.10-11 extinguished acre: W. *erw ddiffoddedig*, i.e. one whose owning kindred had died out. In gwely land, when a kindred died out, its land escheated to the King; in a reckon townland this did not happen, for there no one inherited land as successor to his father, and when an occupier died (whether he left a son or other relative or not), his land returned to the common pool.

100.17 entitled person: W. *dyledog*, the adjective meaning 'rightly entitled', used as a noun.

Regalities (101.1-16)

101.2 This sentence is not a declaration in favour of monarchical government; its force would be conveyed by the paraphrase 'No piece of land is entitled to be independent of the King'. The rest of the paragraph is concerned with the rights retained by the King when franchises are recognised in the Church: 'theft' and 'fighting' refer to the penalties imposed for these offences; 'hosting' means the right to military service from holders of land.

Dadannudd (101.18-104.8)

As the reference to a hearth at 102.7 suggests, *dadannudd* means literally 'uncovering'—of a fire banked up overnight. In Welsh law it becomes the name for a legal action claiming land which was at some previous time held by the claimant's ancestor, whose fire the claimant figuratively uncovers. The action at law, however, is a 'curialisation' of a pre-curial form of self-help, which is not recorded in any Welsh source, but can be deduced from a comparison of the Welsh and Irish sources. The 'three kinds of dadannudd' hardly make sense as different forms of the legal action; their meaning becomes clear when they are recognised as stages in a self-help procedure designed to force the sitting tenant of the land to submit to arbitration of the claimant's case. Dadannudd corresponds in practice to the mort dancestor of English law; and as mort dancestor and the other petty assizes came in practice to replace the writ of right, so there is some reason to believe that dadannudd superseded the procedure by kindred and descent.

101.19 tillage and ploughing: W. *ar ac aredig*. Probably mere hendiadys: in addition to the passage below, *Col* 566

262 *The Law of Hywel Dda*

indulges in this even more exuberantly, with dadannudd of tillage and ploughing and houses and home (W. *ar ac aredig a thai ac anlloedd*); of car and inhabited hearth (*car ac aelwyd cyfannedd*); and of bale and burden and hearth (*bwrn a baich ac aelwyd*): this version shows an insistence on habitation which is missing from *Ior*.

101.20-23 *Col* 567 allows the claimant to bring an action of dadannudd where either his father or he himself has been in occupation; that this was *Ior*'s meaning is implied by the later references in the main text. The provision (added to *Ior* 84/2 from MS *E*) which allows dadannudd to a claimant whose ancestors (W. *rhieni*) have been in occupation is inconsistent with the rest of the text, and is therefore omitted.

101.26 without answering, i.e. without acknowledging a claim made against him.

102.3-5 This sentence is a clear reflection of the growing strength of the state in Gwynedd. In origin, the action of dadannudd tested only the previous occupation of the claimant or his father, and left it open to others to raise questions of title after the expiry of a successful claimant's guaranteed period of occupation; this provision, however, makes a state-approved title a condition for bringing the action. 'Grant and investiture' translates W. *rhodd ac estyn*, an expression also used of the 'gift and transfer' of a woman in marriage: see 54.36n. In relation to land the double expression may be mere hendiadys; the same rule is repeated immediately before the next passage in our text, which is taken from the later part of the same manuscript.

102.21-2 will maintain: the reading of MS. *G* is preferred to that of MS. *B*, 'know it', since maintainers, not knowers, were appropriate for this part of the claimant's case.

102.33 will maintain: from MS. *G*; MS. *B* has 'know it'.

103.16 if . . . equally entitled: W. *o bydd cyhydedd y ddwy blaid*.

103.19-104.8 It does not seem to be significant that in this section the claim is for dadannudd of tillage and ploughing, without mention of house and home, nor that both manuscripts telescope the allegations of maintaining and knowing. The point of the section is the defendant's plea that the issue has already been decided against the claimant, though there is no indication that the defendant was then a party.

Notes: Land Law 263

Claims by Proprietary Right (104.9-107.6)

104.25-6 a proprietor . . . another: W. *cany ddyly priodor ragor rhag ei gilydd*. Other manuscripts, and *Col* 579, have *cany ddyly priodor gychwyn rhag ei gilydd*, 'since a proprietor is not bound to move away from before another'; the contrast between the versions delicately reveals the ambivalence of *dyly*.

104.31 allowance: W. *cynnwys*. The definition in GPC is misleading, for it applies to this text the later use of *cynnwys* for the admission of illegitimate sons to a share in their fathers' land; this is found in Chirkland and the Honour of Denbigh, see *Col* p.147. In the present text the claimant is given, not one half of the land (as he would if he had come a generation earlier) but one share in a distribution per capita among all those entitled, including himself. *Dw* 168 defines *cynnwys* as 'as much as the man who has the greatest occupation', which assumes that the sitting proprietors might have unequal shares in the holding; this would certainly be possible if there had been no re-sharing among cousins.

104.33 *Diasbad uwch Annwfn* is left untranslated because of uncertainty about its form and meaning: the expression does not seem to occur in *Bleg*, and in *Cyfn* occurs only in MS. *U* (WML 316.3, 6, *diaspat uch aduan*), which may well have derived it from a *Ior* text. There is no difficulty over *diasbad*, 'shriek, cry or distress', but the rest of the expression appears in forms ranging from *uch annvyn* to *uchawn*, *vwch aduan*, and *y dannu ffin*. The oldest manuscripts point to our *uwch Annwfn*; Annwfn is the underworld of Welsh mythology, and the expression perhaps implies that the claimant is crying out against being expelled from the human world of landed proprietors.

105.4 contention: W. *ymwrthryn*. The main *Ior* text has no other reference to this type of claim.

105.15 maintain it: following the correcter reading of MS. *G*.

105.17 and unentitled: added from MS. *G*.

105.22-4 If the defendant admits . . . claim: from MS. *G*.

106.23 plea: W. *arddelw*; MS. *G* has *hawl*, 'claim'.

106.31 maintain: following the correcter reading of MS. *G*.

106.37 For 'violence and harm' see 111.13-29.

264　　　　The Law of Hywel Dda

Women and Land (107.8-110.6)

107.12　The *y* inserted from MS. *E* in *Ior* 86/2 is not necessary. The giving in question is the giving in marriage of the woman.

107.16　a wedded husband entitled to land: W. *gŵr priod dylyedog o dir*; see 58.11-13n, 110.28n, for other examples of *priod*.

107.32　since she has not lost her status: W. *cani cholles hi ei braint*. The reasoning is not clear, and the later MS. *D* has *can*, 'since she has', for *cani*; *Col* 602 has *canys o'y hanuot y colles y breynt*, 'since it was against her will that she lost her status', i.e. her status as a virgin. This seems to make the best sense; but the original meaning may have been that she had not lost her status as a member of her kindred. The moral ground for allowing her son's claim is that the kindred have failed in their function of protecting her.

108.5-9　Neither this reading nor that of *Col* 604, according to which a proprietor does not move from before these sons, is wholly satisfactory. The readings are best understood as attempts to state that these sons can claim a share of the patrimony even against other occupiers (not of their maternal kin) who can show full proprietary title: only proprietors could do that.

108.18　innate man: W. *canhwynol*, with adjective used as noun; the adjective usually qualifies *bonheddig*, see the definition at 110.21-3. The point of this rule is that a man from Powys was not an alien in Gwynedd, so that if he begot a son by a woman of Gwynedd, that son, being *canhwynol* in Powys and entitled to patrimony there, would not be entitled to mother-right in Gwynedd. T. P. Ellis (i.455) has misinterpreted this passage, though on the same page he says that 'no free Welshman could be an "alltud" in Wales'. This principle does not seem to be categorically stated in any authentic law text, but is implied by the present passage, and was applied in North Wales under the first English prince, who did not require Welshmen from one patria in Wales to be in advowry in another: *Rec. Caern.* 212.

109.28-110.3　The defendant here puts up a special plea: the claimant is not entitled to mother-right because his father ceased to be an alien after the claimant's mother was given him in marriage. This means that the claimant's

Notes: Land Law 265

father was the son of a Welshwoman and an alien: though an alien by birth, he had become a patrimonial by claiming a share of land alongside his mother's brothers, presumably on the death of his mother's father.

110.4-6 The pedigree would be traced by the distaff (i.e. in the female line) whenever the father was an alien, and it would be theoretically possible to trace it so in one generation after another, but the practical significance of the rule is doubtful.

Miscellanea on Land

110.8 use: W. *defnyddio*. During the father's lifetime, the son has no present entitlement and the father can himself use the land freely; but the paragraph makes it clear that what is in question is the father's right to alienate. In English-law language, the father has only a life interest, so that (except by way of blood-land) he cannot grant an estate for more than his own lifetime to any other person.

110.10 despoil: W. *treisio*, the word also used for rape and robbery.

110.28 wedded wife: W. *gwraig briod*. In this context *priod* must imply a union recognised by the Church, which does not require any particular formality or Christian ceremony. The rule stated is that of English common law rather than canon law, which did however disapprove of inheritance by bastards.

110.33-4 This rule is surely an innovation of fairly recent date, reflecting the strength of the princes of Gwynedd: cf. 102.3-5n. It is not found in the other Redactions.

110.35-6 Though this alleged rule is still given in the fifteenth-century MS. *S* (XI.iv.18), it seems to reflect earlier conditions, under which galanas could arise from 'land-feud': see 94.22n. The rule stated as applicable shows the later narrowing of liability.

112.23,24 monarch: W. *teyrn*. The corresponding passage in *Bleg* (81.27-82.1) has *brenin*, 'king' (*rex* in Lat D 389.33-5).

113.3 alienate: W. *cychwynnu*, the verb usually used of the movement of a person from land (and in this translation usually rendered 'move' or 'move away'). For an orchard the meaning might be that there was no right to move the fruit-trees, but that sense cannot be applied to a mill or a weir.

266   *The Law of Hywel Dda*

113.6 quillets: W. *garddau*, lit. 'gardens', a designation found in North Wales for quillets, see *Col* pp.155-6.

113.9 purchase: W. *prid*, q.v. In this triad the word is used in something like its original sense, for acquiring an interest in land otherwise than by inheritance, which is the technical meaning of 'purchase' in English law. All three cases are of purchase for value: the first is that described in the next paragraph; the second seems to cover on the one hand a simple buying of land, and on the other a payment to a Lord for changing the status of the land from villein land to free land. The third case is that to which the next rules of the main text apply: these set out (in terms of 'holding over') the extent of the interest acquired by an improver of another man's land.

113.13-16 This sentence follows the above triad in *Bleg*. fee for protection: W. *gobr gwarchadw*; without plaint: W. *heb gŵyn*, giving *cŵyn* its technical meaning of a legal action (brought by the returning exile) rather than the general meaning of complaint (by the sitting tenants).

114.1-5 If the brother who clears the woodland has no 'old field' (W. *henfaes*, presumably any kind of established agricultural land) to give the owner of the woodland, the latter will be worse off at the end of four years than if he were a stranger. A stranger would get the whole of the land back, cleared of trees and brought into the agricultural course, though perhaps not in good heart (since there is no requirement that it should be manured); the brother gets only half the land—perhaps on the basis that if his 'woodman' brother had no land, he might be able to claim a share from the woodland owner.

114.6 gage: W. *prido*; let him lease: W. *lloged*. The translation 'gage' is not wholly satisfactory, though it may fairly represent the effect of the transaction in ordinary practice: see the Glossary s.v. *prid*.

7. Aliens

The large additions to this chapter from different points in *Dw* can be taken as a sign that immigration into Wales was increasing in the thirteenth century, so that new problems called for the solutions offered. An alien would come from outside Wales: see 108.18n.

Notes: Aliens   267

114.24 arable land: W. *tir swch a chwlltwr*, lit. 'land of ploughshare and coulter'. The addition 'between them' perhaps implies that the land was held by the newly-matured proprietors in undivided shares, which in turn implies a different tenure from the most usual villein tenure, that of reckon land. Like reckon-land villeins, alien proprietors were bound to their holdings.

116.1-6 Forms of this rule appear in *Col*, *Cyfn*, and *Bleg* in the context of Galanas.

116.9-11 The provisions of Hywel's Book on this matter are not known from any text now extant, and no convincing explanation of *cartomog* has been offered. For *llawedrog* GPC suggests 'heaped, loaded', citing Lat B 246.23-6, which gives the name *carllawedrog* to one who leaves his patrimony and makes his home with a kinsman: he, like the bonheddig in the text, would be taking his goods freely on his sledge (for which see Glossary, s.v. *carr*).

117.29-30 set free: W. *dilysu*; the separation was on this view a valid dissolution of the union.

118.30 servient: W. *gweinyddol*, adjective used as noun. Forms of the same word are used adjectivally for higher grades of slave, see 55.16n, 56.37.

119.23 The text of *DwCol* is emended in the light of other manuscripts, as printed at V.i.9 (AL ii.42). Of the three homagers the resident (W. *adlamwr*, from *adlam*, 'habitation') is the only one whose designation seems self-explanatory; *gwasafwr* seems to be based on the same element as *arwaesaf*, 'voucher/vouchee to warranty' (in the law of theft, see 162.10-11), so that it may imply that the homage creates an obligation in the lord to warrant the homager; *aswynwr* is the subject of notes by Patrick Ford and Eric Hamp in (1976) 26 BBCS 147ff. In the Welsh translation of the Statute of Wales of 1284 *aswyn* renders *essonium*, 'essoin'; there it was no doubt used because of the similarity of sound, and the original meaning was probably not known to the translator. It is not clear from the syntax of the sentence which of the two patrimonials pays the other on the separation: justice seems to require that the gwasafwr should be paid by the landowner, since the latter gets the buildings.

119.35-6 without interruption: W. *yn ddiannod*. While *annod* means 'interrupt' or 'postpone', *diannod* usually occurs in contexts where it must mean 'immediate', e.g. *cyfraith ddiannod*, 'immediate law', 76.37.

8. Royal Rights and Administration

120.5 *Lloegr* is the Welsh name for England: it has been variously explained, most recently by Eric P. Hamp (provisionally) as 'being from near the border', 4 CMCS 83-5.

120.6-21 The account of Dyfnwal Moelmud and his activities resembles, but is far from identical with, that of Geoffrey of Monmouth: the lawbooks must have used, not Geoffrey's work, but some form of the tradition which lay behind it; see *Col* pp.159-60. Of the limits named for the island, Penwith and Grugyll are well known; Shoreham is W. *Soram*, which has also been interpreted as Sarre in Kent: see TYP 235. The headland of Blathaon has not been identified, but should logically be either Cape Wrath or (more probably, since it is sometimes said to be in Caithness) Duncansby Head. 'The Channel' translates W. *Môr Udd*, which seems to have been used for the eastern seas of Britain in a rather wider sense.

120.25-6 The English inch is also traditionally three barleycorns: grains of barley are surprisingly uniform in length, and up to World War II still measured very nearly a third of an inch. The improved strains of recent years may vary from this norm. See also 176.12-13n.

120.28-9 leap: W. *naid*; land, W. *tir*; selion, W. *grwn*, i.e. one of the units into which a field is divided by the normal method of ploughing with oxen or horses. The selion was still traditionally said in Merioneth to be three leaps wide in the present century: 14 BBCS 284. The alleged Old Welsh *tir* for *grwn* may be a back-formation from *milltir*, 'mile', but it must be remembered that 'land' is one of the common English names of the selion.

121.1 two limits: W. *dau eirionyn*, the word used in defining the serjeant's right to corn, see 34.34n.

121.5-6 shareland: W. *rhandir*; holding: W. *gafael*. According to *Col* 649 the shareland comprised four holdings: though all *Ior* manuscripts have the same version as our text, the *Col* version seems to be the more reasonable: T. Jones Pierce, *Medieval Welsh Society* (Cardiff, 1972), 325. The whole account is of course far too schematic.

121.11-13 It is thus assumed that there would be two commotes in each cantred, as there were in Anglesey and some other parts, but most cantreds had more than two commotes: Llŷn had three, Cantref Mawr (Ystrad Tywi) had seven.

Notes: Royal Rights and Administration   269

Commotes varied in size: there were six in Anglesey and only ten in the much larger area of Ceredigion, where (for instance) the commote of Genau'r Glyn reached from the Clarach river to the Dyfi and from the sea to the Pumlumon watershed some fifteen miles to the east.

121.38-122.1 from quarter to quarter: W. *o bedwareran bwygilydd*, i.e. by successive division in quarters.

Maer and Cynghellor (122.7-124.2)

122.18 as two of four: W. *ar eu pedwerydd*; they would no doubt be accompanied by their two servants, but see 129.12-14n.

122.23 legal acre: W. *erw gyfraith*. Ior 91/5 has emended this to the *tir cyfrif*, 'reckon land', of MS. *E*; this perhaps makes clearer the meaning, which is that when a reckonland tenant died his land became available for other tenants of the townland, and that the maer and cynghellor were responsible for the necessary adjustments. The 'legal acre' was not necessarily an area of one acre by measure.

122.25 uses: W. *defnyddio*. As elsewhere (e.g. 110.8n), the word here implies the appropriation of the land to a particular purpose, no doubt usually its grant to tenants. The 'office' of the maer and cynghellor would imply supervision of the tenants.

122.32 four grown pigs: W. *pedair hych mawr. Hych* is the 'numeral' form of *hwch*, which in modern Welsh means 'sow', whereas in medieval Welsh *hwch* is the only singular for *moch*, 'pigs': the plural *hychau* or *hychod* and the singular *mochyn* do not appear until the early modern period.

123.3-4 This does not imply that the cynghellor acted as judge: his function was perhaps that of the sheriff in the medieval English county court (though there is nothing to show whether the Welsh *dadlau*, 'sessions', had the non-judicial functions of the county court or shiremoot). The cynghellor would be responsible for bringing the court together, but the commote judge (if there was one) or the judges by status of land would decide the case. In an action for land, if the King was not present the cynghellor would presumably be 'the man who is in his place' (84.29-30).

123.25-6 Since ebediw, like the English heriot, represented the return to the lord of the vassal's military equipment, it might be expected that the payment would be made from

270   *The Law of Hywel Dda*

the goods left by the chief of kindred. The rule here quoted
(from a small group of rules about ebediw) can be understood
either as implying that some of the chief's goods passed to
his successor (so that the ebediw would be paid from these)
or as indicating that ebediw had become a 'succession duty'
to be paid by the successor in every case.

123.31 Lord: following MS. *E* rather than MS. *C* which has
rhaglaw, 'deputy, viceroy', or MS. *B* which uses the imper-
sonal form of the verb and names no giver. *Rhaglaw* was
latinised as *raglotus* and became the name of an administrative office in later medieval Wales: see Griffiths, *Principality* 49-69.

123.36-7 For the distribution of the supper-money see 14.
11-25. *Cyfn* (WML 292.24-31) has a rather different distribution of what it calls the gwestfa money; since the *Ior*
version gives separate allocations to the King's and the
Queen's officers, the *Cyfn* version is certainly the older.
The assertion that the supper money is shared in the same
way as the twnc pound raises a difficulty, since the twnc
pound was a commutation of the entertainment of the
peripatetic court, in which all shared, from the King to his
needy ones and the unnamed assistant officials. Most, if
not all, of these would expect to share in the commutation,
so that the distribution of the twnc pound would not be the
same as that given for the supper money.

Hostings (124.3-10)

124.5 outside its limits: W. *ohoni ei hun*, lit. 'from itself'.
The manuscripts have various attempts to get round the
difficulty created by the use of *gwlad* for both the territory
and the people.

124.8-9 work on the King's castles: W. *gwaith cestyll y
brenin*. This must be a comparatively late innovation: it is
not found in the other Redactions; see also 41.11n.

King's Villeins (124.11-125.10)

124.17 destroy their swarms: W. *lladd eu bydafau*; see
183.20-184.21n.

124.21 Queen: following MS. *C* for consistency with the
references to the King: MSS. *B, E* have *arglwyddes*, 'Lady'.

125.4-7 See the similar passage at 41.12-15 and the notes
to it.

Notes: Royal Rights and Administration   271

The Dung Maer (125.11-126.16)

For the dung maer see 33.12-34.5 and the Glossary, s.v. *maer biswail.*

125.16 when he is invested with the office of maer: W. *pan estynner maeroniaeth iddo.* There seems to be no reason to suppose (with *Bleg* p.172) that this refers to a promotion to the office of the more honourable maer: in the context, *maeroniaeth* will mean 'office of [dung] maer'.

125.35 repair: W. *diwallu,* which AL translates 'supply'; this is the more usual meaning of the word, and is found elsewhere in our text, e.g. 25.18; 27.6. But the verb is derived from *di-wall,* 'faultless', so that its primary meaning is 'render faultless' (though GPC's earliest example of this sense is dated 1595) and in the present passage the *reficere* of LW must be correct. At 16.32 'equip' and at 202.9 'provide' translate *diwallu.*

126.2 to dry: W. *crasu;* the service was the drying of corn in the kiln. With the often unsettled weather at harvest, drying in the sheaf was still necessary at times in the nineteenth century. A rudimentary kiln would be put up near the farmstead: as a result many farms in Ceredigion have a field called *Cae'r Odyn,* 'the kiln field' near the farmyard.

126.10 The consent or acquiescence is of course that of the aillt's lord.

Boundaries (126.17-128.5)

127.17 three stays of boundary: W. *tri argae terfyn.* It seems impossible to convey the sense of the original in translation. The triad is paralleled by that of the three stays of blood (197.11-16), which gives a basis for liability for bloodshed varying according to the 'stay', i.e. the point to which the blood descends. In the present triad the stays are the grounds which entitle one party to set the boundary against another: higher status, proprietorship as against non-proprietorship, priority of occupation.

Food Renders (128.6-129.27)

128.11-12 single-bound oats: W. *ceirch unrhwym.* This seems to mean that each sheaf was bound with its own straw in its natural length, i.e. not twisted so as to make a longer bond.

272   *The Law of Hywel Dda*

128.14-15 without the heap: W. *heb y foel*, i.e. without the rounded 'head' above the level of the vessel. It is not clear whether this means that the quota was a level vessel-ful, or only that the head was not counted in measuring the vessel.

128.20 of the King's: W. *i'r brenin*, which could equally well mean 'to the King'.

129.4 two bare fistbreadths: W. *dau foelddyrnfedd*. *Cyfn* (WML 57.3-9) makes the butter mass nine fistbreadths in breadth and a fistbreadth with the thumb standing (W. *dyrnfedd a'i fawd yn ei sefyll*) in thickness. There is no evidence to show whether this bare fistbreadth was regarded as different from the palmbreadth (*lled y balf*) of the measurements for land at 120.26, 198.37.

129.9 brew: W. *brag*, which normally means 'malt'; 'brew' is offered as appropriate to mead and bragget as well as beer.

129.12-14 Ct. 122.18 (see note), according to which the maer and cynghellor are entitled to circuits twice a year, but with only two companions in all.

129.19 cwynos. *Arian y gwynos* has been translated 'supper money'. It seems to have begun as a supplement paid to some of the court officers at a time when the court was 'supported' in kind: the right to cwynos was then the right of the court to a feast provided by the district responsible. The present rule seems to imply that bond maenolydd did not provide a feast, but the references (128.35-7, 129.10-11) to lighting a fire in the hall 'that night' clearly link the winter food-gift with the feast. See also 123.36-7.

9. Family Law

129.32-130.2 This 'division of the period of pregnancy into three trimesters corresponds to a traditional medical practice, and its description of the foetus as white in the first trimester . . . and red in the second . . . may have a basis in the appearance of the foetus': WLW 204.

130.18 inadvertence: W. *anoddau*; other manuscripts add 'nor for the act of an insane person' (W. *ynfyd*).

Sons (130.25-131.32)

131.20-27 It is clear from these provisions that the section is concerned with sons of the breyr (or uchelwr) class: as we

Notes: Family Law 273

saw that it was hardly contemplated that a bonheddig would have a daughter of marriageable age while his father was still alive, so it seems to be assumed here that the father who commends his son to a lord has ascended to breyr status. The reference to the status of knight (W. *marchog*) suggests Anglo-Norman influence; cf. 9.34n.

Daughters (131.33-132.21)

132.14-21 Cf. 58.32-3; 60.8-12n.

Affiliation (132.22-137.33)

132.29 his burial-place: W. *ei wyddfa*, where 'he' is the putative father. The word *gwyddfa* (best known in the Welsh name of Snowdon, *Yr Wyddfa*), meant originally a mound or monument over the grave; in the present passage it suggests a family grave as identifying the location of the father.

133.17 till the morrow: W. *hyd drannoeth*. MS. *E* inserts *namyn*, 'save' before the phrase, but there seems to be no point in allowing a delay at all; if the putative father is present to ask for a delay, he is present so as to be able to take the oath.

134.8-9 secured cattle: W. *gwartheg dyfach*, cf. 58.8-9n, where the expression has been translated 'cattle of dark ancestry': see the note. A different translation is given here because of the explanation offered in the text, which implies that *dyfach* is the suffixless verbal adjective from the adjoining verb *dyfeichiaf*, 'give surety'. That the commentator was groping in the dark is indicated by the fact that other texts assert that no surety was given, so that the cattle are *di-fach*, 'suretyless'. See notes at *Ior* pp.110, 122; *Col* p.52; WLW 205.

134.23-4 he cannot . . . in the clear: W. *ni ellir ei wadu yn yr ing cani wadwyd yn yr eang.*

134.27-135.5 A different triad of the Three Dire Losses of a Kindred (*Tri Dyngoll Cenedl*), from another part of *Dw*, is given below at 146.11-27.

135.10 For provisions about a daughter rejected by her alleged father see 56.5-15.

136.16 acre: W. *erw*, here symbolising the patrimony in land: other manuscripts have *yr eiddo*, 'what is his'.

136.22-6 A modern jurist would quote this as an example of the credibility of a declaration against interest.

274   *The Law of Hywel Dda*

137.19-30 This paragraph appears, in Welsh, at Lat D 372. 3-11; it is not in *Bleg*. Lat D adds to the first case that of 'another woman', who swears on a consecrated altar if the affiliation is not accepted without oath; it also makes it clear that the kindred who swear are those of the woman.

137.31-3 This provision of course contravenes the rule of 136.12-18.

Book III: THE JUSTICES' TEST BOOK

In contrast to many of the names used for versions or parts of the Welsh law texts, the name *Llyfr Prawf Ynaid*, 'Justices' Test Book', is found in the texts themselves, which speak of it as put together as a textbook of the 'core subjects' of Welsh legal training. Though normally found as the third part of the Iorwerth Redaction, it may have existed as a separate text: some manuscripts preface it with a version of the account of Hywel's assembly, but the original nucleus of its prologue was probably the material given here. MS. *B* has only two sentences of prologue: 'Here begins the Test Book. That is this, the nine columns of law and the value of wild and tame and what pertains to them'; *Col* has discarded parts of the prologue in such a way that the text does not make sense (see *Col* pp.86-7). Our Book III certainly includes more than the original Test Book: quite apart from any material which may have been added to the original treatment of the core subjects, there is the 'Appendix' (see 190. 4-8): it seems quite likely that it is only the addition of this Appendix which should be credited to the thirteenth-century jurist Iorwerth ap Madog (for whom see CLP 123-33).

141.9-11 the judgment . . . judged: W. *yn farnedig y frawd a farno yntau o hynny allan*.

141.30 the old book of the White House: this is named only in MS. *F* (of the fifteenth century) and in MS. *H*, a manuscript in a cursive hand now thought likely to be considerably earlier than the fifteenth century to which it is ascribed in Gwenogvryn Evans's *Report on Manuscripts in the Welsh Language* (Historical Manuscripts Commission), i.956-7. For the White House book see the Introduction and 94.1-25n.

Notes: The Justices' Test Book   275

1. Homicide

Though the 'Three Columns of Law' are defined as the Abetments of Homicide, Theft, and Fire, the Abetments are only introductions to tractates which in their extant form deal in great detail with the principal offence. This material must be an addition to the original form of the Test Book, for in the Homicide tractate it takes two forms —the 'B' form found in MS. *B*, and the 'A' form found in all other thirteenth-century manuscripts; moreover, a form without any of the additional material on homicide is found in the fifteenth-century manuscript *F*. Our main text translates the 'B' form; some 'A' form material is added, mainly from *Col*, whose text is an edited version of the 'A' form.

143.2 abetments: W. *affaith*. This is usually translated 'accessory', but 'abetment' (which is less a term of art in English law) seems preferable. In the thirteenth-century texts the *affeithiau* are indeed offences subsidiary to the act of the principal offender, but *affaith* was originally applied to anything which created enmity between kindreds: see 94.22n.

143.7-9 There is some confusion in the *Ior* text at this point; this may be a sign that this part of the law was no longer important when the manuscripts were written, but it does seem that the text originally corresponded quite closely to our translation. *Col* agrees with the *Cyfn* and *Bleg* versions in coupling a penalty for admitted abetment with a denial of actual killing, supported by a very large body of compurgators, whereas in the *Ior* manuscripts the compurgators are required to support denial of the abetment. The difference is reflected in the difference between the *Ior* and *Bleg* rules for denial of the principal offence of homicide: see 149.1-9n.

143.37 assault and battery: W. *dyrchaf a gosod*, lit. 'raise and set' (a limb or a weapon, on a victim); this corresponds to the original meaning of the English pair, where 'assault' is the gesture and 'battery' the blow. In modern Welsh the reflexive form of *gosod*, *ymosod*, means 'attack' (with the preposition *ar* in transitive use).

144.3-4 three dirwy pennies: W. *tair ceiniog dirwy*, where 'penny' is perhaps to be understood as referring to payment in money: cf. the use of 'acre' for land, 136.16n. By the time

276 The Law of Hywel Dda

our extant texts were written, the larger penalty of dirwy was payable in other cases also. The name *camlwrw*, lit. 'track of wrong', for the smaller financial penalty suggests that it was an innovation; cf. the English 'misdemeanour' for smaller offences, as contrasted with 'felony' with its sinister overtones.

144.15-16 The 3:1 ratio for galanas to sarhaed applies only to the King and his 'members'; all other cases specified in the texts give the ratio 15¾:1.

144.21-38 The detailed rules for the levying and distribution of the galanas payment vary much from text to text, no doubt because the detailed rules were not applied in practice when the surviving texts were written. Some general principles seem to emerge: (a) sharing between relatives on the father's side and those on the mother's side in the ratio 2:1; (b) payment (if any) by women at half the rate of payment by men; (c) payment by each degree of kin at double the rate for the next degree. Since the blood-feud goes back to the pre-curial age, the enforcing third taken by the Lord must be an innovation: it conveniently absorbs the homicide's contribution, which would logically go to the victim, who is not alive to receive it.

144.30-31 two pence . . . a sister. This and other like expressions must be understood as 'two pence . . . for every penny . . .'.

145.2 shaft penny: W. *ceiniog paladr*, usually rendered 'spear penny', since the reference is no doubt to the shaft of a spear (cf. 1 Sam. xvii.7). In modern Welsh *paladr* is still used for the shaft of a mill-wheel.

145.4-7 This calculation of the seven degrees is almost certainly wrong: it follows the canonist scheme, under which collateral relationship is reckoned by counting the number of generations to the common ancestor in the longer line only. This scheme does indeed put the fifth cousin's son in the seventh degree of relationship, but it also puts the sixth cousin in that degree, and we should expect the sixth cousin to be named in preference to the fifth cousin's son. If the Roman-law scheme is adopted, under which generations are counted from one of the relatives up to the common ancestor and down to the other, the seventh degree is reached at the second cousin's son, and it is necessary to name him because the third cousin is related in the eighth degree.

Notes: Homicide 277

145.15 four kindreds . . . derives. This expression (found also in V.C.III.i.13A) has never been critically examined. The obvious explanation is that the four kindreds are the descendants of the homicide's four great-grandfathers; but all these descendants, as far as the second cousins' children, will be related to the homicide in the seventh degree or less, and so will be liable to contribute a normal share of the galanas: only grandchildren of the second cousins will be in eighth degree and liable to pay the shaft penny, and they can hardly be so numerous that it will be worth while to collect contributions from them. Perhaps the four kindreds are the descendants, not of the four great-grandfathers, but of the four pairs of parents of the great-grandfathers: these would include third cousins (in the eighth degree) and children of third cousins (in the ninth degree). The *Col* text (of 'A' form) is substituted for the 'B' form of *Ior* 106/ 9-11 because the latter requires from the alleged kinsman only an oath 'that he does not derive from his [the homicide's] kin'.

145.25 stock inquiry: W. *cyfarch cyffyll*. This statement of the correct meaning of the term, which follows two other suggested interpretations, is attributed by MSS. *A*, *E* to Iorwerth ap Madog.

146.11 Cf. 134.27-135.5.

146.30 discharge: W. *dilysu*. The word, which is usually translated 'validate', seems here to imply a rejection of the homicide. When property is transferred, the validity (W. *dilysrwydd*) of the transaction is formally assured; perhaps the implication of the present passage is that the homicide is handed over to his victim's kin with a formal assurance that his former kinsmen will not take vengeance in respect of him.

147.8 oldest men: W. *hynafgwyr*. The expression does not seem to imply any official status.

147.11 gwely. The word (lit. 'bed') seems to have first meant the descendants of a common great-grandfather (the *derbfine* of Irish law), and this meaning probably lies behind the concept of gwely land: see 100.5n. Here the gwely is a narrower group, the descendants of the homicide's parents.

147.14-18 The father who pays is presumably the fifth cousin's son, so that the son who does not pay is the fifth

278   *The Law of Hywel Dda*

cousin's grandson, who would be related to the homicide
only in the eighth (canon-law) degree.

147.22 Though the text could be translated 'even if they do
not pay it', the whole context implies that the failure to pay
is the homicide's, and that the rule being stated is that the
kindred cannot be compelled to pay the homicide's share,
though they may do so voluntarily in order to save his life
from the vengeance of the victim's kin, and thus save. themselves from a 'dire loss': see 146.11-17.

147.38 married women: W. *gwragedd*, which may here
mean 'non-virgins'. They take no share of the galanas because
they are presumed to have fulfilled (or to have definitively
failed to fulfil) the function of bearing avengers: the pre-
sumption in relation to receiving galanas, like that in relation
to paying it, is against the woman. Virgins take a share of
galanas in right of their prospective male descendants.

148.6-11 The oldest men of father-kin and mother-kin
share between the two kins; each set of them then shares
out what has fallen to it.

149.1-9 The wording of the corresponding passage in *Col* is
confused, suggesting that these provisions for oaths of forgiveness were dead law; but the Act 1 Hen.5, c.6 complains
that after Glyndŵr's wars the Welsh were requiring persons
loyal to the English crown to 'excuse them of the death of
[Welsh] rebels . . . by one assache, after the custom of
Wales, that is to say, by the oath of 300 men': Bowen, *The
Statutes of Wales* 38.

149.12 galanas . . . dispersion: W. *galanas gwasgarog*, where
gwasgarog is an adjective used as noun (in the genitive), not
an adjective qualifying *galanas*. In modern Welsh *y Cymry
ar Wasgar* are the Welsh diaspora.

150.30-31 an ambush or rout: W. *cynllwyn neu gyrch*. In
modern Welsh, under the influence of *cynllun*, 'plan', *cynllwyn* has acquired the meaning 'conspiracy'; the translation
'ambush' (influenced by the equivalence of *llwyn* and 'bush')
is not wholly satisfactory, for the essence of *cynllwyn*
seems to have been secret killing: see M. E. Owen, (1968)
22 BBCS 346-50.

150.34 murder: W. *murdwrn*, a borrowing from England,
where at the period it meant secret killing, a more serious
offence than killing by open violence.

Notes: Homicide   279

150.37   three kine of violence: W. (MS.) *teyr buy gorthy*,
where *gorthy* represents *gorddwy*, found also in *porthorddwy*, (q.v.), 143.17. It is not clear how this involvement
in homicide differs from the ninth abetment, 143.19-20.
The spelling *gorthy* may reproduce that of the source of the
passage, which was probably a Latin manuscript: see *Col*
p.95.

151.18   manner of death: W. *dihenydd*, 'putting to death'.
English has no word for this: 'execution' properly refers to
the sentence of death, not to the man sentenced.

152.13-14   the innocent . . . the son: W. *ni ddylyir lladd
mab o genedl wirion*. The translation printed makes the
best sense, though 'innocent kindred' is an unusual expression for the kindred of the victim. Other defensible translations are 'there is no right to kill a son from an innocent
kindred' and 'there is no right to kill an innocent son of
kindred'. However translated, the statement is an application of the rule laid down at 146.28-30.

Measure of Galanas and Sarhaed (153.34-156.30)

154.8-11   As appears from 154.29-31, this limitation is too
narrow.

154.12-20   a gold plate for him: W. *clawr aur iddo*. *Cyfn*
and *Bleg* give the king a gold cup (W. *ffiol aur*) with a gold
cover (W. *clawr aur*) to it, and the *iddo* of our text would
refer more naturally to a vessel for which the plate was a
cover; LW (III.ii.1, p.199) accordingly supplies the words
Cwppan aur, 'a gold cup': a masculine word is needed, and
ffiol is feminine. The statement of the king's sarhaed in the
Ior version of the Laws of Court, however, does not mention
the cup, and MS. *B* omits the plate: see the note to 5.30-6.2.

154.14   nine years: the qualifying period is usually seven
years; see 6.1n.

154.18,19   coloured: W. (MS.) *dewyl, dywylion*. GPC
understands the word as *dywyl* and gives the interpretations
'black, coloured'; there are too few examples to allow cert-
ainty, but a contrast with white animals seems indicated,
though we might expect something more dramatic than
'coloured'.

154.25   sovereign tribute: *mechdeyrn ddylyed*, which might
be better translated 'vassal tribute', since it seems likely
that *mechdeyrn* is a name for a subordinate ruler rather than

280 The Law of Hywel Dda

a suzerain: see the comparison with the Breton *machtiern* by J. G. T. Sheringham, (1981) 58 *Mémoires de . . . Bretagne* 61-72. The passage recognises the feudal relation of Welsh princes to an English king, but ties it to the old tradition of the unity of Britain under a ruler throned in London, which must pre-date the suzerainty of the Wessex kings and probably goes back to the Roman organisation.

155.10-17 The provisions of the 'A' form of *Ior*, and those of *Col*, differ from those of the 'B' form here printed, and vary from manuscript to manuscript: their interest was for the owners of the manuscripts no doubt mainly antiquarian. The most noteworthy divergences are two: (a) the officers of 'nine-unit' standard include the chief huntsman according to *Col* and several *Ior* manuscripts, and also the chief groom, the court judge, the pencerdd and chamberlain according to *Col*; (b) a maer and an uchelwr are given a galanas and sarhaed equal to those of two officials (*swyddwyr*) by the *Ior* manuscripts or two officers (*swyddogion*) by *Col*: this is hard to interpret and harder to justify. The augmenting (W. *dyrchafael*) of galanas and sarhaed needs more detailed examination than it has yet received: the schematic provisions of the texts can hardly have been practicable.

155.17 It is of course to be understood that the man's galanas would be four kine and four score kine.

155.34-6 There are minor differences between our text and others in the allocation of the money. *Col* gives a penny for gloves instead of brogues (cf. Maitland, *Domesday Book and Beyond* 31 n.9, 'His hedger's gloves and bill-hook are the arms appropriate to the serf'), and there is in several texts a provision that if the slave is a woodman (W. *coedwr*), an axe replaces the hedging-bill.

2. Theft

156.34 provisions: W. *bwyllwrw*, 'food for journey'.

157.2 receiving: W. *erbyniaid*. For adviser (W. *cynghorwr*) other manuscripts have a different word; the best reading seems to be that of MSS. *C, E,* and *Col* (340), *odwr*, which probably means 'receiver' (of stolen goods): see *Col* p. 105.

157.5 What is concealed seems to be the fact of the theft rather than the stolen property.

157.18 *Ior* adds here, from MS. *C*, 'Others say of that com-

Notes: Homicide 281

purgation that it is five men, without aliens, without designated men, that deny it; and that is properly the law of Hywel'.

157.23 competent: W. *addfwyn*, the word corresponding to the 'meek' of Matt. v.5 ('of a gentle spirit' in NEB); it has in the lawbooks the technical meaning of 'competent' in English law, i.e. legally acceptable as appropriate for the purpose in hand. In the present case competence is defined by the next sentence: according to *Dw* 345 a compurgator's oath that he was competent in this sense was conclusive.

157.31-2 back burden: W. *baich cefn*, following MSS. *C*, *E*, and *Col*, where MS. *B* has *baich cychwyn*, 'movable? burden'.

159.8 deny it: other manuscripts of *Ior*, and *Col* (363) have 'cannot lead it away from him'.

159.16-17 The order of words in *Ior* 112/6 is corrected in the light of other manuscripts.

159.21-2 sufficient information: W. *dogn fanag*. According to *Cyfn* (see 62.33-4) the informer was one of the testifiers whose unconfirmed evidence could be accepted; and that 'sufficient information' was an old procedure is suggested by the variations between the texts. In *Col* (366-8) the informer makes his first statement to the victim; in the *Ior* manuscripts *arglwydd*, 'lord' and *rhaglaw*, 'deputy, viceroy', alternate in a confused way which may reflect the compilers' recognition that the ruler no longer acted in person: their failure to make the text consistent has been rectified in this translation. The *Col* text, which omits the lord and his deputy alike, seems to record a logical development of the procedure.

159.35 he: apparently the Lord, as the grammar implies; he is of course claiming to punish the offender, and there is no mention of compensation to the victim. According to *Col* 368 it was the evidence of the priest, confirmed by a triple oath, which was conclusive, and the victim received what the priest swore to.

159.37 his life: that of the man named by the informant.

159.39 price: W. *gwerth*, which normally means (in relation to a person) galanas, and has been translated 'worth'; in the present passage it means the standard price of a sale thief, £7.

160.1 Other forms of law: W. *Ereill o'r cyfreithiau*.

282   *The Law of Hywel Dda*

160.8-9 presents: W. *lliwo*, which is not the same word as
lliwo, 'to colour', though perhaps affected by it. A semantic
parallel with the use in English law of 'colourable' suggests
itself.

160.26 sharing: W. *gwaddol*, used in modern Welsh for
endowment of any kind. It seems to have acquired that sense
through its use for a daughter's share of her father's goods,
see WLW (s.v.) 203-4, and cf. 107.15.

160.27 *cyhyryn canastr:* no really convincing explanation
or translation has yet been offered; the translation 'a muscle
of a hundred hands' seems rather too plausible to be true.
The triad *Tri Chyhyryn Canastr* (WML 127.2-7, *Bleg* 114.
23-7) offers no help in interpreting the expression: see the
note at *Bleg* p. 228-9.

161.22-3 The manuscripts vary, perhaps in an attempt to
reduce the four classes deposit, hire, loan, and favour to the
promised three: the simplest explanation is that 'loan' and
'favour' (W. *cymwynas*) mean the same thing. Loan (W.
benffyg, mod. W. *benthyg*), from Latin *beneficium*, is
(strictly understood) a loan for use, the Roman law *commodatum*; the loan for consumption (Roman *mutuum*) is in
earlier Welsh *echwyn*, as in Luke xi.5, where the new translation has *benthyg*.

161.27 surreption: W. *anghyfarch*, 'taking without permission'; see the definition at 166.21-2. This use of 'surreption', which is not recognised in SOED, is traditional in
studies of Welsh law.

162.1 who had power to: W. *a feddai; meddu* has come to
mean 'possess', but originally meant something like 'control',
and has such a meaning in the law texts: see 7 CMCS 105-6.

162.9 three pleas: W. *tri arddelw*, see Glossary, s.v. *arddelw*.
The point of the present rule is that the general plea of denial
is not open to the defendant taken with the property: he
cannot rely on compurgation and must offer one of the
specific defences. Birth and rearing, and keeping before loss,
if proved, show that the defendant is the true owner; voucher
to warranty frees him from the guilt of theft, but does not
give him the right to keep the property, since the claimant
can follow it in the hand of the warrantor.

163.12-13 and he vouches a warrantor in another place:
this translation follows the other manuscripts; MS. *B* has

Notes: Theft   283

'or will plead a warrantor in another place', which is inconsistent with what follows.

163.33 he: i.e. the defendant who has vouched the warrantor. The point seems to be that the defendant is not imputing any wrong to the warrantor, since the latter may in turn rely on any of the pleas.

164.11 throne: W. *gorsedd*, to be understood here as meaning the court of law.

165.29 lord: W. *arglwydd*, perhaps reflecting a Latin source with *dominus*; there seems to be a play on the two senses, 'lord' and 'owner', of the Latin word.

165.36 bar: W. *llys*, q.v. Because the thief was legally put to death, the law would not recognise the killing as a ground for feud, nor (consequently) as a bar to testimony under the rule stated at 94.20-22.

166.1 marauders: W. *gwynwyr*, cognate with Irish *fian*, *fiana*, 'which means a "band of roving warriors"' (GML xi-xiv, 183). In the light of the many references to marauding expeditions and to the King's share of the spoil, these marauders were evidently the bodyguards of other rulers. They were protected by the rules of war; if taken prisoner they could be sold into slavery (and since the W. *caeth*, 'slave', is regularly derived from Latin *captus*, they were no doubt at one time the main source of slaves), but as in modern international law, they were not to be killed by civilians.

166.18 everything done: W. *pob peth o'r a wneler*. Other manuscripts have *a ddyger*, 'taken'; this is of course the norm case of theft, but other passages (especially in the law relating to fire) make it clear that the Welsh concept of *lladrad* was not confined to unlawful taking. As the semantic development of derivatives of *lladrad* suggests, the essence of *lladrad* was secrecy, i.e. stealth: to take something with denial, but with force rather than stealth, was not *lladrad* but *trais*, 'robbery, violence'.

167.14 Cf. the provisions of 118.10-16 for the case of the alien whose lord does not defend him.

167.16 weak: W. *gweiniaid*; other manuscripts have *anghyfiaith*, 'not of the same speech'; anything: W. *dim*; MS. *C* has *diod*, 'drink'.

167.25-6 wedded husband: W. *gŵr priod*; see Glossary, s.v. *priod*. The triad follows four others (at *Bleg* 122.8-25)

284　　The Law of Hywel Dda

which set out in turn the thieves liable to camlwrw, to dirwy, to sale and to hanging.

167.26-7 According to *Col* 407 there was no penalty for stealing a tame bird or dog, but compensation must be paid to the owner: cf. 183.16-18.

167.35-8 robbery: W. *trais;* perhaps the rule should be read as applying to all violence, including in particular rape, which was not a capital offence. This sentence, which all *Ior* manuscripts put at the end of the next chapter, is put here for consistency with *Llyfr Iorwerth* (where it has been moved to 115/21) and with *Col*, where it is the last sentence (411) of the tractate on theft in both manuscript and printed edition.

168.15 two penalties: W. *dwy boen*, 'two pains'. This rule against 'double jeopardy' appears repeatedly, e.g. in relation to a wife's offences against her husband.

169.6 treasure does not arise under deprivation: W. *nid â swllt a dan diebryd*, a proverbial expression; *swllt* is the Latin *solidus*, and means on the one hand 'shilling', and on the other (in middle Welsh) 'treasure', perhaps with something of the particular sense of money or precious metals: cf. 40.2n; *diebryd* is the verb-noun of *diaberaf:* while it can have the effective meaning 'delay' (payment), the verb's essential meaning seems to be 'deprive, refuse'. The proverb then means that when a person has been deprived of his property, that property cannot generate 'treasure' for him. The practical justification for the rule seems to be that the wrongful possessor of the cow has cared for her and gets her progeny in right of that care: cf. Graf and Dietherr, *Deutsche Rechtssprichwörter*, 111.

3. Fire

169.11 cresset: W. *rhwyll*. MSS. *A, E* have *bwyllwrw*, 'provisions' (see 156.34 and note), but the consensus of the Redactions favours *rhwyll:* the fire would be carried in the cresset rather than lit on the site of the burning.

169.14 As Aled Wiliam points out (*Ior* p.126), the addition 'without doing anything to prevent or extinguish it' must be understood.

169.17 by stealth: W. *yn lladrad*, see 166.18n.

170.14-16 Payment for his act must mean (on the principle

Notes: Fire   285

of the next sentence) payment for any damage caused by the fire; *Col* 427 makes it clear that payment for the surreption meant a penalty to the Lord: cf. 171.11-13 (where the word *anghyfarch* is not used).

170.18-19 According to this rule the borrower is not burdened by any liability incurred by the fire before he received it; *Col* 429 gives what seems a more necessary rule, that the fire returns to the lender without claim and without surclaim against it, which implies that the borrower indemnifies the lender against liability arising from the fire while lent.

170.20-24 Though there is broad agreement between different texts of this triad, there are several differences in detail. In *Bleg* (114.4-8) the kiln replaces the bath; in both *Bleg* and *Cyfn* (WML 130.21-5) the roof is to be of broom (W. *banadl*) or turf, and the distance from the houses nine paces, while muirburn is permitted from mid-March to mid-April. *Col* 430 requires a distance of nine cubits and a roof of shingles, broom, or turf.

170.28-31 The principle seems to be that each owner is required to prevent fire from escaping from his house, no matter how it reached the house: hence, though he may be entitled to compensation for his own house, the owner is liable to compensate his neighbour.

171.11-13 Cf. 170.14-16n.

4. The Value of Wild and Tame

Horses (171.28-175.5)

171.31 until a year is up: W. *hyd ym mhen y flwyddyn*, lit. 'until the end of the year'—not the calendar year, but a year of the foal's life.

172.2 *Ior* 122/1,2 (from MS. *C*) sets out an alternative scheme ('Others say'), under which the value rises every quarter, to 120d. when the horse is bridled; the scheme of *Bleg*, *Cyfn*, and the Latin texts is similar, but is not identical with this alternative scheme.

172.6 According to Lat A 154.28-30, if a destrier (qualified as having been stall-fed for a month and a half) was stolen or killed, compensation was paid according to the owner's sworn appraisal: this is more consistent with the economic circumstances of the thirteenth century than the low standard

286　　　　　　　*The Law of Hywel Dda*

price of £1. See R. H. C. Davis, 'The Medieval Warhorse' in F. M. L. Thompson (ed.) *Horses in European Economic History* (British Agricultural History Society, 1983), 4-20.

172.9-10 The rouncey (W. *rhwnsi*) and sumpter-horse (W. *swmerfarch*) are distinguished in some texts, the sumpter-horse being given the lower value of 80d., which accords with the fact that in the thirteenth century, the rouncey was not a mere beast of burden but carried the trooper to war: J. E. Morris, *The Welsh Wars of Edward I* (Oxford 1901), 53.

172.34 without irregularity: W. *yn ddirrwysg*; there seems to be no material for comparison as a basis for estimating the exactness of this interpretation.

173.21 damaged: W. *llygrwys*, 'corrupted', from MS. *U*; WML 68.7 (from MS. *V*) has *prynwys*, 'bought'.

173.25-9 These three sentences from MS. *C* are printed as *Ior* 126/4 (i.e. at the end of the material on Horses). Since this part of the *C* text seems to be a borrowing from another source than the main text, the sentences are inserted here as an addition to the very similar text from *Cyfn*, which *Bleg* also resembles. *Ior* 126/1-3,5,6 (from MS. *C*) which give prices for destrier, palfrey, rouncey, and mare, are not translated here.

174.2-3 *Cyfn* (WML 69.4) and *Bleg* (92.15) charge four-pence for dismounting.

174.22 three natural diseases: W. *tri haint anianol*, i.e. the three diseases against which the seller warranted the horse.

Neat Cattle (175.6-178.12)

175.8 sixpence. The *iiii k'*, 'fourpence', of *Ior* 127/2 has been amended to conform with the other Redactions, in the light of the persuasive reasoning of J. G. T. Sheringham, (1982) 29 BBCS 691-708; see particularly p.697. The amendment assumes that the calf in question is not its dam's first calf, whose value would be fourpence, 175.17.

175.9-10 the August when it is right for it to conceive: on the assumption that the calf is born in March or April of year 1, this August is that of the year 3, and the heifer calves for the first time at a little over three years of age: Sheringham, pp.695-6.

175.19 *Ior* 127/6 adds from MS. *E* the statement that the heifer conceives (for the second time) from Midsummer

Notes: The Value of Wild and Tame   287

on; cf. the references to the bulling periods of heifers and mature cows in the tractate on Corn Damage, 206.22-4.

175.24 prime: W. *telediwrwydd*, abstract noun from the root *tâl*, 'payment'; in some contexts the verb *talu* means 'to be worth'. As the next sentence shows, the animal was presumed to be of the standard value only during a limited period: cf. 176.27-9 for the ox, but see 177.12-15n.

176.1 fit: W. *cyfiewin*; the exact force of the Welsh word is undecided: see the note at *Ior* p.127. The same word is applied in *Cyfn* to the cat whose claws are not broken; here it seems appropriate to grass whose stalks are uncropped.

176.12-13 large thumb and small. The Welsh word *modfedd*, 'inch', is literally 'thumb measure'; this provision for resolving a dispute is surprising in the light of the provision (120.25-6n) for basing measurement on the barleycorn.

176.16 'he' must be the buyer: *Ior* 127/15 adds from MS. *C* 'and he wants to claim for it' (i.e. the lost calf).

176.21-2 until he is put under the yoke in February: this will be the February before the ox is three years old: Sheringham, p.696.

177.12-15 Ct. 175.24n, 176.27-9, where different limits are set, and provison is made for appraisal of an animal past its prime. The *Cyfn* text printed is from MS. *W*; MS. *V* puts the ox in its prime until its sixth working year, and the cow until her ninth calf.

177.20-21 The note to the same rule in *Bleg* (87.1-8) reads 'Double payment was necessary for a steer without horns —because it could not defend itself', as though it were the polled beast which had been killed; this view seems to offend against grammar, justice, and agricultural experience. The clear sense of the text is that the contribution of a (living) polled beast is double that of a horned beast; the owner of a dead polled steer would have suffered no extra loss, and there is no reason for giving him extra compensation; the horns are not the steer's only means of defence, and it is a common belief that polled cattle are more irascible than horned cattle. There is a popular saying, 'Mae'n dda nad oes gyrn gan dda moelion'—'It's a good job polled cattle haven't got horns'.

177.25-178.3 St John's Day: 24 June, Midsummer Day. With the whole passage compare the provisions of 63.16-26.

288 *The Law of Hywel Dda*

177.36-178.3 miscellanea: W. (MS.) *amdyryeyt, amdyryet.*
The word is not in GPC, and seems to occur only in this
passage, which in turn is known only from MS. *Col* and the
lost Llanforda manuscript, as transcribed by Moses Williams
in MS. Llanstephan 74, where the reading is *amdyret*. The
translation 'miscellanea' assumes that the word refers to
the head, back, etc.; their value would then rise from 10d.
to 11d. after separation of the hide and meat. For the pig,
the flitch (W. *enhorob, hanerob*) was of course equal to two
quarters.

Pigs (178.13-179.24)

178.19 St John's Day: here 29 August, the feast of the
Decollation of St John the Baptist.

178.24 autumn piglet: W. *cnyw hwch.* The note to the
same passage in *Bleg* (93.20-22) argues that the piglet (W.
parchell) of 178.14 is a young female, and the *cnyw hwch* a
young male; the argument is not convincing, and did not
convince Melville Richards: see *B Bleg* 137-8. The meaning
'autumn piglet' is implied by Lat D 361.33, 'Porcellus
auctumpnalis non habet usque ad annum precium a lege
diffinitum, sed *damdwg* de eo erit'; Lat A 156.10 has 'Porr-
cellus autumpnalis, id est, *kynyw*'. As S. J. Williams said
(*Bleg* p.215), 'The point is that it was after going to the
woods on St John's Day that a little pig got the chance to
fatten, on mast': an autumn-born piglet would not be weaned
until it was almost (if not quite) time for the pigs to leave
the woods.

178.28 domestic pig: W. *hwch tref*, lit. 'townland pig'.

179.4-9 *Bleg* 82.17-21 is a slightly different version of this
paragraph: it does not mention the King, and provides for
killing one of the ten trespassing pigs, until nine have been
killed, and all the trespassers thereafter.

179.12 quinsy: W. *y fynyglog. Cyfn* (WML 76.20-21) and
Bleg (93.26-94.1) require in addition a three-month warranty
against strangles (W. *yr hualog*).

179.23-4 This provision, found also in *Bleg* (94.4-5), contradicts the rule of *Dw* 20, set out at 152.4-9.

Sheep and Goats (179.25-180.14)

179.33 liver-fluke: W. (MS.) *auat*, which must be read as a
trisyllable, just as the lawbooks' *au*, 'liver', is a (very
awkward) disyllable; the awkwardness is avoided in modern

Notes: The Value of Wild and Tame   289

Welsh—in the Bible and in southern spoken Welsh by the insertion of [v], giving *afu*, but in northern dialects by diphthongisation with an introductory [j], giving *iau*, a homophone of the word meaning 'yoke' (and cognate with it).

179.35 threepence: emending the 'twopence' of MS. *B* in the light of other manuscripts, since the total is divided into 2d. and 1d. The other manuscripts value the lamb at 2d. and the milk at 1d., which may be right, since the dry ewe at 3d. would then have the value of the normal ewe less the milk.

180.9-12 The text about goats is presented in a confusing way in AL, which gives the version of MS. *C* as its main text; this is also added to the text of *Ior* 130, but is not translated here, since its only addition of substance is the statement that the goat's properties are half its value. This contradicts the main text, which makes the value of the properties three-quarters of the total value.

180.10-11 dry yearling, W. *hesbin*, 'dry one', from *hesb*, 'dry', primarily applied to a milkable animal which is not in milk, but also to a dried-up stream, especially in the compound *Hafesb*, 'summer-dry', as the name of rivers; *hesbin* designates a young ewe or goat which has not yet given milk; goat-heifer: W. *efyrnig*: like the bovine heifer, the *efyrnig* has been served and may or may not have given birth; unlike the bovine heifer, the *efyrnig* is a yearling. MSS. *A, E* make the point quite clear by adding after 'save being dry' the words *ac euernyc eu vn blyth*, 'and a milch one is an *efyrnig*'.

Cats (180.15-32)

The versions of this sub-tractate in *Cyfn* (WML 82.1-12) and *Bleg* (94.8-22) differ from *Ior* and from each other in wording and to some extent in substance. *Bleg* agrees with *Ior* in the general rule that the 'unclean' animal's properties are worth one third of the animal's value; *Cyfn* omits the general rule and makes the value of the cat's properties equal to its whole value. *Bleg* and *Cyfn* require the cat not to eat its kittens, not to be on heat (*catherig*) every new moon, and to have teeth and claws; *Cyfn* further requires a tail and freedom from marks of fire. The implication seems to be that the smell of singed fur would warn the cat's prey and so make her a poor hunter. In *Cyfn* the requirements in

290   *The Law of Hywel Dda*

respect of physique are set out in a series of adjectives coupling *cyf-* with the noun: 'of perfect claws' is *cyfiewin*, cf. 176.1n.

180.30-32 The punctuation has been emended.

Dogs (181.16-182.34)

A comparison of the material on Dogs in the three Redactions is instructive for the construction of the lawbooks. The *Bleg* tractate (53.1-54.22, corresponding very closely indeed to Lat D 379.31-381.3) brings together material which is all found in *Cyfn*, but in three different places (and even then in different order), though for some of the material the wording is exactly the same. If the three blocks of *Cyfn* material are labelled A (WML 34.6-35.10), B (64.17-65.1), and C (82.13-84.5), and the sections within blocks A and C are numbered, the *Bleg* tractate corresponds to *Cyfn* C1, C4, C2, A1, A5, B, A2, A4, A3, A6, C3, C5, in that order. This must surely mean that the *Cyfn* material cannot have been derived from a *Bleg* text, while the close correspondence of *Bleg* and Lat D makes it fairly certain that the *Bleg* tractate was not composed by extracting material in Welsh from a *Cyfn* manuscript. We must conclude that *Bleg* and *Cyfn* drew independently on the same ultimate sources for their material.

181.17 staghound: W. *gellgi*, where *gell* probably means 'yellow'; the dog in question was certainly large and powerful. For a study of the types of hunting dog known in medieval Wales see W. Linnard, 'The Nine Huntings: a reexamination of *Y Naw Helwriaeth*', (1984) 31 BBCS 119-32.

181.21 The greyhound (W. *milgi*), though less valuable than the staghound, had a special status which was lost if it was without its collar (W. *torch*): see 173.8-10. The values of greyhounds' collars are laid down at 193.25-6, but there is no mention of collars for other dogs.

181.28 pet dog: W. *colwyn*, which sometimes seems to mean 'puppy' and is sometimes used for 'spaniel'. In the present passage it is noteworthy that the uchelwr's *colwyn* is more valuable that his staghound—perhaps because of the *colwyn*'s specially close relation to its owner, which could mean that harm done to the *colwyn* was quasi-sarhaed to its owner.

181.34-182.2 The corresponding passage in *Bleg* (53.28-54.3) adds that the herd-dog (W. *bugeilgi*) should go round

Notes: The Value of Wild and Tame   291

the livestock three times in the night, and that the owner must be able to testify to its qualities with a neighbour from above and a neighbour from below his door.

182.10 guard dog: W. *ci callawedd* (or *callawfedd*). S. J. Williams persuasively suggests (*Bleg* p.192) a connection with *cynllyfan*, 'leash', so that this dog would be one held at the door by a leash nine paces long, and free to bite within that range (but the *vigilans* cited from AL Lat A and Lat B is not relevant, since it is the editor's interpretation of the Welsh word used in the Latin text).

182.13 scenting-hound: W. *bytheiad*. The traditional translation 'harrier' is unacceptable because the *bytheiad* was certainly suitable for larger quarry than hares. Though the Welsh name (with its echo of *bytheirio*, 'belch, bluster', and its modern use for clamouring children) suggests that the dog was named from its baying, its special character seems to have been its hunting by scent, which was perhaps a Norman innovation. The explanation that this type of dog was not known in Hywel's time is rejected by S. J. Williams (*Bleg* p.192) and is omitted by *Cyfn* (WML 35.8-10), which also omits the reference to writing, as does Lat D 380.28-9, which has *Sed rex Howel aliter dixit quod quicquid legali precio caret, de eo damdwng erit.* 'But King Hywel otherwise said that for whatsoever lacked a legal price there should be sworn appraisal'.

182.27 habituated dog: W. *ci cynefodig;* some words, indicating what the dog was habituated to, were perhaps already missing in the archetype of *Cyfn* (since they are missing from all the manuscripts); *Bleg* (54.18-19) has *ci cynefodig ar frathu dynion*, 'a dog accustomed to biting persons', and Lat D 380.40 *canis mordere consuetus.* The occurrence of *arglwydd* for 'owner' in *Cyfn* (alongside *perchennog* in some manuscripts) indicates translation from Latin *dominus*, but the differences in wording suggest translation independent of that of *Bleg*.

182.33 the law of theft is not applied to it: W. *ni wneir cyfraith lledrad arno.* The sentence is not in the *Bleg* tractate, and its force is not clear.

Hawks and Falcons (182.35-183.19)

182.36 falcon: W. *hebog.* For the significance of this and the other names, see the Glossary s.v. *falcon.*

292   The Law of Hywel Dda

Bees (183.20-184.21)

The various forms of this sub-tractate have been very thoroughly examined in Appendix 7 of *Bechbretha* (ed. T. Charles-Edwards and F. Kelly, Dublin, 1983), 192-205; the practical background is dealt with in the section 'Bee-keeping in Early Ireland' of their Introduction, pp.38-49.

Translation has been difficult because in both English and Welsh some words are used in two senses. Explanation of the technical terms can start from *bydaf*, 'colony of bees', which has an Irish cognate (see *Bechbretha* 41) and is translated 'colony of wild bees' at *Bechbretha* 197: this is rather misleading (though *bydaf* is used in some modern dialects for 'wild bees'), since *bydaf* is certainly used for colonies which are as tame as bees ever are: see 124.17n. There is moreover a very real sense in which all bees are wild, and that is no doubt why the hunting of a swarm is free (184.1); cf. also the proverb 'Die Biene ist ein wilder Wurm', Graf and Dietherr III.256 (p.110). In ordinary English 'swarm' has to translate both *haid*, the company of bees which is on the move from its former home, and *bydaf*, the company which has come together in a new home (probably in a hollow tree), the 'clustered swarm' of the present translation.

In the light of the origin of 'colony', that word would be an appropriate translation of *bydaf*, and it has been used in 'queen-colony', which translates *modrydaf* in one of its senses. In the other sense, *modrydaf* is translated 'queen bee'; since *modr-* represents the Indo-European root which means 'mother', *modrydaf* could mean either 'mother of bee-colony' or 'mother-colony of bees'. In the latter sense *modrydaf* is replaced in *Ior* by *henlleu*, 'old colony', for which see *Bechbretha* 202.

There are in manuscripts of the Iorwerth Redaction two versions of the sub-tractate; *Llyfr Iórwerth* prints only the one found in MS. *B*, and it alone is translated here: the relation of the two versions and the *Cyfn* and *Bleg* versions is examined in detail at *Bechbretha* 195-203. In their treatment of the value of successive swarms all versions seem to show the lawyer's schematism in an intense form, but the practical fact lying behind the detailed rules is surely recognition that a swarm must be established well before the winter if it was to be of real value. A late swarm might not amass enough honey to maintain it through the winter: it would certainly not provide a surplus for a human exploiter.

Notes: The Value of Wild and Tame   293

Deer and Hunting (184.22-187.13)

184.26-7 No finality is claimed for the identification of the joints: this list differs at several points from those in *Cyfn* (WML 35.13-16) and *Bleg* (51.24-7), which are identical though the tractates in the two Redactions are not. Aled Wiliam points out (*Ior* p.128) that *Ior* lists only eleven joints (on the assumption that each pair named counts as a single joint), whereas *Cyfn* and *Bleg* have twelve, since they name 'three joints from the neck'. *Ior* has the more accurate arithmetic for the total camlwrw at 36 kine, whereas *Cyfn* has forty kine (an impossible total) and *Bleg* £3 (only four times the single penalty); but the whole sub-tractate has a very antiquarian air. If the joints are worth 60d. each, the theft of any one of them should carry the death penalty; moreover, one might expect that handling a royal animal amounted to sarhaed to the King. However, though we can feel sure that the detailed provisions of the sub-tractate were obsolete in the thirteenth century, we can also feel sure that Welsh and Norman rulers of the period would be glad to refer to its principles as authorising their hunting privileges.

184.29 two pipes: W. *deucorn*. 'The two pipes would presumably be the wind-pipe and the gullet' (Wiliam). Though *corn* usually means 'horn', *corn gwddf* (in various forms) is a living expression for 'throat'.

184.35 champion hart: W. *cylleig*. The Welsh word is found only in *Cyfn*: the ordinary word for 'hart', *hydd*, is used in *Bleg*, perhaps because it is translating from a Latin text which avoided the technical Welsh expression. The etymology of *cylleig* has not been established, and one is tempted to connect it with *cylla*, 'stomach', since the point seems to be that the 'status joints' are found in the hart only when it is in good condition, between 16 June (St Curig's Day) and 1 December (or, according to *Ior* and *Bleg*, between Midsummer and 1 November). We can compare the rule for domestic animals, whose meat is valueless between New Year's Day and Midsummer: see 63.20-26, 177.25-178.3.

The fifteenth-century manuscript Llanstephan 116 (LHDd 109.16) defines *cylleig* as *penhyddgant*, which suggests the leader of a hundred harts; this may reflect the contemporary poets' use of *cylleig* as a laudatory epithet for leaders of men.

294   *The Law of Hywel Dda*

185.4 knifes: W. *cyllella;* the reference is no doubt to cutting out joints, and 'in the manner aforesaid' refers to the payment of a camlwrw for each joint.

185.19 hounds and the skin: other manuscripts have 'meat and skin'. The versions of the passage in *Cyfn* (35.22-36.4) and *Bleg* (51.4-11), which correspond closely to each other, instruct the landowner to 'skin the hart and feed the hounds with the meat and take home the hounds and the skin and the liver and the hindquarter'. The reading of MS. *B* may reflect an increase in the demands of the powerful princes of Gwynedd, but there are several obscurities in the *Ior* tractate: the meaning of the provision for the hindquarter and forequarter (185.30-31) is quite unclear.

185.35-8 This rule (from WML 36.14-17) is repeated in *Cyfn* at WML 98.17-20, in a slightly different form; neither form appears in *Bleg*.

186.1-7 *Cyfn* (WML 113.11-18) and *Bleg* (52.19-25) have a slightly different rule. Both specify the finder's share as the forequarter of a wild pig (*hwch coed*) and the hindquarter of any other edible animal. For an inedible animal, *Bleg* gives the finder a penny; for 'a fox or other inedible beast' *Cyfn* gives him a curt penny if the landowner wants the skin; thus neither Redaction applies the *Ior* exclusion of the unclean wild animal.

186.7-8 *Bleg* (55.21-23) gives the finder 'four pence and his dinner, or the wax'; *Cyfn* (WML 81.18-20) gives him 'a legal penny or the wax, at the landowner's option'.

186.15 idle: W. *segur;* the word may mean no more than 'unoccupied', i.e. these other hounds are not pursuing other quarry. The first branch of the Mabinogi begins with an account of hunting in Dyfed, when Pwyll chieftain of Dyfed drove off the strange hounds which had killed a stag, and fed his own hounds on the stag.

186.36 a person generally: W. *dyn yn gyffredin,* where the idea may be that of a right 'in common', which is a possible translation.

187.7 snare, springe, gin: W. *annel, croglath, yslepan.* The translations should not be taken as more than conventional expressions for three kinds of trap. From the reference at 186.9-13 to opening and closing land when setting an *annel,* it might be supposed that the *annel* was a sort of pitfall; *Dw* 236, which speaks of 'an animal going into an *annel,* and

Notes: The Value of Wild and Tame   295

with that one on him going into another *annel'*, seems to justify the interpretation 'snare'. *Croglath* is literally 'hang-rod', which could imply either a rod hanging ready to fall, or a rod from which the victim would find itself hanging.

187.8-9 There is some variation between the manuscripts, and the punctuation is unhelpful; in the light of the other Redactions, the translation seems to give the right sense. No finality is claimed for the English rendering of the Welsh terms.

187.11-12 roe: W. *iwrch* (which in the *Ior* passage means 'roebuck'); roebuck: W. *caeriwrch*.

Other Animals (187.14-36)

187.22 fox: W. *cadno*; like the French *renard*, this is a personal name (a familiar form of one of the many Welsh names beginning with the element *cad-*, 'battle') adopted as a common noun. The more formal word *llwynog*, used in *Ior* and *Dw* below, does not occur in *Cyfn*.

Skins (188.1-14)

188.1-9 Most of the values given in *Cyfn* are higher: ox, stag, cow, hind, and otter all have skins worth twelve pence; *Bleg* seems to give values only for the skins of ox, hart, hind (all twelve pence) and cow (eightpence). *Cyfn* gives no values for the skins of roebuck, roe, fox, and wolf; its values for marten and beaver skins are the same as *Ior*'s.

188.11 beasts: W. *pryf*, whose usual translation 'vermin' hardly consorts with the dignity of the animals concerned.

188.13 ornamentations: W. *amaerwyau*. Richards (*B Bleg* 106) translates this 'collars', no doubt under the influence of *aerwy*; it seems more likely that the word has the wider meaning of 'borders', for which ermine would be especially appropriate.

5. Trees

188.16-17 twin-forked: W. *dwygainc*, lit. 'two-branched'.

188.18-19 of the same growth: W. *untwf*, so transliterating (as the fifteenth-century scribe of MS. *D* did; cf. LW 261, '*malim legere* un tw' ', with the translation 'ejusdem aetatis') the *untu* of the older manuscripts. This could also represent *untu*, lit. 'on the same side'; GML 284, s.v. *tu*, suggests 'straight', but this interpretation seems rather forced, and

296 *The Law of Hywel Dda*

the natural interpretation would refer to a forking which would normally produce stems of equal thickness; but if unfavourable conditions should hinder the growth of one of the twin stems, this would not affect its status. This may suggest an interpretation of the *cainc uchelfar* which is valued at 60d. in *Cyfn* (WML 104.10-11) and *Bleg* (without specific reference to the oak: 98.9); Wade-Evans (WML 248) translated this 'a branch of a mistletoe'—following a speculation of the Glossary to LW, doubting the translation in the text (LW 263), 'ramus ad cacumen pertigens'.

188.19 cross-branch, W. *trawsgainc*: the corresponding item in *Cyfn* (WML 104.11-12) and *Bleg* (98.2-3) is *cainc arbennig*, 'special branch'; bough, W. *brig:* in modern Welsh *brig* (in relation to trees) is usually a collective name for the top of the tree with its branches, twigs, and leaves; *brigau* (sing. *brigyn*) means 'small branches'.

188.22-3 twenty-four pence. The penalty is 60d. in *Cyfn* (WML 104.9-10) and *Bleg* (98.1-2).

188.24 scrub oak: W. *cegin dderwen*. LW transliterated the *kegyn derwen* of MS. *B* as *cygndderwen*, with the translation 'quercus retorrida', whence perhaps the 'gnarled oak' of AL.

188.25-7 *Cyfn* (WML 104.14) and *Bleg* (98.5) give the hazel a value of 15d. and have no mention of the grove.

189.2-3 This sentence appears as a pendant to the triad *Tri Thlws Cenedl*, 'The three precious things of a kindred, a mill and a weir and an orchard; this is the reason they are so, that all the kindred can be together for them'. The value of a weir is given as £1; no value is given for a mill. For a quite different set of Three Precious Things, see 37.35-6n.

189.6 gardens: W. *garddau*; as at 113.6n, this may mean quillets (which the trees are intended to shelter) rather than gardens in the ordinary sense.

189.6-8 *Bleg* (98.6-7) gives these trees a value of sixpence; for *Cyfn* see 189.14-17.

189.13-14 holy yew: W. *ywen sant*; clearly a yew growing in a churchyard; woodland yew: W. *ywen coed*.

189.16-17 As William Linnard has shown (*Trees in the Law of Hywel*, 10-12), the variations in the treatment of the beech in the law manuscripts are revealing for the provenance of the texts. Beech was virtually unknown in northern

Notes: Trees 297

Wales as late as the eighteenth century, and is not mentioned in *Ior*: it occurred naturally in medieval Wales only along the English border and in the south-east. It is valued at 120d. in two Cyfnerth manuscripts (*W* and *Mk*), and at 60d. in *Cyfn* MS. *U* and most *Bleg* manuscripts.

189.37 windfall: W. *dofod*, elsewhere translated 'casual acquisitions'.

190.4-5 The full name of Iorwerth ap Madog ap Rhawd (for whom see CLP 123-33) is given only in MS. *C*; MS. *B* (alone) has *y doethion*, 'the wise ones', instead of Iorwerth's name.

6. Houses

190.10-14 *Cyfn* has no special provisions for the King's hall; in *Bleg* (95.1-4) the compensation for every timber which supports the roof is 20d., that for the roof 80d., and that for each minor house 20d. The minor houses (W. *godai*) were not necessarily physically 'in' the hall. In *Ior*, MSS. *A*, *C*, *E* price the forks at 40d., which fits with the total of £1.6s.8d. (added to *Ior* 139/2 from MS. *C*) if we assume that 'column' is the same as 'fork'.

190.18 MS. *B* does not refer to the uchelwr's minor houses; MSS. *A*, *E* price them at 30d. each. *Bleg* and *Cyfn* do not mention the uchelwr's hall. MS. *C* prices the roof at 40d.

190.22-4 This list of minor houses appears only in MS. *B*; other *Ior* manuscripts have instead 'A summer house is four legal pence in value; a harvest house eight legal pence' (*Ior* 139 n.9).

190.27-32 The translation of several items in this list is tentative, for there is little medieval material for comparison, and modern usage may be misleading.

end-benches: W. *talfeinciau* (WML 'upper benches', perhaps influenced by the fact that *tâl y fainc* 'the end of the bench' was a place of honour: see 8.2-3 and the note at *Bleg* p.196).

fireback-stones: W. *ystyffylau*, for which see E. Rolant, *Bardos* (ed. R. Geraint Gruffydd, Cardiff, 1982), 58.

porches: W. *cynorau* (WML 'outerdoors', AL 'hatch'; but see the note on 'beerhouse' at 41.12-15, and that on *kynhorty* at *Bleg* p.188).

lintels: W. *gorddrysau*, which suggests either a half-door or an outer door like an Oxbridge 'oak'; but (since *drws* can

298   *The Law of Hywel Dda*

mean either the doorway or the door which closes it, whereas *dôr* can mean only the door) is probably rightly understood
by AL, WML, and *Bleg* as meaning the lintel which is over
the doorway; the Irish cognate means 'lintel' and the variant
form *gwarddrws* is still used in some dialects in this sense
(GPC).

190.34 The significance of the auger hole (W. *twll taradr*)
does not seem to have been explained. The house would
have been of wood; if it was movable (as seems likely), a
hole in the frame could have a peg or stake driven through
it to anchor the house to the ground. The usual translation
'autumn house' for *cynhaeafdy* seems perverse, since in
Welsh the word *hydref*, 'autumn', also means 'October',
and the name for September, *Medi*, means 'reaping'.

191.4 door-frames: W. *amhiniogau*; the same word is used
figuratively for neighbours as witnesses, WML 54.18, 136.14.

191.5 fourpence: correcting the misprint *iii.k'* at the end
of *Ior* 139/5. At the beginning of the next sentence *Ior* adds
from MS. *C* 'for the firestone (W. *pentan*) four legal pence'.

191.8 binder: W. *gwysbren* (a withy for holding thatch in
place?)
     thatch-spar: W. *aseth*, 'stake, spar, sharp-pointed lath,
esp. for fixing thatch on roof' (GPC).

191.9-11 under-thatch: W. *achwre*, cf. 204.17.

191.14 Provisions for securing barns after harvest follow
here in *Cyfn*: cf. 204.30-205.2.

191.23 Provisions relating to fire follow here in *Cyfn*; cf.
170.10-19.

7. Equipment

191.26 boiler: W. *pair*; 'cauldron' would be a more dignified
translation, but that word is needed for the less valuable
(no doubt because smaller) *callor* (191.28), cf. 37.35-6n.

192.9 starting-horn: W. *corn cychwyn*; other manuscripts
add 'which is always with him'.

192.12 Other manuscripts add 'and his horns'.

192.26 cask: W. *gren*; jar: W. *celwrn*, the word corresponding to 'jar' (RSV, NEB; AV 'barrel') in 1 Kings xvii.12. GML
cites *Meddygon Myddfai* as making the measure of the
celwrn four gallons and that of the *gren* sixteen; at AL

Notes: Equipment 299

XIV.iv.5 (ii.584) a *gren* of honey was 'a load for two men on a pole'.

192.34-5 drill: W. *rhwmp*; medium auger: W. *taradr perfedd*; gimlet: W. *ebill*. The corresponding names in *Cyfn* (WML 106.12-14) and *Bleg* (96.22-4), at the same values, are *taradr mawr, perfedd taradr*, and *ebill taradr*; Lat D 363.29-31 has *terebrum magnum, terebrum mediocre*, and *terebrum parvum*.

192.37 hedging-bill: W. *gwddyf*; this was the implement given to the slave as part of his sarhaed, see 155.34-6n.

192.38 hook-knife: W. *gylyf*, 'sharp-pointed instrument, knife' (GPC).

193.1 cropper: W. *croper*; GPC gives the meaning 'chisel' and suggests a derivation from ME. *cropper*, but there seems to be no evidence that this could mean 'chisel'. The usual modern Welsh words *cŷn, gaing*, 'chisel' do not appear in the law texts.

193.9 butter-vessel: W. *rhisgen*; according to *Bleg* 69.10-12, the winter food-gift of a villein townland included a *rhisgen* of butter, three fistbreadths in breadth and thickness, as an alternative to a fat pig.

193.14 costrel: W. *costrel*, the word used in Matt.ix.17.

193.15 crest: W. (MS.) *pyrchuyn*, for which *Ior* p.160 suggests 'Bourgogne, Burgundian helmet'.

193.30 manure-shed: W. *tomdy*, MS. *tomty*; if read as two words, this means lit. 'the dung of a house', and it is translated 'dunghill' by AL and GML (*sterquilinium* in LW); cf. 54.17.

193.31 gauntlet: W. *honffest*, a borrowing from E. 'handfast', for which GPC tentatively suggests 'gauntlet, manacle'; the 'mantle' of GML, 'tunic' of AL, and *tunica* of LW are not acceptable.

193.35 drag-net: W. *ballegrwyd*, the word corresponding in Hab.i.16 to AV 'drag', NEB 'trawl'.

193.39 plates: W. *clorion*; it is not clear what these are, but they can hardly be the 'beams' of AL, since the usual word for weavers' beams, *carfanau*, comes in the next line. *Clorion* is the plural of *clawr*, which occurs in the expressions for 'baking-sheet' and 'throwboard board', and with the meaning 'plate' or 'cover', see 5.30-6.2n, 154.12-20n.

300 *The Law of Hywel Dda*

194.2 wheels: W. *troellau*, which usually means 'spinning wheels'.

194.3-9 The identification of some of the smith's implements must be tentative:

bicorne: W. *einion gyriog*; this was apparently an anvil with horn-like projections.

bender: W. *cameg*; this interpretation, assuming a connection with W. *cam*, 'crooked', is offered as preferable to the 'parer' of AL.

nail-maker: W. *cethrol*; this assumes a connection with *cethr*, 'spike, nail', as does the 'bore' of AL.

furrower: W. *cwysyll*, *cwynsyll*; the translation assumes that *cwysyll* is the original form: the meaning is the same as the 'groover' of AL.

vice: W. (MS) *trooryd*, with variants *troryt*, *tryvoryd*: this passage seems to have the only examples of the word, and it is not found in the early dictionaries; LW offers no translation.

iron file: W. *haearnllif*, lit. 'iron-saw'.

194.10-15 A contrast is evidently to be drawn between the large-scale milling equipment of the quern-house, which used some machinery to transmit power to its large stones, and the hand-operated small quern.

194.18-19 dark-blue-bladed, white-bladed: W. *gwrmsaid*, *gwynsaid*. These adjectives have usually been translated 'blue-hilted' and 'white-hilted', but it seems quite clear that the colour is that of the blade. Since the white-bladed sword is the more valuable, it is likely that the blue-bladed sword had acquired its colour in the process of tempering, whereas the white-bladed one had afterwards been polished and burnished. (I thank Mr A. R. E. North of the Victoria and Albert Museum for this suggestion.)

195.1 Some manuscripts give the value of silvered stirrups as fourpence.

195.4 felt saddle-cloth, W. *panel cynnwgl*, cf. *botasau cynhyglog*, 'felt boots' (195.8), *cynnwgl*, 'quilt' (195.24). The evidence on which to base an interpretation is scanty: there are our passages; there is a citation in an Old Irish glossary which makes O.W. *cintecal* refer to the coarse wool from which a blanket is made; and the form *cynnyglu* occurs in one of Iolo Morganwg's manuscripts for 'to mat' (of hair): NLW MS. 13111, p.78 (printed in Ab Ithel's *Phys-*

Notes: Equipment 301

icians of *Myddfai*, 160). The translations 'felt' and 'quilt' are offered as reconciling all the examples.

195.5-6 horse-brass (W. *canwyl*) follows the editor's gloss *frontale* to Lat B at AL ii. 888 (16), rather than his translation of our passage, 'blinker'.

195.7 long hose, hose: W. *hosanau mawr, hosiaws/hwsiaws*; the two Welsh words seem to be borrowings from O.E. and O.Fr. respectively. The interpretation of 'hose' is left open: if these hose were stockings, they will have been of leather: see I. C. Peate, *Diwylliant Gwerin Cymru* (Liverpool, 1942), 42.

195.8 kneeboots: W. *ystywos* (13th-c. MS. forms *estywaus, estywos, estyaws, ystywos, stiuos*), like German *Stiefel* a borrowing from O.Fr. *estivaux*.

195.11 dagger: W. *honsecs*, from O.E. *hand-seax* or M.E. *hond-sax*.

195.13,14 thrave: W. *drefa*; in twentieth-century Ceredigion the *drefa* consisted of twenty-four sheaves, but from the values of sheaf and *drefa* of oats in our text the medieval Welsh thrave will have had sixteen sheaves.

195.16 corn-measure: W. *hestor*, from Lat. *sextarius*; in recent centuries the hestor was two (Winchester) bushels, but there is no firm evidence for its size in medieval Wales.

195.33-8 There is still room for difference of opinion about the meaning of some Welsh terms for parts of the plough, though most problems in the field were solved by Ffransis G. Payne in *Yr Aradr Gymreig* (Cardiff, 1954); see also the notes on Joint Ploughing, III.9 (p.303).

195.38 thorn-hurdle: W. *draenglwyd*, a medieval counterpart of the chain-harrow.

196.1,2 The same values are given in *Cyfn* at G.C. II.xviii. 44,45 (not printed in WML).

8. The Human Body

196.14-15 Cf. the application of the value of the tongue in an appeal against a judge's ruling on the law, 17.25-9.

196.21-2 The wording of *Ior* implies that this value is that of the thumb-nail; *Cyfn* (WML 42.11-12) has 'a person's nail is worth thirty pence'.

196.22-7 According to our text, with which *Cyfn* (WML 42.12-17) and most *Ior* manuscripts agree, the value of the

302 The Law of Hywel Dda

lowest joint was equal to that of the whole finger, at 80d. (i.e. a cow (60d.) + 20d.) This would mean that the victim got more compensation if he lost his finger joint by joint than if he lost it at one blow.

197.11-16 The distinction drawn is between blood which reaches the ground, which entitles the Lord to a dirwy in any event, and the other two cases, in which the Lord gets the penalty only if the victim sues for compensation. The reference to making the earth bloody suggests a comparison with the pollution of the land by blood, mentioned in Num. xxxv.33; cf. also the Frisian law rule that the blood must reach the ground, cited by Grimm, *Deutsche Rechtsalterthümer* ii.185. For 'stay' see 127.17n.

197.22 . . . of the medication: *Ior* adds from MS. *E* 'from him who wounded him', but the rule is concerned with the fee to which the physician is entitled; our text implies that the wounded man pays it from the £3 to which he is entitled. *Bleg* 57.5-10 gives the wounded man, in addition to the £3 and his sarhaed, 4d. for a pan for making medicaments, 4d. for tallow, a penny a night for light, a penny a day for the physician's food, and a penny a day for his own food.

197.23 blood-clothes: W. *gwaed-dillad*; *Ior* p.131 interprets this as 'dressings, bandages', but other texts (especially WML 25.4, *dillad gwaedlyd*, 'bloody clothes') indicate that the 'bloody clothes' of AL is right.

197.32-7 *Ior* seems to have merged two rules here. The payment of 20d. is for a broken bone, presumably a substantial one but not one of the 'four posts'; the test for size by dropping the bone into a metal bowl applies to splinters of bone. In *Cyfn* (WML 25.8-11) the test is a parenthesis following the blow to the head in the list of the three dangerous wounds; in *Bleg* (57.11-15) the rule is clear: 'Four curt pence are paid to a person for every bone above the skull (*uch creuan*) which is taken from his head, and which sounds in a brass bowl; for every bone below the skull, he gets four legal pence.' The test for size by sounding in a bowl is given in many Germanic law texts: the bowl was originally a shield, and the sound had to be audible from a distance of twelve feet or the like: see Grimm, *Deutsche Rechtsalterthümer* i.109.

198.7 hair uprooted: W. *gwallt bonwyn*, 'white-stocked hair'; the 'white stock' is the root.

Notes: The Human Body 303

198.14-15 free blood: W. *gwaed rhydd;* slave blood: W. *gwaeth caeth.* The expressions certainly refer to the blood of a free person and a slave respectively, but the literal translation has been adopted because the adjective *rhydd* is not found used as a noun.

9. Joint Ploughing

This material has been examined in detail in D. Jenkins, *Agricultural Co-operation in Welsh Medieval Law* (Amgueddfa Werin Cymru, 1982), which includes a translation of the *Col* version of the text. The tractate is found in its developed form only in *Col* and the Iorwerth Redaction (from which it has been borrowed by later manuscripts of the other Redactions); a few of the elements from which it was built up are found in *Cyfn*.

Two patterns of yoking are envisaged, in both of which the oxen are yoked in pairs. In the 'long team' (W. *hirwedd*), all the yokes are of the same length, no doubt that of the short yoke, and each pair of oxen is directly in front of the next. In the other pattern, only the pair nearest to the plough is under the short yoke, and each successive pair is under a longer yoke and is slightly farther out than the one before it: this gives a much more compact team than the 'long team'.

199.8-9 thirty times the rod: W. *deg ar hugain i honno*, lit. 'thirty of that', which may be ambiguous, and has been understood as meaning that the acre is thirty times as long as it is broad. This interpretation is intrinsically unlikely, and was stimulated by the idea that our interpretation made the acre (at 1440 square yards) too small to represent a day's ploughing: this objection fades when it is realised that the 'day' ended at midday, as the rule for the properties of an ox (176.31) shows.

199.11 prime: W. *eithefig*, lit. 'extreme'; the two oxen were extreme in quality, not in position, and would be yoked nearest to the plough.

199.16 *cyfair casnad* is one of the traditional expressions found in the law texts which were clearly obscure to the thirteenth-century scribes: it appears in various forms, all apparently variants of *cyfair asglod* and *cyfair casnad*. The descriptive word seems to be adequately defined in GPC s.v. *casnod, casna[d]d* as 'lath, splinter, wood needed to make or repair a plough', but the interpretation in GPC of

304 *The Law of Hywel Dda*

cyfair asglod as 'ploughbote acre, land set aside to provide timber for making and repairing ploughs and other agricultural implements' is not supported by the passage in Lat B which is cited (AL ii.856, i.e. LTWL 230.11-13), for which (as for our text) the acre is clearly one ploughed for the owner of the 'woodwork'. The point perhaps is that the owner of the woodwork gets an acre ploughed only once a year (though the plough may be used for several 'loops') because what he provides is only raw material, since it is the ploughman's function to make and repair the plough: see 202.3-6.

199.18-20 This rule follows a provision for the order of ploughing, on the same lines as that of *Ior*, and is followed by the rule about the black ox's acre (199.26-30). In the villein townland the order of ploughing may be an order of allocation of acres in a common field (after ploughing); in the voluntary joint-ploughing contract of our tractate the order is certainly that in which the individual acres of the partners are ploughed.

199.24 collars: W. *dôl* (sing.), which has the basic meaning 'curve, loop', and is elsewhere translated 'bow'. By being passed round the ox's neck and through holes in the yoke, the bow formed a collar which held the yoke in place on the neck. The 'closing of collars' was the starting point for the day's ploughing.

199.36-7 support the end of the yoke: this is of course a figurative expression for providing a substitute ox.

200.4 traffic: W. *trafnidro*, perhaps 'exchange' (so AL, *Ior*; LW *permutabit*), but the prohibition should extend to loan and hire; gaging is specifically prohibited, 201.9.

200.17 nothing . . . wrongdoing: so MS. *B*; *Ior* 150/3 follows the other manuscripts, which have 'that he did not do worse for them than for his own'.

200.26 an extra burden: W. *gorysgwr*, lit. 'over-peg'. The peg was that which passed through the 'eye' of the draught-rope from the plough, to hold it in position after it was passed through a hole in the yoke; normally the yoke-hole would be equidistant from the two oxen, but some medieval yokes have more than one hole, so that an advantage could be given to the ox farthest from the hole used.

200.34 wild rough land: W. *tir gwyllt gŵydd*; other manuscripts have only one of the two adjectives.

Notes: Joint Ploughing

202.4 plough: here *gwŷdd*, i.e. the wooden frame.

202.9-11 the yoke-bows and draught-ropes of withes: W. *y pistlau a'r iewyddion o wdyn*; the little rings and the pegs of the bows: W. *y torchau bychain a gwehyll y dolau*. The wording of the manuscripts varies, and the translation is tentative, but has the advantage of accounting for all the equipment of the oxen except the yokes themselves. The little rings were attached to the middle of the yokes and connected the draught-ropes to them; the pegs kept the bows in position in the yokes. Since these were needed only for the long team of oxen in pairs behind each other, we must conclude that with the other arrangement of oxen there were independent draught-ropes for the yokes and that the yokes were attached to the horns of the oxen, so that bows were not needed.

10. Corn Damage

The tractate deals also with damage to other crops, and it might be better to use as a title the technical term of English law, 'Cattle Trespass' (where 'cattle' has its wider meaning); the practical parallels with English law, where the right to impound the trespassing animal is called 'distress damage feasant', are obvious. There is an orderly tractate on Corn Damage in *Cyfn* (WML 83.5-85.3) and a virtually identical one in *Bleg* (85.8-86.32): extracts from this are inserted at appropriate points of our main text. All the sources agree in varying the form of compensation according to the season: the point is most clearly expressed in MS. *S* (2,246): 'There is a right to money in respect of an animal legally taken on corn from when it is sown until it goes into sheaf, and thereafter a sound sheaf in place of the damaged one'. *Cyfn* and *Bleg* provide compensation in money (which in this context includes forfeiture of a trespasser) until the corn is in sheaf, whereas *Ior* requires a replacement of the crop after a specified date which is well before the corn is even in ear.

202.26 pound: W. *carchar*, 'prison'. The owner of the impounded animal is entitled to recover it on payment of the named sum; at the earlier stage this would be his whole liability, but at the later stage the payment must operate as security for his performing his obligation to compensate in kind.

The Law of Hywel Dda

202.30-35 This rule seems never to have been explained: we should expect the compensation to be greater for an unrestrained horse, which could leave its owner's care more easily, wander more freely while trespassing, and escape capture more easily; nor is it clear why unhobbling the horse (which would reduce his compensation) should be an offence in the impounder. He would presumably unhobble it in order to lead it more easily to pound.

203.6 mixed with their dams: this seems to mean that the lambs can be counted as sheep for the purpose of deciding compensation on the scale given below. *Cyfn* (WML 83.25-84.1) and *Bleg* (86.1-2) have a different rule: 'For every lamb, a hen's egg is paid, up to the legal herd, and then a lamb is paid'. *Cyfn* (WML 84.17-19) specifically provides for releasing calves after a day without their mothers' milk: they were no doubt regarded as not consuming any of the growing crop.

203.10 The owner would have first choice, so that the impounder took the second-best animal.

203.20-21 The owner of two pigs would not get pigs (W. *moch*), but only a pig (W. *hwch*, see 122.32n).

203.31 The 'three special beasts' (*tri llydn arbennig*) are defined in *Cyfn* (WML 76.10-12) as those 'whose value never rises or falls: the champion of the pigs, and a herd boar, and a pig for the Lord'; *Bleg* 118.2 makes the last the 'pig for the Lord's gwestfa', and Lat D 375.18 has for the first 'sus maior in grege, id est, arbennid y moch'. *Arbennig*, usually 'special' but here translated 'champion', is the word translated 'suzerain' in its application to the Lord Rhys, 164.24. The 'legal herd of pigs' is effectively fifteen pigs according to *Ior*; that of sheep is thirty according to both *Ior* and *Cyfn* (WML 83.24), but *Cyfn* and *Bleg* give only a farthing for every five sheep taken. Since the legal value of a sheep is fourpence according to all the Redactions, the compensation jumps sharply when the full legal herd is taken, according to *Cyfn* and *Bleg*, but falls (from 5d. to 4d.) according to *Ior*. All this suggests that the scales of compensation were of little practical significance to those who used the surviving copies of *Cyfn* and *Bleg*.

204.11 fodder: W. *gogor*, still a living word in West Wales; there is no confusion with the apparent homonym *gogr*, 'sieve', because the latter becomes *gwagar* in the dialects

Notes: Corn Damage   307

which use *gogor* (usually in the mutated form *ogor*, see GPC s.v. and *Col* p.79).

204.36-8 It is hardly possible to be sure of the detail of these rules, where the technical terms are not well attested elsewhere. *Bleg* (95.24-6) and *Cyfn* (WML 102.15-18) have a simpler rule: 'After All Saints' Day, unless there is a wattling-rod in three places on the wall of a barn, the damage done in it is not paid for'. The walls of the barn were apparently of wattling, which must be strengthened in three places by a wattling-rod (W. *bangor*, which still survives as the name for a thicker spar in a fence: see Bedwyr Lewis Jones, *Iaith Sir Fôn* (Bangor, 1983) 10,15-16); the *bangor* could reach from the ground to the eaves of the barn.

and a board on the doorway: W. *a phlaid ar y drws; plaid* (which has come to mean 'party') had originally the sense 'side of a house', and it seems feasible to transfer the word to the plank or board of which the side might be made. We should probably think of the barn as having a doorway, but no permanently set door: the doorway would then be closed by a board, tied to the wattling with two bonds on the inside and (for obvious practical reasons) with a third bond on the outside.

205.8-9 the foremost and the hindmost: i.e. fore and hind feet.

205.15 fore-oath: W. *llw gweilydd*, 'which is always the unsupported oath of a suspect, taken at the instance of the suspector; if the oath is refused, no counter-oath is required from the suspector before further procedure can follow' (WLW 209). The fore-oath was not appropriate when the animals were not taken on corn because there could be no counter-oath, since the owner's unsupported oath would clear his animals.

205.21-2 It is paid . . . oath: W. (MS.) *Telitor g6edy hala6c 16*, where the archaic verb form *telitor* suggests an early origin for the saying. The oath is befouled because the people of the townland cannot all be telling the truth, since someone's animal must be guilty of the trespass.

205.36-7 the wild one which the tame one catches: W. *y gwyllt a ddeil y dof*. But for the foal's trespass it would be illegal to take in the mare which was not trespassing. *Col* 203 puts the proverb the other way round: (MS.) *e dof a d[e]yly y guyllt*, 'the tame catches the wild'.

308   *The Law of Hywel Dda*

206.29-30 darting colt: W. *saethebol*, lit. 'shooting colt' or 'arrow colt'. *Ior* p.134 cites an explanation from the fifteenth-century manuscript *F*, f.55v, 'This is a darting colt: a colt which does damage following its dam; it is not right to compensate for that damage until it is a year old, since for so long it will be a colt. From a year old on, its value changes and it has value as a horse, and from then on it is right to compensate for its damage though it should do the damage following its dam, since it will then be a horse.'

207.1-4 The translation follows the consensus of the manuscripts, which differs slightly from MS. *B* as punctuated in *Ior*.

207.5 forbidden: W. *fforestir*. This passage was taken into consideration in punctuating the rule against taking pigs on corn, 206.30-32.

207.13-16 enclose: W. *cadw*, lit. 'keep'; paddock: W. *cae cadw*, lit. 'kept enclosure', presumably kept for grazing as the meadow was kept for hay. The Lord's cross would operate here as elsewhere (see *Ior* p.134) to forbid interference, in this case with the fence enclosing a third plot.

207.35 contract: W. *mach*, elsewhere translated 'surety', but here surely referring to a contract made by the procedure explained in II.4.

208.11 his status: W. *ei fraint*, i.e. his status as taker, which entitles him to compensation.

209.10 compensation for damage: W. *diwyn llwgr*. This is contrasted with the flat-rate money payments due for trespass earlier in the growing season. There is no indication whether the plaintiff (owner of the damaged crop) could indeed postpone his claim until after the defendant had harvested the substitute crop, as the mention of the Winter Kalends suggests: we should expect that the duty of harvesting the crop fell on the plaintiff who was to benefit from it and would have had the labour of harvesting his own crop if it had not been damaged.

GLOSSARY AND INDEX TO NOTES

The most important function of the Glossary is to explain the words which have been left in their Welsh form in the translation and those English words which translate Welsh technical terms; as some words of both classes are explained in notes, the Index to Notes is necessarily combined with the Glossary. Many other words are entered under their English versions so that the original Welsh can be traced as a help to further study, or under the original Welsh because readers who are familiar with the Welsh terms will need to know how they are translated in order to trace references: this involves some cross-reference between Welsh and English (e.g. *caib, hoe*). The Glossary is not intended to be exhaustive: while *etc.* of course indicates the existence of more examples of the word listed, the absence of *etc.* does not mean that all examples have been cited.

References to the introductory notes to various divisions of the text are given in the form Pr.n (for the Prologue), In (for a Book), I.5n (for a chapter). In the interest of readers unfamiliar with the Welsh alphabet (in which digraphs such as *ch* and *ll* are treated as single letters, so that *lladrad*, for instance, would follow *luxury-bag* rather than *liver*), entries are in the order of the English alphabet; offended Welsh readers are asked to be forgiving. Italics are used for words of other languages than English; for occasional English words mentioned in linguistic contexts; and for catchwords in cross-references. Welsh words which are not italicised in the text are treated in the same way as English words.

abbot, W. *abad*, 61.24n
Aberffraw, 5.30-6.2n
abetment, W. *affaith*, 143.2n, 7-9n; of homicide, 94.22n
accusations, of a woman, three, 57.25-9n
ach, 'degree' (of kin) q.v., 149.34 etc.
achwre, 'under-thatch', 160. 34; 191.9-11n; 204.17
acknowledge, W. *arddelwi*, see *arddelw*
acquired land, W. *tir cynnif*, 92.22n
acquit, W. *diheuro*, 118.13; 167.13,14; acquit himself, W. *ymddiheuro*, 118.14
acre, W. *erw* (q.v.); measure, 199.8-9n; (day's ploughing) W. *cyfair* (q.v.), see also 99.3-9n, 136.16n; legal acre, W. *erw gyfraith*, 122.23n

310   *The Law of Hywel Dda*

adail, 'building', 99.25n
addfwyn, 'competent', 157.23n
adfer, see *edfryd*
adlamwr, 'resident', 119.23n
admitted thief, W. *lleidr cyfaddef*
adnau, 'deposit', 159.16; 161.22-3n; 170.25
adviser, W. *cynghorwr,* 157.2n
advowry, 108.18n
adze, W. *neddyf,* 192.38
ael, 'litter' (of sow), 179.15
aelwyd, 'hearth', 101.19n
ætheling, see *edling*
affaith, 'abetment' (q.v.), 143.2n,7-9n
affiliation, by kindred, 137.19-30n
agalaen, 'whetstone', 195.12
agweddi (for which the form *egweddi* is also regularly found)
      is in our text the share of the common pool of mat-
      rimonial property to which a woman might be
      entitled if her marriage broke up before it had lasted
      seven years: the measure of agweddi depended on
      the woman's status by birth and had no relation to
      the size of the common pool, whereas after seven
      years the woman's share was half the pool.
      Whether she took any share of the pool at any time
      would depend on the circumstances of the break-
      up. The adjective *agweddïol* (50.16) is used of a
      woman whose potential entitlement is to agweddi;
      agweddi is used in another context for one of the
      nine forms of marital union—perhaps the union
      which, though regularly created by gift of kindred,
      had not reached maturity by lasting for seven years.
      See 45.3-4n; 49.30n; 50.11n; 51.38n; 58.11-13; and
      WLW 23-39 (esp. 28-30), 187-8.
aid, W. *porth* (q.v.), 77.29-78.4n; aid to violence, W. *porth-
      orddwy,* 143.17
aillt, pl. *eilltion,* is one of three words found in the Welsh
      law texts for unfree persons. The other two, *bilain*
      (a borrowing from *villein*), and *taeog* (whose
      Cornish cognate *tyack* became the ordinary word
      for 'farmer') seem to be interchangeable and are
      translated 'villein'; but there are enough indications
      of difference between aillt and *taeog* to make it des-
      irable to mark the distinction by keeping *aillt* in
      the translation: see 50.27-32n; 55.6n; 99.1n; 195.30,

Glossary and Index to Notes 311

31. The original meaning of *aillt* must have been 'client' without any necessary implication of unfree status: *cyfaill*, 'friend', is from *cyf-aillt*, 'fellow-client'. The expression *mab aillt*, meaning 'male aillt' rather than 'aillt's son' has been translated 'aillt'.

alien, W. *alltud*, q.v.; alien having become patrimonial, 109.28-110.3n

alienate, W. *cychwynnu*, 113.3n

allowance, W. *cynnwys*, 104.31n

alltud, 'alien', lit. 'from another country'; yet, though Wales was not one 'country' but many, an alien was one from outside Wales: see 108.18n. The alien's position was insecure: he was required to integrate himself into society as client of some 'lord' (of whatever status), and the clientship could be terminated by either party at any time until it had lasted for four generations. After four generations the status of the breyr's alltud was perhaps indistinguishable from that of his aillt.

allwest, 'stud', 40.4n

altar, oath on, 78.5-79.2n

amaerwyau, 'ornamentations', 188.13n, cf. 41.19n

amaeth, pl. *emeith*, 'ploughman', 6.1 etc.

amaethiaeth, 'ploughmanship', 202.3-4

amarch, 'disrespect', 117.18

ambush, W. *cynllwyn*, 150.30-31n

amddyriaid, 'miscellanea'?, 177.36-178.3n

amhiniogau, 'door-frames, (fig.) neighbours', 191.4n

amhriodor, 'non-proprietor', 91.30 etc., 108.5-9n

amobr (also *gobr*, q.v.): a fee payable to a woman's lord, originally on the loss of her virginity, see WLW 73-5. It is comparable with the English *leyrwite* and *merchet* and with similar dues in most countries; in late medieval Wales the fee (which was originally payable to the patron-lord) was claimed by the territorial Lord in the Marches: WLW 96ff. See 51.38n; 52.22-9n; 55.6n,20n; 56.2-4n; 57.6n,16n.

amod (a) 'contract' in general, 62.32;
(b) (at times *amod ddeddfol*, 'legal amod'), the special form of contract of 79.3-80.33: see note to that passage.

amodwyr (a) 'amod-makers', 79.5;

312   The Law of Hywel Dda

(b) 'contract men', 62.32; 'amodwyr', 79.7, see
    79.3-80.33n.
amryson, 'argument', 142.15; 'dispute', 176.12 etc; 'that
    which is disputed', 95.5
amws, 'destrier', 172.6n: the Welsh word is derived from
    Lat. *admissarius,* 'stallion', but is used for the *dex-
    trarius* of the Latin texts; this was so called because
    it was led by the esquire's right hand until the
    knight mounted it to go into battle.
amyd, 'mixed corn', 195.14
anaf, 'harm', 174.25,30,32
    anaf o faes, 'outward harm', 174.25
anfodd, 'inadvertence', 198.26 (where the harm is done
    without the will of the perpetrator); *o anfodd,*
    'against the will', 116.24, 166.23 (where harm is
    done against the will of the victim), 'unintent-
    ionally', see 60.33n.
anghyfarch, 'surreption', 161.27n; 166.21-2; 170.14-16,
    'unclaimable thing', 61,3,7; see 61.3-9n.
anghyfiaith, 'of foreign speech', 76.4; 167.16n; 'of strange
    speech', 58.17-18
anghyfraith, 'illegality', 63.8 etc.
anghyfrwys, 'unskilled', 142.4; 181.18,22
anghynefin, 'unfamiliar to each other', 207.25
anhepgor, 'indispensable [thing]', 39.30,33,35
anhyys, 'inedible', 182.19
anianol, 'natural', 174.22n; cf. 94.1-25n
animal, W. *anifail,* passim
        wild animal, W. *gwyddlwdn,* 187.33; W. *anifail
        gwyllt,* 189.40
ankles, W. *uffarnau,* 34.20n
annel, 'snare', 187.7n
annilys, 'invalid', 92.22n etc., see *dilys, llys*
annod, 'interrupt, postpone', 119.35-6n; 'postponement',
    96.4
annwfn, 104.33n
anoddau, 'inadvertence', 130.18n; 'misapprehension',
    166.25,27
anolo, 'irregular', 132.25,26; 'void', 87.12 etc.
anosteg, 'non-silence', 89.18-19n
anrhaith, 'booty, spoil', see *rhaith;* 'something to despoil',
    159.9;
        anrhaith gribddail, 'extortionate confiscation', 159.19;
        cwbl o'i anrhaith, 'total confiscation', 83.2

Glossary and Index to Notes   313

anrheithio, 'despoil', 16.10; 'go on a raid', 9.38
anrheithoddef, 'liable to be despoiled', 157.16
antler, W. *ban,* 192.19; see also *throwboard*
anudon, 'perjury', 65.14-15n etc.
anwar, 'uncouth', 41.1; 47.2; see 46.38-47.4n
apple-tree, W. *afallen,* 189.2
    sour-apple tree, W. *afallen sur,* 188.34
    sweet-apple tree, W. *afallen bêr,* 189.1
appraisal, sworn, W. *damdwng,* q.v.
appropriate (v), W. *defnyddio, dywedud,* 58.25n
approve, W. *canmol,* 143.7
âr, 'tilth', 200.30; 209.9
    âr ac aredig, 'tillage and ploughing', 101.19n
arable land, W. *tir swch a chwlltwr,* 114.24n
aradr, pl. *erydr,* 'plough', 111.14 etc.
arbennig, 'champion, special, suzerain', 203.31n
    cainc arbennig, 188.19n;
    eisyddyn arbennig, 99.24, see *toft;*
    gŵyl arbennig, 'special feast', 7.23, 76.18-19 (defn)
    llwdn arbennig, 'special beast', 203.31n
arberygl, 'dangerous wound', 24.18n, 197.17
archenad, 'footwear', 23.32; 36.16,37
archolli, *acholledig,* 'wound, wounded', 24.12,34; 197.20,21
arddelw (n), 'case', 94.38; 'plea', 59.15, 106.23n, 162.9n
etc.; 'warranty', 86.29 etc.; *arddelwi* (v), 'acknowledge', 161.4; 'avow', 162.31; 'plead', 78.2 etc.;
'vouch', 163.12-13n; 'plea' and 'plead' are here
used in their technical English-law sense. The
basic meaning of *delw* is 'image, form': so *delw*
corresponds to 'image' in Gen.i.26 and Ex. xx.4,
and *arddelw* then means the legal form taken on by
the party. The English-law plea best known to
laymen is the general plea of 'guilty' or 'not guilty'
to a criminal charge, but even in a criminal case the
accused may plead autrefois acquit or autrefois
convict (i.e. that he has already been acquitted or
convicted of the charge), and in civil actions
pleading is more detailed, being designed to reduce
the disagreement between the parties to as simple
an issue as possible. With the objective methods of
trial used in medieval law, this was even more
desirable, and the detailed rules of procedure (e.g.
105.5-107.6) are framed to ensure this.

314   *The Law of Hywel Dda*

The secondary meaning 'warranty' arises from the use of *arddelw* in the law of theft for the three pleas of birth and rearing (*geni a meithrin*), keeping before loss (*cadw cyn coll*), and voucher to warranty (*arwaesaf*); since the first two virtually amount to special methods of disproving the plaintiff's ownership, it was perhaps natural to think of *arddelw* as specially appropriate to *arwaesaf*. The use of the verb in the sense 'acknowledge' arises in the same way: this is the sense in which it is still living, particularly in acknowledging (or claiming) relationship.

arddyrchafael, 'augment, augmentation', 16.5; 31.1-2; 32.29n; 33.11n, etc.

ardymheru, 'cook, season', 26.36n; 27.6-7

arffedog, 'guardian', lit. 'apron', 130.35

argae, 'stay', 54.18; 127.17n; 197.11-16n

arglwydd is the ordinary Welsh word for 'lord' in all its senses; it occurs in the law texts most often either (*a*) for the patron of a client: this is the lord to whom a boy is commended at 14 (131.10) and who is primarily entitled to amobr for his client's daughters (see *amobr*); or (*b*) for a territorial ruler; in this sense *arglwydd* alternates with *brenin*, 'king', for by the thirteenth century Welsh rulers found it tactful not to use the same title as the English ruler who claimed suzerainty over them (cf.1.2n); but though the law texts were revised to conform with this practice, the revision was not thorough: see 72.21-3n. In sense (*b*) 'Lord' is spelt with a capital L. For other points see 70.1-2n; 165.29n; 182.27n.

arglwyddes, 'female lord', 60.26, 73.16n; 'Lady', 124.21n

Argoel, 6.6n

argument, W. *ymdaeru*, 205.7; W. *amryson*, 142.15

argyfrau, 46.23-6n; 49.30n; 117.27; see *dower* and WLW 191

arhawl, 'surclaim', 112.2, 170.18-19n, etc.

arian, 'silver, money', passim;
    arian dooddwf, 'lactation money', 175.22
    arian y gwynos, 'supper money', 14.11-25; 123.36-7n; 129.19n
    ariantal, 'money payment', III.10n; 202.21,26n

Glossary and Index to Notes 315

arm, W. *byriad,* 24.22n

Armes Prydain, 20.23-4n

armpit yoke, W. *ceseiliau,* 99.5; 120.35; 199.2

arms, of serf, 155.33-5n

arrange, W. *cyweirio,* 147.28

art, see *celfyddyd, pencerdd*

arwaesaf (n and v, 3 sg.pres.). The noun has the abstract meaning 'voucher to warranty', i.e. the plea (W. *arddelw,* q.v.) in which the defendant calls a person to warrant his title to the property in dispute as derived from that person; it also has the concrete meaning 'vouchee to warranty', i.e. the person so called; 'warrantor' is an alternative translation appropriate when the vouchee accepts the call. Use of the verb, translated 'warrant', implies acceptance of the call. See also 72.36-73.15n; 163.12-13n; cf. 119.23n

arwystl, 'substitute', 63.13; 73.4; the Welsh word is a derivative of *gwystl,* 'gage', and is used when the substitute has been provided to replace another thing temporarily—as a sort of gage for the return of that thing; if it is not returned, the substitute is retained permanently, like a gage which falls forfeit.

aseth, 'thatch-spar', 191.8n

asgellhaid, 'wing-swarm', 183.31,34; 184.18

asgwrn morfil, 'whalebone', 16.26; 192.18

assache, 149.1-9n

assault and battery, W. *dyrchaf a gosod,* 143.37n

assurance, W. *tyllwedd,* 24.33n

aswynwr, 119.23n

atgas, see *cyfraith atgas*

attach (property), W. *dala,* 161.1

attendance (on ox), W. *gwasanaeth,* 199.29

attest, W. *tystio,* 13.28; 65.25; see *tyst*

attestator, attestor, W. *tyst* (q.v.), 83.16-17n; 86.27n

au, 'liver'; *auad,* 'liver-fluke', 179.33n

auger, W. *taradr,* 192.34-5n; W. *trwyddew,* 39.36n; auger hole, W. *twll taradr,* 190.34n

augment, augmentation, W. *arddyrchafael,* 16.5; 31.1-2n; 32.29n; 33.11n; W. *dyrchafael,* 48.4-5; 147.30; 154.21; 155.7-13n

authentic, W. *dilys* (q.v., see also *llys*), 7.26-8.28n; 19.27n; 118.37

autumn house, W. *cynhaeafdy,* 190.34n

316   The Law of Hywel Dda

autumn piglet, W. *cnyw hwch*, 178.24n
avengers, W. *dialwyr*, 148.2
avow, W. *arddelwi*, 162.31
awl, W. *trwyddew*, 39.36n; 193.1

back burden, W. *baich cefn*, 157.31-2n
bad ploughing, W. *drygar*, 200.28-9
baedd, 'boar'; *baedd cenfaint*, 'herd boar', 179.20
baeddredog, 'always on heat' (of sow), 179.10-11
baeol, 'pail', 45.18; 192.30,31
bag, W. *cwd*, 193.19
baich cefn, 'back burden'; *baich cychwyn*, 'movable burden', 157.31-2n
bail, bailsman, bailsmanship, W. *gorfodog, gorfodogaeth*, 80.35-81.26
baking sheet, W. *clawr pobi*, 193.22
ballegrwyd, 'drag net', 193.35n
balog fechni, 'buckle surety', 73.33n
ban, 'antler', 192.19, see also *throwboard*
banadl, 'broom', as roof covering, 170.20-24n
bangor, 'wattling-rod', 204.36-8n
banish, W. *diol*, 157.12 etc.
        banished man, W. *diholwr*, 157.15-16 etc.
bank, W. *clawdd*, 206.35
banquet, W. *cyfeddach* (q.v.), 7.6 etc.
banw, 'pigling', 178.18
bar, W. *corf*, 7.28, see 7.26-8.28n; W. *llys* (q.v.) 165.36n; (pl.) W. *dylaith*, 191.4
bard, chaired, W. *bardd cadeiriog*, 20.10, see *pencerdd*
bard of the household, W. *bardd teilu*, 20.1-32n, see *pencerdd*
bardd cadeiriog, 'chaired bard', 20.10, see *pencerdd*
bardd teilu, 'bard of the household', 20.1-32n, see *pencerdd*
bare fistbreadth, W. *moelddyrnfedd*, 129.4n
barleycorn, W. *gronyn haidd*, 120.25-6n etc., cf. 176.12-13n
barn, W. *ysgubor*; securing, 191.14n; 204.30-205.2
barrel, W. *baryl*, 193.14
barrow, W. *berfa*, 193.31
basket, manuring, W. *cawell deilo*, 193.30
bastard, 110.28n, cf. 104.31n
bath, W. *ennaint*, 170.23, 170.20-24n
battery, W. *gosod*, 143.37n.
battle, trial by, II.6n
battle-axe, W. *bwyall arf*, 194.17

Glossary and Index to Notes 317

beam, (pl.) W. *trostrau*, 191.4; (of plough), W. *rhagarnodd*, 195.35; (weavers', pl.), W. *carfanau*, 194.1; 193.39n
beast, W. *llwdn* (q.v.), 13.5 etc.; W. *pryf*, 188.11n; wild beast, W. *bwystfil gwyllt*, 187.32
beaver, W. *llostlydan*, 188.7,12
Bechbretha (ed. Charles-Edwards and Kelly), 183.20-184.21n
beech, W. *ffawydden*, 189.16-17n
beehive, W. *gwenynllestr*, 184.4
beerhouse, W. *cyfordy*, 41.12-15n
befouled oath, W. *halog lw*, 205.21-2n
beichiog, 'pregnant', 51.5 etc.
beichiogi, (n) 'pregnancy', 55.2, etc.; 'foetus', 130.13; (v) 'make pregnant', 50.36; 56.37 etc.; 'become pregnant', 58.18 etc.
bellows, W. *meginau*, 194.4
belt, W. *gwregys*, 76.29 etc.
bench, W. (pl.) *meincau*, 190.27; at 8.3, 38.9, it is impossible to say whether the MS. *ueyng, ueync* represent mutation of *bainc* or of *mainc*.
bender, W. *cameg*, 194.3-9n
beneficium, 161.22-3n
benffyg, 'lend, loan', 161.22-3n
bequeath, W. *cymynnu*, 46.37-48.7n etc.; bequest, W. *cymyn*, 47.1,3
beriewys, 'short-yoked oxen', 200.22, III.9n, cf. 199.11n
bestowers, W. *rhoddiaid*, 45.3-4n etc.
bettering pleadings, 87.28,34n
bicorne, W. *einion gyriog*, 194.3-9n
bilain, 'villein', 15.10; 41.11n,13; 55.6n; see *aillt*
bileindref, 'villein townland', 7.20n; 41.10, 11n; 125.9
billeting, W. *dofreth*, 121.32
binder, W. *gwysbren*, 191.8n
bird, theft of, 167.26-7
bishop, King and, 18.14-17n
bitter end, W. *dygn:* 'taking it to the bitter end' implied readiness to swear, as at 90.25
black, W. *du* passim; see also *dywyl*
    black-stained, W. *dulys*, 18.30; 194.34 etc. In a note to 18.30 (at *Ior* p.106) Wiliam rightly rejects AL's translation 'cast-off', and suggests that the articles may have been coloured with a dye made from one of the plants called *dulys*.
blaeniaid, 'foremost', 205.8-9n

318   *The Law of Hywel Dda*

blank days, W. *dyddiau dyddon,* 76.25-6; blank time, W.
    amser dyddon, 96.10; see *dyddon*
blanket, W. *teisban,* 195.25
Blathaon, headland of, 120.6-21n
blind man, and Lord, 70.1-2n
blood, reaching earth, W. *gwaedlydu,* 197.11-16n
blood-clothes, W. *gwaed-ddillad,* 10.34; 24.25-6; 197.23n
blood-feud, see *galanas*
blood-land, W. *gwaetir,* 110.8n,16,36; 111.1
blwyddyn: hawl tra blwyddyn, 'superannuated claim',
    97.21,25
boar, W. *baedd;* herd boar, W. *baedd cenfain,* 179.20; wild
    boars, W. *moch coed,* 22.24
board, W. *plaid,* 204.36-8n; throwboard board, W. *clawr
    tawlbwrdd,* 193.16-17; made of boards, W. *ystyll-
    awd,* 192.21
board land, W. *tir bwrdd,* 125.31; for a distinction between
    men of the maerdrèf and men of *tir bwrdd,* see
    Stephenson, *Governance,* 59 n.10
bodyguard, W. *teilu,* see *captain, household,* 166.1n
    man of the bodyguard, W. *gŵr ar deilu,* 9.33-5;
    155.13
boiler, W. *pair,* 191.26n
bonclust, 'box on the ear', 198.22-3
bond maenol, W. *maenol gaeth,* 128.24
bone, size of splinter, 197.32-7n
bonedd, bonheddig. The basic word *bôn,* 'stock' (esp. of a
    tree: 'stump', 189.36; 'base' of the post, 24.8; used
    figuratively, e.g. *yn y bôn,* 'fundamentally') gives
    the abstract noun *bonedd,* 'stock', 110.22;
    'lineage', 183.21, and with the implication 'high
    lineage', 'gentility', 159.24. This in turn gives the
    adjective *bonheddig,* used as a noun for the Welsh-
    man of full free status, the 'free tribesman' of the
    modern historian. In this context 'tribesman'
    implies that his ancestry is known: the bonheddig
    was a man of known stock, as the gentleman was
    originally a man of known *gens;* in modern Welsh
    bonheddig has much the same meaning as English
    'gentleman'. Within the bonheddig class the medi-
    eval Welshman might enhance his status by be-
    coming a *gŵr ar deilu* or gaining a royal office, or by
    succeeding to his patrimony as uchelwr (q.v.).
    For the position of the bonheddig whose patrimony

Glossary and Index to Notes 319

had been given up, see *gwaetir.* See also 7.26-
8.28n, 55.20n.
bonwyn, 'uprooted' (hairs), 198.7n
boon, W. *cyfarws,* 39.1
boots, W. *botysau,* 195.8; see also *ystywos*
booty, W. *anrhaith* passim; see *rhaith*
bore, 194.3-9n
borefwyd, 'breakfast', 36.17
bottom rung (fig.), W. *dilyrbren,* 99.18n
botysau, 'boots', 195.4n,8
bough, W. *brig,* 188.19n
bound, see *dyly*
bounty, W. *cyfarws,* 9.31
bourgogne, 193.15n
bowels, W. *ymysgar,* (human) 10.37; 24.18n; (animal)
177.33
bowl, W. *mail* (MS. *meyl*), 193.10; W. *cawg,* bone
sounding in, 197.32-7n
box on the ear, W. *bonclust,* 198.22-3
bracelet, W. *breichrwy,* 193.16
brag, 'brew', 129.9n
bragawd, 'bragget', 'a drink made of honey and ale fer-
mented together' (SOED), 25.20 etc.
bragget, W. *bragawd*
braint, 'status, right, special right', 32.23n; 107.32n;
208.11n. In modern Welsh used for 'privilege' in a
non-technical sense, *braint* corresponds at Deut.
xxi.17 and Rev. xxii.14 to 'right'; in the Book of
Common Prayer *a'th wasanaeth sydd wir fraint*
translates 'whose service is perfect freedom': cf.
dinasfraint for (Roman) citizenship at Acts xxii.28.
Most often used in the law texts for the general
status of a human being (in right of birth, marriage,
office, etc.), it is also used for human status in
relation to particular circumstances (see 46.19-
20n, 'special right', and 208.11n), and for the
standing of the court, of blank days, of a church, for
the importance of an offence (169.23), and for a
claim to land by manuring ('right', 113.18).
brandail, 'rotten dung', 113.21
brass, W. *efydd, efyddaid,* 194.32 etc.; 197.34
brass vessel, W. *efydden,* 193.11
brawdwr, 'judge', see *ynad*

320   *The Law of Hywel Dda*

break, W. *torri* passim, 80.12-29n
     broken (claws), W. *twn*, 180.21; broken bread, W.
     briwfara, 27.20; broken meat, fragments of meat,
     W. *dihynion*, 11.12; 26.37; 27.20
breakfast, W. *borefwyd*, 36.17
breast, W. *cwll*, 197.12, 11-16n
breast-girth, W. *brongengl*, 195.2
breastplate, W. *llurig*, 193.15
brecicafn, 'wort-trough', 193.37
breeches, without mixed fabric, 34.22n
breichrwy, 'bracelet', 193.16
brenin, 'king', passim; see *arglwydd* and 1.2n
brethynwisg, 'woollen clothing', 5.14-15n
breuan, 'quern', 45.24; 55.16n; 156.1-3; 'hand-quern',
     194.13; *breuandy*, 'quern-house'; *breuanfwth*,
     'quern-shed', 194.10-15n
breuanllif, 'grindstone, 194.8-9
breulif, 'ground on the stone', 194.17-18
brew, W. *brag*, 129.9n
breyr, (from *brogo-rix, 'king of a district') seems to be
     exactly equivalent to *uchelwr*, q.v. Both words
     imply, not a special status of nobility, but a part-
     icular level within the status of bonheddig (q.v.),
     namely that of the freeman who has come into his
     patrimony in land because all his ancestors in the
     direct male line are dead. See also *gwrda* and 50.27-
     32n; 55.20n; 131.20-27n.
bridle-tame, W. *ffrwynddof*, 171.36
briduw, 78.5-79.2n
brig, 'bough', 188.19n
briw, 'wound', 63.3; 'hurt', 174.15
briwfara, 'broken bread', 27.20
brogues, W. *cuaranau* (q.v.), 34.20n
brongengl, 'breast-girth', 195.2
brooch, W. *cae*, 76.29; 193.16
brood goose, W. *gŵydd ôr*, 181.9
broom, W. *banadl*, 170.20-24n
brwydau, 'heddles', 193.39
brycan, a borrowing from O.Ir. *breccan*, 'speckled cloth';
     by 1700 this was for Gaelic Scots the name of 'a
     length of flannel of various colours, which is their
     cloak by day, their bedcloth by night, and their
     shroud in the grave' (*Arch.Brit.* 233, tr.): in the law
     texts this multi-purpose article appears as a

Glossary and Index to Notes   321

blanket for the matrimonial bed (45.31) and as the goodman's indispensable plaid (39.34); the King's brycan is of the same value as his harp (191.25).

bual, 'buffalo', 192.11

buarth, 'fold', 207.17; *buarthdail,* 'folded manure', 113.29

buches, 'cattle pen', 82.26

bucket, W. *hesgin,* 192.30,32

buckle surety, W. *balog fechni,* 73.33n

buddelw, 'tying post', 201.3

budr, 'unclean', 180.27; 186.4

buffalo, W. *bual,* 192.11

bugail, 'herdsman', 62.22; 196.31. Since the modern Welsh *bugail* is a shepherd, it must be noticed that (as the element *bu-,* found also in *buwch,* 'cow', implies) the medieval *bugail* was primarily a herdsman of neat cattle.

bugeilgi, 'herd-dog', 181.34-182.2

building, W. *adail;* (pl.) W. *trefnau,* 99.25n

bull, in royal sarhaed, 5.30-6.2n

bulling (season), W. *terwenydd,* 175.19n,37; 206.22-4; always bulling, W. *rhydderig,* 175.35

bull-swarm, W. *tarwhaid,* 183.27-9

burden, W. *baich* (q.v.)
dadannudd of bale and burden, see 101.18-104.8n; 101.19n
extra burden, W. *gorysgwr,* 200.26n

burial place, W. *gwyddfa,* 132.29n

burwy, 'cow spancel', 193.8

buskins, W. *gwyntysau,* 195.9

butter-vessel, W. *rhisgen,* 193.9n

bwlch, 'opened', 46.11-14n

bwyd treigledig, 'interchangeable food', 76.28n

bwyllwrw, 'provisions', 156.34n; 169.11n

bwystfil gwyllt, 'wild beast', 187.32

bwyty, 'food house', 34.3n; 41.12-15n

bydaf, 'clustered swarm, colony of bees', 124.17n; 183.20-184.21n

bytheiad, 'scenting-hound', 182.13n; 193.13

cabbages, W. *bresych,* 204.15

cabolfaen, 'polishing stone', 193.21

cadno, 'fox', 187.22n

cadw, 'maintain' (by evidence), 86.16 etc., see *tyst;*

322 The Law of Hywel Dda

'enclose', *cae cadw*, 'paddock', 207.13-16n; *cadw cyfraith*, 'legal herd', 203.30,35

cadyd, 'leftovers', 36.5

cae, 'brooch', 76.29; 193.16; 'fence, hedge', 204.18; 205.24; 207.10; 'enclosure', see *cadw*
Cae'r Odyn, 126.2n

caeriwrch, 'roebuck', 187.11-12n

caeth, 'slave', passim, 166.1n; 'restricted', 97.28-31n

cafn, 'trough', 39.36; *cafn traed*, 'foot-trough', 192.28

caib, 'hoe' (q.v.), 192.37

cail, 'sheepcote', 190.23

Calan, 'Kalends' (of any month); *y Calan*, 'New Year'; *Calan Mai*, May Day; *Calan Gaeaf*, 'Winter Kalends', i.e. 1 November, passim, see 22.24-5n

callawedd: *ci callawedd*, 'guard dog', 182.10n

caller, W. *geilwad* (q.v.), 200.13-15

callor, 'cauldron', 191.28, 191.26n, see 37.35-6n

camarferu, 'misuse', 1.3; 5.28-9n

cameg, 'bender', 194.3-9n

camlwrw, 72.36-73.15n; 78.14-18n; 144.3-4n; 185.4n: the smaller of two standard financial penalties for wrongdoing, valued at three kine or 180d. Fr Seamus Cunnane of Cardigan has kindly drawn the editor's attention to the use in the records of the county court of Cardigan in the fourteenth century of *camlour* for penalties of 12d. and 2s., which indicates a widening of meaning; see also *dirwy*.

camp, W. *lluest*, 41.11n

candleman, W. *canhwyllydd*, 5.7,11 etc.

canhwyllydd, 'candleman', 5.7,11 etc.

canhwynol, 'innate', 108.18n, and see *bonheddig*

canine teeth, W. *ysgithredd*, 196.29-30

canllaw. The word is made up of the prefix *can-*, 'with, after', and the noun *llaw*, 'hand'; it is found in the law texts and in modern Welsh for 'handrail', and is clearly appropriate for the advocate (the person 'called up') who is at hand to help the litigant. It is not clear how the canllaw differed from the other helper, the cyngaws (q.v.), nor is it known whether either would be professional as being paid or as having been trained. Both helped litigants with the technicalities of presenting their cases; they are collectively called the litigants' 'aid' (W. *porth*,

Glossary and Index to Notes   323

q.v.). Inasmuch as 'loss and gain' is put in their mouth (85.33-4, 86.5), they seem to have the function of the attorney in medieval English law, who stood in his principal's place and bound him by his acts; other references, however (87.18,34n), show the principal as free to choose his own statement of the case or that of either of his assistants. This means that they do not bind him; thus their function corresponds to that of the Anglo-Norman 'countor' (Lat. *narrator*), whose statement of the case could be disavowed: see J. H. Baker, *The Order of Serjeants at Law* (Selden Society Supplementary Series, vol.v, 1984), esp. pp.8-14. Continental medieval law treated the advocate in a similar way: see (e.g.) Brunner, *Deutsche Rechtsgeschichte*, ii (2nd edn by C. von Schwerin, Berlin, 1928) 465-7.

canmol, 'approve', 143.7

cannwyr, 'plane', 193.2

canon law, canonist, 17.25-9n; 94.15n; 110.28n; 145.4-7n; 147.14-18n

cantred, W. *cantref*, 1.4 etc.; 121.11-13n. The form *cantred* is an old-established and convenient English version of the Welsh word.

Cantref Mawr, 121.11-13n

canwyl, 'horse-brass', 195.5-6n

cap of mail, W. *penffestin*, 193.15

capan, 'cape', 29.34; 34.25 etc.

　　capanau glaw, 'rain capes', 18.28; 32.9

caparison, W. *ystern*, 16.33,34

cape, W. *capan*, q.v.

Cape Wrath, 120.6-21n

capel, 'chapel', 41.26-7n

caplan, 'chaplain', 11.31-2n

captain of the household, W. *penteilu*, lit. 'head of the house-host'; *teilu* (in our translation usually 'bodyguard') had already become *teulu* in many of the law manuscripts, and later came to mean 'family'; the older spelling is retained for the old meaning. See also 8.37-9.1n; 26.10-12n.

car, see *carr*

câr, 'kinsman', 123.23 etc.; pl. *carant*, 'kinsmen', 149.17, *cereint*, 'relatives', 48.14. Cognate with *caru*, 'to love', *câr* is now a rather poetical word for 'friend'.

324 *The Law of Hywel Dda*

carchar, 'prison'; 'pound', 202.26n; *carchar/carcharu amser,* 'prison of time, imprisoned in time', 77.22-3, 25-6

carddychwel, 'car-returning', 57.16n, 102.35-6; 133.27; see *carr.*

care, W. *gwarchadw,* 33.28; 37.6; W. *pryder,* 150.18

carennydd, 'kinship', 145.7 etc.

carfanau, ('weavers') 'beams', 193.39n; 194.1

cargychwyn, 'car-starting', 116.9-11n; see *carr*

carllawedrog, 116.9-11n; see *carr*

carr, 'car'. To reduce confusion, the medieval spelling *carr* is retained for the word which is spelt *car* (with short a) in modern Welsh; the English 'car' is derived from the Celtic word. In medieval Wales the carr was usually (perhaps always) what would be distinguished in modern Welsh as *car llusg,* lit. 'dragged car', i.e. 'sledge': see 45.21n. The compound words *carddychwel, cargychwyn, carllawedrog, cartomog* could (so far as their form goes) be derivatives of *câr,* but are no doubt rightly interpreted as derivatives of *carr:* the vehicle clearly had some symbolic significance, as the concept of dadannudd of car (101.19) indicates. So 'car-starting' implies freedom to leave a place (see 116.9-11n), 'car-returning' freedom to return: 57.16n; 102.35-6; 133.27.

car-returning, W. *carddychwel,* see *carr*

car-starting, W. *cargychwyn,* see *carr*

carthbren, 'cleaning-stick', 195.37

carthwr, 'cleanser', 200.24, the horse used for cleaning the ground in preparation for ploughing

cartomog, see *carr*

carw, 'stag', 22.15 etc.

cas, 'hate', 95.9n

case, W. *cyngaws,* 85.25

caseg dom, 'dung mare', i.e. 'working mare', 172.30,32-3

cask, W. *gren,* 192.26n

cast at, W. *taflu,* 200.18

castell, 'castle', q.v.

castle, W. *castell,* 41.11n;
work on the King's castles, W. *gwaith cestyll y brenin,* 124.8-9n

casual acquisitions, W. *dofod,* 54.10, cf. 189.37n

catherig, 'on heat' (of cat), 180.15-32n

Glossary and Index to Notes 325

cattle disease, W. *clefyd y gwartheg*, 177.7
cattle of dark ancestry, W. *gwartheg dyfach*, 58.8-9n, cf. 134.8-9n
cattle pen, W. *buches*, 82.26
cattle trespass, III.10n (p.305)
cauldron, W. *callor*, 37.35-6n; 191.28; 191.26n
cawell deilo, 'manuring basket', 193.30
cegin dderwen, 'scrub oak', 188.24n
ceibrau, 'rafters', 191.7
ceidwad, 'maintainer', 86.27n; see also *tyst*
ceiniog, 'penny'. *Cyfn* and *Bleg* distinguish between the *ceiniog gyfraith*, 'legal penny', and the *ceiniog gota*, 'curt penny', no doubt so called as having been clipped; in *Ior* the *ceiniog* without addition is the curt penny. As the *dimai*, 'halfpenny', was one third of the legal penny (69.3-4), the legal penny was 1½ curt pence. The pound was equal to 240 pence, but there seems to be no clear statement whether these were curt or legal pence.
  ceiniog baladr, 'shaft penny', 145.2n
  ceiniog ddirwy, 'dirwy penny', 144.3-4n
ceinion, lit. 'fine things', 38.7-8; the word is left untranslated in the Latin texts.
celfi, 'screen', 7.26-8.28n
celfyddyd, 'art', 40.29-34n
cell, woman having, W. *ystafellog o wraig*, 57.6n
celwrn, 'jar', 192.26n
cenau: cenau cath, 'kitten', 180.16; *meithrin canawon,* 'rear kittens', 180.22
cenedl, 'kin, kindred', passim. In modern Welsh *cenedl* means 'nation', and in grammar 'gender'; the modern word corresponding most closely to medieval *cenedl* is *tylwyth*. A modern Welshman may speak of someone who is related to him in any way as of his *tylwyth*; he may also speak of people as being of the *tylwyth* of a named person, their common ancestor. In medieval Wales the *cenedl* of a person for the law of galanas and for compurgation were those related to him in any way; for inheritance of land they were his descendants, normally reckoned through males alone; cf. *degree*.
cenedlelyniaeth, 'kin-feud', 48.5n
cenfaint, 'herd', 40.5n,8-12
cengladur, 'skein-winder', 193.5

326   *The Law of Hywel Dda*

cerdd, 'craft', 40.29-34n; *tri chanu o gerdd amgen,* 'three songs of some other kind', 20.14-15; see also *pencerdd*

cerddor, see *pencerdd*

cerner, 'dormitory', 41.12-15n

cerwyn, 'vat', 23.26 etc.; 126.13 etc.; 192.21-4

ceseiliau, 'armpit yoke', 99.5; 120.35; 199.2

cethr, 'nail', *cethrol,* 'nail-maker', 194.3-9n

chaired bard, W. *bardd cadeiriog,* 20.10; see *pencerdd*

chamber, W. *ystafell,* passim, 57.6n

champion, see *arbennig;* champion hart, W. *cylleig,* 184.35n

Channel, W. *Mor Udd,* 120.6-21n

chapel, W. *capel, sapel,* 12.22; 41.12-15n,26-7n; 65.9-10n

chaplain, W. *caplan,* 11.31-2n

characteristics, W. *teithi* (q.v.), 65.19-20

charge (v), W. *gyrru,* 64.17; 146.23-35 etc.;
       (n), W. *gyr,* 157.39 etc.; take charge of, W. *gwarchadw,* 21.11; 25.11

chest, W. *cist,* 193.11

chief of kindred, W. *pencenedl* (q.v.), 55.7; 123.15-18,25-6n; 136.8 etc.; office of chief of kindred, W. *pencenedlaeth,* 123.28

Chirkland, 104.31n

chisel, 193.1n

Christmas, 76.19

Church, franchise rights, 101.2n
       mother church, W. *mam eglwys,* 41.22,30n
       parish church, 65.9-10n
       sanctuary rights, II.5n (pp.253-4); 83.16-17n

churchman, W. *gŵr eglwysig,* 150.22

churn, W. *buddai,* 192.26

chwarthawr, 'quarter' (of carcase), 185.28 etc.
       chwarthawr dylwr, 'hindquarter', 185.30
       chwarthawr rhag, 'forequarter', 185.31

chwynnogl, 'weeding-hook', 193.4

ci: ci callawedd, 'guard dog', 182.10n; *ci cynefodig,* 'habituated dog', 182.27n

cigddysgl, 'meat-dish', 193.19

cigwain, 'meat-fork', 191.27 etc.

cintecal (O.W.), 195.4n

circuit, W. *cylch,* 122.18n; 129.12-14n

cist, 'chest', 193.11

claf, 'sick', 71.3n; 'damaged', 205.2

Glossary and Index to Notes . 327

clafr, (n) 'scab', 177.8,10; (a) 'leprous', 46.29; 76.8; 150.23
clamour, son by, W. *mab dolef,* 134.15,16
clandestine, W. *llathlud,* q.v.
clarify, W. *amlycáu,* 142.16
clas, 82.24n
clawdd, 'bank', 206.35
clawr, 'board', 193.16-17, see *throwboard;* 'cover', 154.12-
20n; 'plate', 193.39n;
clawr pobi, 'baking sheet', 193.22
clean, W. *glân,* (of animal) 63.5n; (of oath) 95.22
cleaning stick, W. *carthbren,* 195.37
cleanser, W. *carthwr* (q.v.), 200.24
clear, W. *eang,* q.v.
cledren, 'lath', 119.22; 'rail', 191.6
clefyd y gwartheg, 'cattle disease', 177.7
cleric, W. *ysgolhaig,* 145.19; 148.1
clerk, W. *ysgolhaig,* 1.6,7 etc.
cloak, W. *rhuwch,* 195.30,31
clustered swarm, W. *bydaf,* 183.20-184.21n
clustog, 'cushion', 16.20,21n
clwyd, 'hurdle', 195.15; see also *dorglwyd, draenglwyd*
cnyw hwch, 'autumn piglet', 178.24n
coedwr, 'woodlander', 189.33; 'woodman', 113.36; 114.1-
5n; slave as, 155.33-5n
coffers, W. *coffrys,* 6.29
cogail, 'distaff', 120.7; 145.19; 195.16; tracing pedigree by,
110.4-6n
cold case of galanas, W. *oergwymp galanas,* 146.9-10; cf.
dire loss
collar, W. *dôl,* q.v.; W. *torch,* 173.9; 181.21n, etc.
collen, 'hazel'; *collwyn,* 'hazel grove', 188.25-7n
colofn, 'column', of body, see *post;* of house, 7.26-8.28n;
190.10-14n,16; of law, 1.26; 142.37-8; 171.26
colony, of bees, see *bydaf, henlleu, modrydaf*
coloren, 'flesh of (horse's) tail', 172.38 etc.
colourable, 160.8-9n
coloured, W. *dywyl,* 154.18,19n
colt, W. *ebol,* 11.23n; darting colt, W. *saethebol,* 206.29-30n
column, W. *colofn:* of body, see *post;* of house, 7.26-8.28n;
190.10-14n,16; of law, 1.26; 142.37-8; 171.26
colwyn, 'pet-dog', 181.28n
comb, W. *crib,* 193.21
commodatum (Lat.), 161.22-3n
common, right in, 186.36n

328   *The Law of Hywel Dda*

commote, W. *cymwd*, see *cantred*
companionship, company, W. *cyweithas*, 143.10; 156.35;
    see *corn*
compensation, W. *iawn*, 26.17 etc.; compensation for
    damage, W. *diwyn llwgr*, 209.10; contemptuous
    compensation, 18.20-23n; 35.6-8n; 49.30n
competent, W. *addfwyn*, 157.23n etc.
compurgation, W. *rhaith*, q.v.; compurgator, W. *rheithiwr*,
    see *rhaith*
concord, W. *tyllwedd*, 85.21,22; 148.37; 149.5; cf.24.33n;
    W. *cydfod*, 71.38
confine, W. *gwarchae*, 203.3; confined, W. *cyfyng*, 200.14
confiscation, extortionate, W. *anrhaith gribddail*, 159.19;
    total confiscation, W. *cwbl o'i anrhaith*, 83.2
conquest, W. *goresgyn*, 81.30n
conspicuous scar, W. *craith ogyfarch*, 196.34; 197.28
contention, W. *cynnen*, 175.37; W. *ymwrthryn* (for land),
    105.4,5,6
contract (n), W. *amod* (q.v.), 199.23 etc.; by contract, W. *ar
    fach*, 207.35n; see also II.4n; 79.3-80.33n;
    (v) contract for, W. *amodi*, 201.30; contract for joint-
    ploughing, W. *cyfaru*, 201.14
contract-man, W. *amodwr*, 62.32; see *amod*
control (v), W. *meddu*, 162.1n; 182.32; 201.8; (n), W.
    meddiant, 85.20n; 96.23; 201.11
cored, 'weir', 112.19; 113.1; 124.16
corf, 'bar', 7.26-8.28n
corflan, 'enclosure', II.5n (pp.253-4); 82.22n; *tir corflan*,
    'hamlet land', 113.5
corn, 'horn': *corn canu*, 'sounding horn', 195.17; *corn
    cychwyn*, 'starting-horn', 192.9n; *corn cyweithas*,
    'social horn', 40.14-19n;
    'pipe', 184.29n
corn, mixed, W. *amyd*, 195.14
corn measure, W. *hestor*, 195.16n
cost, W. *cost, traul*, 41.11n
costog, 'cur': *costog tom*, 'dunghill cur', 181.31 etc.
costrel, W. *costrel*, 193.14n
coulter, W. *cwlltwr*, 37.35-6n, and see *arable land*
counter-swear, W. *gwrthdyngu*, passim
country, W. *gwlad*, passim; strange country, out of the
    country, W. *gorwlad*, passim
court, W. *llys*, passim; laws of court, In (p.220)
cover, W. *clawr*, 154.12-20n; W. *hwyl*, 23.27,29; 25.12

Glossary and Index to Notes 329

cow, W. *bu, buwch*; pl. *gwartheg*, 40.5n; 201.25,26

cowhouse, W. *beudy*, 190.22

cow-spancel, W. *burwy*, 193.8

cowyll, 46.23-6n; 50.27-32n,33-5n; 51.38n; 58.25n. The word is remotely cognate with English 'cowl', and perhaps gets its meaning of 'morning-gift' from the change of head-dress which often marks change of status from virgin to married woman: see WLW (references in the Index, s.v. *cowyll*).

craith ogyfarch, 'conspicuous scar', 196.34; 197.28

crane (bird), W. *garan*, 15.18; (implement), W. *pergyng* (q.v.), 45.33; 191.27

crasu, 'to dry' (corn), 126.2n

creddyfyn (n), 'religious', 163.38

creditor, W. *dylyawdr*, 66.17, see *dyly*

crefenllyn, 'scraper', 193.6

crefydd, 'religion' (i.e. religious order), 150.23; *dillad crefydd*, 'religious habit', 164.6

cresset, W. *rhwyll*, 169.11n

crest, W. (MS.) *pyrchuyn*, 193.15n

creu moch, 'pigsty', 190.24

creuan, 'skull', 197.32-7n

crib, 'comb', 193.21

cribin, 'rake', 193.7

croesan, 'jester', 18.20-23n

croft, W. *eisyddyn*, 99.24; see *toft*

croglath, 'springe', 187.7n

cropper, W. *croper*, 193.1n

cross, Lord's, 207.13-16n

cross-bed, W. *trawstyle*, 45.32n

cross-branch, W. *trawsgainc*, 188.19n

cross-load, W. *pwn traws*, 175.4

crow (v), W. *canu*, 181.14,15

crozier, W. *bagl*, 127.28

cruse, W. *stên*, 193.13, cf. I Kings xvii.12 (AV: NEB flask)

cryman, 'reaping-hook', 45.34; 192.35-6

cuaranau, 'brogues', 34.20n; *cuaran* is an Irish word, most familiar in the by-name of Olaf Cuaran, the Scandinavian king of Dublin who died in 980: see D. Simon Evans, *Historia Gruffud vab Kenan* (Cardiff, 1977), 48

cudgel-blow, W. *ffonnod*, 68.28

'Culhwch and Olwen', 28.12-13n

330   The Law of Hywel Dda

cup, W. *cwpan,* 154.12-20n; W. *ffiol,* 19.29; 154.12-20n; 192.12,29; 193.4

cur: dunghill cur, W. *costog tom,* 181.31 etc.

curtilage, W. *dible,* 159.11

cushion, W. *clustog,* 16.20,21n

custom, W. *defod,* 31.32; 55.6n, etc.

cwcwyo, 'tread' (of male bird), 181.8; 183.15

cwd, 'bag', 193.19

cwgn, 'joint' (of finger), 196.22-7

cwlltwr, 'coulter', 37.35-6n; *tir swch a chwlltwr,* 'arable land', 114.24n

cwmwd, 'commote', see *cantred*

cwpan, 'cup', 154.12-20n

cwta: *llwdn cwta,* 35.35n; *ceiniog gota,* see *ceiniog*

cŵyn, 'complaint', 111.16; 'plaint', 113.13-16n

cwynos, 'supper', 123.36-7n; 129.19n

cwynsyll, *cwysyll,* 'furrower', 194.3-9n

cychwynnu, 'start, move', passim; 'alienate', 113.3n

cydweddog, 'yoke-fellow', 176.33,34

cyfair, 'day's ploughing, acre', 195.33,34; *cyfair asglod, cyfair casnad,* 199.16n

cyfar, 'joint-ploughing, joint-ploughing contract', III.9n

cyfarch cyffyll, 'stock inquiry', 145.25n

cyfaru (v), 'contract for joint-ploughing', 201.14 etc.

cyfarws, 'bounty', 9.31; 'boon', 39.1

cyfarwydd mywn cyfraith, 'learned in law', 142.34

cyfarwyr, 'joint-ploughing partners', 200.33; 201.1; 'partners', 201.6,38

cyfebrwydd, 'pregnancy' (of mare), 171.29

cyfeddach, 'banquet', 7.6 etc. The root of the Welsh word is *medd,* 'mead', which is also the root of *meddw,* 'drunk': other passages show that it was contemplated that some of the court would get drunk, and *cyfeddach* should perhaps be translated by some such word as 'junketing'.

cyfelin, 'ell' (q.v.), 34.37; 193.23,24; 'forearm', 53.4

cyff, 'stock', 104.11 etc.

cyfiewin, 176.1n; 180.15-32n

cyflafan, 'damage', 60.33n; 171.1; 'harm', 208.6; 'offence', 48.1; 53.23 etc.

Cyfnerth, 92.10-11n

cyfneseifiaid, 'closest relatives', 48.17; 60.5-6

cyfordy, 'beer-house', 41.12-15n

Glossary and Index to Notes 331

cyfraith, 'law, legal', passim, see *rhaith*; pl. *cyfreithiau*, 'forms of law', 160.1;
    cyfraith atgas, 'repellent law', 119.17-20;
    cyfraith eglwys, 'church law', 110.28n; see also *canon law*;
    Cyfraith Hywel, 'the law of Hywel', 52.3; 157.18n
    cyfraith lladrad, 'the law of theft', 182.33n
    tair cyfraith, 'three systems of law', 94.15n

cyfrwys, 'skilled', 181.17,21

cyhydedd, 'equality', 103.16n

cyhyryn canastr, 160.27n

cylch, 'circuit', 11.1 etc.; 122.18n; 129.12-14n

cylleig, 'champion hart', 184.35n

cyllell, 'knife'; *cyllell gell*, 'larder knife', 195.11; *cyllell glun*, 'dirk', 195.11

cyllellu, 'to knife', 185.4n

cyllidus, 'geldable', (as noun) 'villein', 100.5n

cymell, 'compel', 51.16; 'enforce', 78.33; 146.32; 147.21; 'exact', 69.23 etc.; 77.9n
    traean cymell, 'enforcing third', 146.33; 147.35

cymheinio, 'equalise', 100.2n,4

cymod, 'reconciliation', 148.36

cymwd, see *cantred*

cymwynas, 'favour', 161.22-3n

cymydog, 'neighbour', 162.18; 181.34-182.2n

cymyn, 'bequest', 47.1 etc.; *cymynnu*, 'bequeath', 46.38 etc.

cŷn, 'chisel', 193.1n

cynddaredd, 'rabies', 187.18

cynddeiriog, 'rabid, having rabies', 151.34,36; 182.31

cynefodig, see *ci*

cynflith, 'first-calf heifer', 35.3; 206.24

cyngaws: in *Bleg* and *Cyfn*, this usually means 'case, argument'; so also at 85.25 in *Ior*, where it usually names a person who presents the case: 86.27n; 87.34n; see also *canllaw*.

cynghawsedd, cyngheusaeth, 'pleading, set of pleadings', 87.15 etc. In *Ior* these abstract forms usually replace *cyngaws* in the sense of 'case, argument'.

cynghellor. This officer was not a chancellor in any of the modern senses of that word, and the word does not seem to be derived from Lat. *cancellarius*: see 27 BBCS 115-18. The cynghellor was not an officer of the court, but had a special place at the banquet when the court in its peregrinations visited the

332   The Law of Hywel Dda

district in which he (jointly with the maer, q.v.) was concerned with administration on behalf of the King. The district may originally have been a commote, cf. 121-16-34; in the upper Towy valley in the fifteenth century the cyngelloriaeth of Llandovery seems to have been coterminous with the marcher lôrdship, which comprised the two commotes of Hirfryn and Perfedd: (1982) 12 *Carmarthenshire Antiquary* 23.

cyngor, 'decision', 88.7n

cynghorwr, 'adviser', 157.2n

cynhaeafdy, 'harvest house', 190.34n

cynhyglog, 'felt', 195.4n

cynhysgaeth, 'endowment', 59.31n

cynllwst, 'kennel', 181.19,23

cynllwyn, 'ambush', 150.30-31n

cynllyfan, 'leash', 22.11; 193.26-8 etc., see also 182.10n

cynnogn, 'principal debtor', 63.33 etc.

cynnwgl, 'felt, quilt', 195.4n

cynnwys, 'allowance', 104.31n

cynorau, 'porches', 190.27-32n

cynordy, 'porch', 41.12-15n, cf. *cynorau*

cyntedd, 'precinct', 7.26-8.28n

cynutai, 'fueller', 6.27; 32.1; 36.33, 34-37.15n

cynwaith, 'first working', 176.29

cynwarchadw, (n), 'priority of occupation', 92.6-7; (v) 'previously occupying', 108.12

cyrch, 'rout', 150.30-31n

cysefin, 'first', 13.36; 66.5 etc.; 'primary', 82.12

cystadlu, 'divide equally', 99.33; 100.2n

cyweirgorn, 'tuning-horn', 40.23,24; 191.30,31. The literal translation is intended to avoid implying any interpretation. *Cyweirgorn* has long been understood as 'tuning-key', but Thomas Jones's 1688 Dictionary (following the *plectrum* of Davies's *Dict. Dupl.*) has 'a quill, or any such thing to strike on the strings of musick', and Lat D 370.15 has *plectrum* for the *kyweirgorn* of *Bleg* 108.10. GPC's third sense, 'pitch-pipe', seems the most natural, but is not clearly supported by instances.

cyweirio, 'arrange' (galanas), 147.28; 'prepare' (food), 31.9n; 'put in order' (plough irons), 202.7

cyweithas, 'companionship', 143.10; 'company', 156.35
    corn cyweithas, 'social horn', 40.14-19n

Glossary and Index to Notes   333

da, 'goods', passim

dadannudd, 101.18-104.8n; 101.20-23n; 102.3-5n

dadlau, 'sessions', 123.3-4n etc.

daered, 12.2; 46.38-47.4n; 46.39; 61.3-9n; 165.19; 168.28. The word may originally have had the wide general meaning of a payment legally due to any superior: see 46.38-47.4n. In our texts it is used only in two senses: that of a money payment to the King, the 'supper money' of other texts; and that of a payment to the Church from the goods of a dead man: see WLW 198 and D. Howells 8/9 SC 57. The provision at 12.2 that the priest of the household should have the daered of the men of the bodyguard suggests that the payment would normally go to the parish priest.

Dafydd ap Llywelyn, prince, 6.19-7.25n

dagger, W. *honsecs,* 195.11n

dala, 'attach', 161.1; 'hold' (animal), 202.21; 207.17; 'take' (animal), 202.20 etc.

damage (n), W. *cyflafan,* 60.33n; 171.1; (v) W. *llygru,* 173.21; damaged, W. *claf,* 205.2

damdwng, lit. 'swearing about': 'swear, swear to' (as being the swearer's goods), 161.7 etc.; 'appraise, sworn appraisal' (as having a value then named), 164.22-28 etc. The rule of 161.18-20 that if the owner has voluntarily parted with his goods to another he cannot swear to them in the hands of a third party has Germanic parallels: see *Col* p.111; the Roman law *vindicatio* on the other hand enabled the owner to claim his goods from a third party in any circumstances. See 72.36-73.15n; 172.6n; 178.24n; 182.13n.

dangerous wound, W. *arberygl,* 24.18n; *gweli arberygl,* 10.35

dark-blue-bladed, W. *gwrmsaid,* 194.18-19n

darting colt, W. *saethebol,* 206.29-30n

date, due date, W. *oed,* 65.7 etc.; 69.1 etc.

dawn bwyd, 'food gift', 128.25; 129.1

day, blank, W. *dyddiau dyddon,* 76.25-6; see *dyddon*
   day of loss and gain, W. *dydd coll a chaffael,* 97.32-98.7n;
   for a fixed day, on a single day, W. *unddyddiog,* 70.21-2n; 84.1-4

day's ploughing, W. *cyfair,* 195.33,34

dead testimony, W. *marwdystiolaeth,* 98.8

334 *The Law of Hywel Dda*

dead thing, W. *peth marwol* (cf. 'dead stock'), 161.32
dead-house, W. *marwdy,* 34.30n
death, condemn to, W. *barnu dienyddu,* 165.23
    manner of, W. *dihenydd,* 151.18n
    penalty, W. *dihenydd,* 167.29
    put to, *W. dienyddio, dienyddu,* 158.22 etc.
    sentence, W. *dihenydd,* 189.39
debtor-surety, W. *mach cynnogn,* 70.24, 29-38n
December, Kalends of, ninth of, 22.24-5n
decision, W. *cyngor,* 88.7n
deddf, 'rule of law', 80.9-11n
dedfryd, see *edfryd*
defnyddio, 'use, appropriate', 14.7; 58.25n; 110.8n; 122.25n;
    185.29
defod, 'custom', 31.32; 55.6n; etc.
degree (of kindred), W. *ach,* 149.34 etc.; W. *gradd,* 110.18.
    These passages suggest that *ach* is used for a degree
    reckoned outwards, *gradd* for one reckoned down-
    wards: see *cenedl.*
      degrees or orders, W. *graddau neu urddau,* 164.5
Deheubarth, lit. 'southern part'; in its widest sense it
    would have covered all Wales south of a line drawn
    due east from the mouth of the Dyfi, but at most
    periods it meant 'the realm . . . formed by the
    accretion of Ceredigion, Ystrad Tywi and Brych-
    einiog around the ancient kingdom of Dyfed' (HW
    256), so that it excluded Gwent and Morgannwg;
    but Rhys ap Gruffudd as 'suzerain of Deheubarth'
    (164.24) certainly interested himself in the Welsh
    rulers from Morgannwg and Gwent. When the
    lawyers speak (as they sometimes do) of Deheu-
    barth, Gwynedd, and Powys as the three divisions
    of Wales, they probably have no exact idea of the
    boundaries of the three.
      king of Deheubarth, 5.30-6.2n
delay, W. *oed,* passim, 133.17n
    delay for aid, W. *oed wrth borth,* 77.29-78.4n
    delay of claim of surety, 77.3n
Denbigh, Honour of, 104.31n
deposit, W. *adnau,* 159.16; 161.22-3n; 170.25
deprivation, W. *diebryd,* 169.6n
derbfine, 147.11n
designated compurgator, W. *rheithiwr nod,* see 95.20n

Glossary and Index to Notes   335

despoil, W. *anrheithio,* 16.10; W. *treisio,* 110.10,12
    something to despoil, W. *anrhaith,* 159.9
destrier, W. *amws,* (q.v.), 172.6n
destroy, W. *difetha,* 165.20; W. *lladd,* 124.17
devastate, W. *diffeithio,* 111.24
dewyl, see *dywyl*
dialwyr, 'avengers', 148.2
diannod, 'immediate, without interruption', 119.35-6n
Diasbad uwch Annwfn, 104.33n
diaspora, 149.12n
dible, 'curtilage', 159.11
diddim, 'have-not', 70.1-2n; for *barn y diddim* in later
    law, see WLW 99
diebryd, 'deprivation', 169.6n
dienyddio, dienyddu, 'put to death', 158.22 etc., cf.
    dihenydd
difetha, 'destroy', 165.20
diffaith, 'waste', (n), 40.36 etc.; (fig.) 41.16 etc.
diffeithio, 'devastate', 111.24
difwyno, 'spoil', 144.37; 166.11
digasedd, 'love', 95.9n
dihenydd, 'death penalty', 167.29 etc.; 'death sentence',
    189.39; 'manner of death', 151.18n, cf. *dienyddio*
diheuro, 'vindicate', 49.24,30n; 60.6; 'acquit', 118.13;
    167.13,14; *ymddiheuro,* 'acquit himself', 118.14.
    Since 'acquit' suggests a finding that the accused
    did not commit the offence, it might be better to
    translate *diheuro* by 'absolve', and to understand it
    as implying freedom from penalty rather than
    absence of guilt; 'absolve' could also replace
    'vindicate'. In modern Welsh *ymddiheuro* means
    'apologise', i.e. 'ask for pardon', ('absolution'?).
dillad crefydd, 'religious habit', 164.6
dilys, 51.38n; 'authentic', 7.26-8.28n; 19.27-8n; 118.37;
    'unobjectionable', 93.19; 'valid', 63.13n, 69.9-
    11n; 'validly free', 57.13n. All the translations aim
    to present clearly the application to particular cir-
    cumstances of the simple idea conveyed by *dilys,*
    i.e. *di-lys,* 'without objection, without bar'. In
    practice, as has been pointed out for the Irish cog-
    nate *díles* (CG 83), *dilys* has diametrically
    opposite meanings according to the standpoint
    from which a transaction is viewed: if, for instance,
    a transfer of goods is valid, the goods are *dilys* for

336   *The Law of Hywel Dda*

the transferee and they cannot be taken from him;
they are also *dilys* against the transferor and he
cannot reclaim them. It is in the light of this contrast
that some applications of the verb *dilysu* are most
easily understood. See also *llys.*

dilysrwydd, 51.38n

dilysu, 'discharge', 146.30n; 'set free', 117.29-30n; 'validate', 73.22 etc.; see also 81.10-13n. The basic
meaning of the verb is 'validate', i.e. 'declare or
render *dilys'*, so that no legal claim can upset the
situation: the special applications involve some
shift of meaning which is more easily envisaged
than explained, but can be understood when it is
recognised that a title or transaction which is *dilys*
(i.e. valid) in favour of one party is also *dilys* (i.e.
forfeit) against the other party: see *dilys.*

Dinefwr, 5.30-6.2n

dinesig, 'town-made', 195.21,22

Dinlle, 92.10-11n

dinod, 'undesignated', see *rhaith* and 95.20n

dioer (i.e. *Duw a ŵyr*), 'God knows', passim

diol, 'banish', 157.12 etc.; 'exile', 71.7; *diholwr*, 'banished
man', 157.15-16 etc.

dire loss, W. *dygngoll*, 134.27-135.5n; 146.11-27; 147.22n

dirk, W. *cyllell clun* (lit. 'thigh knife'), 195.11

dirrwysg, 'without irregularity', 172.34n

dirwy, passim, the standard financial penalty of twelve
kine or £3, apparently at first imposed only for
theft, fighting, and violence (*trais*, q.v.), but soon
extended to other offences, 144.3-4n. Comparison
with Irish *dire* (CG 84) indicates that dirwy began
as compensation to the victim of wrong; but in the
classical law, and long before, it is a penalty payable to the ruler: the transfer of meaning is perhaps
explained by the statement in *Dw* 436, 'the victim
[of wrong] is entitled to what is his from him who
caused him loss, and it is because loss was caused
to the Lord that the latter is entitled to the
penalty'. See also 28.13-14n; 52.17n

discharge, W. *dilysu*, 146.30n

discretion, W. *pwyll*, 142.1

disease, W. *clefyd*, 177.7; W. *haint*, 172.16; 174.22

disgyfrith, 'unrestricted', 202.32; *disgyfreitho*, 'unhobble',
202.30-35n

Glossary and Index to Notes 337

dish, (of food), W. *saig*, 9.15 etc.

disjudge, W. *difarnu*, i.e. give judgment unfavourable to, 90.32,34; 96.31,32

dismounting, payment for, 174.2-3n

dispersion, one in, W. *gwasgarog*, 149.12n

dispute, W. *amryson*, 176.12 etc.

disrespect, W. *amarch*, 117.18

dissolve, W. *torri*, 80.12-29n

distaff, W. *cogail*, 120.7; 145.19; 195.16; tracing pedigree by, 110.4-6n

distain, 'steward', 5.4 etc., ct. *ystiwart*, 33.15n. The Welsh word is borrowed from an Anglo-Saxon word which would have given *dishthane* in modern English, and the name was appropriate enough for the officer who had charge of the arrangements of the hall. By the thirteenth century the distain had become a political officer: Goronwy ab Ednyfed (an ancestor of the royal Tudors), whom Llywelyn ap Gruffudd called *senescallus noster* in a Latin letter (*Litt. Wall.* 28) was *distain i'r tywysog*, 'steward to the prince' in the Welsh chronicle's notice of his death. In a memorandum of 1305 in the Record of Caernarvon, the Justiciar of North Wales is said to be *loco destein*, 'in the place of the distain': see 22 BBCS 127-8.

distrain on, W. *adafaelha*, 201.10

distress damage feasant, III.10n (p.305)

divide equally, W. *cystadlu*, 99.33; 100.2n

diwall, 'faultless'; *diwallu*, 'equip, provide, repair, supply', 125.35n

diwyn (vn of *diwygaf*), 'compensate', passim; *diwyn llwgr*, 'compensation for damage', 209.10n

docked beast, W. *llwdn cwta*, 35.35n

dock-leaves, W. *tafol*, 179.34

dodrefn, 'equipment', 190.6 etc.

doethion, 'wise ones', 190.4-5n

dofod, 'casual acquisition', 54.10; 'windfall', 189.37n

dofreth, 'billeting', 121.32

dog, see *bugeilgi, bytheiad, ci, colwyn, costog, gellgi, milgi, olrhead, segur*

    theft of dog, 167.26-7n;

    tractate on dogs, pattern and significance, 181.16-182.34n

dogn, 'quota' (q.v.), passim

338   *The Law of Hywel Dda*

dognfanag, 'sufficient information', 62.34; 159.21-2n
dôl, pl. *dolau,* 'yoke-bow, collar', 199.24n; 202.9-11n
dolly, W. *golchbren,* 39.23
domestic pig, W. *hwch dref,* 178.28n
dominus (Lat.), 'lord, owner', 165.29n; 182.27n
dooddwf: *arian dooddwf,* 'lactation money', 175.22
door, doorway, W. *dôr, drws,* 190.27-32n; 204.36-8n
door-frames, W. *amhiniogau,* 191.4n
door-hurdle, W. *dorglwyd,* 190.37-8
dôr, 'door', 190.27-32n; 204.36-8n
dorglwyd, 'door hurdle', 190.37-8
dormitory, W. *cerner,* 41.12-15n
double jeopardy, 168.15n
doubted son, W. *mab amau,* 134.26,31
dower. This technical term of English law is not used in the
     translation, mainly because no Welsh technical
     term corresponds closely enough to it, but also
     because in lay use it is so often confused with
     'dowry'. Both 'dower' and 'dowry' are translated
     dos in Latin, but whereas 'dowry' means the prop-
     erty which the bride brings with her (corres-
     ponding to *argyfrau*), 'dower' means the share of
     her dead husband's property to which a widow is
     entitled: the (very rough) analogy is with Welsh
     agweddi. In English law dower was a right to land:
     hence the Statute of Wales of 1284 speaks of wives
     in Wales as having had no right to dower under
     Welsh law. The Welsh version of that statute in
     MS. Peniarth 41 has *argyfrau* for 'dower': this is
     perhaps evidence that the technical terms no
     longer had practical significance when the trans-
     lation was made.
dowry, W. *argyfrau* (q.v.), 46.23-6n; 59.26-33n; 59.31n;
     see also *dower, endowment.*
draenglwyd, 'thorn-hurdle', 195.28n
drag-net, W. *ballegrwyd,* 193.35n
draught-ropes, W. *iewyddion,* 202.9-11n
draw (milk), W. *dydyllu,* 175.15
drawknife, W. *rhasgl,* 192.38
drefa, 'thrave', 195.13,14n
drill, W. *rhwmp,* 192.34-5n
drud, 'fool', 70.1-2n
drws, 'door, doorway', 204.36-8n, cf. 190.27-32n

Glossary and Index to Notes 339

dry (v) see *crasu*; (a) W. *hesb* (of female animal), 180. 10-11n; dry yearling (goat), W. *hesbin*, 180.10-11n

drych, 'mirror', 193.9

drygar, 'bad ploughing', 200.28-9

du ysgyfaint, 'strangles', 172.18

due date, W. *oed*, 69.1 etc.

dull, 'hank', 193.7

dulys, 'black-stained' (q.v.), 18.30; 194.32 etc.

Duncansby Head, 120.6-21n

dung, rotten, W. *brandail*, 113.21

dung horse, W. *march tom*, 172.30 etc.

dung maer, W. *maer biswail* (q.v.), 33.12-34.5; 124.18-19; 125.11-37

dung mare, W. *caseg dom*, 172.30 etc.

dunghill, W. *tom*, 54.17; cf. 193.30n
  dunghill cur, W. *costog tom*, 181.31 etc.

dwygainc, 'twin-forked' (of tree), 188.16-17n

dyddon: *amser dyddon*, 'blank time', 96.10; *dyddiau dyddon*, 'blank days', 76.25-6. The sense is clear, though no generally-accepted explanation of the word has been offered: but see GML 123-4 and *Ior* p.115. The expression does not seem to occur in *Cyfn* and *Bleg*, and the examples cited in GPC all have the word in combination with *dydd* or the like.

dydyllu, 'draw' (milk), 175.15

Dyfed. Medieval Dyfed was much smaller than the recently-created administrative county. It was bounded on the north by the river Teifi from Llandysul to the sea, on the west and south by the sea, and on the east by the Towy as far as the mouth of the Gwili above Carmarthen, and thence by the Gwili and the Tyweli back to the Teifi.

Dyfnwal Moelmud, 120.6-21n

dygngoll, 'dire loss', 134.27-135.5n; 146.11-27; 147.22n

dygymod, 'be reconciled', 159.6

dylaith, 'bars', 191.4

dyledog, 'entitled', 107.14-16; 119.9 etc.; 'entitled person', 100.17n; see also *dyly.*

dyly, 104.25-6n: this is the 3rd sing. present of a verb (vn *dylyu*) which is modern Welsh has become defective, having only an imperfect or conditional with present meaning (in 3rd sing. *dylai*, 'he ought') and a pluperfect with past (and often present) meaning (in 3rd sing. *dylasai*, 'he ought-to-have', 'he

340   The Law of Hywel Dda

ought'); the analogy with English 'ought' is close. In medieval Welsh the verb has all tenses and a wider meaning, which can often be conveyed by 'it is right': it sometimes happens that a passage has two versions, one with *dylyu* and the other using the adjective *iawn* ('right', but in our translation 'proper', reserving 'right' for dylyu). What is right for a person may be what he is entitled to, or what he is bound to, and it is sometimes impossible to choose between the two senses, which may of course co-exist. The same is true of one important derivative of *dylyu*, the abstract noun *dylyed*: in the modern forms *dylêd*, *dyled*, the sense has narrowed down to 'debt', but in the law texts *dylyed* may mean 'entitlement' as well as 'debt' or 'duty'. The adjective *dyledog* (q.v.) means 'having an entitlement', and by a natural development it comes to be used in literary texts for 'person having a large entitlement'. In our translation 'it is right' is used whenever possible for *dylyu*; 'bound' and 'entitled' are used when necessary. At 66.17 'creditor' translates *dylyawdr*, 'person entitled' (to payment).

dylyed, 'debt, entitlement, right', 32.23n; see *dyly*.

dynawed, 'yearling', 49.28; 176.19,20

dyrchaf a gosod, 'assault and battery', 143.37n

dyrchafael, 'augment', 48.4-5; 147.30; 154.21; 'hang up', 46.12; 'lift', 35.33; 'put up', 92.29; 'raise', 176.20,21; 'rise', 144.20; 175.11,14

dyrnfedd, 'fistbreadth', 128.10 etc.; *moelddyrnfedd*, 'bare fistbreadth', 129.4n

dywedud, 'say, speak', passim; 'appropriate', 58.25n

dywyl, 'coloured', 154.18,19n

eang, 'clear', 134.23-4

ears, steers with horns as long as, 19.31-2n; 50.3-6n

Easter, W. *Pasg*, 5.16 etc.; one of the three special feasts, 76.19

eat, W. *bwyta*, 19.22 etc., W. *ysu*, 63.5; 179.11,13

ebb and flow, W. *llanw a thrai*, 84.20n

ebediw: in practice this had by the thirteenth century become a death duty or succession duty, sometimes related to land-holding, but in origin it is comparable with the heriot of English and other Germanic

Glossary and Index to Notes   341

societies: see 11.23n; 46.38-47.4n; 55.20n; 57.6n;
    123.25-6n.

ebill, ebill taradr, 'gimlet', 192.34-5n

ebol, 'colt', 11.23n

ebran, 'fodder, horse-fodder', 11.23n

echwyn, 'borrow', 161.22-3n

edfryd, vn of *adferaf*, 'restore', is used in the law texts
    much in the technical sense of 'return' in English
    law, and is accordingly translated 'return'. The in-
    tensified form *dedfryd* (vn of *dadferaf*) has become
    in modern Welsh an abstract noun used for 'sen-
    tence' rather than 'verdict'.

edgings, W. *wrlys*, 41.19n

edling, 6.19-7.25n; 11.23n

efyrnig, 'goat-heifer', 180.10-11n

egwyd, 'loop' (of a hobble), 202.35

ehegyr, 'staggers', 172.17

eilltion, (pl.) see *aillt*

einion, 'anvil', 194.4; *einion gyriog*, 'bicorne', 194.3-9n

eirionyn, 'limit, margin', 34.34n; 121.1n

eisteddfa, 'seat', 142.29

eisyddyn, 'croft', 99.24, see 99.18n and *toft*

eithefig, 'prime ox', 199.11n

ell, W. *cyfelin*, 34.37; 193.23,24; this seems to have been
    the single ell of two feet, not the more usual double
    ell of four feet. At 53.4 *cyfelin* is translated 'fore-
    arm ', as the context clearly requires.

ellwng, 'release', 158.34 etc.

elm-bark rope, W. *rhaff lwyf*, 193.23-4

enaid, 'life', 63.22 etc.

enamel: blue enamel, W. *calch lasar*, 194.23; gold enamel,
    W. *eurgalch*, 194.23-4,28

enclose (land), W. *cadw*, 207.13-16n

enclosure, W. *corflan*, II.5n (pp.253-4); 82.22n

end-benches, W. *talfeinciau*, 190.27-32

endowment, W. *cynhysgaeth*, 59.31n; W. *gwaddol*,
    107.15; cf. *dowry*

enforce, W. *cymell*, 78.33; 146.32; 147.21

English law, of inheritance, 110.28n

enhorob, 'flitch', 128.13; 177.36-178.3n

eniwed, 'harm', 106.37n; 111.13-29

enjoy, W. *mwynhau*, 72.31; 89.24, etc.

enllyn, 34.36; 36.17; 124.35; 128.23; this is a still living
    word for anything eaten with bread, such as butter,

342   *The Law of Hywel Dda*

cheese, or meat. The enllyn in the food renders included everything except the bread and drink; so the serjeant, the watchman, and the billeted alien might have to be content with the poorest choice from such items.

enmity, W. *gelyniaeth,* 93.37; see also *galanas*
ennaint, 'bath', 170.23; 170.20-24n
entertainments, W. *gwestfâu,* 33.26
entitled, entitled person, W. *dyledog* (q.v.), 100.17n and
    see *dyly*
entitlement, see *dylyed*
entrenched (fee), W. *muriedig,* 123.30
equalise, W. *cymheinio,* 100.2n,4
equality, W. *cyhydedd,* 103.16n
equally, divide, W. *cystadlu,* 99.33; 100.2n
equip, W. *diwallu,* 125.35n
erbyniaid, 'receive', 157.2n
erlid, erlyn, erlynaf: *erlid* was originally the verb-noun of
    erlynaf, which carries the same root as *canlynaf,*
    dilynaf, 'I follow' and has the broad meaning
    'pursue'. In modern Welsh the verb and verb-noun
    have separated: *erlid* has generated a verb *erlidiaf,*
    'I persecute', and *erlynaf* a verb-noun *erlyn,* 'to
    prosecute'. This development has already begun in
    some of the law texts.
    erlid cyfraith anudon arno, 'prosecute him for
        perjury', 65.14-15n; 158.16
    erlyn, 'follow', 76.28n
ermine, W. *carlwng,* 188.10,13
erw, 'acre', passim; see also *cyfair*
    allocation after ploughing, 199.18-20n
    erw ddiffoddedig, 'extinguished acre', 100.10-11n
    erw gyfraith, 'legal acre', 122.23n
    erw yr ych du, 'black ox's acre', 199.18-20n, 24-30
    measure, 99.3-12; 120.30-121.3; 199.8-9n
escheat, see 34.30n; 100.10-11n
escort, W. *hebrwng,* 82.11,13,14n
esgidiau: esgidiau careiog, 'thonged shoes', 195.9
estyn, see *rhodd ac estyn*
euraid, 'gilt', 193.15 etc.
ewig, 'hind', 187.11
ewyllys, 'free will', 200.27; 206.17; 'will' (of God), 71.36;
    (sexual), 59.6
exact (v), W. *cymell,* 69.23; 77.9 etc.

Glossary and Index to Notes 343

examine, 1.14n
exchange, W. *cyfnewid,* 163.25; 174.12
    exchanged goods, W. *da cyfnewid,* 174.11
excommunication, 78.14-18n
execution, see *dihenydd*
exile (v), W. *diol,* 71.7
extinguished acre, W. *erw ddiffoddedig,* 100.10-11n
extortionate spoliation, W. *anrhaith gribddail,* 159.19
extra burden, see *gorysgwr*

fabric, mixed, W. *tenllif,* 34.22n
face-shame, face-value, see *wynebwerth*
falcon, W. *gwalch.* The Welsh vocabulary of hunting with
    birds has not been fully studied, and English
    translations have tended to be arbitrary. *Hebog* has
    been translated by 'hawk' because both words
    were derived from A.S. *heafoc,* and *gwalch* by
    'falcon' because the two words looked as though
    they might be cognate. It can now be said with
    some confidence that they are not cognate, and
    that *gwalch* seems to be the original word used for
    a hunting bird of any kind, whereas *heafoc* was
    borrowed specifically for the falcon after falconry
    was introduced as a sport from England. It seems
    certain that the bird which could kill a heron
    (15.18,19) was a peregrine falcon (*Bleg* p. 228), and
    it must be significant that the *hebog* was more
    valuable than the *gwalch,* and that only *Cyfn*
    names a legal value for the *gwalch*: in the
    translation 'goshawk' follows the suggestion of
    Bleg p. 228. In later Welsh *hebog* is used in
    a more general sense, as *hawk* is in English.
    'Sparrowhawk', the traditional translation for
    llamysten, is supported by the *nisus* of the Latin
    texts; 'tiercel', the usual English word for the male
    bird (because it is a third smaller than the female
    which is normally used for hunting) translates
    hwyedydd, which the Latin texts explain as
    meaning the male. *Gwalch,* which is normally
    masculine, is sometimes feminine in the
    Romances (e.g. WM 140.18) as though it was
    realised that the hunting bird was the female.

344 The Law of Hywel Dda

falconer, W. *hebogydd,* 5.4n; 14.30-31n; see *falcon;* for land reserved for falconers, see 92.10-11n; chief falconer, 10.14n

family, W. *rhieni,* 147.37

fault (in horse). W. *twyll,* 174.21

faultless, W. *diwall,* 200.11-12

favour, W. *cymwynas,* 161.22-3n

fawn, W. *elain,* 187.9,33

feast: of saints, see *Gŵyl;* special, see *special feasts*

fee, W. *gobr,* q.v.; fee for protection, W. *gobr gwarchadw,* 113.13-16n
   physician's fee, 197.22n

feeble, W. *gwan,* 71.3n

feed, W. *porthi,* 15.8 etc.

felt, W. *cynhyglog, cynnwgl,* 195.4n

female compurgators, W. *rheithwragedd,* 60.1

female Lord, W. *arglwyddes,* 60.26; 73.16n

fence, W. *cae,* 204.18; 207.10

fetter, W. *hual,* 193.10; 195.15; 202.30

ffawydden, 'beech', 189.16-17n

ffiol, 'cup', 19.29; 154.12-20n; 192.12,29; 193.4

ffonnod, 'cudgel-blow', 68.28

fforch, 'fork' (implement) 193.7; (house-cruck) 190.20,26, see also *gafael*

fforddol, 'wayfarer', 186.25,31

fforestu, 'forbid', 207.5n

ffunen, 'neck-kerchief', 195.26

ffyrnig, 'furious'; *ffyrnigrwydd,* 'fury'; *ffyrnigwr,* 'furious man', 151.16; 166.7-17

field, old, W. *henfaes,* 114.1-5n

fighting, 101.2n

file, iron, W. *haearnllif,* 194.3-9n

final word, see *gair*

fine flour, W. *peilliaid,* 128.31

finger, value of, 196.22-7n

fireback-stones, W. *ystyffylau,* 190.28n

firestone, W. *pentan,* 39.36n; 191.5n

fistbreadth, W. *dyrnfedd,* 128.10 etc; bare fistbreadth, W. *moelddyrnfedd,* 129.4n

fit (a), W. *cyfiewin,* 176.1n; 180.15-32n

flax, W. *llin,* 204.15; flax-garden, W. *gardd lin,* 204.23

flesh of tail, W. *coloren,* 172.38 etc.

flitch, W. *enhorob,* 128.13; 177.36-178.3n

flour, fine, W. *peilliaid,* 128.31

Glossary and Index to Notes 345

fodder, W. *gogor*, 204.11n; W. *ebran*, lit. 'horse-share', passim

foetus, W. *beichiogi*, 130.13

fold, W. *buarth*, 207.17
  fold-hurdles, two, W. *dwyglwyd buarth*, 195.15
  folded manure, W. *buarthdail*, 113.29
  folded steer, W. *eidion buarth*, 202.29

follow, W. *erlyn* (q.v.), 76.28n

fondle, W. *gofysio*, 48.2n

food, interchangeable, 76.28n

food-gift, W. *dawn bwyd*, 128.25; 129.1

food-house, W. *bwyty*, 34.3n; 41.12-15n

fool, W. *drud*, 70.1-2n

footholder, W. *troediog*, 33.11n

foot-trough, W. *cafn traed*, 192.28

footwear, W. *archenad*, 23.32; 36.16,37

forbid, W. *fforestu*, 207.5n; W. *gwahardd*, 78.32

forces, (pieces in throwboard game), W. *gwerin*, 191.35 etc.; see *throwboard*

foreign speech, of, W. *anghyfiaith*, 76.4

forearm, W. *cyfelin*, 53.4, see *ell*

fore-oath, W. *llw gweilydd*, 205.15n

forelock, W. *talgudyn*, 173.6 etc.

foremost, W. *blaeniaid*, 205.8-9n

forequarter, W. *chwarthawr rhag*, 185.31

forfeit, fall, W. *digwydd*, 69.5-6 etc.; life . . . forfeit, W. *eneidfaddau*, 151.17 etc.

fork (implement), W. *fforch*, 193.7; (house-cruck), W. *fforch*, 190.20,26; W. *gafael*, 190.12,15,19; roof-fork, W. *nenfforch*, 189.34

foul house, W. *halawcty*, 159.14-15

fourth man, W. *pedwarygwr*, 104.12 etc.

fox, W. *cadno*, 187.22n; W. *llwynog*, 186.1-7n; 187.22n; 187.33

frame (weaving woman's), W. *prenial*, 193.38

franchise rights, 101.2n

free blood, W. *gwaed rhydd*, 198.14-15n

free will, W. *ewyllys*, 200.27; 206.17

fueller, W. *cynutai*, 6.27; 32.1; 36.34-37.15n

furious, W. *ffyrnig*; furious man, W. *ffyrnigwr*; fury, W. *ffyrnigrwydd*: 151.16; 166.7-17

furniture, (of quern house), W. (MS) *keluyd*, 194.14: the translation is tentative, understanding the word as *celfydd*, perhaps a variant of *celfi*. LW emends to

346   *The Law of Hywel Dda*

cilwydd and translates *materia; Ior* (Index) treats
the word as *celwydd*, with translation 'rods (?)',
following AL VC III.xxii.159, 'kiln rods'.
furrower, W. *cwysyll*, 194.3-9n

gaeafar, 'winter tillage' 122.34; 'winter tilth', 202.25
gaeafdy, 'winter house', 40.12n; 190.25,31
gafael, 'fork' (pair of crucks), 190.12,15,19; 'holding',
       121.5-6n
gaflaweg, 'young-salmon net' (q.v.), 193.34
gage, (n) W. *gwystl* (q.v.), 68.24,25n; 68.37-69.8n; (v) W.
       gwystlo, 63.37 etc.; (v) W. *prido*, 114.6n, and
       see *prid*.
gaing, 'chisel', 193.1n
gair, 'word': *gair yw ei air*, 'his word is final', 61.32n etc.;
       gair cyfarch, 'word of inquiry', 87.34n
galanas, 'enmity, homicide, compensation for homicide'.
       The root of the word is *gal*, 'heat, valour, steam':
       dial (lit. 'without *gal*'), 'vengeance', is that which
       removes the heat. Hence the primary meaning of
       galanas is 'feud' or 'enmity' between kindreds.
       The meaning of 'homicide' develops because
       homicide is in the developed law the only recog-
       nised ground of feud, though it is clear that in ear-
       lier days feud could arise from a dispute over land
       or from wrong done to a woman, and probably from
       other causes as well: see 94.22n; 143.2n; and WLW
       61-5.
       The compensation for killing depended on the
       status of the victim; hence the occasional use of
       gwerth, 'worth', for *galanas* in this sense. For dis-
       tribution of the galanas, as asset or as liability,
       among the kindreds of the victim and the homicide
       respectively, see 144.21-38n; for the special case of
       the *gwasgarog*, a person away from his homeland,
       149.12n
gaol, W. *geol*, 33.26
garan, ' crane' (bird), 15.18
gardd, 'quillet', 113.6n; 'garden', 189.6n; 204.15,18,19;
       gardd lin, 'flax-garden', 204.23
garden, see *gardd*
garderobe, W. *geudy*, 30.6; see also *latrine*
garment, W. *tuddedyn*, 195.23
gate, W. *porth*, 16.35 etc.

Glossary and Index to Notes 347

gauntlet, W. *honffest,* 193.31n

gefel, 'tongs', 193.9; *gefel gof,* 'pincers', 194.5

gefyn, 'handcuff', 193.32

geilwad, 'caller', the man in charge of the plough-team, who cannot be called 'driver' since he walked backwards before the oxen, 200.13-15; see also *Agricultural Co.operation* (III.9n, p.303 above) 11.

geldable, W. *cyllidus,* 100.5n

gellgi, 'staghound', 181.17n

Genau'r Glyn, 121.11-13n

gentility, W. *bonedd* (q.v.), 159.24

Geoffrey of Monmouth, 120.6-21n

geol, 'gaol', 33.26

geudy, 'garderobe', 30.6

gift and transfer, W. *rhodd ac estyn,* 54.36n

gilt, W. *euraid,* 193.15 etc.

gimlet, W. *ebill, ebill taradr,* 192.34-5n

gin (trap), **W.** *yslepan,* 187.7n

girth, W. *cengl, torgengl,* 194.36; 195.3; see also *breast-girth*

glân, 'holy', 1.12n; 'clean', 63.5n etc.

glanders, W. *llynmeirch,* 172.19

gleisiad, 'sewin' (i.e. sea-trout), 193.35

gleisiadeg, 'sewin net', 193.33

Glewlwyd Gafaelfawr, 28.12-13n

gloves, 155.33-5n

Glyndŵr, Owain, war of, 149.1-9n

goat, properties of, 180.9-12n

goat-heifer, W. *efyrnig,* 180.10-11n

gobennydd, 'pillow', 16.20,21n

gobr, 'fee', 36.2 etc.; 'reward', 95.10; when untranslated it is equivalent to *amobr,* q.v. For the etymology see WLW 203

    gobr gwarchadw, 'fee for protection', 113.13-16n

God knows, W. *dioer,* a contraction of *Duw a ŵyr,* 64.9 etc.

godaeog, 99.1n; see also *aillt*

goddaith, 'muirburn', 170.21,34: this is the technical term for burning off heather etc. for the improvement of mountain pasture. The corresponding verb occurs in Ps.lxxxiii.14 and Joel i.19

gody, pl. *godai,* 'minor house', 190.10-14n,18n,22-4n

gofud, 'trouble', 74.25

gofysio, 'fondling', 48.2n

gogor, 'fodder', 204.11n

gogr, 'sieve', 45.23; 54.16; 193.20; see also 204.11n

348   *The Law of Hywel Dda*

gogyfurdd, 'of equal rank', 196.6-7,13-14

golwyth, 'joint' (of meat): *golwyth breiniol,* 'status joint', *golwyth cyfreithiol,* 'legal joint', 22.21; 184.26-7n, 35n,37

goodman, W. *gwrda.* The word has parallels in other legal systems in Europe, and in the plural corresponds to the *degion* of the oldest Welsh legal document, the '*Surexit* memorandum': see 7 CMCS 101,110-11 and notes 5-7. While *gwrda* sometimes seems to correspond to *breyr* or *uchelwr* (e.g. 40.8; 49.37; 50.27-32n), the references to *gwyrda* in court procedure suggest that they were a special group or class who were suitors of court and as such would at an early stage have made the court's decisions in legal cases, though by the thirteenth century their functions 'seem to have been advisory and concerned with policy in the exercise of discretion' (7 CMCS 111 n.7): see 84.36; 96.27.

goose, brood, W. *gŵydd ôr,* 181.3-4

gordd, see *ordd*

gorddrysau, 'lintels', 190.27-32n

gorddwy, 'violence', 150.37n; see also *porthorddwy*

goresgyn, 'conquest', 81.30n

goreth, 'tent' (medication), 197.24

gorfodog, 'bailsman', 80.35-81.26; see 78.28

gorfodogaeth, 'bail', 80.36; 81.4,10; 'bailsmanship', 81.17

gorsedd, 'throne', 164.11n

gorysgwr, 'extra burden', 200.26n

gosber, 'vespers', 185.23

goshawk, W. *gwalch,* see *falcon*

gosod, 'battery', 143.37n

gosodedigaethau, 'ordinances', 142.9

gowyn: compensation to a wife for her husband's infidelity, 53.10,23-7; see also 46.23-6n; 52.34n

gradd, 'degree' (of kindred), q.v., 110.18; (holy orders), 164.5

graddwr, 'man in orders', 29.10; 163.38

gradell, 'griddle', 193.12

graft, W. *imp,* 188.29

grant and investiture, W. *rhodd ac estyn,* 102.3-5n; cf. 110.33-4n

grassland, W. *gwyndwn,* 209.13

grayling net, W. *penllwydeg,* 193.33

gre, 'stud', 40.4n

gren, 'cask', 192.26

Glossary and Index to Notes 349

greyhound, W. *milgi,* 181.21n
griddle, W. *gradell,* 193.12
grindstone, W. *breuanllif,* 194.8-9
groats, W. *rhynion,* 128.32
ground on the stone, W. *breulif,* 194.17-18
grove, hazel, W. *collwyn,* 188.25-7n
growth, of the same, W. *untwf,* 188.18-19n
grubbing (of pig), W. *tonfo,* 178.15
grwn, 'selion', 120.28-9n
guard (v), W. *gwarchadw,* 180.27
guard dog, W. *ci callawedd,* 182.10n
guardian (of child), W. *arffedog* (lit. 'apron'), 130.35
guest, W. *gwestai,* 6.14-15n
guiding-thong, W. *llywgroen,* 193.8
gwaddod, 'lees', 18.35,37
gwaddol, 'endowment', 107.15; 'sharing', 160.26n
gwaed-ddillad, 'blood-clothes', 10.34; 24.16; 197.23n
gwaedlydu, 'make bloody', 197.11-16n
gwaetir, 'blood-land', 110.8n,16,36; 111.1
gwalch, 'hawk, goshawk', see *falcon*
gwallt bonwyn, 'uprooted hair', 198.7
gwan, 'feeble', 71.3n; 'weak', 167.16n
gwanhwynar, 'spring tillage', 122.34; 'spring tilth', 202.23
gwarchadw (v), 'be in possession of', 161.3 etc.; 'guard',
        180.27; 'occupy', 87.4,6; 'supervise', 33.14;
        'take charge of', 21.11; 25.11;
        (n), 'care', 33.28; 37.6; 'occupancy', 108.14; 'occu-
        pation', 91.31 etc.; 'possession', 162.16
       gobr gwarchadw, 'fee for protection', 113.10
gwarddrws, 190.27-32n
gwarthafl, 'stirrup', 37.35-6n; 194.35-7; 195.1n
gwartheg, 'cows', 40.5n; 201.25,26
       gwartheg dyfach, 'cattle of dark ancestry', 58.8-9;
       'secured cattle', 134.8-9n
gwasafwr, 119.23n
gwasanaeth, 'service', 12.13n; 'attendance', 199.29
gwasgarog, 'one in dispersion', 149.12n
gwasgawd, gwasgawdwydd, 'shelter', 189.4,6
gwayw, 'spear', 194.16
gwddyf, 'hedging-bill', 155.33-5n; 192.37n
gwdyn, 'withe', 202.10
gwe, 'web', 170.36
gwedd, 'team', 201.3; 'yoke', 35.3; 130.23
gweddw, 'single', 47.12; 156.26. In modern Welsh *gweddw*

350   *The Law of Hywel Dda*

has the meaning of its English cognate 'widow', but in medieval Welsh it can mean a single woman who has never been married.

gwehyll, 'pegs', 202.9-11n

gweinyddfarch, 'working horse', 172.2,10

gweinyddiol, *gwenigol,* 'servient', 55.16n; 56.37; 118.30n; 156.1

gweirglawdd, 'meadow', 206.33 etc.

gweli, 'wound', passim; *gweli angheuol,* 'mortal wound', 24.18n; *gweli arberygl,* 'dangerous wound', 10.35

gwellau, 'shears', 192.36

gwellt, 'sward', 176.37,38; 202.1

gwelltpawr, 'pasture', 207.12

gwely, gwely land, 100.5n; 147.11n

    Gwely Hebogyddion, 'the falconers' gwely', 92. 10-11n

gwelygordd, 'kin-stock', 97.13,14

gwenigol, see *gweinyddiol*

gwercheidwad, 'occupier', 84.14,15; 127.9; 'possessor', 161.9,11

gwerin, 'forces', 191.35-192.1; see also *throwboard.* In modern Welsh *gwerin* is an emotive word, used for 'folk' (as in *canu gwerin,* 'folk singing') and for 'ordinary people' as contrasted with 'gentry'; from this sense is derived *gweriniaeth,* 'republic, democracy'. The use of *gwerin* in our text for the non-royal pieces is paralleled by the modern use of *gwerin gwyddbwyll* for 'pawns' in chess and figuratively. The basic meaning is 'people', perhaps considered primarily as fighting men: *Cyfn* has a rule for sarhaed committed by one of the *gwerin* of the four countries, Deheubarth, Gwynedd, Powys, and Lloegr (WML 113.5, translated 'people', 256.13).

gwerth, 'worth' (q.v.), see *galanas;* 'value' of animal, slave, or other chattel, passim; 'price' of sale thief, 159.39

    gwerth cyfraith, 'legal value', •164.22 etc.; cf. *damdwng*

gwerthyd, 'spindle', 193.5

gwestai, 'guest', 6.14-15n

gwestfa, 'entertainment', 33.26; 'hospitality', 167.23; the food render so called, 121.35 etc.: the basic idea is that of hospitality.

Glossary and Index to Notes 351

gwestfa money, 123.36-7n

gwïalen, 'rod', 99.5 etc.; 'withe', 204.8

gwir, 'law', 80.9-11n; the basic sense of *gwir* (cognate with Lat. *verus*) is 'true'.

gwirod, pl. *gwirodau*, 'liquor', 13.29; 14.33, etc.; *gwirod gyfreithiol*, 'legal liquor', 25.19n; see also *ceinion*

gwlad, 'country', 124.5n

gŵr, 'man, husband': the basic meaning is 'male human being', as at 130.4, and at many points either 'man' or 'husband' would be an appropriate translation.

gŵr ar deilu, 'man of the bodyguard, 9.33-5; 155.13

gŵr dinod, 'undesignated man', 169.18; see *rhaith*

gŵr dyfod, 'incomer', 92.3

gŵr nod, 'designated man', 169.18; see *rhaith* and 95.20n

gŵr priod, 'wedded husband', 107.16n

gwraig, 'woman, wife': the basic meaning is 'female human being' as at 130.4 ('woman'), but there are two specialised meanings:

(a) 'non-virgin' (or perhaps 'mature woman') as contrasted with *gwyryf*, 'virgin', or *morwyn*, 'maiden', as at 37.26; 49.22 ('woman'); 147.38n ('married woman');

(b) 'wife' of a named man: in this sense the use of the word *gwraig* does not imply any particular form of marital union, and a girl may be a wife while still a virgin; see *morwynwraig*.

gwraig briod, 'wedded wife', 58.11-13n; 110.28n, and see *priod*

gwraig bwys, 'woman of weight', 46.35-6n

gwraig wriog, 'married woman', 47.11 etc., but see 147.38n

gwrda, 'goodman', q.v.

gwreictra, 'woman-feud', 94.22n

gwreigog (of man), *gwriog* (of woman), 'married', without necessary implication of a formally established union

gwrmsaid, 'dark-blue-bladed', 194.18-19n

gwrthod, 'repudiate', 80.12-29n

gwrthrychiad, 'heir-apparent', 6.19-7.25n

gwybyddiad, 'knower', 86.27n, see also *tyst*

gwyched, 'wicket', 16.37n

352 *The Law of Hywel Dda*

gŵydd: three homophones must be distinguished—

(a) 'goose'; *gŵydd ôr*, 'brood goose', 181.3-4;

(b) 'presence', 5.27; 68.33; etc.

(c) 'wild', 200.34n; at 113.24 the same word is translated 'scrub' in the light of the following line. The translation at WML 211, 'break up fresh soil on another's land' strains the grammar of the Welsh passage.

gwŷdd, 'trees', 189.11; 'woodwork', 194.12; 199.16n; 'plough', 202.4n,5; 'plough-frame', 126.20

gwyddfa, 'burial place', 132.29n

gwyddlwdn, 'wild animal', 187.33

gwyddwaledd, 'thickset hedges', 97.19; 106.38

gŵyl, 'feast, festival':

Gŵyl Badrig, 'St Patrick's Day' (17 March), 177.8; 206.34

Gŵyl Fair gyntaf, 'first feast of St Mary' (Assumption, 15 August), 206.22-3

Gŵyl Fihangel, 'Michaelmas' (29 September), 13.34; 176.7,8; 179.4; 206.27

Gŵyl Gurig, 'St Curig's Day' (16 June), 176.6,7; 184.38

Gŵyl Ieuan, 'St John's Day' (a) 'at Midsummer' (Nativity of St John the Baptist, 24 June), 22.7,15; 63.20,23-4; 177.25-178.3n; 183.23-5; (b) 'when the pigs go to the woods' (Decollation of St John the Baptist, 29 August), 178.19n,21,30; 206.32

Gŵyl Sanffraid, 'St Bride's Day' (1 February), 83.36-84.1; 202.22,23

y tair gŵyl arbennig, 'the three special feasts', 7.23 etc.; defined at 76.19 as Christmas, Easter, and Whitsun

gwyllt, 'wild', passim

gwyndwn, 'grassland', 209.13

Gwynedd: medieval Gwynedd at its smallest covered much the same ground as the modern administrative county of the same name; when its rulers were powerful, Gwynedd took in much of the modern Clwyd and encroached on Powys.

King of Gwynedd, 5.30-6.2n; state power in Gwynedd, 102.3-5n; 110.33-4n

gwynsaid, 'white-bladed', 194.18-19n

gwynwyr, 'marauders', 166.1n

gwysbren, 'binder', 191.8n

Glossary and Index to Notes 353

gwystl, 'gage' (of thing), 68.25n etc.; measure of, 68.25n;
redemption and forfeiture, 68.37-69.8n; validity,
69.9-11;
'hostage': in this sense the word seems to occur in
the law texts only in derivatives: see *gwystloriaeth;*
'pledge' (person), 85.18,20n; 88.38
gwystlo, 'give as hostage', 58.17,19; 'gage', 63.37 etc.
gwystloriaeth, 'hostageship', 107.34
gwythwch, 'wild pig', 178.27
gygus, 'offensive', 52.34n
gylyf, 'hook-knife', 192.38n
gyr (n), *gyrru*, (v), 'charge', passim

habit, religious, W. *dillad crefydd,* 164.6
habitation, importance in dadannudd, 101.19n
habituated dog, W. *ci cynefodig,* 182.27n
haddock, W. *penwaig,* 35.21n
haearnllif, 'iron file', 194.3-9n
hafdy, 'summer house', 40.12n; 190.22-4n
Hafesb, 180.10-11n
haid, 'swarm', 183.20-184.21n
hair, of horse's tail, W. *rhawn,* 172.38 etc.; uprooted, W.
gwallt bonwyn, 198.7n; hair rope, W. *rhaff flew,*
193.23
halawcty, 'foul house', 159.14-15
halfpenny, W. *dimai,* 68.25n
halog, 'befouled'; *halog fechni,* see *balog fechni*; *halog lw,*
'befouled oath', 205.21-2n
hamlet, W. *trefgordd,* 62.22; 170.21,23; 205.17;
hamlet land, W. *tir corflan,* 113.5, see II.5n (p.253)
and 82.22n
hammer, W. *morthwyl,* 193.13
handcuff, W. *gefyn,* 193.32
hand-quern, W. *breuan,* 194.13, see also *quern*
hand-sax, 195.11n
hanerob, see *enhorob*
hank (of flax), W. *dull,* 193.7
harlot, W. *putain,* 60.29
harm, W. *anaf,* 174.25,30,32; W. *cyflafan,* 208.6
violence and harm, W. *twrf ac eniwed,* 106.37n;
111.13-29
harness, W. *ystern,* 32.12; W. *harneis,* 11.24; (weaving)
harnesses, W. *rhwyllau,* 194.1

354   *The Law of Hywel Dda*

harrowing-horse, W. *march llyfnu*, 200.25
hart, W. *hydd*; champion hart, W. *cylleig*, 184.35n
harvest house, W. *cynhaeafdy*, 190.22-4n,34n
hate, W. *cas*, 95.9n
have-not, W. *diddim*, 70.1-2n
hawk, W. *gwalch*, see *falcon*
hawl tra blwyddyn, 'superannuated claim', 97.21,25
hazel, W. *collen*; hazel grove, W. *collwyn*, 188.25-7n
head, (on pile of food), W. *moel*, see 128.14-15n; (so many)
     head (of animals), W. *llwdn, llydn*, 178.34 etc.;
     according to the number of head of steers, W. *i rif
     eidon llwdn*, 205.20-21
headcloth, W. *penguwch*, 54.15; 195.27
headkerchief, W. *penlliain*, 54.12; 195.26
heap, W. *moel*, 128.14-15n
heart (of animal), 15.7n
hearth, W. *aelwyd*, 101.19n
heat, on: cat, W. *catherig*, 180.15-32n; cow, heifer, 175.19n;
     206.22-5; sow, 179.10-11
hebog, 'falcon', q.v.
hebogydd, 'falconer', see *falcon*; *Gwely Hebogyddïon*,
     92.10-11n
hebrwng, 'escort', 82.11,13,14n
heddles, W. *brwydau*, 193.39
hedge, W. *cae*, 205.24; thickset hedge, (fig.), W. *gwydd-
     waledd*, 97.19; 106.38
hedging-bill, W. *gwddyf*, 155.33-5n; 192.37n
he-goat, W. *bwch*, 187.13
heifer, first calf, W. *cynflith*, 35.3; 206.24
heir-apparent, W. *gwrthrychiad*, 6.19-7.25n
helmet, W. *helm*, 193.15
hen, sitting, 35.6-8n
hendiadys, 101.19n; 102.3-5n
hendref, 'main home', lit. 'old settlement', 40.12n
henfaes, 'old field', 114.1-5n
henlleu, 'old colony', 183.20-184.21n
Henry V, legislation of, 149.1-9n
herd, W. *cenfaint*, 40.5n,8-12; W. *praidd*, 178.12;
          legal herd (of cattle), W. *praidd cyfreithiol*, 178.12;
          (of pigs), W. *cadw cyfraith*, 203.30,35;
          herd boar, W. *baedd cenfaint*, 179.20;
          herd dog, W. *bugeilgi*, 181.34-182.2n
herdsman, W. *bugail*, 62.22; 196.31
herechan, 'latrine', 41.12-15n

Glossary and Index to Notes 355

heriot, see *ebediw*

herring, 35.21n

hesb, 'dry', 180.10-11n

hesbin, 'dry yearling', 180.10-11n

hestor, 'corn measure', 195.16n

hind, W. *ewig,* 187.11

hindmost, W. *oliaid,* 205.8-9n

hindquarter, W. *chwarthawr dylwr,* 185.30

hire, W. *llog,* 161.22-3n

hiriau, 'long yoke', 99.3-9n; 120.36; 199.3; cf. III.9n

hirwedd, 'long team', III.9n (p. 303)

hobble, W. *llawethyr,* 202.30

hoe, W. *caib,* 192.37; in modern Welsh *caib* is used for 'mattock' or even 'pickaxe'.

hold (animal), W. *dala,* 202.21; 207.17

holding, W. *gafael,* 121.5-6n

holy, W. *glân,* 1.12n; holy yew, W. *ywen sant,* 189.13

home-made, W. *pentan,* 195.23

homicide, (offence), W. *galanas,* q.v.; (offender), W. *llofrudd,* 58.8-9n etc.; principal offence of homicide, W. *llofruddiaeth yr alanas,* 144.9

honffest, 'gauntlet', 193.31n

honsecs, 'dagger', 195.11n

hoofrasp, W. *carnllif,* 194.8

hook-knife, W. *gylyf,* 192.38n

horn, king's, 40.14-19n; 77.3n; steers', see *ears;* sounding-horn, W. *corn canu,* 195.17

horse, W. *march,* passim; see also *amws, dung horse, dung mare, palfrey, rouncey, working-horse;* horse in attendance, W. *march preswyl,* q.v.

horse-brass, W. *canwyl,* 195.5-6n

horse-cloth, W. *suder,* 195.4

hosanau, 'hose', 32.11; 195.7n

hose, W. *hosanau, hwsiaws,* 32.11; 195.7n

hospitality, W. *gwestfa,* (q.v.), 167.23

host, W. *osb,* 6.25n

hostage: give as hostage, W. *gwystlo,* 58.17-19

hostageship, W. *gwystloriaeth,* 107.34

hostings, W. *lluydd,* 24.37; 77.3n; 101.2n,5,6; 124.5n

house, W. *tŷ,* passim; minor house, W. *gody,* 190.10-14n, 18n,22-4n

household, W. *teilu, teulu.* In modern Welsh *teulu* is the ordinary word for 'family', and it is convenient to use the older form *teilu* for the older sense, 'bodyguard, household troops'; in combination, *teilu* is often translated 'household', since the reference seems to be to the whole royal entourage:

bard of the household, W. *bardd teilu*, 5.5-6 etc.
captain of the household, W. *penteilu*, 5.3-4 etc.
priest of the household, W. *offeiriad teilu*, 11.26 etc.

From the references to *anrhaith*, 'booty', it is clear that marauding expeditions into other countries were an important function of the *teilu*; from the viewpoint of the victims in the other country, the *teilu* were no doubt regarded as *gwynwyr* (q.v.), 'marauders'. Galanas was not payable for the victim of the *teilu*'s activities: 'Nyt a galanas yn ol teulu6ryaeth', WML 311.20.

hual, 'fetter', 193.10; 195.15; 202.30

hualog, 'strangles', 179.12n

humerus, W. *byriad*, 24.22n

hundy, 'sleephouse', 41.12-15n; 125.4-7n

huntsman, W. *cynydd* (lit. 'houndsman'), passim;
chief huntsman, W. *pencynydd*, 10.14n

hurdle, see *door-hurdle, fold-hurdle, thorn-hurdle*

hurt, W. *briw*, 174.15

hwch, *hych* (form with numeral), 'pig, sow', 122.32n; 203.20-21n
hwch coed, 'wild pig', 186.1-7n, cf. *gwythwch*
hwch dref, 'domestic pig', 178.28n

hwsiaws, 'hose', 195.7n

hwyedydd, 'tiercel', see *falcon*

hwyl, 'cover', 23.27,29; 25.12

hych, see *hwch*

hydd, 'hart', 184.35n

hynaf, 'senior', 84.32-3n

hynafgwyr, 'oldest men', 147.8n

Hywel, king, 182.13n; see also *cyfraith Hywel*

iaen, 'icicle, piece of ice', 70.1-2n

iau, 'liver', see *au*

iau, 'yoke', 45.21n; see 176.21-2; 179.33n; 199.36-7n

iawn (n), 'compensation', 26.17 etc.; (a, adv), 'proper', see *dyly*

icicle, stone in place of, W. *maen dros iaen*, 70.1-2n

idle, W. *segur*, 186.15n, 23; idle trinkets, W. *oferdlysau*, 16.28 and see *tlws*

Glossary and Index to Notes   357

iewyddion, 'draught-ropes', 202.9-11n
ignorance, oath of, W. *llw diarnabod,* 177.19; 205.20,21-2n
illegality, W. *anghyfraith,* 63.8 etc.
immediate, W. *diannod,* 76.36 etc., see 119.35-6n
immunity, W. *rhyddid,* 91.17n
imp, 'graft', 188.29
important: most important, W. *pennaf,* In (p.220); 182.1
imprisoned in time, W. *carcharu yn amser,* 77.22-3
inadvertence, W. *anoddau,* 130.18n; see also *anfodd*
inch, W. *modfedd,* 120.25-6n; 176.12-13n
incomer, W. *gŵr dyfod,* 92.3
indispensables, three, W. *tri anhepgor,* 39.30,33,35
inedible, W. *anhyys,* 182.19
information, W. *manag;* sufficient information, W. *dogn-
         fanag,* 62.34; 159.21-2n
informer, W. *managwr,* 62.33; 159.21-2n
ing, 'strait', 134.23-4
iniuria (Lat.), see *sarhaed*
innate, W. *canhwynol,* 108.18n, see also *bonheddig*
inquiry, word of, W. *gair cyfarch,* 87.34n; stock inquiry,
         W. *cyfarch cyffyll,* 145.25n
insane, W. *ynfyd,* 151.27
inseil agored, 'patent seal', 12.3; 29.1
install, W. *llehau,* 142.28
interchangeable, W. *treigledig,* 76.28n
interest, declaration against, 136.22-6n
interruption, 119.35-6n
intervene, W. *ymyrru,* 123.23; 135.28
intestines, W. *penhygen,* 185.30
invalid, invalidate, see *dilys, dilysu, llys*
investiture, W. *estyn,* see *grant and investiture*
Iorwerth ap Madog ap Rhawd, 92.10-11n; IIIn; 145.25n;
         190.4-5n
iron file, W. *haearnllif,* 194.3-9n
irregular, irregularly, W. *anolo,* 132.25,26; without irreg-
         ularity, W. *yn ddirrwysg,* 172.34n
irresponsible thing, W. *meredig,* 171.8
iwrch, 'roe, roebuck', 187.11-12n
iyrchell, 'roe', 187.9

jar, W. *celwrn,* 192.26n
jester, W. *croesan,* 18.20-23n
Joan, queen of Llywelyn the Great, In (p.220); 6.19-7.25n

358 *The Law of Hywel Dda*

joint, of finger, W. *cwgn*, 196.22-7n; of meat, W. *golwyth*, 22.21; 184.26-7n;35n,37

joint-ploughing, joint-ploughing contract, W. *cyfar*, III.9 passim; make joint-ploughing contract (intrans.), put into joint-ploughing contract (trans.), W. *cyfaru*; joint-ploughing partners, W. *cyfarwyr*

judge, (n), W. *brawdwr*; (v) W. *barnu*; see *ynad*

judgment: challenge to, 17.25-9n; properly judged, 141.9-11

July, 13.34-7n

June, 13.34-7n

justice, W. *ynad*, q.v.; commote justice, senior justice, 84.32-3n

justiceship, W. *yneidiaeth*, see *ynad*

kennel, W. *cynllwst*, 181.19,23

Kidwelly, lordship, 17.25-9n

kiln, W. *odyn*, 126.2n; 170.10-13,20-24n; 191.15-23,23n

kin, kindred, W. *cenedl* (q.v.), passim. References to degrees of kindred are confused, probably because of a confounding of the canon-law and Roman-law methods of computing, see 145.4-7n; the confusion suggests that the rules were becoming obsolete when the texts were written. The problems are not yet resolved, but it seems likely that the basis of the system was the four-generation group (from progenitor to great-grandchildren), the *derbfine* of Irish law; this seems to be the original meaning of *gwely:* see 145.15n. For inheritance, kinship is measured downwards from the ancestor, through males alone; for galanas (q.v.), it is measured outwards from the homicide and his victim, through males and females. Exactly computed payment of galanas was probably obsolescent, but the rules were retained because liability (or right) to galanas was the qualification for a compurgator, see 68.11-16.

innocent kindred, W. *cenedl wirion* (i.e. the victim's kin), 152.13-14n

kindred and descent, W. *ach ac edryf*, 86.17 etc. The translation is conventional: *ach* usually means 'degree [of kindred]' (q.v.), but it has been suggested that *ach* and *edryf* refer to ancestry on the mother's and father's side respectively: see Col 577n.

Glossary and Index to Notes 359

kin-feud, W. *cenedlelyniaeth*, 48.5n
kin-stock, W. *gwelygordd*, 97.13,14
kindred, see *kin*; four kindreds, 145.15n
king, W. *brenin*, 72.21-3n; 112.23,24n; see also *arglwydd*.
In theory, all Welsh kings were equally sovereign,
no matter what the size of their dominions might
be, but the surviving law texts clearly show that
there were grades among them. For the suzerainty
of the 'King of London', see 154.25n; for a king's
rights over enfranchised land, 101.2n
kinship, W. *carennydd*, 145.7 etc.
kinsman, W. *câr* (q.v.), 123.23 etc.
kitten, W. *cenau cath*, 180.16; rear kittens, W. *meithrin
canawon*, 180.22; cat not to eat its kittens,
180.15-32n
kneeboots, W. *ystywos*, 195.8n
knife, (v), W. *cyllellu*, 185.4; (n), see *hook-knife, larder-knife*
knight, W. *marchog*, 9.34n; 131.20-27n
knower, W. *gwybyddiad*, 86.27n; 102.21-2n; see also *tyst*

lactation money. W. *arian dooddwf*, 175.22
land (i.e. selion), W. *tir*, 120.28-9n
land and earth, W. *tir a daear*, 9.32n etc; cases on, 9.32n; 13.8n
land-feud, W. *tirdra*, 94.22n; 110.35-6n; cf. 143.2n
larder, W. *cell*, 46.16 etc.; larder knife, W. *cyllell gell*, 195.11
lath, W. *cledren*, 119.22
latrine, W. *herechan, peiriant, trefn fechan, tŷ bychan*,
41.12-15n
law, W. *cyfraith*, passim, see *rhaith*
church law, W. *cyfraith eglwys*, 110.28n
forms of law, W. *cyfreithiau*, 160.1
learned in law, W. *cyfarwydd mywn cyfraith*, 142.34
of Hywel, W. *cyfraith Hywel*, 157.18n etc.
of theft, W. *cyfraith lladrad*, 182.33n
repellent law, W. *cyfraith atgas*, 119.17-20
rule of law, W. *deddf*, 80.9-11n
three systems of law, W. *tair cyfraith*, 94.15n
lawbooks, structure of, 181.16-182.24n
laxity, W. *llesgedd*, 161.26
leap, W. *naid*, 120.28-9n
learned in law, W. *cyfarwydd mywn cyfraith*, 142.34
lease, W. *llogi*, 114.6n
leash, W. *cynllyfan*, 22.11 etc.; 182.10n; 193.26-8
lees, W. *gwaddod*, 18.35,37

360   *The Law of Hywel Dda*

leftovers, W. *cadyd,* 36.5
legal, W. *cyfraith, cyfreithiol,* passim; see also *ceiniog, gwirod, gwerth, golwyth, joint, tyst*
life, W. *enaid,* 63.22 etc.
limit, W. *eirionyn,* 34.34n; 121.1n
lineage, W. *bonedd* (q.v.), 183.21-184.21n
linen, for serjeant's breeches, 34.22n
lintels, W. *gorddrysau,* 190.27-32n
liquor, W. *gwirod,* 13.29; 14.33 etc.; legal liquor, W. *gwirod gyfreithiol,* 25.19n; see also *ceinion*
litter (of sow), W. *ael,* 179.15
liver, liver-fluke, W. *aü, aüad,* 179.33n
livestock, W. *ysgrubl,* passim; small livestock, W. *mân ysgrubl,* 203.15; 208.22
lladrad, lledrad, 'theft, stealth', 166.18n; 169.17n etc.; 'stolen property', 157.4; see also *cyfraith lladrad*
llamysten, 'sparrowhawk', see *falcon*
llanw a thrai, 'ebb and flow', 84.20n
llathlud, 'clandestine', passim. The word occurs in various forms and in slightly varying contexts, so that it sometimes implies seduction or even rape; the essential element is, however, absence of consent by the woman's kin; the first element in the word may be the same as in *lladrad,* meaning 'stealth'.
llawethyr, 'hobble', 202.30; this is the living form of the word in some dialects, the standard literary form being *llyffethair.*
llawfaeth, 'full time', 137.21, following WML and adopting the suggestion of GPC that the manuscript readings may be an error for *llawnaeth.*
llawgydau, 'purses', 46.2n
llawn, 'full', passim; (of animal) 'in good condition', 63.5n
lledfegin, 'tamed animal', 187.26-34; as the definition shows, the name means 'partly reared'.
lledrad, see *lladrad*
llehau, 'install', 142.28
lleidr, 'thief', passim; *lleidr gwerth,* 'sale thief': here *gwerth* is the stem of the verb *gwerthaf,* 'I sell', used as adjective, and the expression means that the thief is liable to be sold into slavery. As the references show, the thief could be expected to redeem himself by paying his 'value' (£7) himself.
llesgedd, 'laxity', 161.26
lliwo, 'present', 160.8-9n

Glossary and Index to Notes   361

Lloegr, 120.5n, see also *gwerin*
llofrudd, 'homicide', 133.31 etc; 'principal offender',
    81.7n etc.; 'principal', 95.8n
llofruddiaeth, 'principal offence', 144.9, and see 81.7n; 95.8n
llog, 'hire', 161.22-3n
llogi, 'lease', 114.6n
llosgwrn, 'tail', 49.28; 175.26 etc.
llostlydan, 'beaver', 188.8,12
lluest, 'camp', 41.11n
llumaniaeth, llumenyddiaeth, 'office of standard-bearer',
    92.10-11n
lluydd, 'hostings', 24.37; 77.3n; 101.5,6 etc.
llw, 'oath', passim; *halog lw,* 'befouled oath', 205.21-2n;
    llw diarnabod, 'oath of ignorance', 177.19; 205.20,
    21-2n; *llw gweilydd,* 'fore-oath', 205.15n
llwdn, 'beast', 13.5 etc.; 'head', 178.34 etc.; *i rif eidon
    llwdn,* 'according to number of head of steers',
    205.20-21; *llwdn cwta,* 'docked beast', 35.35n;
    llydn (form used with numeral, cf. *hych*), 122.32n
llwgr, (n), 'damage', 190.7; 209.10n etc.
llwyg, 'restiveness' (q.v.), 172.19
llwynog, 'fox', 187.22n; 187.33
llyffethair, see *llawethyr*
llygru, 'damage', 173.21; *llygredig,* 'corrupted', 49.12 etc.
Llŷn, 121.11-13n
llynmeirch, 'glanders', 172.19
llys, 'court', passim
llys, 'bar, objection', was the most useful word of the med-
    ieval Welsh lawyer's vocabulary, and is the most
    troublesome for the translator, because it generated
    so many derivatives. The basic meaning is seen at
    94.1: certain facts operate as a bar against a proposed
    testifier, and are made the ground of the litigant's
    objection to him: see 94.1-25n; 165.36n. From the
    basic word comes first the verb *llysu,* 'object to',
    93.16 etc.; this is the verb used in Acts iv.11, cor-
    responding to 'rejected' in RSV and NEB. It gives
    the participle-adjective *llysiedig,* 'rejected', 94.27,
    and the abstract noun *llysiant,* 'ground of objection',
    94.35.
        With the negating prefix *di-, llys* becomes *dilys,*
    'without objection', variously translated 'authentic'
    (7.26-8.28n), 'unobjectionable' (93.19), 'valid',
    (63.13n; 69.9-11n etc.), 'validly free' (57.13n) in

362   *The Law of Hywel Dda*

the attempt to show the application to particular
circumstances of the basic idea. In practice, as has
been pointed out for the Irish cognate *diles* (CG
83), *dilys* has opposite meanings according to the
standpoint from which a transaction is viewed. If,
for instance, a transfer of goods is valid, the goods
are *dilys* against the transferor, and he cannot
reclaim them from the transferee; as against the
transferor, the validity of the transfer makes the
goods *dilys* for the transferee. From *dilys* we have
the verb *dilysu*, essentially 'to render *dilys*', 'to
prove as *dilys*'; in different contexts this is
translated 'validate' (73.22 etc.), 'set free' (117.29-
30n), 'discharge' (146.30n), but in all contexts the
result of the *dilysu* is that no legal claim can upset
the relation created. *Dilys* has also the abstract
nouns *dilysrwydd* and *dilystod*, 'the state of being
dilys'; both nouns have also the concrete sense of
compensation for loss of that state: see 51.38n.

A second negating prefix gives *annilys*, 'invalid'
(69.10; 72.36-73.15n etc.), with its verb *annilysu*,
'invalidate' (73.1 etc.) It may well happen that a
transaction valid between the two parties is upset
by a third party: the transfer of property may be
effective to give the transferee the property as
against the transferor, but if a third party can show
that he, rather than the transferor, is the true
owner of the property, he may be able to reclaim it
from the transferee.

Llywelyn the Great (Llywelyn ab Iorwerth, ob. 1240), In
   (p.220), 6.19-7.25n

llywgroen, 'guiding thong', 193.8

llywiadur, 'ruler', 193.8

loan, W. *benffyg*, 161.22-3n

London, King of, 154.25n, 26

long team, W. *hirwedd*, III.9n

loop, W. *magl*, 198.34, 199.22: this is a living word for a
   snare and for a stitch in knitting; the figurative use
   in relation to joint ploughing seems to come from
   the idea that the team returns to its starting point
   after going round all the acres.
   W. *egwyd*, 202.35

lord, W. *arglwydd*, q.v.

Glossary and Index to Notes 363

lordship, W. *arglwyddiaeth,* (authority) 114.13,14; (territory) 147.26; 167.32

loss by laxity, W. *coll o lesgedd,* 161.26

loss, dire, W. *dygngoll,* 134.27-135.5; 146.11-27; 147.22n

love, W. *digasedd,* 95.9n

lungs, of animal, 15.7n

luxury-bag, W. *trythgwd,* 46.2n

mab, 'son', passim
    mab aillt, see *aillt*
    mab amau, 'doubted son', 134.26,31
    mab anwar, 'uncouth son', 46.38-47.4n
    mab dioddef, 'son by sufferance', 134.15-16,19,24
    mab gwâr, 46.38-47.4n

mach, 'surety, contract', II.4n; 72.36-73.15n; 207.35n
    mach ar gyfraith, 'surety to abide law', 77.29-78.4n
    mach cynnogn, 'debtor surety', 70.24,29-38n

machtiern (Breton), see *mechdeyrn*

macwyaid, 'pages', 6.26; 124.1,24

maen dros iaen, 'a stone in place of an icicle', 70.1-2n

maenol, pl. *maenolydd,* 121.7 etc. The word which has this form in manuscripts written in Gwynedd appears as *maenor* (pl. *maenorau*) in those written farther south; both forms have given rise to place names, such as *y Faenol* ('Vaynol') near Bangor, *Cefn-faenor* near Aberystwyth, and *Maenor Bŷr* ('Manorbier') in South Pembrokeshire. The meaning corresponds roughly to that of English 'manor', but the words are not cognate: see *Col* pp.161-2. The lawbooks are at their most schematic in dealing with these land-divisions, which are far from corresponding to the facts on the ground.

maer, pl. *meiri.* In modern Welsh *maer* (from Latin *maior*) means 'mayor'; the medieval maer was a royal official who shared with the cynghellor (q.v.) the local administration of land occupied by self-employed husbandmen (whether free or unfree), who paid dues in kind to the King and might owe certain services. His functions resemble those of the English reeve, but whereas the English name (A.S. *gerefa,* 'servant', whose German cognate is *Graf,* 'count') sees the functionary from the viewpoint of the lord whom he served, *maer* sees him from that of the men over whom he exercised

364 The Law of Hywel Dda

authority. There is little to show how far the functions of maer and cynghellor differed; both officers were surely freemen, for their status (as measured by their sarhaed and the amobr of their daughters) was high: see 55.3,4; 155.8. The cynghellor ranked above the maer, for when they had to share anything, it was for the maer to divide and the cynghellor to choose—and the general rule gave the choice to the person of a higher rank: *Dw* 488; the rule is clearly being applied at 23.11-13

maer biswail, 'dung maer', was one of the Additional Officers (I.5n); he exercised the same kind of functions as the maer, but in relation to the unfree tenants of the maerdref, which would be a smaller area than that under the care of the maer and cynghellor. Like the English reeve, the dung maer was unfree (see 124.18-19), and the higher officials' contempt for him is indicated by the name and by the rule of 33.34-8; but the fact that he did not get even a derisory compensation (see 18.20-23n; 35. 6-8n) suggests that his office was not of very long standing.

maer cynghellor, 55.3: the two offices could evidently be combined in one man when this passage was written, as they certainly sometimes were in the fourteenth century: see (1976) 27 BBCS 117-18

maerdref, i.e. 'maer's townland', 33.19 etc. This was the townland surrounding the court, held in demesne by the Lord: cf. *tir bwrdd.* Place-names incorporating *maerdref* (e.g. *Llanilltud Faerdre,* 'Llantwit Vardre' near Pontypridd) or *maerdy* (e.g. *Mardy* in the Rhondda Valley) are an indication of the site of a court.

maestir, 'open land', 189.31

magl, 'loop' (q.v.), 198.34,35; 199.22

maiden, W. *morwyn* (q.v.), passim; as tongue-bearer, 62.16-21n; maiden-wife, W. *morwynwraig,* 60.17, see *gwraig.*

mail (MS. *meyl*), 'bowl', 193.10

mail, cap of, W. *penffestin,* 193.15

maintainer, W. *ceidwad,* 86.27n; 102.21-2n,33n; 105.15n; 106.31n; see also *tyst.*

Maitland, F.W., 155.33-5n

mâl, 'tribute', 120.23

Glossary and Index to Notes 365

mallet, W. *orddwyn*, 193.6
malt, W. *brag*, 129.9n
mam-eglwys, 'mother church', 41.22,30n
mamwys, 'mother-right', 58.3,15; 107.22 etc.
manag, 'information', 62.34; 159.21-2n
managwr, 'informer', 62.33; 159.21-2n
manure-shed, W. *tomdy*, 193.30n
manuring basket, W. *cawell teilo*, 193.30
manwydd, 'minor trees', 189.9
marauders, W. *gwynwyr*, 166.1n
march, 'horse', passim; in modern Welsh *march* is in some
        parts of the country the ordinary word for
        'stallion'; it is nowhere now used as it is in the
        law texts for 'horse' in general
        march gwyllt, 'wild horse', 172.11
        march llyfnu, 'harrowing-horse', 200.25
        march preswyl, 'horse in attendance', 11.27; 12.26
        etc.; 'horse in residence' would be a more literal
        translation. In the corresponding expressions
        march bidoseb (*Cyfn*, in various forms) and
        march yn woseb (*Bleg*), the emphasis seems to
        be laid on the character of the horse as a gift (see
        GPC s.v. *goseb*) rather than on its constant
        availability.
        march tom, 'dung horse', 172.30
marchdy, 'stable', 41.12-15n
marchog, 'knight', 9.34n; 131.20-27n
margin, W. *eirionyn*, 34.34n; 121.1n
marry, W. *gwra* (of woman), *gwreica* (of man). At an early
        stage, Welsh custom seems to have recognised
        nine grades of marital union (see Charles-
        Edwards, 'Naw Kynywedi Teithiawc', WLW 23-
        39): 'marry' is used as a shorthand translation
        for *gwra* or *gwreica*, without any implication of
        any particular grade of union or of any formality.
        See also *gwraig, priod, wedded.*
        married, W. *gwreigog* (of man), *gwriog* (of woman):
        this again does not imply any particular form of
        marital union.
marten, W. *belau*, 187.36; 188.12
marwdy, 'dead-house', 34.30n; 40.35-9n
marwdystiolaeth, 'dead testimony', 98.8
May, 13.34-7n
mead-brewer, W. *meddydd*, 7.32-3n

366 *The Law of Hywel Dda*

meadow, W. *gweirglawdd,* 206.33 etc.
measure, corn, W. *hestor,* 195.16n
 of acre, 199.8-9n
 of bone size, 197.32-7n
meat, rights to, 34.30n
meat dish, W. *cigddysgl,* 193.19
meat-fork, W. *cigwain,* 191.27 etc
mechdeyrn: mechdeyrn ddylyed, 'sovereign tribute', 154.25n
meddu, 'control', see 162.1n; 182.32; 201.8; 'have power', 162.1n
meddiant, 'control', 85.20n; 96.23; 201.11; 'wealth' (q.v.), 159.25
meddydd, 'mead-brewer', 7.32-3n
meddyg, 'physician', 7.32-3n; 24.3-25.5n
meddyginiaeth, 'medical attention', 24.15; 'medication', 24.28 etc.; 197.22n
medical attention, medication, see *meddyginiaeth*
medium auger, W. *taradr perfedd,* 192.34-5n
meiiau, 'mid-yoke', 99.4; 120.35; 199.2
mennai, 'trough', 192.27
menstruate, W. *blodeuo,* 49.20; 60.5; 131.37-132.1
meredig, 'irresponsible', 171.8
mess, W. *saig,* 6.26; 14.31
Michaelmas, W. *Gŵyl Fihangel,* 13.34 etc.
midday, W. *hanner dydd,* passim
mid-yoke, W. *meiiau,* 99.4; 120.35; 199.2
mile, W. *milltir,* (q.v.), 120.29n
milgi, 'greyhound', 181.21n
milltir, 'mile', 120.29n. According to this measure the Welsh mile was 6,750 English yards, or some 3¾ English miles.
minor houses, W. *godai,* 190.10-14n,18n,22-4n
minor trees, W. *manwydd,* 189.9
mirror, W. *drych,* 193.9
misapprehension, W. *anoddau,* 166.25,27; see 130.18n
miscellanea, W. *amddyriaid,* 177.36-178.3n
mistletoe, 188.18-19n
misuse, W. *camarferu,* 1.3; 5.28-9n
mixed corn, W. *amyd,* 195.14
mixed fabric, W. *tenllif,* 34.22n
moch, 'pigs', 122.32n; 203.20-21n,31n; *arbennig y moch,* 'champion of the pigs', 203.31n; *moch coed,* 'wild boars', 22.24
modfedd, 'inch', 120.25-6n; 176.12-13n

Glossary and Index to Notes   367

modrwy, 'ring', passim
modrydaf, 'queen bee, queen colony', 183.20-184.21n
moel (n), 'head, heap', lit. 'bald (head)', 128.14-15n;
    (a), 'polled' (of cattle), 177.20-21n
moelddyrnfedd, 'bare fistbreadth', 129.4n
monarch, W. *teyrn,* 38.24; 112.23,24n
Monarchy of Britain, W. *Unbeiniaeth Prydain,* 20.23-4n
money, W. *arian,* passim; money payment, W. *ariantal,*
    III.10n; 202.21,24n
Môr Udd, 'the Channel', 120.6-21n
Morgannwg: medieval Morgannwg corresponded to the
    pre-1974 county of Glamorgan, with its county
    boroughs, but excluding the Swansea Valley and
    the Gower peninsula: its boundaries were thus
    very much those of the present diocese of Llandaff.
Morgenau, 92.10-11n
morthwyl, 'hammer', 193.13
morwyn, 'maiden', passim; cf. *gwyryf,* 'virgin'. In later use,
    morwyn means 'maid (servant)' more often than
    'virgin', though the Virgin Mary is *y Forwyn Fair.*
morwynwraig, 'maiden-wife', 60.17; see *gwraig*
mother church, W. *mam-eglwys,* 41.22,30n
mother-right, W. *mamwys,* 58.3,15; 107.22 etc.
mow, W. *lladd,* 126.3; 206.37
muirburn, W. *goddaith,* (q.v.), 170.21,34
murder, W. *murdwrn,* 150.34n; W. *llofruddiaeth,* 81.7n
murdwrn, 'murder', 150.34n
muriedig, 'entrenched', lit. 'walled', 123.30
mutuum, 161.22-3n
mwynhau, 'enjoy', 72.31; 89.24 etc.; 'take', 92.36 etc.;
    'use', 63.18. The sense is close to the technical
    legal sense of English 'enjoy'.
mwyniant, 'use', 63.12
Myddfai, physicians of, 24.3-25.5n; 195.4n
mynwent, 'churchyard', 82.22n
mynyglog: y fynyglog, 'quinsy', 179.12n; the name implies
    an affection of the throat (W. *mwnwgl*).

nai, 'nephew', 6.23n
naid, 'leap', 120.28-9n
nail (finger or thumb), 196.21-2n
nailmaker, W. *cethrol,* 194.3-9n
natural, W. *anianol,* 174.22, cf. 94.1-25n
nawdd, 'protection, sanctuary', II.5n (pp.253-4)

368   *The Law of Hywel Dda*

nawn, 'nones' (q.v.), 185.21,22
neck-kerchief, W. *ffunen,* 195.26
negyddiaeth, 'refusal', 68.33n
neighbour, (W. *cymydog*) as witness, 162.18; 181.34-182.2n;
     cf. 191.4n
neillwyr, 'separate men', 192.2
neithior, 'wedding celebration', 39.1n
neithiorwyr, 'wedding guests', 39.1n; 49.4,15
nen, 'roof', 190.14,16,20,21
nenbren, 'roof-tree', 189.33; 190.25-7
nenfforch, 'roof-fork', 189.34
nephew, W. *nai,* 6.23n
net, W. *rhwyd* (fig), 40.4,8,11
     various nets for fish, 193.33,34,35n
nithlen, 'winnowing sheet', 192.25
noddfa, 'sanctuary', II.5n (pp.253-4)
noe, 'platter', 130.26; 131.37; 193.22
nones, W. *nawn,* 185.21,22, i.e. the ninth hour, or 3 p.m.
     In modern Welsh *prynhawn* (from *pryd-nawn*) is
     the ordinary word for 'afternoon'.
non-proprietor, W. *amhriodor,* 91.30 etc.; 108.5-9n
non-virgin, 147.38n, see also *gwraig*
November, Kalends of, W. *Calan Tachwedd,* 22.24-5n; see
     also *Winter Kalends*

oak: scrub oak, W. *cegin dderwen,* 188.24n
oath: as proof in Welsh law, II.6n (pp.254-5)
     befouled oath, W. *halog lw,* 205.21-2n
     oath of ignorance, W. *llw diarnabod,* 177.19; 205.20,
     21-2n
     see also *fore-oath*
object to, W. *llysu,* see *llys*
objection, W. *llys* (q.v.), 94.1-25n; ground of objection, W.
     llysiant, 94.35
occupancy, W. *gwarchadw,* 108.14
occupation, W. *gwarchadw,* 91.31 etc.
occupier, W. *gwercheidwad,* 84.14,15; 127.9
occupy, W. *gwarchadw,* 87.4 etc.
odwr, 'receiver', 157.2n
odyn, 'kiln', 126.2n; 170.10-13,20-24n; 191.15-23,23n
oed, 'age', 58.34 etc.; 'date', 65.7 etc.; 'delay', 78.2 etc.;
     133.17n; 'due date', 69.1 etc.; 'fixed term',
     81.11

oed wrth borth, 'delay for aid', 77.1; 77.29-78.4n
etc., cf. *canllaw*

oergwymp galanas, 'cold case of galanas', 146.9-10, cf.
dygngoll

oferdlysau, 'idle trinkets', 16.28, see *tlws*

offeiriad, 'priest', 41.30n; 62.5-8n
offeiriad teilu, 'priest of the household', 5.4n etc.

offence, W. *cyflafan,* 48.1 etc., see 60.33n

offender, principal, W. *llofrudd,* 81.7n etc.

offering, W. *offrwm,* 6.30n

office, W. *swydd,* passim; in right of land, 33.11n

officer, W. *swyddog;* official, W. *swyddwr.* Because two
different words are used in Welsh, care has been
taken to use two different words in English,
though the usage in Welsh is not wholly consistent
and the difference in meaning is never explained. A
swyddog is usually one of the named officers of or
about the court, while *swyddwyr* seem to have
been assistants who were not separately specified.
Bleg (8.3-4) and *Cyfn* (WML 6.2-4) include a
swyddwr llys, 'court official' among the twenty-
four; his protection, 'from when he begins to distribute the food until the last gets his food' indicates
that he was an assistant to the steward. He was perhaps brought in to make up the number of 24, for
he was discarded in *Ior,* which needed places for
additional officers of the Queen. The *swyddwyr*
were under the supervision of the steward, 12.34.

Officers, Additional ('by use and by custom'), I.5n (p.231)

offrwm, 'offering', 6.30n

ointment, red, W. *rhuddeli,* 197.25

oldest men, W. *hynafgwyr,* 147.8n

oliaid, 'hindmost', 205.8-9n

olrhead, 'tracker-dog', 193.28-9

open land, W. *maestir,* 189.31

opened, (cheese, etc.), W. *bwlch,* 46.11-14n

ordd, 'sledge-hammer', 194.5; the usual modern form is
gordd.

orddwyn, 'mallet', 193.6

ordeal, II.6n (pp.235-6)

order, put in, W. *cyweirio,* 202.7

orders, holy, W. *graddau,* 164.5; W. *urddau,* 40.33; man in
orders, W. *graddwr,* 29.10; 163.38

ordinances, W. *gosodedigaethau,* 142.9

370   *The Law of Hywel Dda*

orles, (Fr.), W. *wrlys,* 41.19n
ornamentations, W. *amaerwyau,* 188.13n, cf. *orles*
osb, 'host', 6.25n
outside the skin (fault), W. *eithr croen,* 174.21-2
outward harm, W. *anaf o faes,* 174.25
overtake, W. *goddiwes,* 47.35; 205.11; 207.2-3
owner, W. *arglwydd,* 182.27n, cf. 165.29n; W. *perchen,* 72.30 etc.; W. *perchennog,* 25.14 etc.
ownership, W. *perchenogaeth,* 162.16

packhorse, W. *pynfarch,* 124.20; (fig.) 40.35-9n etc.
pack-saddle, W. *ystrodur,* 193.36
paddock, W. *cae cadw,* 207.13-16n
pages, W. *macwyaid,* 6.26; 124.1,24
pail, W. *baeol,* 45.18; 192.30,31
pair, 'boiler', 191.26n
pais, 'smock', 34.22; 51.21; 155.34
paladr, 'shaft', 145.2n
palf, 'palm'; *lled y balf,* 'palmbreadth', 120.26; 129.4n etc.
palmbreadth, W. *lled y balf,* 120.26; 129.4n etc.; cf. *fist-breadth*
panel, 'saddle-cloth', 195.4n,5
parish priest, W. *periglor,* 46.37 etc.
parson, W. *person,* 41.30n; 81.31; make parson, W. *personi,* 12.21
partners, W. *cyfarwyr,* 201.6,38; joint-ploughing partners, W. *cyfarwyr,* 200.33, 201.1
party, W. *plaid,* 64.2 etc.; cf. 204.36-8n
pasture, W. *gwelltpawr,* 207.12
patent seal, W. *inseil agored,* 12.3; 29.1
patrimonial, W. *treftadog,* 92.1 etc.
patrimony, W. *treftad,* lit. 'father's townland', i.e. inheritance in land, 58.3 etc.; acre (W. *erw*) as symbolising, 136.16n
pawl, 'pole', 191.6; *polion syfagau,* 'weather-poles', 191.6-7
peg, W. *ysgwr,* 99.7; 120.37; 199.5; 200.26n; pl., W. *gwehyll,* 202.9-11n
peilliaid, 'fine flour', 128.31
peiriant, 'latrine', 41.12-15n
peithyndo, 'roof of shingles', 170.20-24n
peithynnau, 'reeds' (of loom), 193.39
pellennau, 'balls of yarn', 170.36
penalty, W. *poen,* 168.15n; death penalty, W. *dihenydd,* 167.29 etc.

Glossary and Index to Notes 371

pencenedl, 'chief of kindred', 55.7; 123.15-18,25-6n etc.
No detailed study of the *pencenedl* has ever been
made, and it is not even known for how large a
group of kindred he was chief. The references in
the text give some indication of the functions of
the office, but for the mode of appointment we
have only the hint given by the rules of 123.25-9. In
spite of these rules the office may have become
hereditary: in 1318-19 Llywelyn ap Gruffudd
claimed that he and his father and ancestors had
pencenedlaeth over their coparceners of the lineage of Hwfa ap Cynddelw: W. Rees, *Calendar of
Ancient Petitions*, 84-5.

pencenedlaeth, 'office of chief of kindred', 123.28

pencerdd: see also 8.37-9.1n; 38.16-39.17nn. Two men
who seem to the modern mind to be poets are mentioned in the lawbooks: the *bardd teilu*, 'bard of the
household', and the pencerdd, usually translated
'chief of song', because in modern Welsh the usual
sense of *cerdd* is musical, though the word often
means 'poem'. It has usually been assumed that
both were officers of the court and had their places
in a professional hierarchy, that of the pencerdd
being the higher; there have been many attempts
to show that their respective functions corresponded to those of two grades in the later scheme of
bardic organisation and training, but these have
hardly been supported by the lawbook evidence.
   In point of constitutional status the pencerdd
should be compared, not with the bard of the household but with the court smith, as a leader in a skilled
craft. The Welsh *cerdd* means originally 'craft'; the
craft of music and verse came to be the *cerdd* par
excellence, but smithcraft was on the same level as
bardism as one of the three arts (*tair celfyddyd*) forbidden to villeins: 40.29-34n. The pencerdd is
given an honoured place at the banquet, not as an
officer of the court but as a distinguished visitor,
the leader of a locally-based group of men of the
craft; to the compiler of *Ior* he was probably the recognised head of the bardic order in a considerable
area: see 39.14n. The bards certainly formed an
independent order, older than the 'state' organisation with which the Laws of Court are primarily

372   *The Law of Hywel Dda*

concerned; see 'Pencerdd a Bardd Teilu' (1988) 14
    Ysgrifau Beirniadol 19-46.
pencynydd, 'chief huntsman', 10.14n
penffest aradr, 'plough-head', 195.34
penffestin, 'cap of mail', 193.15
penguwch, 'headcloth', 54.15; 195.27
penhebogydd, 'chief falconer', 5.4n; 10.14n; see *falcon*
penhyddgant, 184.35n
penhygen, 'intestines', 185.30
penlliain, 'headkerchief', 54.12; 195.26
penllwydeg, 'grayling net', 193.33
pennaf, 'most important', In (p.220), 182.1
pennill, 'stall', 172.6n
penny, W. *ceiniog,* (q.v.), passim; see also 144.30-31n; curt
    penny, W. *ceiniog gota,* see *ceiniog;* dirwy penny,
    W. *ceiniog ddirwy* (representing money pay-
    ment?), 144.3-4n; shaft penny, W. *ceiniog baladr,*
    145.2n
pentan, 'firestone', 39.36n; 191.5n; 'home-made', 195.23
penteilu, 'captain of the household' (q.v.), passim; see
    8.37-9.1n
penwaig, 'haddock', 35.21n
perchen, perchennog, 'owner', 25.14; 72.30 etc; 182.27n
perchenogaeth, 'ownership', 162.16
perfedd, 'middle', (n) 85.3; 176.10; (a) 11.4; 99.7; 196.24;
    'medium' (a) 192.34-5
pergyng, 'crane', apparently a device for holding a cauldron
    over the fire, see WLW 213; 45.33, 191.27
periglor, 'parish priest', 46.37 etc.
perjury, W. *anudon,* 65.14-15n
person, W. *dyn,* passim; see pp.xli-xlii
person, 'parson', 41.30n; 81.31
personi, 'make parson', 12.21
pet dog, W. *colwyn,* 181.28n
physician, W. *meddyg,* 7.32-3n; 24.3-25.5n; fee, 197.22n;
    assurance, 24.33n
piben: odyn biben, 'piped kiln', 191.15 etc.
pig, W. *hwch,* pl. *moch,* 122.32n; 203.20-21n,31n; domestic
    pig, W. *hwch tref,* 178.28n; wild pig, W. *hwch
    coed,* 186.1-7n; W. *gwythwch,* 178.27
piglet, W. *porchell,* 164.19; 178.14; autumn piglet, W.
    cnyw hwch, 178.24n
pigling, W. *banw,* 178.18
pigsty, W. *creu moch,* 190.24

Glossary and Index to Notes 373

pillow, W. *gobennydd,* 16.20,21n
pincers, W. *gefel gof,* 194.5
pipe, W. *corn,* 184.29n; piped kiln, W. *odyn biben,* 191.15 etc.
pistlau, 'yoke-bows', 195.36; 202.9-11n
pitfall, 187.7n
plaid, 'board', 204.36-8n; 'party', 64.2 etc.
plaint, W. *cŵyn,* 113.13-16n
plane, W. *cannwyr,* 193.2
plate, W. *clawr,* 193.39n
platter, W. *noe,* 130.26; 131.37; 193.22
plea, W. *arddelw,* (q.v.), 59.15; 70.25; 88.9; 106.23n; 162.9
    etc.
plead, W. *arddelwi,* 78.2; 162.30; W. *ymddywedud (o gyf-raith),* 85.29n
pleading, W. *cyngheusaeth, cynghawsedd* (q.v.), 87.15 etc.
pledge, W. *gwystl,* 85.18,20n; 88.38
plot, standard, W. *tu a thâl,* 91.14n
plough, W. *aradr,* pl. *erydr,* 111.14 etc.; 195.33-8n; W. *gwŷdd,* 202.4n,5; cf. 199.16n
plough-bote acre, W. *cyfair casnad,* 199.16n
plough-frame, W. *gwŷdd,* 126.20, cf. 202.4n
plough-head, W. *penffest aradr,* 195.34
ploughing, day's, W. *cyfair,* 195.33,34; cf. 99.3-9n
ploughman, W. *amaeth,* 6.1 etc.; pl. *emeith,* 202.8: in this
    context the caller (W. *geilwad*) seems to be included.
ploughmanship, W. *amaethiaeth,* 202.3-4
ploughshare, W. *swch,* q.v.
poen, 'penalty', 168.15n
pole, W. *pawl,* 191.6; weather-poles, W. *polion syfagau,*
    191.6-7
polishing-stone, W. *cabolfaen,* 193.21
polled (steer), W. *moel,* 177.20-21n
porch, W. *cynnor, cynordy,* 41.12-15n; 190.27-32n
porchell, 'piglet', 164.19; 178.14
porter, W. *porthor,* 16.35 etc.; 26.10-12n
porth. There are three words *porth* in Welsh, of which *porth*
    (f), 'port, bay', does not occur in the law texts,
    and *porth* (m), 'gate, gateway', 16.35 etc.,
    presents no difficulties. The third *porth* (m),
    'help', (see Ps.cxv. 9,10,11) occurs in a general
    sense, translated 'support', at 85.26, and in a
    technical sense in the recurring expression *oed
    wrth borth,* 'delay for aid', see 77.29-78.4n; the

374   *The Law of Hywel Dda*

meaning of 'aid' is explained at 97.1-2; see also *canllaw*.

porthorddwy, 'aid to violence' 143.17; cf. 150.37n

porthi, 'feed', 15.8 etc.; 'support', 121.31 etc. In today's Welsh the verb is used of feeding livestock, and figuratively of orally expressed approval of sermons and other public utterances.

porthor, 'porter' (i.e. gatekeeper), 16.35 etc.; 26.10-12n

possess, possession, W. *gwarchadw*, 161.3; 162.16

possessor, W. *gwarcheidwad*, 161.9,11

post, 'post', 21.6 etc.; (fig., of body, cf. *column*), 24.21,22n

postponement, W. *annod*, 96.4, see 119.35-6n

pound (for animals), W. *carchar*, 202.26n

power, have, W. *meddu*, 162.1

precinct, W. *cyntedd*, 7.26-8.28n; 9.19 etc.

precious thing, W. *tlws*, 189.2-3n, cf. 37.35-6n

pregnancy, W. *beichiogi*, 129.29; 129.39-130.2n; (of mare) W. *cyfebrwydd*, 171.29

pregnant, W. *beichiog*, 51.5 etc.; become pregnant, make pregnant, W. *beichiogi*, 50.36; 58.18 etc.

prenial, (weaving woman's) 'frame', 193.38

present, (v), W. *lliwo*, 160.8n

price, W. *gwerth*, 159.39

prid, 'purchase', 113.9n. By the fourteenth century, *prid* transactions were used as a means to evade the rule of Welsh law (continued under the Statute of Wales, 1284) against alienation of land beyond the alienor's lifetime: the land was gaged as security for a sum which could in theory be repaid at any time, but in practice was not repaid. See Llinos Beverley Smith, (1977) 27 BBCS 263-77, (1976) 29 Econ HR (second series) 537-50

prido, 'gage', 114.6n

priest, W. *offeiriad*, 41.30n etc.; as tongue-bearer, 61.24n; 62.5-8n; parish priest, W. *periglor*, 18.15; 46.37; priest of the household, W. *offeiriad teilu*, 5.4n etc.

prifai, 'privy thing', 53.9-27n

primary, W. *cysefin*, 82.12

prime, (n), W. *telediwrwydd*, 175.24n etc.; prime ox, W. *eithefig*, 199.11n

prince, W. *tywysog*, 1.2n

principal, (n), W. *llofrudd*, 95.8n; principal debtor, W. *cynnogn*, 63.33 etc.; principal offence, W. *llofrudd-*

Glossary and Index to Notes   375

iaeth, 143.29; 144.9 and see 81.7n; 95.8n; principal
   offender, W. *llofrudd,* 81.7n etc.

priod, priodolder, priodor. The basic word *priod,* from Latin
   privatus, means 'proper to a particular person', and
   gives rise to the noun *priodor,* 'proprietor' for the
   holder of the fullest admissible right to land, and
   priodolder, 'proprietorship', for that right: see 104.
   25-6n; 108.5-9n. The greatest difficulty arises over
   the application of *priod* to *gŵr,* 'man, husband',
   and *gwraig,* 'woman, wife': see 58.11-13n; 107.16n;
   110.28n

priority of occupation, W. *cynwarchadw,* 92.6-7

prison, W. *carchar,* passim; prison of time, W. *carchar
   amser,* 77.25-6

privy thing, W. *prifai,* 53.9-27n

probwyllau, 'stilts' (of plough), 195.35

procedure, II.6n; proof of due following, 97.32-98.7n

proctor, W. *procurator,* 74.33, 75.2

procurator, 'proctor', 74.33; 75.2

proof, II.6n (p.254)

proper, W. *iawn,* see *dyly;* W. *priod,* q.v.

properties, W. *teithi,* 172.16 etc.

proprietor, W. *priodor,* 86.15; 104.25-6n; 108.5-9n etc.; see
   priod

proprietorship, W. *priodolder,* 86.16-17 etc.; see *priod*

prosecute him for perjury, W. *erlid cyfraith anudon arno,*
   65.14-15n; 158.16; see also *erlid*

protection, W. *nawdd,* II.5n (p.253); fee for protection, W.
   gobr gwarchadw, 113.10

provide, W. *diwallu,* 125.35n

provision himself, W. *ymogorio,* 204.11-12n

provisions, W. *bwyllwrw,* 156.34n; 169.11n; stolen provisions , W. *lledrad ymborth,* 167.24

pryf, 'beast', 188.11n

puppy, 181.28n

purchase, W. *prid,* (q.v.), 113.9n

purse, W. *llawgwd,* 46.2n

putain, 'harlot', 60.29

pwn traws, 'cross-load', 175.4

Pwyll, Mabinogi, 186.15n

pwyllog, 'sane', 151.27 etc.

pwys: *gwraig bwys,* 'woman of weight', 46.35-6n

pynfarch, 'packhorse', 124.20; (fig.) 40.35-9n etc.

376 The Law of Hywel Dda

pyrchuyn, (MS.), 'crest', 193.15n
pystl, pl. *pystlau,* 'yoke-bow', 195.36; 202.9-11n

quarter: from quarter to quarter, W. *o bedwareran bwy-gilydd,* 121.38-122.1n; (of carcase) W. *chwarthawr,* 185.28 etc.
Queen, 124.21n
queen-bee, queen-colony, W. *modrydaf,* 183.20-184.21n
quern, W. *breuan,* 45.24; 55.16n; 156.1-3; hand-quern, W. *breuan;* quern-house, W. *breuandy;* quern-shed, W. *breuanfwth,* 194.10-15n
quillet, W. *gardd,* 113.6n; cf. 189.6n
quilt, W. *cynnwgl,* 195.4n,24
quinsy, W. *y fynyglog,* 179.12n
quota, W. *dogn,* passim, alternating with *digon,* 'enough'; in modern Welsh *dogn* is used for 'ration'.

rafters, W. *ceibrau,* 191.7
rail, W. *cledren,* 191.6
rake, W. *cribin,* 193.7
rank: of equal rank, W. *gogyfurdd,* 196.6-7,13-14
rape (n), W. *trais* (q.v.), 167.35-8n etc.; (v) W. *dwyn trais ar,* passim; W. *treisio,* 52.4; see 51.38n; 59.11-18n
reaping-hook, W. *cryman,* 45.34; 192.35-6
receiving, W. *erbyniaid,* 157.2n
reckon land, W. *tir cyfrif;* reckon townland, W. *tref gyfrif,* 100.5n; 114.24n; 122.23n
reconcile, W. *dygymod,* 159.6
reconciliation, W. *cymod,* 148.36
redeem, W. *prynu,* 167.12
red-handed, W. *llofrudd,* 81.7n
red-tongued, W. *tafodrudd,* 143.4-5, see *Ior* 104.4n, p.123
reeds (weaving), W. *peithynnau,* 193.39
refusal, W. *negyddiaeth,* 68.33n
rejected, W. *llysiedig,* 94.27; see *llys*
relatives, W. *ceraint,* 48.14; closest relatives, W. *cyfnes-eifiaid,* 48.17; 60.5-6; W. *rhieni* (q.v.), 150.19-20
release, W. *ellwng,* 158.34; released blood, W. *gwaed ellyngedig,* 197.9
religion, W. *crefydd* (i.e. a religious order), 150.23
religious, (n), W. *creddyfyn* (i.e. member of a religious order), 163.38; religious habit, W. *dillad crefydd,* 164.6
renard, (Fr.), 187.22n
repellent law, W. *cyfraith atgas,* 119.17

Glossary and Index to Notes 377

repudiate, W. *gwrthod, ymwrthod â,* 80.12-29n
resident (n), W. *adlamwr,* 119.23n
restiveness, W. *llwyg,* 172.19. Because 'restive' is so commonly used today as though it were a variant on 'restless', it may be as well to emphasise that a restive horse is one which insists on remaining at rest.
restricted, W. *caeth,* lit. 'captive, enslaved', 97.28-31n
return (v), W. *adferaf* (vn *edfryd,* q.v.), in physical sense (also translated 'repay, restore'), 172.23; 180.23; in technical legal sense, 79.12; 81.34; W. *dedfryd,* 66.30
rhaff, 'rope', 155.34; 193.23,24
rhaffan, 48.22: at *B Bleg* 71.37 translated 'rope-playing', with the note (p.133) 'presumably a game like "Kiss-in-the-ring" in which a rope takes the place of linked arms'.
rhagarnodd, 'beam' (of plough), 195.35
rhaglaw, 'deputy, viceroy', 123.31n
rhaith is the Welsh form of the word which appears in most Indo-European languages, e.g. Irish *recht,* 'law', German *Recht,* 'law, right', English *right.* The Welsh word means 'compurgation' (both in the abstract sense and in that of the body of human compurgators); in *rhaith gwlad,* 'compurgation of country', the meaning approaches 'jury' in the modern sense, for 'Where a compurgation of country is appropriate, it is right for the King to compel compurgators to a relic, to swear with the denier or against him, at their option', *Bleg* 106.22-4. The individual compurgator was *rheithiwr* (which in modern Welsh means 'juror', though 'jury' is *rheithgor,* not *rhaith*).

The true compurgator was called by his principal, and swore in support of him; the classical law distinguished between the designated compurgator (W. *rheithiwr nod,* see 95.20n) and the undesignated compurgator (W. *rheithiwr dinod*). In some cases (e.g. 52.11-15) compurgators were required to have special qualifications; it was a general rule that compurgators should be so nearly related to the principal that they would pay and receive galanas in respect of him: see e.g. 68.11-13.

378   *The Law of Hywel Dda*

Two other derivatives of *rhaith* appear frequently in the law texts. *Cyfraith* is the ordinary word for 'law', most often in the sense of Latin *ius*, French *droit*, and German *Recht*, but occasionally in the sense of *lex*, *loi*, *Gesetz*, for which *deddf* (translated 'rule of law' at 80.9-11n) is preferred in modern Welsh. *Anrhaith*, etymologically 'non-right' is used for the plundering expeditions of the bodyguard, and also for the confiscation of an offender's goods: hence *anrhaithoddef*, 'liable to spoliation', *anrhaith gribddail*, 'extortionate spoliation' (i.e. total confiscation), and the paradoxical *anrheithio o gyfraith*, etymologically 'non-righting by co-right', for 'despoiling by law'. By a different transfer of meaning *anrhaith* comes to be used in medieval Welsh verse for the object of a poet's love.

rhandir, 'shareland', 92.13n; 121.5-6n

rhasgl, 'drawknife', 192.38

rhaw, 'shovel', 192.36; 193.7

rhawn, 'hair of (horse's) tail', 172.38 etc.

rheithiwr, 'compurgator, member of rhaith', see *rhaith*

rhidyll, 'riddle,' 45.22; 193.20

rhieni, 'family', 147.37; 'closest relatives', 150.19-20: in modern Welsh *rhieni* means 'parents', but the medieval meaning was less definite: where translated 'closest relatives' it approximates to the meaning of *gwely*, for which see 147.11n; 'ancestors', 101.20-23n

rhingyll, 'serjeant', 34.6-35.13n; 46.38-47.4n; 85.4,9,16

rhisgen, 'butter vessel', 193.9n

rhodd ac estyn, 'gift and transfer', 54.36n; 'grant and investiture', 102.3-5n; 110.33-4n

rhoddiaid, 'bestowers', 45.3-4n etc.

rhuddeli, 'red ointment', 197.25

rhuwch, 'cloak', 195.30,31

rhwmp, 'drill', 192.34-5n

rhwnsi, 'rouncey', 172.9-10n

rhwyd, 'net' (fig.), 40.4,8,11

rhwyll, 'cresset', 169.11n; pl. *rhwyllau*, 'harnesses', (weaving), 194.1

rhwymo, 'tie' (animals), 207.22,23

rhychwant, (MS. *ry6hant*), 'span', 182.29

rhyddid, 'immunity', 91.17n

rhynion, 'groats', 128.32

Glossary and Index to Notes 379

rickyard, W. *ydlan*, 204.8
riddle, W. *rhidyll*, 45.22; 193.20
right: it is right, see *dyly*; special right, W. *braint*, 46.19-20n; cf. 61.3-9n; right (n), W. *dylyed*, 32.23n, and see *dyly*
ring, W. *modrwy*, passim; little rings, W. *torchau bychain*, 202.9-11n
rob, W. *treisio*, 167.36
robbery, W. *trais*, 167.35-8n etc.
robe, W. *ysgin*, 195.27,28
rod, W. *gwialen*, 99.5 etc.
roe, W. *iwrch, iyrchell*, 187.9,11-12n
roebuck, W. *iwrch, caeriwrch*, 187.8,11-12n
Roman law, 94.15n; 95.35; 145.4-7n; 161.22-3n
roof, W. *nen*, 190.14,16,20,21; W. *to* (q.v.), 191.9
roof-fork, W. *nenfforch*, 189.34
roof-tree, W. *nenbren*, 189.33; 190.25-7
rope, W. *rhaff*, 155.34; 193.23,24
rotten dung, W. *brandail*, 113.21
rough (land), W. *gŵydd*, 200.34n
rouncey, W. *rhwnsi*, 172.9-10n
rout, W. *cyrch*, 150.30-31n
ruler (measurer), W. *llywiadur*, 193.8

saddle-cloth, W. *panel*, 195.4-5
saethebol, 'darting colt', 206.29-30n
said, 'blade', 194.18-19n
saig, 'dish' (of food), 9.15 etc.; 'mess', 6.26; 14.31
St Bride's Day, W. *Gŵyl Sanffraid* (1 February), 83.36-84.1; 202.22,23
St Curig's Day, W. *Gŵyl Gurig* (16 June), 176.6,7; 184.38
St John's Day, W. *Gŵyl Ieuan* (a) Nativity (24 June), 22.7,15 etc.; (b) Decollation (29 August), 178.19n etc.
St Mary, first feast of, (Assumption, 15 August), 206.22-3
St Patrick's Day, W. *Gŵyl Badrig* (17 March), 177.8; 206.34
sale thief, W. *lleidr gwerth* (q.v.), 62.31n; 159.39n; 166.1n,3
same: of the same growth, W. *untwf*, 188.18-19n
sanctuary, W. *nawdd, noddfa*, II.5n (pp.253-4)
sane, W. *pwyllog*, 151.27
sapel, 'chapel', 12.22; 41.26-7n
sarhaed is the medieval form of the abstract noun from *sarhau*, 'to insult': it is used in preference to the modern form *sarhad* (and the baseless form *saraad* of the translation in AL) because it has a technical

sense in law; it corresponds to the Irish *sarugud*, see WLW 216. Its primary legal sense is similar to that of the Roman-law *iniuria*, which 'embraced any contumelious disregard of another's rights or personality' (Nicholas, *Introduction to Roman Law* (Oxford, 1962), 215-16): *iniuria* appears in the Latin texts for *sarhaed*. The word has the secondary meaning of the compensation payable, which varies according to the status of the victim and is the usual measure of status. For ordinary males, sarhaed is related to galanas as 1:15¾, for the royal 'members' as 1:3, 144.15-16n; for women, galanas always depended on status by birth, but the sarhaed of a married woman followed her husband's: 47.10-12. See 5.30-6.2n; 52.1-2n.

Sarre, 120.6-21n

saw, W. *serr*, 193.2

scab, W. *clafr*, *clefri*, 177.8,10

scenting-hound, W. *bytheiad*, 182.13n

scholar, W. *ysgolhaig*, 76.5n

scraper, W. *crafell*, 37.24; W. *crefenllyn*, 193.6

screen, W. *celfi*, 7.26-8.28n

scrub land, W. *tir gŵydd*, 113.24, and see *gŵydd*

scrub oak, W. *cegin dderwen*, 188.24n

seal, W. *insail*, 12.3; 29.1

season (v), W. *ardymheru*, 26.36n; 27.6-7; (n) W. *tymor*, passim

seat, W. *eisteddfa*, 142.29

secured cattle, W. *gwartheg difach*, 134.8-9n; see 58.8-9n

segur, 'idle', 186.15n,23

selion, W. *grwn*, 120.28-9n

senedd, 'synod', 11.33; 29.9; 168.13

senior, W. *hynaf*, 84.32-3n

separate: separate men, W. *neillwyr*, 192.2

serjeant, W. *rhingyll*, 34.6-35.13n; 46.38-47.4n; 85.4,9,16

serr, 'saw', 193.2

service, W. *gwasanaeth*, passim; 12.13n

servient, W. *gweinyddol*, *gwenigol*, 55.16n; 56.37; 118.30n; 156.1-3

sessions, W. *dadlau*, 123.3-4n etc.

sewin (i.e. sea-trout), W. *gleisiad*, 193.35; sewin net, W. *gleisiadeg*, 193.33

shaft penny, W. *ceiniog baladr*, 145.2n

shareland, W. *rhandir*, 92.13n; 121.5-6n

Glossary and Index to Notes   381

sharing, W. *gwaddol,* 160.26n; W. *cyfran, rhannu,* passim
shears, W. *gwellau,* 192.36
sheepcote, W. *cail,* 190.23
sheet, baking, W. *clawr pobi,* 193.22
shelter, W. *gwasgawd, gwasgawdwydd,* 189.4,6
shield, W. *tarian,* 194.23; use in assessing size of bone,
　　197.32-7n
shieling-land, W. *hafotir,* 121.10-11
shingles, roof of, W. *peithyndo,* 170.23
Shoreham, W. *Soram,* 120.6-21n
short-yoked oxen, W. *beriewys,* III.9n; 200.22; cf. 199.11n
shovel, W. *rhaw,* 192.36; 193.7
shriek, W. *diasbad;* see *Diasbad uwch Annwfn,* 104.33n
sick, W. *claf,* 71.3n
side-posts, W. *tubyst,* 190.30
sieve, W. *gogr,* 45.23; 54.16; 193.20; see also 204.11n
silvered, W. *ariannaid,* 193.16; 194.32
single, (of woman), W. *gweddw* (q.v.), 47.12; 156.26; single-
　　bound (oats), W. *unrhwym,* 128.11-12n
skein-winder, W. *cengladur,* 193.5
skiff, W. *ysgraff,* 193.12
skilled, W. *cyfrwys,* 181.17,21
skin, (of animal): value, 188.1-9n; value relative to meat,
　　177.25-178.3n; cattle skins of the dung maer,
　　33.29-30n
slave, W. *caeth,* passim, 166.1n; see also *servient;* slave
　　blood, W. *gwaed caeth,* 198.14n
sledge-hammer, W. *ordd,* 194.5
sleephouse, W. *hundy,* 41.12-15n; 125.4-7n
smock, W. *pais,* 34.22; 51.11; 155.34
snare, W. *annel,* 187.7n
Snowdon, 132.29n
social horn, 40.14-19n
sofl, 'stubble', 209.12
son, W. *mab,* q.v.
Soram, 'Shoreham', 120.6-21n
sounding horn, W. *corn canu,* 195.17; cf. 40.14-19n
sovereign tribute, W. *mechdeyrn ddylyed,* 154.25n
Sovereignty of Britain, W. *Unbeiniaeth Prydain,* 20.23-4n
sow, W. *hwch,* q.v.
span, W. *rhychwant,* 182.29
spancel: cow spancel, W. *burwy,* 193.8
spaniel, 181.28n
sparrowhawk, W. *llamysten,* see *falcon*

382 *The Law of Hywel Dda*

spatula, W. *ysbodol,* 193.6

spear, W. *gwayw,* 194.16

special, W. *arbennig;* special beast, W. *llwdn arbennig,* 203.31n; special feast, W. *gŵyl arbennig,* 28.12-13n; 76.18-19 (defn), etc.; special right, W. *braint,* 46.19-20n

spindle, W. *gwerthyd,* 193.5

spinning wheels, W. *troellau,* 194.2n

spoil, (n), W. *anrhaith,* q.v.; (v) W. *difwyno,* 144.37; 166.11

spoliation, W. *anrhaith,* q.v.; extortionate spoliation, W. *anrhaith gribddail,* 159.19

spring, end of, 13.34-7n

springe, W. *croglath,* 187.7n

stable, W. *marchdy, ystabl,* 41.12-15n

stack, W. *tas,* 209.13; turn his back on the stack, W. *ymchwelyd ei gefn ar y das,* 101.26

stag, W. *carw,* 22.16 etc.

staggers, W. *ehegyr,* 172.17

staghound, W. *gellgi,* 181.17n

stall, W. *pennill,* 172.6n, see *Ior* 121.11n at p.126

stallion, W. *ystalwyn,* 172.13; see also *amws, march*

standard-bearer, office of, W. *llumaniaeth, llumenyddiaeth,* 92.10-11n

standard plot, W. *tu a thâl,* 91.14n

starting horn, W. *corn cychwyn,* 192.9n

State, growing strength of, 102.3-5n; 110.33-4n; (prince) 185.19n

status, W. *braint,* 46.19-20n; 107.32n; 208.11n. At 107.10 the correct Latin plural *status* is used, as less repulsive than any alternative.

status joints, W. *golwython breiniol,* 184.26-7n, 35n,37

status of land, 113.9n

status toft, W. *tyddyn breiniol,* see *toft*

stay, W. *argae,* 54.18; 127.17n; 197.11-16n

stên, 'cruse' (q.v.), 193.13

stealth, W. *lladrad,* 166.18n; 169.17n

steward, W. *distain* (q.v.), 5.4 etc.; W. *ystiwart,* 33.15n

Stiefel (Germ.), 195.8n

stilts (of plough), W. *probwyllau,* 195.35

stirrup, W. *gwarthafl,* 37.35-6n; 194.35,37; 195.1n

stock (livestock), W. *ysgrubl,* 177.16 etc.; (family origin), W. *cyff,* 104.11 etc.; W. *bonedd,* 110.22; stock inquiry, W. *cyfarch cyffyll,* 145.25n

Glossary and Index to Notes 383

stolen property, W. *lladrad,* 157.4

stone, Lord as, 70.1-2n; polishing, W. *cabolfaen,* 193.21

stool, W. *ystôl,* 193.36

strait, W. *ing,* 134.23-4n

strangles, W. *du ysgyfaint,* 172.18; W. *hualog,* 179.12n

straw, W. *celefryd* (treated by GPC as a variant on *calafrwd,*
    which is analysed as *calaf,* 'stalks' + *rhwd,* 'rust',
    i.e. 'dirty worthless straw'), 209.27

stubble, W. *sofl,* 209.12

stud, W. *allwest,* 40.4n; W. *gre,* 40.8; 173.34;
    stud mare, W. *caseg rewys,* 173.32

submit, (to law), W. *ymroddi,* 164.3 etc.

substitute, W. *arwystl* (q.v.), 63.13; 73.4

suder, 'horse-cloth', 195.4

sufferance, son by, W. *mab dioddef,* 134.15-16,19,24

summer, months of Welsh, 13.34-7n

summer house, W. *hafdy,* 190.22-4n,35,36

sumpter horse, W. *swmerfarch,* 172.9-10n

superannuated claim, W. *hawl tra blwyddyn,* 97.21 etc.

supervise, W. *gwarchadw,* 33.14

supper money, W. *arian y gwynos,* 14.11-25; 123.36-7n;
    129.19n

supply, W. *diwallu,* 125.35n

support (n), W. *porth,* 85.26; (v) W. *porthi,* 121.31 etc.;
    support end of yoke, W. *cynnal pen yr iau,* 199.36-7n

surclaim, W. *arhawl,* 112.2; 170.18-19n etc.

surety, W. *mach,* 59.31n; II.4n; 72.36-73.15n; surety to
    abide law, 77.29-78.4n

surreption, W. *anghyfarch,* 161.27n; 166.21-2; 170.14-16n

suzerain, W. *arbennig,* 164.24; see 203.31n

sward, W. *gwellt,* 176.37,38; 202.1; prime sward-ox, W.
    eithefig y gwellt, 199.12

swarm, W. *haid, bydaf,* 124.17n; 183.20-184.21n; clustered
    swarm, W. *bydaf,* 183.20-184.21n

swear to, (property or its value), W. *damdwng,* (q.v.), 161.7
    etc.

swch: tir swch a chwlltwr, 'arable land', 114.24n

swllt, 'treasure', 40.2n; 169.6n

swmerfarch, 'sumpter horse', 172.9-10n

sworn appraisal, W. *damdwng,* (q.v.), 164.22-8 etc.

syfagau: polion syfagau, 'weather poles', 191.6-7

synod, W. *senedd,* 11.33; 29.9; 168.13

384 *The Law of Hywel Dda*

taeoctref, 'villein townland', 41.11n etc.; see *aillt*

taeog, 'villein', 41.11n; 50.27-32n; 55.6n; 100.5n; see *aillt*

tafodiog, 'tongued one', 49.2; II.2n (p.246); 95.35-96.2n

tafodrudd, 'red-tongued', 143.4-5

tafol, 'dock-leaves', 179.34

tail, W. *llosgwrn,* 49.28; 175.26 etc.; flesh of (horse's), W. *coloren,* 172.38 etc.; hair of (horse's), W. *rhawn,* 172.38 etc.

take (animals on corn), W. *dala,* 202.20 etc.; (witnesses) W. *mwynhau,* 92.36 etc.;
take charge of, W. *gwarchadw,* 21.11; 25.11

talbren, 'backlog', 39.36n

talfeinciau, 'end-benches', 190.27-8

talgudyn, 'forelock', 173.6 etc.

tame: tame catches wild, 205.36-7n; tamed animal, W. *lledfegin* (q.v.), 187.26-34

taradr, 'auger', 192.34-5n; *twll taradr,* 'auger hole', 190.34n

tarian, 'shield', 194.23

tarwhaid, 'bull-swarm', 183.27-9; cf. Ir. *tarbsaithe,* Breton *tarvhed,* see *Bechbretha* (183.20-184.21n, p.292 above) 116.17

tas, 'stack', 209.13; *ymchwelyd ei gefn ar y das,* 'turn his back on the stack', 101.26

tawlbord, tawlbwrdd, 'throwboard', (q.v.), 16.26 etc.

team, W. *gwedd,* 201.3; long team, W. *hirwedd,* III.9n

teddf, 'socket', 37.35-6n

teilu, 'bodyguard, household', see *household*

teiluwriaeth, 'the activity of the bodyguard', see *household*

teisban, 'blanket', 195.25

teithi, 'characteristicts', 65.19-20; 'properties' 172.16 etc.: if anything was to be a true specimen of its kind for legal purposes, it must show the *teithi* of that kind.

telediw, 'of full value', 63.14-15n; *telediwrwydd,* 'prime', 175.24n

Telitor wedi halog lw, 205.21-2n

tenllif, 'mixed fabric', 34.22n

tent (medication), W. *goreth,* 197.24

terwenydd, 'bulling', 206.22-4

Test Book, W. *Llyfr Prawf,* IIIn (p.274)

testifier, W. *tyst,* (q.v.), 57.23 etc.

testimony, dead, W. *marwdystiolaeth,* 98.8 etc.

tether (v), W. *tido,* 205.32

teyrn, 'monarch', 38.24; 112.23,24n

Glossary and Index to Notes 385

thatch, W. *to* (q.v.), 204.16

    thatch-spar, W. *aseth*, 191.8n

theft, W. *lladrad, lledrad*, 166.18n; claim of theft, 77.3n; rights to profit of, 101.2n

thickset hedges, W. *gwyddwaledd*, 97.19

thief, W. *lleidr*, passim; see also *sale thief*; triads on thieves, 167.25-6n

third man, W. *trydygwr*, 91.38; 108.11,13

third person, W. *trydydyn*, 58.5

thong: guiding thong, W. *llywgroen*, 193.8; thonged shoes, W. *esgidiau careiog*, 195.9

thorn-hurdle, W. *draenglwŷd*, 195.38n

thrave, W. *drefa*, 195.13,14n

three nights, 50.11n

threshold, W. *trothwy, trothau*, 39.36; 190.29

throne, W. *gorsedd*, 164.11n

throwboard, W. *tawlbord, tawlbwrdd*, 16.26 etc. The translation assumes that the first syllable comes from W. *taflu*, 'to throw', though it has been argued that it is from Lat. *talus*, 'a die': see *Ior* p.129. The article has often been explained as a chequer-board serving the purpose of an abacus, like the cloth which gave its name to the English Exchequer: see *Dialogus de Scaccario* (ed. C. Johnson, Edinburgh, 1950) xxxv-xxxvi; in the light of the values set out in 191.33-192.7, however, it seems clear that the name is applied to the apparatus for a board game of the 'hunt' type: see F. R. Lewis, 'Gwerin Ffristial a Thawlbwrdd', [1941] *Tr. Cym.* 185-205. Since sworn appraisal is provided for the 'throwboard board' (W. *clawr tawlbwrdd*, 193.16-17) and the pieces make up the whole legal value of the King's throwboard, it must be taken that it was the pieces which were of the materials named: it is much easier to believe in pieces (comparable with chessmen) carved from a hart's antler than in a board made of that material. See also *gwerin*.

thumb, W. *bawd*; in measurement of inch, 176.12-13n

tido, 'tether', 205.32

tie, W. *rhwymo*, 207.22,23

tiercel, W. *hwyedydd*, see *falcon*

tiles, W. *tyglys*, 170.23

tillage: tillage and ploughing, W. *âr ac aredig*, 101.19n;

386   The Law of Hywel Dda

spring tillage, W. *gwanhwynar,* 122.34; winter
tillage, W. *gaeafar,* 122.34

tilth, W. *âr,* 200.30; 209.9; spring tilth, W. *gwanhwynar,*
202.24; winter tilth, W. *gaeafar,* 202.26

timber, W. *pren,* 189.32; big timber, W. *pren bras,* 191.2;
made of a single·timber, W. *un pren,* 192.23

time, full (of pregnant woman), W. *llawfaeth* (q.v.), 137.21

tin: of tin, W. *ystaenaid,* 194.31 etc.

tir, 'land', passim; 'land' (sc. selion), 120.28-9n;
   tir a daear, 'land and earth' (esp. as object of legal
      rights), passim;
   tir corflan, 'hamlet land', 113.5, and see II.5n; 82.22n
   tir cyfrif, 'reckon land', 100.5n; 114.24n; 122.23n
   tir cyllidus, 'geldable land', 100.5n
   tir cynnif, 'acquired land', 92.22n
   tir gwelyog, 'gwely land', 100.5n
   tir gŵydd, 'scrub land', 113.24
   tir swch a chwlltwr, 'arable land', 114.24n

tirdra, 'land-feud', 94.22; 110.35-6n; cf. 143.2n

tlws, pl. *tlysau,* 'precious thing, trinket'. *Tlws* has the
broad sense of something precious, and it is therefore translated 'precious thing' at 192.11 and in the
triad *Tri Thlws Cenedl* (189.2-3n; cf. 37.35-6n). In
modern Welsh the noun is used as a general term
for 'trophy' (in the sense of prize in any kind of
competition), while the adjective means 'pretty'.
'Trinket' is a traditional translation for the precious things given to the justice and others; the 'idle
trinkets' (W. *oferdlysau*) were presumably so
called because they had no relation to the recipient's functions. For 'interchangeable trinkets',
see 76.28n

toft, W. *tyddyn.* Etymologically *tyddyn* implies a plot of
land carrying a house (*tŷ*), and 'toft' is used as a
rough equivalent, though some passages suggest
that the *tyddyn* did not necessarily have buildings
on it; perhaps the essential feature of the tyddyn
was that the land was enclosed, for it is clear from
references in III.10 that most land would not be
permanently fenced. The 'status toft' (W. *tyddyn
breiniol*) would no doubt be the parcel directly
occupied by the previous holder; it corresponds to
the 'special croft' (W. *eisyddyn arbennig*) of 99.24;
see 99.18n, which deals with distribution of hold-

Glossary and Index to Notes   387

ings on succession. It is not intended to imply that
the Welsh names have exactly the same force as
the English: the latter are used for convenience as
rough equivalents.

tomdy, 'manure-shed', 193.30n

tongs, W. *gefel*, 193.9

tongue, value of, 196.14-15n

tongued one, W. *tafodiog*, 49.2; II.2n; 95.35-96.2n

torch, 'collar', 173.9; 181.21n etc.; *torchau bychain*, 'little
rings', 202.9-11n

torri, 'break, cut', passim; 'dissolve', 80.12-29n

townland, W. *tref*, passim. In modern Welsh *tref* means
'town'; the medieval sense (which is reflected in
many farm names in some parts of Wales) corresponds to the medieval Latin *villa*, and is least mis-
leadingly rendered by 'townland'.

town-made, W. *dinesig*, 195.21,22

tracker dog, W. *olrhead*, 193.28-9

traffic, (v), W. *trafnidro*, 200.4n

trafnidro, 'traffic', 200.4n

trais, 167.35-8n; 'rape', 107.31 etc.; 'robbery', 166.22;
167.35-8n; 'violence', 144.5 etc.; *dwyn trais ar*,
'rape' (v), 51.24 etc.

trawsgainc, 'cross-branch', 188.19n

trawstyle, 'cross-bed', 45.32n

tread, W. *cwcwyo*, 181.8; 183.15

treadles, W. *troedlasau*, 194.2

treasure, W. *swllt*, 40.2n; 169.6n; W. *tryzor*, (q.v.), 19.28

tree, W. *pren*, passim; (collective), W. *gŵydd*, 189.11;
minor trees, W. *manwydd*, 189.9

tref, 'townland', q.v.; *tref gyfrif*, 'reckon townland', 100.5n;
114.24n; *tref tad*, 'patrimony', passim

trefgordd, 'hamlet', 62.22; 170.21,23; 205.17

trefn: *trefnau*, 'buildings', 99.25n; *trefn fechan*, 'latrine',
41.12-15n

treftadog, 'patrimonial', 92.1 etc.

treigledig, 'interchangeable', 76.28n

treisio, 'despoil', 110.10,12; 'rape', 52.4; 'rob', 167.36

trespass, cattle, III.10n (p.305)

triads: Three Accusations of a Woman, W. *Tair Enllib
Gwraig*, 57.25-9n

Three Names of the Serjeant, W. *Tri Enw Rhingyll*,
34.6-35.13n

388 *The Law of Hywel Dda*

Three Powerful Ones of the World, W. *Tri Chadarn Byd*, 70.1-2n

Tri Chyhyryn Canastr, 160.27n

tribute, W. *mâl*, 120.23; sovereign tribute, W. *mechdeyrn ddylyed*, 154.25n

trinket, W. *tlws*, q.v.

trivet, W. *trybedd*, 193.11

troediog, 'footholder', 33.11n

troedlasau, 'treadles', 194.2

troellau, 'wheels, spinning wheels', 194.2n

troorydd, 'vice', 194.3-9n

trostrau, 'beams', 191.4

trothau, trothwy, 'threshold', 39.36n; 190.29

trouble, W. *gofud* (mod. *gofid*), 74.25

trough, W. *cafn*, 39.36; W. *mennai*, 192.27; foot-trough, W. *cafn traed*, 192.28; wort-trough, W. *brecicafn*, 193.37

trumpet: claim of trumpet, W. *hawl utgorn*, 77.3n

trunk, W. *cyff*, 197.1,2

trwyddew, 'awl', 39.36n; 193.1

trybedd, 'trivet', 193.11

trydydyn, 'third person', 58.5; 'one of three persons', 7.5 etc.

trydygwr, 'third man', 91.38 etc.

trydywaith, 'working for the third time', 176.25

trythgwd, 'luxury bag', 46.2n

tryzor, 'treasure', 19.28: the form with z for the s of later Welsh suggests borrowing from French. The word does not occur in *Cyfn* or *Bleg.*

tu a thâl, 'standard plot', 91.14n

tubyst, 'side-posts', 190.30

tuddedyn, 'garment', 195.23

tun, W. *tunnell*, 193.12

tuning-horn, W. *cyweirgorn* (q.v.), 40.23,24; 191.30,31

turf, W. *tywyrch*, 170.20-24

turning-lathe, W. *turnen*, 193.5

twin-forked, W. *dwygainc*, 188.16-17n

twisting-frame, W. *ystyllawd dirwyn*, 193.5-6

twll taradr, 'auger hole', 190.34n

twnc, 21.16 etc., 123.36-7n

twrf ac eniwed, 'violence and harm', 106.37n; 111.13-29

tŷ, 'house', passim; *tŷ bychan*, 'latrine', 41.12-15n

Tŷ Gwyn ar Daf yn Nyfed, 'Whitland', Pr.n; *hen lyfr y Tŷ Gwyn*, 94.1-25n; 141.30n

tyddyn, 'toft', q.v.

Glossary and Index to Notes 389

tyglys, 'tiles', 170.23

tying-post, W. *buddelw*, 201.3

tyllwedd, 'assurance', 24.33n; 'concord', 85.21,22; 148.37; 149.5

tymor, 'season', passim

tyst, 'attestor, testifier'. In modern Welsh *tyst* (from Lat. *testis*) is the ordinary word for 'witness', and gives the verb *tystio*, 'to testify'. Classical Welsh law knew three kinds of testifier, see 86.27n; and in the texts *tyst* is used in two senses: (*a*) the narrow sense 'attestor', i.e. the attesting witness who is specially called to witness a specific transaction; (*b*) the wide sense 'testifier', which includes the attestor, the maintainer (W. *ceidwad*), who testifies to a particular state of affairs, and the knower (W. *gwybyddiad*), who testifies to an event from his own knowledge.

    tystion deddfol, 'legal witnesses', 83.16-17n

tystio, 'attest', 13.28; 65.25; 'call to witness', 96.26-7; 'testify', 49.16

tywyrch, 'turf', 170.20-24n

tywysog, 'prince', 1.2n

uchelfar, 188.18-19n

uchelwr, passim; the word is apparently an exact synonym for *breyr* (q.v.), but is used in modern Welsh for a member of the nobility or squirearchy, and this meaning tends to be read back into the lawbooks (with some support from the *nobilis* and *optimas* of the Latin texts). Though in practice there were certainly economic differences between one uchelwr and another, in legal theory all had the same status. See also 50.27-32n.

uffarnau, 'ankles', 34.20n

Unbeiniaeth Prydain, 'The Sovereignty of Britain', 20.23-4n

unclaimable thing, W. *anghyfarch*, 61.3,7; see 61.3-9n

unclean (animal), W. *budr*, 180.27; 186.4

uncouth, W. *anwar*, 41.1; 47.2; see 46.38-47.4n

unddyddiog, 'for a fixed day', 70.21-2n; 'on a single day', 84.1,4

under-thatch, W. *achwre*, 160.34; 191.9-11n; 204.17

undesignated (compurgator, man), W. *dinod*, see *rhaith* and 95.20n

390   *The Law of Hywel Dda*

unfamiliar to each other, W. *anghynefin,* 207.25
unhobble, W. *disgyfreitho,* 202.30-35n
unobjectionable, W. *dilys,* q.v., see also *llys*
unrestricted, W. *disgyfrith,* 202.32
unrhwym, 'single-bound', 128.11-12n
unskilled, W. *anghyfrwys,* 142.4; 181.18,22
untwf, 'of the same growth', 188.18-19n
uprooted (hairs), W. *bonwyn,* 198.7n
use (v), W. *defnyddio,* 14.7; 110.8n; 122.25n; 185.29; W.
     mwynhau (q.v.), 63.18; (n), W. *mwyniant,* 63.12
utgorn, 'trumpet', 77.3n

valid, W. *dilys,* q.v.
validity, W. *dilysrwydd,* q.v.; validity of title and
     transfer, 72.36-73.15n
value, W. *gwerth,* q.v.; of full value, W. *telediw,* 63.14-15n
vat, W. *cerwyn,* 23.26; 126.13; 192.21-4 etc.
vespers, W. *gosber,* 185.23
vessel, W. *llestr,* passim; butter vessel, W. *rhisgen,* 193.9n
vice, W. *troorydd,* 194.3-9n
villein, W. *bilain,* 15.10; 41.13; W. *taeog,* 39.37; 41.11n;
     50.27-32n etc.;
     villein land, status of, 7.20; 113.9n
     villein townland, W. *bileindref,* 7.20n; 41.10,11n;
         125.9; W. *taeoctref,* 41.11n; 199.18-20n etc.
vindicate, W. *diheuro,* 49.24,30n; 60.6 etc.
violence, W. *gorddwy,* 150.37n; W. *trais,* 77.3n; 144.5;
     167.35-8n
     aid to violence, W. *porthorddwy,* 143.17
     violence and harm, W. *twrf ac eniwed,* 106.37n;
         111.13-29
virginity, maiden as tongued one, 48.36-49.4; 62.16-21n
vouch, W. *arddelwi,* 163.12-13n; see *arddelw*
vouchee, W. *arwaesaf* (q.v.), 96.4; 119.23n
voucher to warranty, W. *arwaesaf,* q.v.
voluntarily, W. *o'i fodd,* 202.13; cf. 60.33n
vow, W. *gofuned,* 80.13 etc.

warrant, (v), W. *arwaesaf,* 162.31 etc.; W. *bod y dan,*
     172.25
warrantor, W. *arwaesaf* (q.v.), 73.5,6; 162.31; 163.12-13n;
     33n; cf. *vouchee*

Glossary and Index to Notes 391

warranty, W. *arddelw* (q.v.), 86.29,37; 106.18; W. *arwaesaf* (q.v.), *arwasogaeth*, 164.12; see also *vouchee*

waste, W. *diffaith*, 40.36; 114.16; 121.10; 122.24; (fig.) 41.16; 56.10; 101.11

wattling-rod, W. *bangor*, 204.36-8n

wax, right to, 23.29-31n; 186.7-8n

wayfarer, W. *fforddol*, 186.25,31

weak, W. *gwan*, 167.16n

wealth, W. *meddiant*, 159.25; in the light of 162.1n, *meddiant* could perhaps be here translated 'power'.

weather poles, W. *polion syfagau*, 191.6-7

web, W. *gwe*, 170.36

wedded, W. *priod*, (q.v.), 107.16n; 110.28n; 167.25-6n

wedding celebration, W. *neithior*, 39.1n

wedding-guests, W. *neithiorwyr*, 39.1n; 49.4,15

weeding-hook, W. *chwynnogl*, 193.4

weir, W. *cored*, 112.19; 113.1; 124.16

whalebone, W. *asgwrn morfil*, 16.26; 192.18

wheels, (spinning?), W. *troellau*, 194.2n; (plough), W. *olwynau*, 195.35

whetstone, W. *agalaen*, 195.12

White House (Whitland), Pr.n; Book of the White House, 94.1-25n; 141.30n

white-bladed, W. *gwynsaid*, 194.18-19n

Whitsun, one of the three special feasts, 76.19

wicket, W. *gwyched*, 16.37n

wife, W. *gwraig*, q.v.; cf. *woman*; rights on separation, 34.30n; 45.21n; wedded wife, W. *gwraig briod*, 110.28n; cf. 58.11-13n

wild, W. *gŵydd* (q.v.), 200.34n; W. *gwyllt* passim
wild animal, W. *anifail gwyllt*, 189.40; W. *gwydd-lwdn*, 187.33
wild beast, W. *bwystfil gwyllt*, 187.32
wild horse, W. *march gwyllt*, 172.11
wild pig, W. *gwythwch*, 178.27; W. *hwch coed*, 186.1-7n
wild taken by tame, 205.36-7n

will, W. *ewyllys*, 59.6; (of God), 71.36; of his own will, W. *o'i fodd*, 201.22-3; free will, W. *ewyllys*, 200.27; 206.17

windfall, W. *dofod*, 189.37n

wing-swarm, W. *asgellhaid*, 183.31,34; 184.18

winnowing-sheet, W. *nithlen*, 192.25

winter house, W. *gaeafdy*, 40.12n; 190.27,31

392   The Law of Hywel Dda

Winter Kalends, W. *Calan Gaeaf*, 22.24-5n etc. *Calan Gaeaf* now falls on 13 November, i.e. 1 November (Old Style).

winter tillage, tilth, W. *gaeafar*, 122.34; 202.21

wise ones, W. *doethion*, 190.4-5n

withe, W. *gwialen*, 204.8; W. *gwdyn*, 202.10

witness: legal witnesses, W. *tystion deddfol*, 83.16-17n; see also *tyst;* for classes of witness see *tyst* and 86.27n

woman, W. *gwraig* (q.v.), as contrasted with man (W. *gŵr*) and with virgin (W. *gwyryf*) or maiden (W. *morwyn);* married woman, W. *gwraig wriog*, 47.10 etc., but see 147.38n; woman of weight, W. *gwraig bwys*, 46.35-6n

woman-feud, W. *gwreictra*, 94.22n

woodlander (owner of woodland), W. *coedwr*, 189.33

woodman, W. *coedwr*, 113.36; 155.33-5n; slave as, 155.33-5n

woodwork, W. *gwŷdd*, 194.12; 199.16n

woollen clothing, W. *brethynwisg*, 5.14-15n etc.

word, W. *gair;* final word, 61.32n; word of inquiry, W. *gair cyfarch*, 87.34n

working: first working, W. *cynwaith*, 176.29; working age, W. *oed gweini*, 175.1; working for the third time, W. *trydywaith*, 176.25; working horse, W. *gweinyddfarch*, 172.2,10

worth, W. *gwerth:* this translation is reserved for *gwerth* when used as a synonym for *galanas* in the sense of the compensation for killing the person concerned. For a slave the payment made to the owner is *gwerth*, 'value', like that for an animal: 'he has no galanas, but his value is paid to his owner like the value of a beast': J 89.34-5

wort-trough, W. *brecicafn*, 193.37

wound (n), W. *gweli*, passim; (v), W. *archolli*, 197.20,21 dangerous wound, W. *gweli arberygl*, 10.35; W. *arberygl*, 24.18n; 197.17 wounded man, W. *archolledig*, 24.34; wounded person, W. *dyn archolledig*, 24.12

wrlys, 'edgings', 41.19n; cf. 188.13n

wynebwerth, lit. 'face-value', *wynebwarth*, lit. 'face-shame': both forms occur in the manuscripts, but *wynebwerth* has been uniformly used in the translation. At 26.8 *wynebwerth* seems to be no more than a variant on *sarhaed*, but in the Law of

Glossary and Index to Notes   393

Women *wynebwerth* is reserved for the compensation for sexual misbehaviour within marriage; see WLW 220 and 46.23-6n, 51.38n.

yarn, balls of, W. *pellennau,* 170.36
ydlan, 'rickyard', 204.8
yearling, W. *dynawed,* 176.19; dry yearling (goat), W. *hesbin,* 180.10
yew, W. *ywen,* 189.7,12; holy yew, W. *ywen sant,* 189.13-14n; woodland yew, W. *ywen coed,* 189.14
ymborth, 'provisions', 167.24
ymdaeru, 'argument', 205.7
ymddiheuro, 'acquit himself', 118.14; see also *diheuro*
ymddywedud, 'plead', 85.29n
ymogorio, 'provision himself', 204.11-12; see also *gogor*
ymroddi, 'submit', 164.3 etc.
ymryson, see *amryson*
ymwrthod â, 'repudiate', 80.12-29n
ymwrthryn, 'contention', 105.4,5,6
ymyrru, 'intervene', 123.23; 135.28
ynad, 'justice'; *ynad cwmwd,* 'commote justice'; *ynad llys,* 'court justice', 5.4-5n. Because *Ynad Heddwch* is used in modern Welsh for 'Justice of the Peace', so that *llys ynadon* means 'magistrates' court', *ynad* has been translated 'justice', in order to make clear the difference between this word and *brawdwr,* 'judge'. Since *brawd* (pl. *brodiau*) means 'judgment', *brawdwr* essentially refers to a judicial officer, and it is clear that the *ynad* often (or indeed usually) exercised judicial functions. The name may however have originally meant 'jurist, one learned in the law', so that the king who grants justiceship (see 141.9) is conferring status rather than admitting to office; the older spellings of the word represent *yngnad* and may derive from the root *gna-,* 'know'; see WLW 220-21. It may be significant that *brawdwr* is very much commoner than *ynad* in the manuscripts written in southern Wales, where there were said to be no professional judges: the landowners who sat in the southern courts would be judges (for they gave judgment), but they were not learned in the law.
yoke, W. *iau,* 45.21n; 179.33n; W. *gwedd,* 35.3; 130.23 date of putting ox under, 176.21-2n

394   *The Law of Hywel Dda*

long yoke, W. *hiriau*, 99.3-9n; holes in, 200.26n
    supporting the end of the yoke, 199.36-7n
yoke-bow, W. *pystl*, 195.36; 202.9-11n
yoke-fellow, W. *cydweddog*, 176.33,34
young-salmon net, W. *gaflaweg*, 193.34: no view of the
    meaning of 'young salmon' is implied.
ysbodol, 'spatula', 193.6
ysgadan, 'herrings', 35.21n
ysgin, 'robe', 195.27,28
ysgithredd, 'canine teeth', 196.29-30
ysgolhaig, 'clerk', 1.6,7; 11.32; 90.13; 'cleric', 145.19;
    148.1; 'scholar', 76.5n
ysgraff, 'skiff', 193.12
ysgrubl, 'livestock', passim; 'stock', 177.16 etc.
ysgwr, 'peg', 99.7; 120.37; 199.5; 200.26n
yslepan, 'gin' (trap), 187.7n
ystabl, 'stable', 41.12-15n
ystaenaid, 'of tin', 194.31 etc.
ystafell, 'chamber', passim; see 57.6n
ystafellog, 'having a cell', 57.6n
ystalwyn, 'stallion', 172.13; see also *amws, march*
ystern, 'caparison', 16.33,34; 'harness', 32.12
ystiwart llys, 'court steward', 33.15n
ystôl, 'stool', 193.36
ystrodur, 'pack-saddle', 193.36
ystyffylau, 'fireback-stones', 190.27-32n
ystyllawd, (a) 'made of boards', 192.21; (n) *ystyllawd dirwyn,*
    'twisting-frame', 193.5-6
ystywos, 'kneeboots', 195.8n
ysu, 'eat', 63.5; 179.11,13
ywen, 'yew', 189.7,12; *ywen coed,* 'woodland yew',
    189.14; *ywen sant,* 'holy yew', 189.13-14n

INDEX TO SOURCES

Ancient Laws: references to Book, chapter, and section; numbers following a stroke refer to unnumbered sentences in the section. All references to Book III are to the 'Venedotian Code'; the letter A indicates the text on the upper half of the page.

III.pr. (vol.i, 216.23-218.13)	141.1-35
III.i.16A	148.16-38
III.i.17A	149.1-9
IV.iii.12,13	151.15-26
VII.i.10/4,5	86.28-87.2
VII.i.13	95.18-19
VII.i.22,23	105.5-107.6
VII.i.24,25	108.21-110.3
VII.i.26/3,4; 27	102.6-103.18
VII.i.29	103.19-104.8
XI.v.48	112.6-10

Damweiniau Colan: references to numbered sentences

2,3	151.27-33	217	187.30-34
6	151.34-152.3	233,234	186.35-187.5
20	152.4-9	235	118.10-16
22-24	186.14-30	240	152.10-17
77	38.30-33	246	153.29-33
82-85	145.25-36	250,251	168.1-10
113	169.1-6	255	160.5-6
117,118	76.7-16	268,269	135.25-30
124-127	55.24-56.4	274	116.26-34
130	153.2-10	275	117.4-9
138,139	197.11-16	276-278	166.30-167.4
140,141	127.17-20	286	166.14-17
142-144	178.29-179.3	291	97.13-21
147	189.2-3	292	116.35-117.3
149-151	134.25-135.5	298,299	163.21-34
152-4	135.17-24	300-302	146.11-27
158-161	119.22-38	304	164.29-165.5
163	171.22-5	305,306	100.23-30
164	189.39-190.3	308	146.34-5
169-172	153.11-28	309	152.24-8
173-176	206.1-15	313	152.29-34
177b (i.e.		314-317	56.5-18
second half)	54.21-3	321,322	65.32-9
183	54.3-8	324	70.9-14
192-4	10.15-27	325	68.5-16
199-201	82.33-83.10	328	118.1-4
213,214	129.17-23	331	174.26-32
216	100.14-17	334	198.22-5

[Damweiniau Colan]

337,338	117.19-24	423	187.6-7
339-342	98.8-31	424,425	56.19-36
344	69.35-70.4	428,429	118.17-29
354	136.19-21	437,438	80.12-29
355,356	117.25-35	443,444	165.22-31
357	112.27-39	445-448	160.29-40
358,359	135.31-136.2	452	167.5-10
363	70.5-8	453	118.30-35
369	97.32-98.7	454,455	127.21-9
370	117.13-18	458-460	118.36-119.21
372	168.11-15	462-468	73.33-75.18
373	97.22-7	471	47.14-30
382	117.10-12	472	163.35-164.12
387	79.1-2	473-475	126.29-127.11
402-405	66.33-67.28	476,477	114.25-115.8
407	73.30-32	478-482	115.16-116.13
410	110.24-6	484	88.21-36
411	52.36-53.5	485	77.10-28
412-414	191.33-192.7	495-498	111.19-36
415-419	177.25-178.3	499	127.30-37
420	141.36-142.3	503,504	168.16-17

J: reference is to page and line

91.4-8   115.9-15

LHDd: reference is to page and line

63.29-31   80.30-33

Llyfr Blegywryd: references are to page and line

4.1-5	6.3-7 (= WML 3.7-11)	55.18-21	184.4-8
		57.15-19	198.1-6
6.1-15	8.11-28	61.10-13	48.25-9
13.15-20	12.5-10	61.20-22	53.6-8
16.16-17.18	142.4-36	63.10-14	49.5-10
30.29-30	149.10-11	63.31-2	52.3-4
31.28-32.25	149.30-150.21	67.1-5	48.30-35
32.27-33.3	150.22-9	75.19-25	107.14-20
34.11-18	169.32-170.3	78.8-10	113.13-16
37.26-8	95.35-96.2	91.16-17	173.16
37.29-30	61.21-2	93.23-4 +	
39.25-9	66.17-21	154.11-15	164.22-8
41.16-25	70.29-38	94.8-14	180.27-32
41.26-31	81.21-6	97.12-14	196.1-2
51.1	185.7-8	98.21-7	189.23-30
51.30-52.3	185.3-6	122.26-32	167.20-27
52.6-10	187.25-9	135.12-13	166.19
52.28-9	187.35-6	154.11-15	164.24-8
54.7-11	182.13-16		

Index to Sources   397

Llyfr Colan: references are to numbered sentences

17-19	55.16-23	323-326	155.28-33
22	48.19-24	331	156.1-3
24	53.28-32	333	156.4-8
42-45	61.10-16	358 (end of	
63-66	52.22-35	sentence)-360	158.24-32
67	53.33-7	396 (end of	
89,90	67.36-68.4	sentence)	166.5-6
146	81.18-20	410	167.31-4
268-271	145.10-24	459	86.7-9
273	148.12-15	528-531	94.1-25
277	150.30-33	544	95.28-30
278,279	150.38-151.4	558	97.7-12
291	152.18-23	576	112.11-12
292,293	151.5-14	592	100.20-22
304,305	153.34-154.4	613,614	111.15-18
318,320	155.23-7		

Llyfr Iorwerth: because (with one exception) all the passages from this text appear in the same order in the printed text and in this translation, they can be easily traced in the table of Source References and are not indexed here. The one exception is Ior 126/4, which at 173.25-9 comes between 124/2 and 124/3.

Welsh Medieval Law: references are to page and line

3.7-11	6.3-7	35.3-8	182.7-12
14.1-5	14.1-4	35.11-12	184.35-36
15.15-16	17.1-2	35.19-27	184.37-185.2
15.23-5	17.7-9	36.11-14	185.9-12
17.10-13	17.33-6	36.14-17	185.35-8
17.14-23	15.19-28	36.21-4	186.31-4
18.4-6	16.7-9	37.17-20	41.31-4
18.15-19	15.29-33	41.8-13	62.16-21
18.21-3	16.10-12	41.19-23	62.32-6
20.10-12	21.36-8	42.7-9	196.16-17
22.13-15	19.31-2	42.17-20	196.32-5
22.19-22	38.24-7	42.21-5	198.17-21
25.14-15	24.22	43.4-7	198.10-13
26.20-22	33.8-9	46.19-22	150.34-7
28.14-29.1	122.27-123.2	50.5-13	99.23-31
29.5-16	123.3-14	50.23-51.3	111.37-112.5
32.7-8	35.25-6	51.11-13	112.13-16
32.19-20	36.18-19	51.13-15	110.4-6
33.4-5	33.32-3	53.2-6	113.9-12
33.7-10	33.34-7	56.10-13	129.24-7
33.16-20	39.1-5	62.4-6	113.32-4
33.20-25	39.8-13	62.12-15	113.25-8

398 The Law of Hywel Dda

[*Welsh Medieval Law*]

64.17-20	182.3-6	97.12-21	52.11-19
67.19-68.2	173.7-15	98.16-17	188.10
68.2-10	173.17-24	99.2-4	125.1-3
68.10-14	172.30-34	100.6-11	123.25-9
68.22-69.2	173.30-33	100.14-101.5	160.7-21
69.10-11	174.25	101.16-102.8	190.25-37
69.11-15	172.25-9	102.9-12	191.12-14
74.7-20	177.12-24	102.19-103.7	191.15-23
74.20-21	178.4-5	103.15-18	170.7-9
75.6-7	180.4-5	104.1-2	169.25-6
75.16-18	180.13-14	104.8	189.13
76.16-19	178.24-6	104.12-13	189.1
77.2-3	179.23-4	104.14-105.2	189.14-22
	= Bleg 95.4-5	105.2-5	189.35-8
77.10-13	187.10-13	105.6-9	194.20-22
77.13-14	178.27-8	105.10-11	194.25-6
77.15-78.2	187.14-21	108.4-6	199.18-20
78.4-6	178.6-7	110.12-18	179.4-9
78.6-8	179.20-22	111.20-112.2	118.5-9
78.8-11	187.22-4	112.4-7	198.26-9
79.13-15	183.9-12	114.11-13	112.23-6
79.19-24	183.13-19	117.7-9	189.31-4
81.1-4	183.20-24	117.14-15	165.20-21
81.12-18	184.9-15	117.20-22	202.12-15
81.21-6	184.16-21	117.23-118.3	207.5-9
82.13-83.5	182.17-34	118.16-19	209.25-8
83.8-15	202.29-36	129.6-16	137.19-30
83.15-21	203.30-35	131.4-7	188.11-14
84.3-10	204.3-10	140.13-16	178.8-11
84.10-16	204.23-9	143.3-5	137.31-3
84.19-24	205.17-22	293.19-23	130.35-131.3
84.24-85.3	207.25-9	295.2-4	205.6-9
85.7-11	65.27-31	300.20-21	194.28-30
89.13	80.11	301.17	173.34
89.18-20	50.33-5	301.17-18	178.12
95.14-19	54.29-34	315.19-20	52.19-21
95.20-96.5	52.5-10		

INDEX TO TEXT AND INTRODUCTION

The reader is reminded that fuller references to some subjects will be found in the Glossary and Index to Notes.

abbey: land, abbot land, 101, 127
  law manuscript at, xxi
abbot, 41,82,101,114,127
  men under, 114
Aberffraw, king of, xxxvii, 5,6,
  153,154
abetments, of fire, homicide,
  theft, 143ff
abortion, of cow or mare, 201
acquittal by lord, 118,166,167
acre, 82,99,100,120-22,136,
  198-201
act, objection for, 94
Act of Union (1536), xvii
Adam, 133
advice, void, 88
adviser, 157
advocate, xxx
affiliation, 132-7
Africa, xxxiii
age, for appointment as justice,
  141; legal, 58
agweddi, xxix, 45-52,61, see also *delay*
aid, 84,97,143, see also *delay*
aillt (pl. eilltion), 55,99,121,
  124-6,129,155,181,195
alder, 189
Alfred, English king, xii
alien, 55-8,89,94,104,107-10,
  112,114-19,133-6,152,155,
  167
allowance, 104
alms, 167
altar, 65,70,132,133,142,159,160
ambush, 150
amobr, xxix, 15,19,21,33,35,38,
  39,49-61,101,122,123,125,
  132
amod, 79,80
amod-makers, amodwyr, 79, see
  also *contract-men*
ancestors, 98
anchor, 112
angels, law between, 71
Anglesey, 120

Anglo-Norman consort, xxvii;
  law, xxxii, rule, xxvi
Anian, bishop of St Asaph, xxi
animal, claim to, 162
  clean, 63,177,180
  flesh of, 160
  four-footed, 164
  injury to, xxiv, 63
  kills a bonhedding, 152
  king's, 40, 187
  small, 26
  small wild, 10
  stray, 40
  tamed, 187
  unclean, 180
  wild, 10,186,189
answer, 84
  void, 87
anthropology, social, xxxiv
apple-tree, 188,189
appraisal, sworn, 164,165,175,
  176,182,192,193,195,196
April, 172,206
arbitration, xviii
archaism, xxxiv
Arfon, xix
Argoel, 6
argyfrau, 117, see also *dowry*
arm (of body), 24
arms, 61,151,see also *weapons*
arrow, 153,186,194
arts, three forbidden to villein's
  son, 40
Arwystli, xix
ash, 189
assault and battery, 143,153
assurance, 24
aswynwr, 119
attachment and swearing, 161,162
attest, 65
  liquors, 13
attestator, attestor, 95,151
auger, 192
  hole, 190
augmentation, 156

400   The Law of Hywel Dda

August, 40,83,84,175,183,206
  ninth day before, 184
autumn piglet, 178
avengers, 148
axe, 34,37,45,192
  man with, 41,125

back, horse's, 173
back-burden, 157,182
badger, 187
bail, bailsman, bailsmanship,
  80,81
bakeress, 37,39
banishment, 104,151,157-9, see
  also *exile*
bank, 206
banquet, 7,25,32
baptism, 78,130-32
bar, 7,13,191
  to compurgation, or evidence,
  68,79,165,166
bard, 8,20
  chaired, 8,20,39
  from a strange country, 39
  of the household, 8-10,16,20,
  26
bardism, xix, 40
barley, 176,181
barleycorn, 120,198
barn, 14,29,41,46,125,190,204,
  206
  breyr's, 191
  cat which guards king's, 180
  king's, 14,180,191
bath, hamlet, 170
battery, assault and, 143,153
battle: killing in, 151
  trial by, xxxii
beams, 191
beard, 141
  blemish on, 52,53
beast, clean, 186
  milking, 129
  unclean, 186
beaver, 187,188
bed, 14,19,30,37,49,53,54,58,
  61, see also *cross-bed*
  legitimate, 135
bedclothes, 19,45
bee, 183,184
  lineage, 183

queen, 183
swarm, 183,184
beech, 189
beehive, 184
beer, 25,34,126,128,129
belt, 76,195
bench, 190
  end of, 8,38
Benedicamus, 65
bequest, 47,165,201
berries, 35
best men of kindred, 137,148
bestower, 45,49,50,132
betrayer, 166
bettering, of pleadings, 87
billeting, 121,123,129
binder, 191
bird, notable, 15
  properties of, 183
  thief of, 167
birth and rearing, plea, 162
bishop, 12,18,101,127
  chapter, 164
  land, 101,112,127
  men under, 114
bitter denial, 160
bitter end, 90,93,134,158
bittern, 15
black ox, acre, 199
blank days, time, 76,77,96
Blathaon, headland of, 120
Bleddyn ap Cynfyn, 98,165
Blegywryd, xx
  Redaction, xxii,xxiv-xxvi,
  xxviii; translation from Latin,
  xxv
blemish, 51
  on beard, 52,53
blood, 143,153
  and wound, 149,150,198
  free, 198
  from nose, 197
  from scab, 197
  from teeth, 197
  God's, 198
  human, 198
  letting, 24
  released, 197
  sacral, xxxi
  slave, 198
  three stays, 197

Index to Text and Introduction 401

blood-clothes, 10,24,197
blood-feud, xxx,94,104
blood-land, 110,111
bloody, earth, 197
blow, inadvertent, 198
boar, 122,179,203,206
   herd, 178,179
   testes, 179
   wild, 22
body, 197
   alienage of own, 119
   human, xxiv, 196-8
bodyguard, 6,8-12,16,17,20,24,
   39
   man of, 9,131,155
   three parts, 11
bondage, 116
bone, broken, 197
bonedd, 131
bonheddig, 36
   animal kills, 152
   entitled, 119
   innate, 110,131,134,135,149
   155
   patrimonial, 116
   woman, 152
book, of Cyfnerth and Morgenau,
   141
   of Goronwy ap Moriddig, 141
   of Gwair ap Rhufawn, 141
   of Hywel, 116
   of the White House, xxvii,94,
   141
   some say, 117
   this to be known, 141
boon, neithior, 39
booty, 10,14,17-20,29,35
bottom rung, 99
bough, 188
boundary, 5,8,34,126,206
   between townlands, 126
   fixing, 97,127
   stone, 128
   three stays, 127
bounty, 9
bowels, 10,24,197
bowl, brass, 197
bows, pegs of, 202
box, on ear, 198
boy, 145
   seven-year-old, 78

bragget, 25,34,126,128,129
brain, 10,24,197
branch, 188,189
bread, 128,129
   broken, 27,31
   mass, 133
breaking ploughs, 111
breast, 184
breath, stinking, 46
breeches, 34,124,155
breed, 178
brew, 129
breyr, 38
bridle, 18,173
bridle-tame, 171
briduw, 65,73,78,79
   hands meet, 78
brogues, 22,34,155
brooch, 76
brood goose, 181
brooding, property of female bird,
   183
brother, 68,99,110,113,114,136,
   144,145,147,149
   can deny sister, 136
   eldest, 99
   second-youngest, 99
   share land, 98
   youngest, 99
brycan, 39,191,192·
buckle, 75
   suretyship, 73-5
buck, 13
buffalo horn, 40,192
building, 118,125,127,189
Builth, xxii
bull, 5,6,35,154,178,206
   hamlet, 178
bull-swarm, 183
burden, back, 157,182
   extra, 200
   horse's, 157
burial-place, church of, 132
burning, 111,151,169-71
   by stealth, 169
bush and brake, woman of, 50,
   135,137
butler, 25
butter, 34,46,126,128,129

The Law of Hywel Dda

cabbages, 204
cache, 160
Cadell, xii
cake, 37
calf, 175-7,188,203,206
caller (of oxen), 120,126,127,
   199,200,202
camlwrw, 13,19,26,33,36,40,
   52-4,61,78,85,87-9,101,125,
   127,128,130,141,143,144,166,
   167,171,174,182-6,188,189,
   202,206
   double, 41,87
camp, 41
candle, 14,27,31,33
candleman, 5,14,27,31
canllaw, 85,86,96,97
cantred, 65,121,122,154,158,160
cape, 18,29,32,34,36,195
captain of the household, 8-11,
   13,20,24,36,92,153,154
car, 45,172,175
Cardiganshire, xxi
carllawedrog, 116
car-returning, 57,59,102,133
carouse, 48
carrion, 63
car-starting, 116
castles, king's, 124
cat, 34,46,180,204
   guarding king's barn, 180
   mousing in flax-garden, 204
cattle, neat, 175-8
   of dark ancestry, 58 .
   payments made in, 134
   secured, 134
cattle-pen, 82
cauldron, 39,45,99,191,192
causation, xxxvi
ceinion, 38
cell, woman having, 57
Celtic law, society, xxxiv
cerddor, 38,39
chair, in hall, 7,8
chamber, 14,16,19,23,27-30,41,
   113,128
   sharing by chambers, 113
chamberlain, 5,14,19,29,30
champion-hart, 184,185
chancel, 159
Channel, 120

chapel, king's, 12
chaplain, 142
chaps, 184
chapter, 101,164
charge, 64,146,157,158,160
chase, legal, 206
cheese, 36,46,126,129
chick, 181,182
   red (of hawk), 182
chief of kindred, 108,123,136,
   137,155
chieftain, alien, 58,108
child, 58,60,132,148,165
   care for, 150
   carried, 52
   childbearing, signs of, 49
   of homicide, 150
Christmas, 5,11,22,23,76
church, 8,29,41,65,78,81-3,101,
   133,136,142
   burial-place, 132
   daered, 165
   disrespect, 117
   door, 159,160
   influence on Blegywryd Red-
      action, xxv
   land, 82,97
   mother, 41,135
   protection, 81-3
   vestments of, 101
churchman, 150
churchyard, 41,82,160
Cilmin Droetu, tribe of, xix
circuit, 11,15,23,121-4,129
Cistercians, xiv
claim, 112,208
   and surclaim, 56,170,208
   extinguished, 111
   of surety and debtor, 77
   sudden, 84
   superannuated, 97,106,111
clamour, son by, 134
clas, 41,82
claws, cat's, 180
cleanser, 200
clear, denial in, 134
cleric, 145,147,148,168
clerks, 1,11,90
clerkship, 40
close season, 96
cloth of one colour, 189

Index to Text and Introduction   403

clothes, clothing, 7,10,12,20,26,
     29,30,36,37,39,195
  king's, 9,41,188
  linen, 5,9,11,12,14,16,18-21,
     23-32
  ornamented, 41,188
  woollen, 5,11,12,14,16,18-21,
     23-32
clustered swarm, 184,186
Clwyd, xix
cock, 181,204
codification, xxxv
coffers, 6,30
coins, Hywel's, xii
cold case of galanas, 146
collar, closed on oxen, 199
  dog's, 193
  greyhound without, 173
colony, of bees, 183,184
colt, 203,206
  darting, 206
column, 7,190
  of body, 10
  of law, 1,141,142,171
Commandments, Ten, xxii
commentary, xxxiv
commission, on Welsh law, etc.,
     xix,xx
common law, English, xxx
commote, 84,88,116,121,122,
     133,160,163,201
company, king's, 6
compensation, 26,171,191
  and punishment, xxx
  and vengeance, 53,165
  for damage, 202,205,207,209
  for fire, 170
  mocking, xxix
  owner's, 167,174
complaint to country and Lord,
     111
compurgation, 65,78,95,157,
     162,163,168,169,189
  delay allowed for, 79
  due date of, 78
  of country, 170
compurgator, xxxiii, 68, 73,
     95
  bar to, 68,79
  designated, xxxiii,95
  female, 60

male, 60
  oath of, 95
  undesignated, 95
concord, 85,148,149
confiscation, total, 83
connexion, 59
conquest, 81
consecrated ground, burial
  refused, 166
contempt, 96
contention: for land, 105-7
  about milk, 175
contract, II.4 passim, 62,199-201,
     207
  joint-ploughing, 198-202
contract-man, 62
control, 201
cook, 5,11,13,14,26-8,31
copulation, 46,48
corn, 34,46,51,122,171,202-9
  damage, xxiv,190,202-9
  of one year, 208
  pigs on, 206
  ripe, 207
Cornwall, 120
corpse, 116,122,159
corruption, maiden, 49
coulter, 37,45,99,196
counterswearing, 64-6,78,79,93
country, and Lord, complaint to,
     111
  compurgation of, 170
  law of, xxiv,41,61
  strange, 10,14,17,20,35,39,
     48,97
court, book, 41
  of Dinefwr, 6
  King comes to, 126
  laws of, xxiv,xxvii,5,41;
     omitted from lawbook, xxiii
  officers, 5
  order of, 7
  royal, xv
  persons who belong to, 12
cousin, fifth, 145,149,150
  first, 99,100,110,136,145,
     149,150
  fourth, 145,150
  second, 100,110,136,145,
     149,150
  third, 145,150

cover, 23,25
cow, 20,21,33,34,40,51,154,178,
  187,201
  bulling, 175,206
  each cow of dog's value, 182
  in calf, 176
  prime, 175,177
  skin, 22,188
  stolen, 169
cowhouse, 190
cowyll, 46,50,51,53,58,60,61
crane (of bird), 15; (implement)
  45,191
cresset, 169,195
crime, xv; charge, xxxiii
croft, special, 99
cross, 123,159,207
cross-bed, 45
cross-branch, 188
cross-examination, xxxi,xxxiii
cross-load, 175
crown, of London, 120
crowing, cock, 181
crozier, oath by, 127
crudity, in Welsh law, xxix,xxx
cuckold, compensation to, xxvi
cudgel-blow, 68
cup, 14,19,192,193
cur, 52,181
curlew, mountain, 15
curtilage, 159
cushion, 16
custom, 31,142,158,179
  of Welshwomen, 52
  officers by, 31,39
cwynos, 129
cyfair casnad, 199
Cyfeiliog, xix
Cyfnerth ap Morgenau, book of,
  xviii,141
  Redaction, xxiv,xxv,xxviii
cyfraith gyhydedd, xxxv
cyhyryn canastr, 160
cyngaws, 85,86,96,97
cyngelloriaeth, 123
cynghellor, 7,16,33,34,90,100,
  121-3,125,129,155
  office of, 91,92
  townland with office of, 129
Cynyr ap Cadwgan, xix

dadannudd, xxxiv,101-5
  of bale and burden, 101
  of car, 101
  of tillage and ploughing, 101-3
daered, 12,46,47,165
Dafydd Llwyd ap Gwilym, roll of,
  xx
Dafydd Ysgrifennydd, xxii
damage, 207
  by woman, 60
  compensation for, 202,205,
    207,209
  corn, II.10
  great, to corn, 209
Danes, in England, xii
date, 66,69,75,78,84,96,207
daughter, 55,56,58,114,131,132
  heir of land, 107
  King's, 154
Davies, R. R., xxix,xxxvi
day, fixed, 66,70
  full, 84
  of loss and/or gain, 88,92,96,
    97,108
  part of, 84
  single, 84
dead thing, plea, 162
dead testimony, 98
dead-house, 34,130,131
death, 46,96
  penalty, 167,189
  to which God went, 62
death-clod, 57
debt, 46,47,68-70,78,165
  admitted, 67
debtor, principal, 63-72,76-8
debtor-surety, 70
December, Kalends of, 22
degrees (orders), 164
  (of kindred) 149,150
Deheubarth, xxiii,108,141,164
  books from, xxvii,141
  suzerain of, 164
delay, 77,88,92,94,96,116,147,
  159,163
  for aid, 77,78,84,97
  for compurgation, 79
  for galanas, 147,148
  for memory, 65,67,96
  for oath, 133
  for seeking relics, 133

Index to Text and Introduction   405

denial, 63,64,66,67,110,136,143,
  160,161,166
  bitter, 160
  of son, 132-7
  plus payment, not proper, 143
deposit, 159,161,162,170
designated compurgator, man,
  51,95,157,158,167,169
despoiling, 157,159
  by law, 16
destrier, 40,172,173
devil: authority for Hywel's law,
  xxii
  no law between, 71
dewfalls, three, 172
Diasbad uwch Annwfn, 104
dilysrwydd, dilystod, 51,52
Dinefwr, 6
  New Town, xxii
Dinlle, xix
dirt in his teeth, 52
dirwy, 13,15,19,21,28,33,36,40,
  51,52,61,101,125,130,131,
  143,144,156-8,160,166,167,
  182,183,185,189,197
  for fighting, 143,144
  for theft, 144
  for violence, 144
  pennies, 144
discharge, of homicide, 146
discretion, 142
disease, 152,172,174,177
dish, (vessel) 129,193; (of food)
  9,11,21,26,34,35,37,39
dispersion, galanas of one in, 149
dispute, 176,200,205
disrespect, to Church, 117
distaff, 120,145,195
  pedigree by, 110
distraint, 201
ditch, work on land, 98
divine, literate, 41
dock-leaves, new, 179
docked beast, 35
doctrine, juristic, xxxv
doe, skin, 13,15
dog, 6,7,9,11,154,160,167,181,
  182,187,206
  guard, 182
  habituated (to bite), 182
  herd, 181

neighbour's, 206
  pet, 181
  rabid, 182
  tracker, 193
dolly, 39
donor, 62
door, doorway, 190,191,204
  frames, 191
  hurdle, 190
doorkeeper, 11,14,25,26,30
dormitory, 41
dosbarthwr, xx
double galanas, penalty, penance,
  149-151
doubted son, 134
dowry, 46,50
draught-ropes, 202
drink, 13,18,128
drying, 126,170
dry sheep, 15,179
dumb, 135,150
dung, 113,203
dung horse, 172
dung maer, xxix,21,26,33,34,
  100,124,125
  wife, 60
dung mare, 172
dunghill, 54
dunghill cur, 181
Dyfed, xii,xiv
Dyfnwal Moelmud, 120

ear, 173,175,180,196
  box on, 198
earth, making bloody, 197
Easter, 5,76
ebb and flow, 84,88
ebediw, 6,11,17,33,40,55-57,
  101,122,123,125,131,165
edling, 6,7,13,39,59,154
Ednywain, xix
Edward I, king of England, xix,
  xxii,xxviii
Edwards, J. Goronwy, xxxvi
eel, 13
egg, 35,203,204
  laying, 181
eggshell, 35
egweddi, see *agweddi*
eilltion, see *aillt*
Einion ap Gwalchmai, xix,xx

406   *The Law of Hywel Dda*

Einion ap Madog, xx
elder, 13,84
elements (sacred), 142
encampments, 125
enclosure, 82
end-benches, 190
endowment, 52,59,107
enforcing third, 146,147
England, Hywel and, xii
    king of, xix,xxii
English, administration, xxviii
    courts, xxviii
    law, xvii,xviii,xxviii,xxxiii,
       xxxvi,xxxvii
    lawyers, xxvi,xxx
    procedure, xxv
    the, 120
enllyn, 34,36,124,128
enmity, 93,94
enthroned ones, three, 101
entrails, 26
entreaty, 142
Epiphany, 179
equalisation, equality, etc., 91,
    93,95,99,100,103,104,106,171
    law of, xxxv,95,104,171
equipment, 21,45,190,191-6
ermine, 188
errands, 19,29,34,36,71,122
escort, 82
evidence, xxxi
ewe, 175,180
exchange, 163
excommunicate, 47,94
exile, 71,113, see also *banish*
extinguished acre, 100
extortionate spoliation, 159
extra burden, 200
eye, 36,172,173,175,180,182,196
eyelid, 198

fabric, mixed, 34
face, 197
fairness, of law, 157
falcon, 9, 11, 15, 16, 40, 154, 182,
    183
    nest, 15, 182
    tiercel, 13, 183
falconer, 5-7,13-18,124
    office of, 92
fallow, 113

family group, 56
Family Law, 129-37
farthing, 69,193,195
father, 45,48,49,51,52,55,56,60,
    61,71,72,80,99-102,107-11,
    130-37,144,147-9,152,168
favour, 161
fawn, 13,187
feast, 14,25
    day, 77
    three special, 7,9,12,15,19,
       20,26,30,76,123
February, 13,22,34,83,176
fee, 36,91,141
    entrenched, 123
    King's, 92
fellow-heirs, 150
fellow-kinsmen, 145
fellow-thief, 62
fence, 207
fetter, 193,195,202
fighting, 33,68,101
    dirwy for, 143,144
filly, 174,203
finger, 196,198
fire, 6,36,128,129,169-171
    carrying, 171
    covering, 50, see also *dadan-
       nudd*
    from hollow tree, 171
    galanas does not follow, 170
    giving, 171
    lending, 170
    lighting, 6,128,129
    nine abetments, 169
    pigs, 171
fireback-stones, 190
firestone, 39
firewood, 35
fish, 123,124,186,187
flax, 45,204,209
    garden, cat mousing in, 204
    green, 34
flesh, horse, cut to the bone, 173,
    see also *tail*
flitch, 128,178
flour, 46,128
foal, 18,29,171,175,205
fodder, horse fodder, 7,9,13,16,
    18,37,128,129,204
foetus, 130

Index to Text and Introduction 407

fold, 113,207
  hurdles, 195
folded manure, 113
fondling, 48
food, 13,39
  in attendance, 36,37
  official, 11
  person's act on another's, 168
  physician's, 197
  renders, 128,129
food-gift, 128,129
food-house, 34,37,41,125
foot, 120,126,127,196,197,199
  horse's, 172
  king's, 32
  wife's, one in bed, 47
footholder, 7,13,32,33
footwear, 23,36
fore-oath, 205
forelock, 173
forequarter, 185
forest, king's, 186
forfeit, gage, 75
forgiveness, 148,149
fork, 190,193
fossils, legal, xxxiv
fosterage, 126
foul house, 159
fourteen, age, 130-32,145,165
fourth man, 104,114
fox, 184,187,188
fragments, meat, 27,31
frame, weaving-woman's, 193
free will, 200
freeman, 118,181
French, influence, xxxvii
  words in lawbooks, xxvii
fright, 153
fruit, 188
fuel, 37,126,169
fuel-axe, 34,37,45,99,192
fuel-horse, 37
fueller, 6,36,37
furious man, thief, etc., 149,
  151,166
furrow, 126,176,202

gage, 63,68-71,76,99,112,114,
  201,207,208
  date for, 207

for corn, 207
forfeit, 75
  invalidating, 208
  legal, 68
  validity of, 75
galanas, 35,47,58,60,65,68,79,
  111,129,130,132-5,144-57,
  165,166,179
  charge, 146
  cold case, 146
  delay for, 148
  double, 149-151
  legal measure of, 144
  fire, does not follow, 170
  of one in dispersion, 149
  surety for, 133,135
gander, 181
gangway, 84,85
gaol, 33
garden, 189,204,209
garderobe, 30
gate, 25,35,36
  great, 16
geldable land, 100
gentility, 159
Germany, xxxv
gibbet, 62
gift, 35,62,160,162,163
  and transfer, 54
  by wife, 53,54
gilt, 194,195
gin (trap), 187
Gladstone, xix
glanders, 172
gloss, xxxiv
gloves, 15,124
Glyn, Glynllifon, Glynne, xix
goat, 45,179,180,187,188,203,208
goat-heifer, 180
gobr, 50
God, 38,41,183
  blood, 198
  cross, 159
  death, 62
  protection of, 8,64,93
  swearing to, 132,133
  taken as surety, 78
  tempting, xxxii
  will of, 71
  yoke of, 130
godaeog, 99

gold, 5-7,9,32,41,46,154,194
    ring, 16,20,123,142
    treasure, 41
goodman, 6,8,40,49,50,84,85,
    96,151,193
goods: alien's, 116,118
    claim to, 111
    father's, 58
goose, 181,203,204,207
gorfodog, 78, see also *bail*
Goronwy ap Moriddig, xix,xxvi,
    48,141
goshawk, 183
gospel, oath by, 127
gowyn, 46,53
graft, 188
grandfather, 102,112,115
grandson, 114,115
grant and investiture, 102
grass, 207,209
grave, payer's, 70
Gray's Inn, xxvi
grazing, 172
great-grandfather, 102,112
great-grandson, 114,115
great-great-grandson, 115
great-great-great-great-grand-
    father, 149
greed of property, 75
greyhound, 173,181,193
    collar, 173,193
groats, 128
groom, 18,19
    chief, 5,8,13,16-19,29,32
    money, 15,17,18
    of the rein, 31,32
grove, 57
    hazel, 188
grubbing, pig, 178
Gruffudd ab yr Ynad Coch, xx
Gruffudd ap Llywelyn (ab Ior-
    werth), xx
Gruffudd ap Llywelyn (ab Seisyll),
    xvi
Grugyll, 120
guard-dog, 182
guardian, 130,131
guests, 6
Gwair ap Rhufawn, book of, 141
Gwalchmai, xx
gwasafwr, lath of, 119

gwely, 147-9
    kindred, 149
gwely-land, 100
gwestfa, 118,121,128
Gwilym Wasta, xxii
Gwynedd, xxiii,xxv,8,49,107,
    108,141,149,160
    centre of legal study, xix,xxvii
    lawbooks written in, xxvii
    princes of, xviii,xxxxvi; fall
    of, xxvi
    men of, 8,160

habit, religious, 164
habituated dog, 182
haddock, 35
hair, see also *tail*
    from horse's back, 173
    uprooted, 198
hall, 10,23,30,33,41,125,128,190
halter, 18,29,173,175
hamlet, bath, 170
    bull, 178
    corn damaged beside, 205
    herdsman, 62
    land, 113
    smithy, 170
    stock of, 177
hand, 73,126,127,132,133,137,
    161,196,197
    amodwyr, 79
    hundredth, 160
    justice's, relic in, 64
    Lord's, land in, 127
    meeting hand, 73-5,78,79,198
    priest's, 78,130
    receiving goods, 161
    surety's, 73-5
handmaid, 5,14,30
handsbreadth, 18,27
hanging, 151
hare, 187
harlot, 60
harm, 208
    outside the skin, outward, 174
    violence and, 106,111
harness, 11,32
harp, 9,20,38,39,40,123,191,192
harrow, 126,172
harrowing-horse, 200
hart, 22,184,185

Index to Text and Introduction 409

antler, 192
champion, 184,185
    skin, 13,14,15,185,188
    tame, 187
harvest, 77,83,103
harvest house, 190
hate, 95,142
haunches, 184
hawk, see *falcon, goshawk*
hay, 204,206,207
He paid who gave surety, 135
he-goat, 187,206
headings, in lawbooks, xxv
headland, 34
hearing on the land, 84
heart, 15,184
    breaking, oxen, 200
    mother's, woman's, 132,133
hearth, 101,102
hedge, 205
    thickset (fig.), 97,106
hedging-bill, 37,45,155,192
heifer, first-calf, 35,206
heir, 107,131,150
heir-apparent, 6
hen, 34,46,181,183,203,204,207
herbs, 24,27,197
herd, 40,178,203
    boar, 178,179
    legal, 178,203
herd-dog, 181
herdsman, 62,176; (fig.) 196
hermit, 76
Heroic Age, xxvii
heron, 15
hide, 63,177, see also *skin*
highway, King's, 189
hind, 22,187,188
hindquarter, 185
hire, 161,174
historians, social, xxix
hobble, 202
holding, 86,102,105,121
homage, 51,114,115,118,119,131
home-made garment, 195
homicide, (offence) xxx,60,71,
    143,144; (offender) 111,133,
    134,144-6,150,152
    children of, 150
    principal offence of, 144
honey, 40,123,124

horn, 14,19,22,23,36,40,41,175,
    180,192,195
    buffalo, 22,40,41,192
    steer's, 192
    swearing by, 22
horse, 6,9,11-21,23-32,35,37,40,
    41,61,69,97,121,125,154,157,
    171,202
    back harmed, 173
    borrowed, 173,174
    burden, 157
    court justice's, 32
    fastest, 18,29
    foot, 172
    fuel, 37
    harrowing, 200
    hired, 174
    in attendance, 11,12,14,16,
        18-21,23-32
    lamed, 174
    lodging, 32
    properties of, 172
    sumpter, 172,173
    taken without leave, 173
    wild, 172
    working, 172
    worth ten pounds, 69
horse-load, 128
horseshoe, 9,13,32,174
hose, 32,36,195
hospital, 101,117
hospitality, 167
host, 6,7,13
hostage, hostageship, 58,107
hosting, 24,41,101,124,125
hounds, 22,23,121,124,129,185,
    186
    idle, 186
house, 99,190,191
    aillt's, 190
    burning, 111,112,169
    damage to, 191
    empty, 57
    foul, 159
    harvest, 190
    keeping, 118
    legal, 191
    making, for king, 41,125
    minor, 190
    stolen property traced to, 159
    summer, 190

410　　　　The Law of Hywel Dda

uchelwr's, 118
winter, 190
within townland, 170
household, 124, see also *body-guard*
hundredth hand, 160
hunt, hunting, 13,16,22,184
huntsman, 13,21,22,124,185,186
chief, 5,8,10,14,21-3
greyhound, 21,22
staghound, 21,22
hurdle, door, 190; fold, 195
husband, entitled to land, 107
last, 156
Hywel, Hywel Dda, Hywel the
Good, xi-xvii,xxii,xxiii,1,
120,123
back to, xxxvii
book, xxiii,116
justices, 187
law, xi,xvi,xvii,xix,xxi,xxii
52,94,110,157,164,165
Hywel Fychan, xxii

icicle, stone in place of, 70
ignorance, oath of, 177,205
illegality, 82,117,125,146,205
immunity,91
inadvertence, 130,153
blow received from, 198
inch, 120,176,198
incomer, 92
indispensables, 11,12,17,39
Indo-European, xxxiv
inedible beast, 182
information, payment for, 40
sufficient, 62,159,160
informer, 62
innate, 108,110, see also *bon-heddig*
innocent, 146,152
inquiry, stock, 145
word of, 87,88
insane, 150,151
instruction, 38
intention, xxxvi
intercourse, 48
intervention, 123,135
intestine, 184,185
investiture, 82,103,110

Iorwerth ap Llywelyn ap Tudur,
xxii
Iorwerth ap Madog, xx,xxiv-xxvii,
141,190
Iorwerth Fychan, xix,xxvii
Iorwerth Redaction, xxiv-xxvii
irons (plough), 126,127,200,202
irregularity, 132
irresponsible things, 171
It is paid after a befouled oath, 205

jesses, 15
jester, 18
Jesus Christ, 41
joint, of finger, 196
of meat, legal, 22,184,185
joint ploughing, 190,198-202
contract, 198,199,201
partners, 201
tractate, xxvi,III.9
joint theft, with husband, 167
judge, xix,142, see also *justice*
challenge to, xxxi
court, 5,41,142
function of, xxxi
wrong decision, xxxi
judgment, 17,64,66,79,91,96,142
and trial, xxxi,xxxii
better, 141
false, 141,142
justice on, 61
of the law, 110
place of, 91
properly judged, 141
seat, 85,96
judicial oath, 1
June, 206
jurist, xix
conflict of opinions, xxiii
jury, xxxi,xxxii
justice, 17,64,66,77,84-91,93,
96,98,141,161,176, see also
Test Book
at Westminster, xix
commote, 84,85
court, 8,11,16,17,32,38,39,
84,85,91,141
from country, 142
Hywel's, 187
on his judgement, 61

Index to Text and Introduction   411

some of, 51,67,203
justiceship, 17,141
Kalends of December, 184
keeping before loss, 162
kennel, 181
keys, 30
kid, 13,126,164,180,187,203,206
killing, corpse, 159
   fury, 149
   horse, by stealth, 173
   in battle, 151
   messenger, 154
   person, 149
kiln, 21,41,125,171,190,191
   burning, 168
   fire in, 170
   piped, 191
kin, kindred, 51,56,57,60,65,79,
   92,107,108,133-6,143-9,151,
   152,156
   and descent, 86,87,98,101,
    102,104
   bar between, 165,166
   best men of, 136,137,148
   chief of, 123,136,137
   degrees of, 149
   denial by, 135,137
   dire losses, three, 133,134,146
   discharge homicide, 146
   enmity of, 94
   father's, 58,68,78,134,147,
    148,149,157
   four, 145
   gwely, 149
   homicide's, 133
   innocent, 152
   Lord's, 72
   mother, 55,58,68,72,78,133,
    134,147-9,157
   nearer, 93,94
   oldest men of, 147,148
   principal debtor's, 72
   vengeance of, xxx,156
kin-feud, 48
kin-stock, 97
king, passim
   as state, xv
   daughter, 50,154
   forest, 186
   Germanic, xxxv
   marcher lord, status, xxviii

member, 7,11
nephew, 6,7,154
of Aberffraw, 5,6,153,154
of England, as feudal superior,
   xxviii,154
of Lloegr, 120
of London, 154
prison, 88
son, 6,7,153
status of, xv
wife, 153
woods, 179
kingship, personal union, xii
kinship, 145,147,158
kinsman, 123,145,149,155
kinswoman, 123
kiss, 48,137
kitchen, 13,26,28,31,33,35,125
kitten, 180
knees, errand done on, 26
knife, 76,192,195
knight, 131
knower, 86,88-90,98,103-5,107,
   109,163

labour, applied to land, 113
lactation money, 175
lamb, 13,126,164,175,179,180,
   203,206
land, 7,11,12,14,16,18-21,23-38,
   50,54,55,61,120
   abbey, abbot's, 101,127
   acquired, 92
   alongside shore, 112
   and earth, 5,12,13,17,33,77,
    83-6,91,92,96,97,102,103,
    110,111,126
   arable, 114
   bishop's, 101,112,127
   blood, 110
   carrying office, 92
   carrying status, 91
   case, claim, of land and earth,
    9,84,92
   church, 82,97
   court, 33
   daughter as heir, 107
   ditches, works on, 98
   fee from, king's, 92
   geldable, 100
   hearing on, 84

412   *The Law of Hywel Dda*

hospital, 101
joint holder, 92
king's, 117
law, season for, 83,105
Lord's, 112
measures of, 120
office in right of, 32,108
procedure in action for, 83-98,
   101-10
quarter, 185
reckon, 100
sharing, 98-100,113
status from, 108
sureties for, 85
without office, 91,92
without status, 91
women and, 107-10
land-feud, 93,94
language, technical, of law, xxxvi
lard, 33
larder, 46,54,190,195
lash, eye, 198
lath, of gwaesafwr, 119
Latin, texts of Welsh law, xxi,xxv
latrine, 41,125
laundress, 32,39
law: adaptability of, xxxvii
amod and, 80
barbarian, xxxv
Biblical, xxxi
change, by ruler, xxxv
Church, 110
classical, xviii,xxvi-xxviii,
   xxx
closed, 83,112
common, English, xxx
constitutional, xv
customary, xxxv
development and change, xviii,
   xxviii
enforcement, private, xviii
English, xvii,xviii,xxviii,
   xxxiii,xxxvi
fair, 157
finding and application, xxxii
Hywel's, xi,xvi,xvii,xix,xxi,
   xxii,xxxiv,52,94,110,157,
   164,165, see also *Welsh*
decline of, xxviii
immediate, 76-8, 163
Irish, xv,xxxiv

judgment of, 110
language of, xxxvi
Lombard, xxxv
Lord's, 164
of synod, 168
of women, xxiv,xxix,45-61
open for land and earth, 83
person unskilled in, 142
pre-curial, xxxv
principles, xxxvii
public, xv,xxvii
repellent, 119
Roman, xxxiv,95
surety for, 77,78
three columns of, 1,141,142,
   171
three systems, 94
Welsh, xv,xxviii; specialists in,
   xviii,xx,xxi; suppression,
   xxvi
written, xxxiv
written statement of, xxxii
worldly, 71
lawbooks, xvii-xix,xxi,xxvi,xxix-
   xxii,xxxiv-xxxvi
illustrations to, xxi,xxii
Irish, xxxiv
order and disorder in, xxiv
Scandinavian, xxxv
variability of Welsh, xxxv
law-day, adjudged, 89
lawful aid, 97
lawmaker, xxxv
lawman, Scandinavian, xxxv
lawyers: conservatism of, xxiii
English, xxx
family of, xviii-xix
interest in exceptional cases,
   xxx
professional, professionalism,
   xxi,xxvii
laxity, loss by, 161
laying, eggs, 183
layman, 1,101,141
of status, 90
leash, 22,23,193
leeks, 204
lees, 18
leftovers, 36
legal charge, 157
legalism, xxxv

Index to Text and Introduction 413

Leges Hoeli, xi
legislation, xxviii,xxxiv
Lent, 1,12,29
leprous, 46,76,150
letters, 12
Lichfield, Gospels, xvii
life, 63,118,197
   and limb, 118,130
   animal's, value of, 63,177,178
   forfeit, 151,158,159,164-9
lifetime, right limited to, 123
   three men's, 111
light, lighting, 24,25,197
limb, 166,173, see also *life*,
   member
limits, 121,199
lineage, of bees, 183
linen, 195,see also *clothes*
linseed, 45
lintels, 190
lips, 196
liquor, 14,25,30,38
   attesting, 13
   legal, 25
listening, 87
litigation, 61,77
litter, sow's, 179
liver, 184
liver fluke, 179
livestock, 82,111,113,122,160,
   181,202-9
   chasing from corn, 206
   King's, 125
   not overtaken on corn, 205
   owner of, 209
   small, 13,203,208
   taking, 208
Llan Daf, Book of, xvii
Llandeilo Fawr, xvii
Lloegr, King of, 120
Llyfr Colan, xxvi,xxvii
Llyfr Gwyn Rhydderch, xx
Llyfr Teg, xxii
Llyfr y Damweiniau, xxiv-xxvi,
   xxviii
Llywarch ap Hyfaidd, xii
Llywelyn ap Gruffudd, xvi-xix
Llywelyn the Great (ab Iorwerth),
   xix,xx,xxvii
loaf, 34,36,128,129
loan, 161-3

lock, 25,193
lodging, 6,9,11,12,14,16,18-21,
   23-32,34,39
   horse's, 32
logic, xxxv
loins, 184
London, crown of, 120
   King of, 154
loop, 198,199,202
lord, 51,52,61,116,131
   acquits, 118,166,167
   goods of man to, 116
   man, of his father, 115
   of his wife, 53,165
   proprietor, 115
Lord, 34,69,70,72,75,79,83,96,
   98,103,110,114,123,141,143,
   144,146,147,151.156-9,164-8,
   174
   betrayal of, 82,166
   complaint to, 111
   cross from, 207
   female, 60
   investiture from, 110
   land, 112
   law, 164
   man in his place, 137
   protection of, in oath, 64
   throne, 164
   will not allow right, 97
lordship (territory), 147,148;
   (authority), 114
loss, and/or gain, 85,86,88,92,
   96,97,108
   by laxity, 161
   of properties, 176
   sharing, 71
love, 95,142
Low Sunday, Tuesday after, 76
lungs, 15

mace, 26
mach, xviii, see also *surety*
maenol, 121,123,127
   bond, 128
   free, 123,126,128
maer, 13,16,21,33,90,100,121,
   122,125,129
   office, 91,92,129
   townland carrying office, 129

maerdref, 33,60,121
  land of, 100
  men of, 33,36,124,125
  serjeant in, 35
magic, xxxi
maiden, 39,46,48,49,51,52,55,
  58-62; false, xxix
maidenhood, 62
maiden-wife, 60
maintainer, 86,88-91,95,98,103,
  105,106,162
maintenance, lord's, 51
Maitland, F. W., xxxi, xxxiii
man, of bodyguard, 9,131,155
  of maerdref, 33,36,124,125
  with axe, 41,125
mane, 173,175
mantle, 15,34,46,57,185,195
manure, land held in right of, 113
marauders, 166
March (month), 13,34,170,175
March (of Wales), marcher lordship, xviii,xxviii,xxix
mare, 172,201,205
  pregnancy of, 171
  properties of, 175
  stud, 173
margins, 34
marten, 187,188
mass, 12,39,142,183
  bread, 65,133
materials, 89
Maurice, William, xxviii
May, 83,84,172,175,176
  shower, 175
May Day, 40,84,179,183,184,
  202,203
mead, 14,25,30,34,123,126,128,
  129
  vat, 23,25
mead-brewer, 5,23
mead-cellar, 25,33
mead-store, 13
meadow, 206,207
measuring vessel, 176
meat, 63,177,178
  and hide, 63,177
  fragments, 27,31
  opened, 34,46
medical attention, care, 10,24,63
medication, 197

Meilyr, xx
meiri, pl., see *maer*
member, of body, 196-8, see also
  limb
  of kin, 6,7,150,155
memory, delay for, 65,67,96
Merioneth, xxii
messages, 25
messenger, killing, 154
mew, hawk in, 16,183
Michaelmas, 176,179,206
mid-yoke, 99,120,199
midday, 77,84,88
Midsummer, 22,206
milch animal, 63,129,209
mile, 120
milk, 126,129,175,176,179,180,
  see also *milch animal*
  contention about, 175
  useless, 180
mill, 113
misapprehension, 166
miscellanea, 178
mistake, 166
monarch, 38,112
money, 72,76,111,208
  money payment, 202
  supper money, 14
monk, 61,76,90
moons, three, 172
Morgenau, xviii,xix
mother, 52,56,110,137,144,147,
  149,152, see also *kin*
  goods of, 136
  kin, 65
mother-church, 41,135
mother-right, 58,107-10,114,
  115,123
mouse, mousing, 180,204
mowing, 126
muirburn, 170
murder, 150
musicians, 6

nail, 196
  of ploughman, 6,154
name, 130
nationhood, xxxvi
nature, objection for, 94
  of disease, 152
neat cattle, 175-8

Index to Text and Introduction 415

neck, 37
needy person, 6,40
negligence, xxxvi
neighbour, 162
neithior, 39
nephew, 6,7,150,154
  son of fifth cousin, 145,147
nest, 181
  falcon's, hawk's, sparrow-
    hawk's,15,183
net (fig.), 40; (fishing, various),
  193
New Year, 63,177,178,206
  Day, day after, 76
nine, abetments, 143,156,169
  days, 83,84,88
  days and nights, 47
  fistbreadths, 128
  houses, 41
  members of equal rank, 196
  men, 150
  paces, 175,182
  tongued ones, 49,61
ninth day, 54,83,96,101,102
  before August, 184
  second, 101
ninth person, 104
non-proprietor, 91,103,104,108
nones, 185
nose, 196
  blood from, 197

oak, 188,189
oath, xxxii,xxxiii,48,51,52,55,
  57,60,61,66,68,78,79,91,95,
  131,132,137,143,145,150,
  158,168,174,200,209
  as one of seven, 65,157
  befouled, payment after, 205
  by crozier and gospel, 127
  clean, xxxiii,95,136
  compurgator's, 79,95
  delay for, 133
  false, 64
  herdsman's, 176
  judicial, 1
  lord's, 118
  mother's, 137
  of fifty, 51,52,57,149,151,169
  of five, 157
  of forty, 60

of fourteen, 60
of ignorance, 177,205
of one hundred, 143,148,150
of one person, single person,
  61-2,78-80,158,182
of seven, 60,65,136,157
of six hundred, 151
of taker of animal, 205
of three hundred, 143,149
of twelve, 157,158,169
of twenty-four, 160,167,173
of two hundred, 143
owner's, 205
oatmeal, 176
oats, 35,128,181,193
objection, to testifiers, 89,93,94
occupancy, sufficient, 108
occupation of land, 105
  priority, 92,127
October, 13,14,172
Offa's Dyke, 116
offence, 134
  gross, 48
  objection for, 94
  principal, 143
offering, 6,11,12,29,142
office, and land, 32,92,108
  person having, 155
officers, by use and custom, 31,39
  court, 5
  twelve special court, 142
officials, 12,14
ointment, 24,197
old field, 114
old persons, 142
oldest men of kindred, 147,148
oppressor, 105,106
orchard, 113,189,204
ordeal, xxxii
orders, 40,164,168
  alien, 117
  man in, 29,163
  sacred, 150
ordinances, 142
ornamentations, ornaments,
  101,188
otter, 184,188
ox, 20,34,63,126,127,187,199-201
  black, acre, 199
  collars closed on, 199
  prime, 177

prime furrow, 199
short-yoked, 200
skin, 22,188
stolen, 201
sward, 199
value, 177

packhorse, 124; (fig.), 40,112
paddock, 207
pages, 6,124
palfrey, 172,173
palmbreadth, 120,198
pan, 24,45,51
pannage, 178,179
Paradise, 183
parson, 12,41,81
party, 64,66,84-7,89-91,94,126, 127
partners, joint-ploughing, 201
paternoster, 7,11,87
patrimonial, 92,108,119
   in another place, 109
   legal, 109
   Welshman, 89
patrimony, 58,82,99,100,107, 109,110,112,119,136
   by mother-right, 58,107,109
payment, and denial, not proper, 143
   and second payment, 165
   made in cattle, 134
   releases surety, 63
pays de droit coutumier, écrit, xxxiv
peace, 8
Peckham, John, xxii
pedigree, 104
   by distaff, 110
peg (of bow), 202; (of yoke), 99, 120,199
penalty, basis of, xxxi
   double, 150,151
   mitigation of, xxxi,157
   two for one cause, no right, 168
penance, 12,29,94
   double, 150
pencerdd, 38-40
   harp, 38,40,191
penis, 197
penny, 128,130

curt, 180,187
dirwy, 144
last, 47,54,59,68,116,146
legal, 69,180
one, 59,146
scores of, augmentation, 156
shaft, 58,60,111,145,146,149, 152
tenth, 160
wrong worth one, 82
Penwith, headland of, 120
pepper, 27
perjury, 65,94,158
Peuliniog, xiv
physician, 5,7,10,24,25,197
Pictland, 120
pig, 35,40,122,157,177-9,203, 206-8
   domestic, 178
   fire, 171
   killing person, 179
   life, 178
   on corn, 206
   three-year-old, 128
   wild, 178
pillow, 16
pipes (of hart), 184
plaint, 66
platter, 193
   father's, 130-32,165
plea, 70,160,162
pleading, 85,87,91,96
   bettering, 87
pledge, 85,88,89,91,141
plot, standard, 91
plough, 176,195,201,202
   breaking, 111,112
plough-frame, 126,127
plough-ox, 63,176,177,199-202
ploughing, 83,113,114,125-7
   afar off, 200
   bad, dispute about, 200
   day's, spring and winter, 195
   joint, 198-202
   near at hand, 200
   without leave, 126
ploughman, 6,126,127,154,199, 200,202
   acre, 199,200
   nail of, 6,154
ploughmanship, 202

Index to Text and Introduction 417

ploughshare, 45,196, see also
  irons
poison, 151
pole, 191
Pope, protection of, 64
porch, 41,125,190
porter, 16,26,30,31,35,36,125
post, 21,24,34,197; tying, 201
postponement, 96
poultry, 181
pound, 121
  twnc, 122,123,128
pound, stock, 202
Powys, xix,xxiii,108,136,137,
  141,149
  books from, xxvii,141
practice, xxiv,142
precinct, lower and upper, 9
pregnancy, 129,137; mare, 171
priest, 5,39,41,61,82,84,85,87,
  90,159,163
  hand, 78,130
  king's, 18,28
  of household, 7,11,16,21,38
  parish, 18,46,78,137
  Queen's, 28,29
prime, 175,176
  of cow, 175,177
  of ox, 176,177
principal, 95
principal debtor, 63-72,76,77
principal offence, 143,149
  of homicide, 144,152
principal offender, 81,157,158
Principality of Wales, English,
  xviii,xxviii
priod, 58
priority of occupation, 92,127
prison, 88,91, see also *gaol*
  of time, 77
prisoner, 33,35
privy things, 53,61
procedure, xxxi
proctor, 74,75
profession, learned, in medieval
  Wales, xix,xxviii,xxxvii
profit, 174
progeny, 169
prohibition, 123,126
prologue, xiii,1,141
promise, 79,81,93,95,96

proof, xxxi,xxxii
  form of, xxxii
  irrational, xxxii
  objective, xxxii
properties: bird, 183
  greater than animal's value,
    178
  horse, 172
  loss of, 176
  mare, 172,175
  sheep, 179
  sow, 179
property, invalidating, 73
  rescuing, 167
proprietary holding, 86,102,105
proprietary right, claim by, 104
proprietor, 86,91,102-6,108,
  114-116
  by kindred and descent, 87
  lord, 115
proprietorship, 87,91,92,104-6,
  114,127
  by kindred and descent, 86
  extinguished, 104
prosecution, by state, xxxi
protection, 5-9,13,15,17-21,23-
  34,36-39,70,81-3,151,154
  church, 81-3
  fee for, 113
  of God, 8,64,93
  of Lord, 64,151
  of Pope, 64
provision, 6,156,167
publican, 47
punishment, xv,xxx
purchase of land, three kinds, 113

quarter (of carcase), 177,185,186
queen bee, 183
queen-colony, 184
quern, quern-house, quern-shed,
  34,45,156,194
quillet, 113
quinsy, 179,187
quota, 59,65,78,95,98,162,176

rabid dog, rabies, xxxvi,151,182,
  187
rafters, 191
raid, 9
rail, 191

418   *The Law of Hywel Dda*

raiment, 15
ram, 180,206
rape, xxix,51,52,55,58-60,62,107
readiness, 93
reaping, 83,126
rearing, 51,135, see also *birth
   and rearing*
rebound, 153
reckon land, reckon townland,
   100,129
reconciliation, 148,159
rectum, 184
Red Book of Hergest, xxii
Redactions, xxiv,xxv,xxxv
red-tongued, 143
refusal, 68
relatives, 48,119
   closest, 48,60,150
release, of stock from pound, 202
relic, 8,64,82,83,88,90,91,132,
   133,142,145,161,164,177,
   199,205
   delay for seeking, 133
   putting lips to, 64
religion, religious, 150,163
repudiation: of amod, 80
   of wife, 48
rescission, of transfer, 40
rescue fee, 167
resident, 119
restiveness, 172
retinue, 6
returners, 67
reward, 95
rhaffan, 48
Rhodri Mawr, xii
Rhol Dafydd Llwyd, xx
Rhydderch ab Ieuan Llwyd, xx
Rhys ap Gruffudd, xiv,xviii,xxvi,
   164
rickyard, 204
ring, 6,19,192,193
   gold, 16,20,123,142
   little, 202
river, tree falling across, 189
road, 128,186
robbery, xxx,166,167
rod, 99,120,121,191,199
   blows with, three, 53
   gold, 5,154
   silver, 52

roe, roebuck, 187,188
Rome, law of, xxxiv,95
roof, 160,190,191
roof-fork, 189
roof-tree, 189,190
rope, 155,193
rough land, 200
rouncey, 172,173
rout, 150
rye meal, 176

Sachsenspiegel, xxxv
saddle, 18,30,32,194
St Asaph, xix
   bishop of, xxi
St Bride's Day, 83,84,202
St Curig's Day, 176,184
St. Davids, pilgrimage to, xiv
St John's Day, 63,177,184,206
   at Midsummer, 22
   when the pigs go to the woods,
     178
St Mary, first feast of, 206
St Patrick, xiii
   Day, 206
sale thief, 118,159,164-6
sanctuary, 81-3
sarhaed, 5-7,9,11,12,16,17,19-21,
   23,25-39,47,48,51-3,57,59,
   60,131,134,144,147,153-6,
   167,197,198
scab, 177,197
Scandinavia, lawbooks and law-
   men, xxxv
scar, 196-8
scenting-hound, 182,193
sceptre, 120
scholar, from school, 76
scraper, 37,193
scratching, 33
screen, 7,8,11,18,21,24
scribes, of Welsh lawbooks, xxii
Scripture, 1
scrub land, 113
scrub oak, 188
sea, 40,112
seal, patent, 12,29
season, close, for land cases, 83,
   84,105
seasoning, 27

Index to Text and Introduction 419

second man, 91
security, 91,170
selion, 120
selling, land, 114
Senchas Már, xiii
serjeant, xxix,16,31,34,35,85,
  87,89
servant, 7,122,129,145
  act of, 168
  alien, 167
service, 7,12,15,21,28,30
  of uchelwr, 116
servient, 55,118,156
sessions, 12,122,123,125
seven, persons, 145
  years, 45,50,83
  years old, 78,130,131
seventh degree, 145,150
  person, 145,148,149
sexton, 11,28
shaft penny, 58,60,111,145,146,
  149,152
shame, 52,156
  in respect of wife, 154
  of maiden, 61
sharing, 23,45,92,100,103,104,
  118,160
  buildings, 118
  equality and, 93
  land, 98-100
  loss, 71
  stolen property, 157
  three places in law for, 71,127
shareland, 92,121,174
sheaf, sound instead of damaged,
  205
sheep, 13,45,126,157,179,180,
  188,203,208
  and goats, 45,179
  dry, 15,179
  properties of, 179
sheepcote, 190
sheet, 16,59
shelter, 189
shieling, 121,125
shingles (roofing), 170
ship, 112
shoeing, 32
shore, land alongside, 112
Shoreham, 120
short-yoked oxen, 200

shower, May, 175
shriek, 104
side-posts, 190
silence, 21,85,89
silver, 41,46,154,194
  rod, 52
sin, father's, 110
sister, 109,136,144,147
six kine, of corpse, 116
six ways in which person's goods
  go, 161
skin, 11-15,18,22,23,26,33,35,
  173,185,188, see also *hide*
  harm outside, 174
skull, 197
slaughter, 63
slave, 155,166,167
  daughter, 55
  servient, 55,56
  value, 167
  woman, 156
sleephouse, 41,125
smith, 38
  court, 8,9,13,32,37,38
  implements, 194
smithcraft, 40
smock, 155
smoke, 14
snake, delivery of, 137
snare, 186,187,189
snatching, 6,154
society, simple, xxxiii
  trust within, xxx
soliciting, by bards, 38,39
son, 45,46,59,61,80,100,114,
  115,126,130,131,134,135,
  152,168
  acceptance, 133,135-7
  alien's, 136
  by clamour, 134
  by sufferance, 134
  denial, 132-7
  doubted, 134
  eldest, 99,110,113,137,148
  entitlement, and father, 110
  in father's place, 76
  king's, 6-8,154
  laying to father, 132,133,137
  of dead surety, 71,72
  of principal debtor, 72
  uncouth, 47

420 *The Law of Hywel Dda*

youngest, 99,100,110,113
song, 20,38
sophistication, in law, xxix,xxx
sour-apple tree, 188
Southern Wales, xxvi,49
sovereign tribute, 154
Sovereignty of Britain, 20
sow, 179,206
sowing, 125
spade, 156
sparrowhawk, 15,17,183
spear, 34,194
    head of, 37
speech, foreign, strange, 58,76
spoil, 144
spoliation, extortionate, 159
spring, 77,83
    ploughing, 195
springe, 187
spurs, 18,194
stable, 41,125
stack, 101,103,209
stag, 22,184,187
staggers, 172,177
staghound, 181,182,185, see
    also *huntsman*
stall, 172
stallion, 178,206, see also *destrier*
standard-bearer, office of, 92
state: in medieval Wales, xv
    king as, xv,xxx,xxxv
    power, xxxv
    prosecution by, xxxi
status, 7,8,23,30,32,47,50,55,
    57,60,72,82,83,89,90,92,95,
    107,112-15,127,130,133,134,
    144,160,162,167,169,172,
    173,184,187,191,198,203,
    208,209
    father's, 131
    from land, 7,108
    joints, 184,185
    land without, 91
    lord's, 131
    mother's, 135
    of court, 17,41
    of gage, 69
    of kindred, 29
    of land, 7
    primary, 127
    thief's, 164

toft, 58,108
    woman's, 47,60
Statute: of Wales, xviii,xxviii
    preamble, xiii
stay, of blood, 197
    of boundary, 127
    of wife, 54
stealth, xxx
    burning by, 169
    killing horse by, 173
steer, 14,17,49,50,62,97,128,
    157,168,172,177,202
    polled, 177
step, 120
steward, 5,8-10,12-14,23,26-8,
    31,33,41,92,155
    office, 92
    queen's, 28
stock (family), 104,110; inquiry,
    145
    (livestock), 177,202,207,209;
    milch, 209; not to be mixed,
    207
    (of tree), 190
stolen property, 160, 163-5
    attachment, 161
    provisions, 167
    share of, 157
    traced to house, 159
stomach, 184,185
stone, 171
    in place of icicle, 70
    work, 98
strait, denial in, 134
strangles, 172
straw, 19,36,126,209
striking, 6,154
stubble, 209
stud, 40
    legal, 173
    mare, 173
substitute, 63,73
sucking, 178,203
suet, 33
sufferance, son by, 134
sufficient information,
    62,159
summer food-gift, 129
summer house, 190
sumpter horse, 172,173
Sunday, 65,76,77

Index to Text and Introduction   421

supper money, 14,19,25,27-31,
123
support, for end of yoke, 199-201
surclaim, 112,170,208
surety, xviii, 49,50,52,59-77,79,
81,89,132-4,163,165
208, see also *mach*
admitted, 66,68,77
and contract, 63
and principal debtor, claim
of, 63-77
denial of, 68
for fixed day, 70
for galanas, 133-5
for land and earth, 85
for law, 77,78,85
God taken instead of, 78
hand of, 73-5
he paid who gave, 135
in absence, 74
many, 67,68
persons not entitled to be, 76
son of dead, 72
two, 67
woman, 57,73
suretyship, 63-78,81
blemishes of, three, 73
buckle, 73-5
vain, 72-3
surreption, 161,162,166,170
fee, 126
fine, 174
suzerain, of Deheubarth, 164
sward, furrow and, ploughing,
176,202
swarm, 124,183,184
bull, 183
clustered, 184,186
wing, 183,184
swearing, 130,137,161
and attachment, 162,163
to God, 132,133
sweet-apple tree, 189
sword, 124,194
sworn appraisal, 164,165,175,
176,193,195,196
synod, 11,29
law of, 168

tail, 175,177,180,182
flesh of, 172,173

greased, 49
hair of, 172,173
of lawbook, following Redaction, xxv
taker, of livestock, 207-9
tallow, 26
tame, wild and, see *wild and tame*
tamed animal, 187
tasting, 26
teacher, 90,141
teat, 175,180
tent, medication, 197
tenth penny, 160
term, fixed, for bail, 81
test, 141
Test Book, Justices', xxv,xxvii
141,142,190
testes, testicles, 18,52,172,179,
180,196
testifier, 89,92-6,163
better, 90
objection to, 93
status of, 90
woman, 57
testimony, 93
dead, 98
of one person, 95,96
thatch, 204
thatch-spar, 191
theft, xxx,33,60,71,101,118,
156-69
dirwy for, 144
in hand, 160
law of, xxiv,118,182
nine abetments of, 156,157
presenting, 160
thickset hedge (fig.), 97,106
thief, 40,62,94,122,156-60,164-7
admitted, 160,164
furious, 166
release of, 158
sale, 118,159,164-6
status, 164
thigh, 24,48
third share, 5-7,9-15,17,18,20,
21,23,28,29,59,144,151,154,
171,174
third man, 91,108
third person, 108
third wind, 116
third, enforcing, 146,147

422   The Law of Hywel Dda

thirds, sharing, 166
thorn-bush, 189
thrave, 128,195
three acceptances of a son, 135
three ancestors' lifetimes, 112
three animals whose properties
  are more than their legal
  value, 178
three beasts to whose value the
  King is entitled, 188
three blemishes of suretyship, 73
three buckle suretyships, 73-5
three cattle diseases, 177
three columns of law, 1,141,142,
  171
three conspicious scars, 197
three dangerous wounds, 24,197
three dead testimonies, 98
three dewfalls, 172,177
three dire losses of a kindred,
  133,134,146
three diseases, 172
three enthroned ones, 101
three fires for which no compensation, 170
three flows and three ebbs, 112
three free huntings, 184
three free huntings for a villein,
  187
three indispensables, 11,39
three kinds of blood not compensated, 197
three kinds of dadannudd, 101
three kinds of homage, 119
three kinds of objection, 94
three kinds of purchase of land,
  113
three kine of the corpse, 116
three kine of violence, 150
three legal points, 93
three men's lifetimes, 111
three moons, 172
three natural diseases, 174
three nights, 45
three nights and three days, 101,
  102,116,167,170,171,172,179
three pence instead of three
  pounds, 157
three persons not to be buried in
  consecrated ground, 166

three places where law shares,
  71,127
three pleas, 162
three points, 156
three precious things of kindred,
  113
three privy things, 53,61
three reasons a surety will be free,
  63
three seasons, 172
three shames of a maiden, 61
three special beasts, 203
three stays of blood, 197
three stays of boundary, 127
three stays of a wife, 54
three systems of law, 94
three thieves who escape from
  admitted theft, 167
three things, 37-8,122,124,154
three things from which there is
  no right to protection, 81
three things which a person can
  take without leave, 171
three timbers which are free to
  every builder on open land,
  189
three times, 53,110,170,182,185
three townlands, 167
three unclaimable things, 61
three vain suretyships, 72
three ways a son cannot be denied
  by a kindred, 135
three ways sarhaed is done, 6,154
three women whose sons are
  entitled to mother-right, 58,
  107
threshing, 126
threshold, 39,190,191
throne, Lord's, 164
throw, rebound, 153
throwboard, 16,20,123,142,191-3
thumb, 176,196,198
tiercel, 13,15,17,183
tiles, 170
tillage, tilth, 122,200,202,209
timber: big, 191
  three free, 189
time, prison of, 77
tithe, 12,28
toe, 196

Index to Text and Introduciton   423

toft, 98,99,113,114,121,122
   legal, 100
   status, 58,108
toll, 112
tongue, 17,118,141,184,196
tongued-one, 49,61
tooth, 174,178,180,196
   blood from, 197
   wear of teeth and side, 50
   wishing dirt on teeth, 52
townland, 9,100,121,129,143,
   167,177,205
   boundary, 126
   house within, 170
   reckon, 100,129
   villein, 41,125,129,199
   with office of maer or cyng-
     hellor, 129
   without office, 129
town-made garment, 195
tracker dog, 193
tractate, xv,xxiv,xxv
training, 172
transfer rescinded, 40
treading, by male bird, 181,183
treasure, 19,40
   does not arise under depriv-
     ation, 169
   gold, 41
tree, 113,184,188-90
   bridge of a single, 76
   falling, xxxvi,153
   falling across river, 189
   pigs going under, 178
   without labour, 189,190
trial by battle, xxxii
tribute, 120
   sovereign, 154
trinkets, 6
   idle, 16,142
   interchangeable, 76
trough, 39,192,193
trunk, 197
truth, 95
Tudor, Henry, xvi
tuning-horn, 40,191,192
turf, 170
twelve legal joints, 184
twelve years old, 131,132
twenty-five years old, 141

twnc, 21,118,123,125,129
   pound, 122,123,128
two penalties for same cause, no
   right to, 168
tying-posts, 201

uchelwr, 8,98,114,115,118,121,
   123,126,155,182,192,195
   alien of, 114,118
   daughter of, 55
   homage of, 115
   service of, 116
   wife of, 54,195
unclaimable things, three, 61
uncle, 108,150
unclean animal, beast, 180,186
under-thatch, 160,191,204
unreadiness, 93
unskilled, 181
upper precinct, 13
usher, 5,8,20,21,122,125
utter payment after utter
   swearing, 177

value, 95,142,158
   legal, 73,164,165,177,178,
     182,193,194,196,203
   of thief, 165
   of wild and tame, 1,141,142,
     171-88
vat, 128,192
   of mead, 23,25
vengeance, 150
   compensation and, 53,165
   of kindred, 156
vespers, 185
vessel, measuring, 176
vestments, 101
villein, 15,23,38,39,122,123,125,
   182,183, see also *aillt*
   barn, 191
   daughter, 50
   king's, 41,124
   land, 7
   nets, three, 40
   tamed animal, 187
   townland, 41,125,129,199
violence: aid to, 143
   and harm, 106,111

dirwy for, 144
three kine of, 150
virginity, 61,62
void, advice, answer, 87,88
vouchee, 96
voucher to warranty, 162,163
vow, 52,80

Wales, 110
never pagan, xxxii
politics in, xi
warning, 153
warrantor, 73,92,162-4
warranty, 106
two, 86
voucher to, 162,163.
waste, 40
king's, 41,56,101,114,121,122
watchman, 36
water, 171,172
holy, 65,133
wattling-rods, 204
wax, 23,27,183,186
wayfarer, 186
wealth, 159
weapons, 83, see also *arms*
weather-poles, 191
weaving-woman, 170,193
web, 170
wedding-guest, 49
weir, 112,113,124
Welsh (language, old, newer),
116,120
Welshman, 94,114,132
patrimonial, 89
Welshwoman, 56-8,108,117,
134,135
custom of, 52
entitled, 108
wether, three-year-old, 129
whalebone, 16,20,192
wheat, 128,180
White House (on Taf), 1
Book of, xiv,xxvii,94,141
Whitland, xiii,xxiii
Abbey, xiv,xxvii
Whitsun, 5,76
Tuesday after next Sunday to,
76
wicket, 16

wife, see also *woman*
alien's, 117
gaging, 208
gift by, 54
goods of, 54,165
king's, 54
misuse of, 5
second, xxvi,45,47
shame in respect of, 154
uchelwr's, 54
villein's, 54
wedded, 110
wild and tame, value of, 1,141,
142,171-88
wild animal, beast, 186,187,189
wild horse, 172
wild one which the tame catches,
205
wild pig, 178
will, 59
free, 200
willow, 189
wind, 124,204
first, 116
third, 116
windfall, 189
wing-swarm, 183,184
winter: food-gift, gwestfa, 128
house, 40,190
Kalends, 22,34,83,84,101,103,
175,176,179,183,184,188,
203,204,206,207,209
ploughing, 195, see also *tillage*
wise men, 1
witnesses, xxxi-xxxiii,79
legal, 83
wolf, 187,188
woman, see also *wife*
feud, 94
galanas, 47,155,156
killing person, 152
land, 107-10
laws of, xxiv,45-61
married, 37,47,59
of bush and brake, 50,135,137
sarhaed, 37,47,155,156
shameful, 53
surety, testifier, 57
woodland, wooded land, woods,
113,114,189

Index to Text and Introduction   425

king's, 179
 preserving, 178
 yew, 189
woodlander, 189
woodman, 113
woodwork, 199
wool, 45,175,180, see also
 clothing, woollen
word: is no word, 93
 is the final word, 61
 of inquiry, 87,88
 of mouth, 90,93,134,158
 uncouth, 41
working age, 175
working horse, 172
worth, 5,7,9,12,16,17,19-21,
 23-39,118,134,154,155
 double, 150
wound, 143
 blood and, 150,198
 dangerous, 10,24,197
wounded person, 24
woven materials, 46
wrongdoer, 81
wynebwerth, 26,45,46,51,53,
 61,129,141
Wynn, family, xix

yarn, balls of, 46,170
year and day, 75,81,97,111,117,
 119,126,134
year, corn of one, 208
yearling: dry (goat), 180
 female, male, 49,176
yew, 189
yoke, 45,176,195
 armpit, 99,120,199
 God's, 130
 long, 99,120,199
 mid, 99,120,199
 short, 99,120,199
 supporting end of, 199-201
yoke-bows, 195,202
yoke-fellow, 176
yoking, 35,176
young persons, 142
Ystrad Tywi, xvii
Ystrwyth, xix

www.ingramcontent.com/pod-product-compliance
Lightning Source LLC
Chambersburg PA
CBHW031409230426
43668CB00007B/254